Originally published:
Baltimore, Maryland
2016

Reprinted by:

Native Study LLC
Gallipolis, OH
www.nativestudy.com

Library of Congress Control Number: 2020911767

ISBN: 978-1-64968-013-6

Made in the United States of America.

This series is dedicated to
Mike Marchi,
who keeps my spirits up.

CREEK CENSUS.

SECOND NOTICE.

Members of the Dawes Commission will be present at the following times and places for the purpose of enrolling Creek citizens, as required by Act of Congress of June 10, 1896:

At Muskogee, Nov. 8 to 30, 1897, inclusive.
At Wagoner, Nov. 8 to 13, " inclusive.
At Eufaula, Nov. 8 to 13, " inclusive.
At Sapulpa, Nov. 15 to 20, " inclusive.
At Wetumpka, Nov. 15 to 20, " inclusive.
At Okmulgee, Nov. 22 to 30, " inclusive.

All persons who have not heretofore enrolled before the Dawes Commission should appear and enroll. Parents and guardians can enroll their families and wards.

TAMS BIXBY,
FRANK C. ARMSTRONG,
A. S. McKENNON,
THOS. B. NEEDLES,
Commissioners.

The above illustration is similar in nature to what was found throughout Indian Territory for different tribes as far as postings on bulletin boards, public centers, or wherever they could be read so people would be notified of where and when they needed to be for enrollment with the Dawes Commission.

This is a picture of the Dawes Commission at Camp Jones in Stonewall, Indian Territory on September 8, 1898.

The images below are of two of the original cards given on the microfilm. The cards given in this book have been formatted to fit on one page and still give all the information found on the original cards.

Introduction

This series of Choctaw Enrollment Cards for the Five Civilized Tribes 1898-1914 has been transcribed from National Archive Film M-1186 Rolls 39-46.

The series contains more than 6100 Choctaw enrollment cards. All of the cards list age, sex and degree of blood, the parties' Dawes Roll Numbers, and date of enrollment by the Secretary of Interior for each person. The contents also give the enrollee's parents' names as well as miscellaneous notes pertaining to the enrollee's circumstances, when needed. Most entries indicate whether or not a spouse is an Intermarried White, with the initials I.W.

Enrollment wasn't as simple a process as most would think just by going through these pages. The relationships between the Five Tribes and the Dawes Commission were weak at best. There were political battles going on between the tribes and the U.S. Government as it was, but the struggles didn't stop there. Each tribe had its own political factions pulling it from every direction. On top of everything else, people from every corner of the United States were trying to figure how to get in on the spoils (Money and Land Allotment) by means of political favor. Kent Carter, author of *The Dawes Commission*, describes the continuous effort required to enroll the different tribes and the pressure the Commission incurred from people all over the country who tried to insinuate themselves into the equation:

"In May 1896 the Dawes Commission Returned To Indian Territory for its third visit, establishing its headquarters at Vinita in the Cherokee Nation. It now had to process applications for citizenship in addition to negotiating allotment agreements; these circumstances make the narrative of events more confusing because the commission attempted the two tasks concurrently. The commissioners resumed making their usual speeches to tribal officials and public gatherings to promote negotiations, but now they inevitably had to respond to questions about how the application process for citizenship would work. They also began receiving letters from people all over the United States asking how they could 'get on the rolls' so they could 'get Indian land'."[1]

For the actual process of Choctaw enrollment, "A commission was appointed in each county of the Choctaw Nation under an act of September 18 to make separate rolls of citizens by blood, by intermarriage, and freedmen; it was to deliver them to recently elected Chief Green McCurtain by October 20, but he rejected them even before they were completed because of charges that people were being left off for political reasons. On October 30, the National Council authorized establishment of a five-member

---

[1] *The Dawes Commission* by Kent Carter, page 15, para. 1

commission to revise the rolls within ten days and then directed McCurtain to turn them over to the Dawes Commission on November 11, 1896. The Choctaws hired the law firm of Stuart, Gordon, and Hailey, of South McAlester to represent the tribe at all proceedings held by the Dawes Commission,"[2] another indication that throughout the Commission's efforts there was always controversy between the tribes and the negotiators.

When completed, this multi-volume series will contain thousands of names, all of them accounted for in the indexes carefully prepared by the author. Hopefully this work will help many researchers find their ancestors and satisfy the questions that so many have had about their Native American heritage.

Jeff Bowen
Gallipolis, Ohio
NativeStudy.com

---

[2] *The Dawes Commission* by Kent Carter, page 16, para. 5

Choctaw By Blood Enrollment Cards 1898-1914

RESIDENCE: Sans Bois COUNTY. **Choctaw Nation** Choctaw Roll CARD NO.
POST OFFICE: Milton, I.T. *(Not Including Freedmen)* FIELD NO. 2701

Dawes' Roll No.	NAME	Relationship to Person First Named	AGE	SEX	BLOOD	TRIBAL ENROLLMENT		
						Year	County	No.
7802	1 Talipoose, Simeon DIED PRIOR TO SEPTEMBER 25 1902	First Named	23	M	Full	1896	Sans Bois	11850
	2							
	3							
	4							
	5							
	6							
	7							
	8							
	9							
	10							
	11							
	12							
	13							
	14	ENROLLMENT						
	15	OF NOS. 1 HEREON						
	16	APPROVED BY THE SECRETARY OF INTERIOR JAN 17 1903						
	17							

TRIBAL ENROLLMENT OF PARENTS

	Name of Father	Year	County	Name of Mother	Year	County
1	Sampson Talipoose	Dead	Skullyville	Tema Talipoose	Dead	Skullyville
2						
3						
4						
5						
6	Not died before Sept 25, 1902 Enrollment cancelled by Department May 2, 1906					
7			On 1896 roll as Simeon Tallipoose.			
8						
9						
10						
11						
12						
13						
14						
15					Date of Application for Enrollment.	
16					6/14/99	
17						

Choctaw By Blood Enrollment Cards 1898-1914

RESIDENCE: Skullyville		COUNTY. **Choctaw Nation**				**Choctaw Roll** *(Not Including Freedmen)*	CARD NO.	
POST OFFICE: Brazil, I.T.							FIELD NO. 2702	

Dawes' Roll No.	NAME	Relationship to Person First Named	AGE	SEX	BLOOD	TRIBAL ENROLLMENT		
						Year	County	No.
7894	1 German, Rena 17	Named	14	F	1/2	1896	Skullyville	11911
	2							
	3							
	4							
	5							
	6							
	7							
	8							
	9							
	10							
	11							
	12							
	13							
	14	ENROLLMENT						
	15	OF NOS. 1 HEREON						
	16	APPROVED BY THE SECRETARY OF INTERIOR JAN 17 1903						
	17							

TRIBAL ENROLLMENT OF PARENTS

Name of Father	Year	County	Name of Mother	Year	County
1 Robert Trahern	Dead	Skullyville	Cornelia Trahern	Dead	Skullyville
2					
3					
4					
5					
6		On 1896 roll as Czarma Trahern			
7					
8					
9					
10					
11					
12					
13					
14				Date of Application for Enrollment.	
15					
16				6/14/99	
17 McCurtain I.T. 12/16/02					

2

Choctaw By Blood Enrollment Cards 1898-1914

RESIDENCE: Skullyville COUNTY.
POST OFFICE: Ward, I.T

Choctaw Nation

Choctaw Roll
(Not Including Freedmen)

CARD NO.
FIELD NO. 2703

Dawes' Roll No.	NAME	Relationship to Person First Named	AGE	SEX	BLOOD	TRIBAL ENROLLMENT		
						Year	County	No.
7895 ₁	Merryman, James F ²²	First Named	19	M	1/4	1896	Skullyville	8455
I.W 269 ₂	" Ruth	Wife	18	F	I.W			
7896 ₃	" Earl Q ³	Son	1mo	M	1/8			
7897 ₄	" Lillian Joanna ¹	Dau	6wk	F	1/8			
₅								
₆								
₇								
₈								
₉								
₁₀								
₁₁	ENROLLMENT OF NOS. 2 HEREON APPROVED BY THE SECRETARY OF INTERIOR SEP 12 1903							
₁₂								
₁₃								
₁₄	ENROLLMENT OF NOS. 1,3,4 HEREON APPROVED BY THE SECRETARY OF INTERIOR JAN 17 1903							
₁₅								
₁₆								
₁₇								

TRIBAL ENROLLMENT OF PARENTS

	Name of Father	Year	County	Name of Mother	Year	County
₁	John Merryman	1896	Skullyville	Joanna Merryman	Dead	Skullyville
₂	Polk Howell	1896	Non Citz	Manda Howell	1896	Non Citz
₃	No1			No2		
₄	No1			No2		
₅						
₆						
₇			No1 on 1896 roll as Jas F Merryman			
₈			No.4 Enrolled October 15, 1901			
₉						
₁₀			For child of Nos 1&2 see NB (Mar 3-05) Card #184			
₁₁						
₁₂						
₁₃						
₁₄						
₁₅				No3 enrolled Nov 24/99		
₁₆				Date of Application for Enrollment.	6/14/99	
₁₇	P.O. Saylor I.T. 1/21/03					

3

Choctaw By Blood Enrollment Cards 1898-1914

RESIDENCE: Skullyville   COUNTY. **Choctaw Nation**   **Choctaw Roll**   CARD No.
POST OFFICE: Milton I.T.   (Not Including Freedmen)   FIELD No. 2704

Dawes' Roll No.		NAME		Relationship to Person	AGE	SEX	BLOOD	TRIBAL ENROLLMENT		
								Year	County	No.
DEAD.	1	Dwight Simon	23	First Named	20	M	Full	P.R. 1893	Skullyville	153
7898	2	" Albert	12	Bro	9	M	"	P.R. 1893		155
	3									
	4									
	5	No. 1 HEREON DISMISSED UNDER								
	6	ORDER OF THE COMMISSION TO THE FIVE								
	7	CIVILIZED TRIBES OF MARCH 31, 1905.								
	8									
	9									
	10									
	11									
	12									
	13									
	14	ENROLLMENT								
	15	OF NOS. 2 HEREON								
	16	APPROVED BY THE SECRETARY OF INTERIOR JAN 17 1903								
	17									

TRIBAL ENROLLMENT OF PARENTS

	Name of Father	Year	County	Name of Mother	Year	County
1	Eden Dwight	Dead	Skullyville	Lizzie Dwight	Dead	Skullyville
2	" "	"	"	"	"	"
3						
4						
5						
6		No1 On Skullyville Co P.R. P #15 No 153, 1893				
7		No2 On " " " " 15 No 155, 1893				
8		No.1 also on 1896 Choctaw roll as Limon Pearson, page 255, #10076				
9		No.2 " " " " " Albert Pearson, " " #10078				Sept. 27th, 1900
10		N°1 Died Oct. 15, 1901, Proof of death filed Dec 24 1902				
11						
12						
13						
14						Date of Application for Enrollment.
15						
16						6/14/99
17						

Choctaw By Blood Enrollment Cards 1898-1914

RESIDENCE: Sans Bois   COUNTY. **Choctaw Nation**   **Choctaw Roll** *(Not Including Freedmen)*   CARD No.
POST OFFICE: Iron Bridge, I.T.   FIELD No. 2705

Dawes' Roll No.	NAME		Relationship to Person First Named	AGE	SEX	BLOOD	TRIBAL ENROLLMENT		
							Year	County	No.
7899	1 Perry, Eastman	48	First Named	45	M	Full	1896	Sans Bois	10070
7900	2 " Eve	56	Wife	53	F	"	1896	" "	10071
7901	3 " Campbell	20	Son	17	M	"	1896	" "	10072
7902	4 " Caroline	19	Dau	16	F	"	1896	" "	10073
7903	5 " Joseph	14	Son	11	M	"	1896	" "	10074
7904	6 " Leo	11	"	8	"	"	1896	" "	10075
	7								
	8								
	9								
	10								
	11								
	12								
	13								
	14	ENROLLMENT							
	15	OF NOS. 1,2,3,4,5,6 HEREON							
	16	APPROVED BY THE SECRETARY OF INTERIOR JAN 17 1903							
	17								

TRIBAL ENROLLMENT OF PARENTS

	Name of Father	Year	County	Name of Mother	Year	County
1	Boland Perry	Dead	Skullyville	Nancy Perry	Dead	Sans Bois
2	Harris	"	Sugar Loaf	Lizzie Harris	"	" " "
3	No1			No2		
4	No1			No2		
5	No1			No2		
6	No1			No2		
7						
8						
9			No4 on 1896 roll as Catherine Perry			
10			No6 " 1896 " " Newton "			
11						
12						
13						
14						
15						
16				Date of Application for Enrollment.	6/14/99	
17						

5

Choctaw By Blood Enrollment Cards 1898-1914

RESIDENCE: Sans Bois COUNTY. **Choctaw Nation** **Choctaw Roll** CARD NO.
POST OFFICE: Iron Bridge I.T.   *(Not Including Freedmen)* FIELD NO. 2706

Dawes' Roll No.	NAME	Relationship to Person First Named	AGE	SEX	BLOOD	TRIBAL ENROLLMENT Year	County	No.
7905	1 Lucas Joshua 31	First Named	28	M	3/4	1896	Sans Bois	7685
7906	2 " Jennie 31	Wife	28	F	Full	1896	" "	7687
7907	3 " Frank 18	Bro	15	M	3/4	1896	" "	7686
	4							
	5							
	6							
	7							
	8							
	9							
	10							
	11							
	12							
	13							
	14	ENROLLMENT						
	15	OF NOS. 1,2,3 HEREON						
	16	APPROVED BY THE SECRETARY						
	17	OF INTERIOR JAN 17 1903						

TRIBAL ENROLLMENT OF PARENTS

	Name of Father	Year	County	Name of Mother	Year	County
1	Lewis Lucas	Dead	Sans Bois	Mary Lucas	Dead	Sans Bois
2	Edmond McCurtain	"	Skullyville	Surie McCurtain	"	Gaines
3	Lewis Lucas	"	Sans Bois	Mary Lucas	"	Sans Bois
4						
5						
6						
7						
8						
9						
10						
11						
12						
13						
14						
15						
16				Date of Application for Enrollment.	6/14/99	
17						

6

Choctaw By Blood Enrollment Cards 1898-1914

RESIDENCE: Sans Bois COUNTY. **Choctaw Nation** Choctaw Roll CARD No.
POST OFFICE: Iron Bridge I.T. *(Not Including Freedmen)* FIELD No. 2707

Dawes' Roll No.	NAME	Relationship to Person First Named	AGE	SEX	BLOOD	TRIBAL ENROLLMENT		
						Year	County	No.
DEAD.	1 Lucas Sally		80	F	Full	1896	Sans Bois	7684
2								
3								
4								
5								
6								
7								
8	No. 1 HEREON DISMISSED UNDER							
9	ORDER OF THE COMMISSION TO THE FIVE CIVILIZED TRIBES OF MARCH 31, 1905.							
10								
11								
12								
13								
14								
15								
16								
17								

TRIBAL ENROLLMENT OF PARENTS

	Name of Father	Year	County		Name of Mother	Year	County
1	Milton McCoy	Dead			Shemohoyo McCoy	Dead	
2							
3							
4							
5							
6							
7							
8	No 1 Died in August 1900 – Proof of death filed Decr 23rd 1902						
9							
10							
11							
12							
13							
14							Date of Application for Enrollment.
15							
16							6/14/99
17							

CANCELLED

Applicant died prior to ratification of Choctaw-Chickasaw agreement Sepr 25 1902

| RESIDENCE: Tobucksy | COUNTY. | **Choctaw Nation** | **Choctaw Roll** | CARD No. |
| POST OFFICE: Stewart I.T. | | | (Not Including Freedmen) | FIELD No. 2708 |

Dawes' Roll No.	NAME	Relationship to Person First Named	AGE	SEX	BLOOD	TRIBAL ENROLLMENT		
						Year	County	No.
0	1 Pryor Olivia	Named	36	F	1/16			
0	2 Douglass Kyle	Son	17	M	3/16			
0	3 Jordan Henry	Son	14	M	1/32			
0	4 " Rhoda	Dau	12	F	1/32			
0	5 " Lora	Dau	10	F	1/32			
0	6 Pryor George	Son	8	M	1/32			
0	7 " James	Son	6	M	1/32			
0	8 " Mary E	Dau	3	F	1/32			
DP	9 " Sallie	Dau	1	F	1/32			
DP	10 " Vernon	Son	1mo	M	1/32			
DP	11 " Earl	Son	1mo	M	1/32			
12	Nos1 to 8 incl Denied in 96 Case 850							
13	Judgement[sic] of U.S. Ct admitting Nos 1 to 8 incl vacated and set aside by Decree of Choctaw Chickasaw Citizenship Court Dec 11 '02							
14	Nos 1 to 8 incl now in C.C.C.C. Case No 58							
15								
16	#9-10-11 DISMISSED							
17	JAN 19 1905							

TRIBAL ENROLLMENT OF PARENTS							
Name of Father	Year	County	Name of Mother	Year	County		
1 Samuel J Cowart	Dead	Non Citz	Rhoda Cowart	Dead	Choctaw		
2 Kyle Douglass	"	Choctaw	No 1				
3 Henry Jordan	"	Non Citz	No 1				
4 " "		" "	No 1				
5		" "	No 1				
6 Samuel V. Pryor	1896	" "	No 1				
7 " " "	1896		No 1				
8	1896		No 1				
9 " " "	1896	" "	No 1				
10 " " "	1896	" "	No 1				
11 " " "	1896	" "	No 1				

DENIED CITIZENSHIP BY THE CHOCTAW AND CHICKASAW CITIZENSHIP COURT Dec 3 '04

12 Nos 1-2-3-4-5-6-7 and 8 admitted by U.S. Court at S. McAlester
Jan 1-1898 Case No 101. As to residence and birth of child
13 Sallie O. see testimony of Oliver Pryor
14 No9 Born April 21st 1898
15 No1 Admitted as Paior

Father of No.11 is Saml V Pryor and mother Olivia Pryor

Date of Application for Enrollment.
6/14/99

16 Nos 10 and 11 enrolled Aug 18, 1900
17 Nos 10 and 11 are twins

Choctaw By Blood Enrollment Cards 1898-1914

RESIDENCE: **Sans Bois**   COUNTY.   **Choctaw Nation**   **Choctaw Roll**   CARD No.
POST OFFICE: **Cowlington, I.T**   *(Not Including Freedmen)*   FIELD No. **2709**

Dawes' Roll No.		NAME	Relationship to Person First Named	AGE	SEX	BLOOD	TRIBAL ENROLLMENT Year	County	No.
0	1	Edwards, Ophelia S	Named	39	F	1/4			
0	2	" Charles	Son	19	M	1/8			
0	3	" Lula J	Dau	16	F	1/8			
0	4	" Martha J	"	14	"	1/8			
0	5	" David L	Son	12	M	1/8			
REFUSED.	6	" Luther W	"	3	"	1/8			
	7								
	8	DISMISSED							
	9								
	10	JAN 21 1905							
	11								
	12	McCurtain 6/28/04							
	13	No.6 refused, born August 25, 1896 prior to filing of original application and not included therein							
	14								
	15								
	16	See Pet #C-130							
	17	Duplicate record found							

TRIBAL ENROLLMENT OF PARENTS

	Name of Father	Year	County	Name of Mother	Year	County
1	J.M. Lewis	Dead	Choctaw	Zora P. Lewis	1896	Choctaw
2	Joseph M Edwards	1896	Non Citz	No1		
3	" " "	1896	" "	No1		
4	" " "	1896	" "	No1		
5	" " "	1896	" "	No1		
6	" " "	1896	" "	No1		
7						
8	Nos1 to 5 incl. denied in 96 Case #850					
	Nos1 to 5 incl. now in C.C.C.C. Case #58					
9	DENIED CITIZENSHIP BY THE CHOCTAW AND					
10	No1,2,3,4,5 CHICKASAW CITIZENSHIP COURT					
11	Admitted by U.S. Court, Central District January 19/98, Case No 101					
12	Judgement[s] of US Ct admitting Nos1 to 5 incl vacated and set aside by Decree of Choctaw Chickasaw Cit Court Dec 17'02					
13	As to residence see testimony of No1					
14	DEPARTMENT OF THE INTERIOR, COMMISSION TO THE FIVE CIVILIZED TRIBES.					
15	JUDGMENT RENDERED AND COPY MAILED APPLICANT.			Date of Application for Enrollment.		
16				6/14/99		
17	*Tams Bixby* ACTING CHAIRMAN					

Choctaw By Blood Enrollment Cards 1898-1914

RESIDENCE: Skullyville   COUNTY. **Choctaw Nation**   **Choctaw Roll**   CARD NO.
POST OFFICE: Shady Point, I.T.   *(Not Including Freedmen)*   FIELD NO. 2710

Dawes' Roll No.	NAME	Relationship to Person First Named	AGE	SEX	BLOOD	TRIBAL ENROLLMENT Year	County	No.
1	Hicks, Ulric Z	Named	23	M	1/16			
2								
3								
4								
5								
6								
7								
8								
9								
10								
11								
12								
13								
14								
15								
16								
17								

TRIBAL ENROLLMENT OF PARENTS

	Name of Father	Year	County	Name of Mother	Year	County
1	Stephen P. Hicks	1896	Nan Witz	Mollie Hicks	Dead	Choctaw
2						
3						
4						
5	No1 Denied in 96 Case #850					
6	Admitted by U.S. Court, Central District,					
7	Jany 19/98, Case No 101, as Ulric C Hickes					
8	As to residence, see his testimony					
9	Judgement[s(e)] of U.S. Court admitting No1 vacated and set aside by Decree of Choctaw Chickasaw Cit Court Dec 17'02					
10	No1 now in C.C.C.C. Case #58					
11						
12						
13						
14						
15					Date of Application for Enrollment.	
16					6/14/99	
17						

10

Choctaw By Blood Enrollment Cards 1898-1914

RESIDENCE: Sans Bois   COUNTY. **Choctaw Nation**   **Choctaw Roll** (Not Including Freedmen)   CARD NO.
POST OFFICE: Panther, I.T.   FIELD NO. 2711

Dawes' Roll No.	NAME		Relationship to Person First Named	AGE	SEX	BLOOD	TRIBAL ENROLLMENT		
							Year	County	No.
I.W.121	1 Wyers, John W	34	First Named	31	M	I.W			
7908	2 " Irene	32	Wife	29	F	1/4	1896	Sans Bois	12671
7909	3 " Belle	14	Dau	11	"	1/8	1896	" "	12672
7910	4 " Bailey	12	Son	9	M	1/8	1896	" "	12673
7911	5 " Effie	10	Dau	7	F	1/8	1896	" "	12674
7912	6 " John N	8	Son	5	M	1/8	1896	" "	12675
7913	7 X " Pearl	6	~~Dau~~ Son	3	~~F~~ M	1/8	1896	" "	12676
7914	8 " Sampson	4	Son	1	M	1/8			
7915	9 " Corena	2	Dau	9m	F	1/8			
7916	10 " Edna	1	Dau	1mo	F	1/8			

X 12/21/1910 Designation of sex of No 7913 changed from "F" to "M" per Dept authority of Dec 12, 1911

12	ENROLLMENT
13	OF NOS. 1 ~~~~ HEREON APPROVED BY THE SECRETARY
14	OF INTERIOR JUN 13 1903
15	ENROLLMENT
16	OF NOS. 2,3,4,5,6,7,8,9,10 HEREON APPROVED BY THE SECRETARY
17	OF INTERIOR JAN 17 1903

TRIBAL ENROLLMENT OF PARENTS

	Name of Father	Year	County	Name of Mother	Year	County
1	William Wyers	Dead	Non Citz	Ellen Wyers	1896	Non Citz
2	Turner Brashears	"	Skullyville	Katie Brashears	Dead	" "
3	No1			No2		
4	No1			No2		
5	No1			No2		
6	No1			No2		
7	No1			No2		
8	No1			No2		
9	No1			No2		
10	No.1			No.2		

11 No 6 on 1896 roll as Norman Wyers

12   No.9 Enrolled January 31, 1901.

13 As to marriage of parents of No2, see testimony of Leathy Smith

14 No8 Affidavit of birth to be supplied. Recd 6/22/99   #1 to 8

15 No.1 As to marriage, see his testimony.   Date of Application for Enrollment.

16 No.10 Born Feby 7, 1902; enrolled March 25, 1902   6/14/99

For child of Nos 1&2 see NB (March 3, 1905) #1235

17

McCurtain I.T.

RESIDENCE:	Sugar Loaf	COUNTY.	**Choctaw Nation**		Choctaw Roll	CARD NO.	
POST OFFICE:	Kulli Chaha, I.T				(Not Including Freedmen)	FIELD NO.	2712

Dawes' Roll No.	NAME	Relationship to Person First Named	AGE	SEX	BLOOD	TRIBAL ENROLLMENT		
						Year	County	No.
✓	1 Harper, Edgar B		17	M	1/32			
	2							
	3							
	4							
	5							
	6							
	7							
	8							
	9							
	10							
	11							
	12							
	13							
	14							
	15							
	16							
	17							

TRIBAL ENROLLMENT OF PARENTS

	Name of Father	Year	County	Name of Mother	Year	County
1	W.W. Harper	1896	Non Citz	Leathy A Harper	Dead	Choctaw
2						
3						
4	No1 Denied by C.C.C. Case #50 March 18th 04					
5	No1 Denied in 96 Case 1335 No Appeal					
6	No1 " " 96 " 355 Appealed.					
7	Admitted by U.S. Court, Central District, August 24/97, Case No7					
8						
9	As to residence, see evidence of father, W.W. Harper					
10						
11	See original paper in 1896 Choctaw Cases 355 and 1335					
12	Judgement(s) of U.S. Ct admitting No1 vacated and set aside by Decree of Choctaw Chickasaw Cit Court Decr 17/02					
13	No appeal to C.C.C.C. Error					
14						
15					Date of Application for Enrollment.	
16					6/14/99	
17						

Choctaw By Blood Enrollment Cards 1898-1914

RESIDENCE:	Skullyville	COUNTY.	**Choctaw Nation**	**Choctaw Roll** (Not Including Freedmen)	CARD NO.
POST OFFICE:	Shady Point, I.T				FIELD NO. 2713

Dawes' Roll No.	NAME		Relationship to Person	AGE	SEX	BLOOD	TRIBAL ENROLLMENT		
							Year	County	No.
7917	₁ Wilkins, Adam	23	First Named	20	M	Full	1896	Skullyville	12736
	2								
	3								
	4								
	5								
	6								
	7								
	8								
	9								
	10								
	11								
	12								
	13								
	14								
	15	ENROLLMENT OF NOS. 1 HEREON APPROVED BY THE SECRETARY OF INTERIOR JAN 17 1903							
	16								
	17								

TRIBAL ENROLLMENT OF PARENTS

	Name of Father	Year	County	Name of Mother	Year	County
₁	Henry Wilkins	Dead	Skullyville	Wicey Wilkins	Dead	Skullyville
2						
3						
4						
5						
6						
7			On 1896 roll as Adams Wilkins			
8						
9						
10						
11						
12						
13						
14						
15					Date of Application for Enrollment.	
16					6/14/99	
17						

13

Choctaw By Blood Enrollment Cards 1898-1914

RESIDENCE: Skullyville	COUNTY.	Choctaw Nation	Choctaw Roll	CARD NO.
POST OFFICE: Bokoshe I.T.			(Not Including Freedmen)	FIELD NO. 2714

Dawes' Roll No.	NAME		Relationship to Person First Named	AGE	SEX	BLOOD	TRIBAL ENROLLMENT		
							Year	County	No.
7918	1 Stacy Andrew J	30	Named	27	M	1/8	1896	Skullyville	11138
7919	2 " Henry J	8	Son	5	M	1/8	1896	"	11140
7920	3 " William F	5	Son	2	M	1/8		"	
7921	4 DIED PRIOR TO SEPTEMBER 25 1902 Julius V		Son	4mo	M	1/8		"	
	5								
	6								
	7								
	8								
	9								
	10								
	11								
	12								
	13								
	14								
	15	ENROLLMENT OF NOS. 1,2,3,4 HEREON							
	16	APPROVED BY THE SECRETARY OF INTERIOR JAN 17 1903							
	17								

TRIBAL ENROLLMENT OF PARENTS

	Name of Father	Year	County	Name of Mother	Year	County
1	Andrew J Stacy	Dead	Non Citz	Lucretia Stacy	Dead	Skullyville
2	No 1			Susie E Stacy	"	"
3	No 1			" " "	"	"
4	No 1			" " "	"	"
5						
6						
7	No1 On the 1896 roll as Andrew Stacy					
8	No3 Affidavit of birth to be supplied Recd June 16/99					
9						
10	No4 died July 5, 1899 Proof of death filed Dec 20 1902					
11	No.4 died July 5, 1899 Enrollment cancelled by Department July 8, 1904					
12						
13						
14						
15						
16				Date of Application for Enrollment.		6/14/99
17						

14

Choctaw By Blood Enrollment Cards 1898-1914

Choctaw Nation

Choctaw Roll (Not Including Freedmen)

CARD No. FIELD No. 2715

Dawes' Roll No.	NAME	Relationship to Person First Named	AGE	SEX	BLOOD	TRIBAL ENROLLMENT Year	County	No.
7922	1 Anderson, David 43	First Named	40	M	Full	1896	Sans Bois	14
7923	2 " Isabelle DIED PRIOR TO SEPTEMBER 25, 1902	Wife	24	F	"	1896	" "	15
7924	3 " Levisey 9	Dau	6	"	"	1896	" "	16
7925	4 " Newman 3	Son	2mo	M	"			
7926	5 Colbert, Jasper 15	Ward	12	"	"	1896	Sans Bois	2132
	6							
	7							
	8							
	9							
	10							
	11							
	12							
	13							
	14							
	15	ENROLLMENT OF NOS. 1,2,3,4,5 HEREON APPROVED BY THE SECRETARY OF INTERIOR JAN 17 1903						
	16							
	17							

TRIBAL ENROLLMENT OF PARENTS

	Name of Father	Year	County	Name of Mother	Year	County
1	Sam Anderson	Dead	Skullyville	Meh-yo-lo-na	Dead	Sans Bois
2	Winchester Colbert	"	Sans Bois	Sophie Colbert	"	" "
3	No1			No2		
4	No1			No2		
5	Joe Colbert	Dead	Sans Bois	Nancy Colbert	Dead	Sans Bois
6						
7						
8						
9	No5 on 1896 roll as Joseph Colbert					
10						
11	No4 Affidavit of birth to be supplied Recd June 15/99					
12	No.2 died March 11, 1901; Enrollment cancelled by Department July 8, 1904					
13						
14						
15						
16				Date of Application for Enrollment.	6/14/99	
17						

15

Choctaw By Blood Enrollment Cards 1898-1914

| RESIDENCE: Sans Bois COUNTY. | POST OFFICE: Iron Bridge, I.T | **Choctaw Nation** | Choctaw Roll (Not Including Freedmen) | CARD NO. FIELD NO. 2716 |

Dawes Roll No.	NAME	Relationship to Person	AGE	SEX	BLOOD	TRIBAL ENROLLMENT		
						Year	County	No.
7927	1 Scott, Daniel 44	First Named	41	M	Full	1896	Sans Bois	11117
7928	2 " Phoebe 56	Wife	53	F	1/2	1896	" "	11118
7929	3 Simson, Walter 20	Ward	17	M	Full	1896	" "	11119
	4							
	5							
	6							
	7							
	8							
	9							
	10							
	11							
	12							
	13							
	14							
	15	ENROLLMENT OF NOS. 1, 2,3 HEREON						
	16	APPROVED BY THE SECRETARY OF INTERIOR JAN 17 1903						
	17							

TRIBAL ENROLLMENT OF PARENTS						
Name of Father	Year	County	Name of Mother	Year	County	
1 Henry Scott	Dead	Sans Bois	I-yo-no	Dead	Sans Bois	
2 Mitchell LeFlore	"	Sugar Loaf	Martha LeFlore	"	Sugar Loaf	
3 Willis Simpson	"	Skullyville	Sarah Simpson	"	Wade	
4						
5						
6						
7						
8						
9						
10						
11						
12						
13						
14						
15						
16			Date of Application for Enrollment.	6/14/99		
17						

16

Choctaw By Blood Enrollment Cards 1898-1914

RESIDENCE: Sans Bois COUNTY.
POST OFFICE: Stigler, I.T.

Choctaw Nation
(Not Including Freedmen)

Choctaw Roll CARD No.
FIELD NO. 2717

Dawes' Roll No.	NAME	Relationship to Person First Named	AGE	SEX	BLOOD	TRIBAL ENROLLMENT Year	County	No.
I.W. 648	1 Dodson, John W 46	First Named	44	M	I.W	1896	Skullyville	14454
7930	2 " Emma 34	Wife	31	F	1/8	1896	"	3215
7931	3 " Sudie 12	Dau	9	"	1/16	1896	"	3216
7932	4 " Willie E 14	Son	11	M	1/16	1896	"	3217
7933	5 " Elisha Thomas 5	"	2	"	1/16			
7934	6 " Charlie 2	Son	3mo	M	1/16			
	7							
	8							
	9							
	10							

ENROLLMENT
OF NOS. 1 HEREON
APPROVED BY THE SECRETARY
OF INTERIOR MAR 26 1904

ENROLLMENT
OF NOS. 2,3,4,5,6 HEREON
APPROVED BY THE SECRETARY
OF INTERIOR JAN 17 1903

TRIBAL ENROLLMENT OF PARENTS

	Name of Father	Year	County	Name of Mother	Year	County
1	Rolly Dodson	Dead	Non Citz	Eliza Dodson	Dead	Non Citz
2	Thos. Stark	1896	" "	Flissie Stark	"	Sans Bois
3	No1			No2		
4	No1			No2		
5	No1			No2		
6	No.1			No.2		
7						
8						
9	No3 on 1896 roll as Ludie Dodson					
10	No4 " 1896 " " Willy E "					
11	No1 " 1896 " Jno W "					
	No5 Affidavit of birth to be supplied					
12	No.6 Enrolled Dec 6th 1900					
13	For child of No.3 see NB (Apr 26,1906) Card No. 250.					
	" " Nos1&2 " (March3,1905) " " 1220					
14					#1 to 5	
15					Date of Application for Enrollment.	
16					6/14/99	
17	Bennington I.T. 10/18/02					

17

Choctaw By Blood Enrollment Cards 1898-1914

RESIDENCE:	Sans Bois	COUNTY.				
POST OFFICE:	Whitefield, I.T.					

Choctaw Nation

Choctaw Roll (Not Including Freedmen)

CARD NO.
FIELD NO. 2718

Dawes' Roll No.	NAME	Relationship to Person First Named	AGE	SEX	BLOOD	TRIBAL ENROLLMENT		
						Year	County	No.
7935	1 McKinney, Adam 39	First Named	36	M	Full	1896	Sans Bois	9330
I.W. 307	2 " Bertha W. 35	Wife	35	F	I.W			
	3							
	4							
	5							
	6							
	7							
	8							
	9							
	10							
	11	ENROLLMENT						
	12	OF NOS. 2 HEREON APPROVED BY THE SECRETARY						
	13	OF INTERIOR MAR 14 1905						
	14	ENROLLMENT						
	15	OF NOS. 1 HEREON						
	16	APPROVED BY THE SECRETARY OF INTERIOR JAN 17 1903						
	17							

TRIBAL ENROLLMENT OF PARENTS

	Name of Father	Year	County	Name of Mother	Year	County
1	John McKinney	Dead	Gaines	Martha McKinney	Dead	Sans Bois
2	Geo E Whitehead	dead	non-citizen	Ann M. Whitehead	dead	non-citizen
3						
4						
5	No.1 is now the husband of Bertha W McKinney on Choctaw card #D765					
6	On July 23 1902 No 2 was married to Adam McKinney No.1 July 25, 1902					
7						
8	Nos 1 and 2 lived together until the					
9	first of August, 1902 When they separated but were not divorced					
10	No.2 originally listed for enrollment on Choctaw card D-765 July 25, 1901:					
11	transferred to this card Jan 28, 1902. See decision of Jan 12, 1905.					
12	Record as to enrollment of No. 2 forwarded Department Mar 14, 1906					
	Record returned. See opinion of Assistant Attorney General of March 15, 1906 in case of Omer A Nicholson					
13						
14						
15				#1		
16				Date of Application for Enrollment.	6/14/99	
17	No/2 P.O. Stringtown I.T. 12/25/03					

18

Choctaw By Blood Enrollment Cards 1898-1914

RESIDENCE: Skullyville   COUNTY. **Choctaw Nation**   Choctaw Roll   CARD NO.
POST OFFICE: Milton, I.T   *(Not Including Freedmen)*   FIELD NO. 2719

Dawes' Roll No.	NAME		Relationship to Person First Named	AGE	SEX	BLOOD	TRIBAL ENROLLMENT		
							Year	County	No.
7936	1 Smith, Letha	59	First Named	56	F	1/4	1896	Skullyville	11147
7937	2 Cox, Letha	20	Dau	17	"	1/8	1896	"	2183
7938	3 " Joseph	16	G.Son	13	M	5/16	1896	"	2184
	4								
	5								
	6								
	7								
	8								
	9								
	10								
	11								
	12								
	13								
	14								
	15	ENROLLMENT OF NOS. 1,2,3, HEREON							
	16	APPROVED BY THE SECRETARY							
	17	OF INTERIOR JAN 17 1903							

TRIBAL ENROLLMENT OF PARENTS

	Name of Father	Year	County	Name of Mother	Year	County
1	Alfred Daniels	Dead	Non Citz	Mary Daniels	Dead	Tobucksy
2	Charley Cox	"	" "	No1		
3	Don Trahern	1896	Skullyville	Emma Cox	Dead	Skullyville
4						
5						
6						
7						
8						
9						
10						
11						
12						
13						
14						
15					Date of Application for Enrollment.	
16					6/15/99	
17						

Choctaw By Blood Enrollment Cards 1898-1914

RESIDENCE: Skullyville COUNTY. **Choctaw Nation** Choctaw Roll CARD NO.
POST OFFICE: Milton, I.T. (Not Including Freedmen) FIELD NO. 2720

Dawes' Roll No.	NAME		Relationship to Person First Named	AGE	SEX	BLOOD	TRIBAL ENROLLMENT		
							Year	County	No.
7939	1 Cox, Joseph R	25	First Named	22	M	1/8	1896	Sans Bois	2152
I.W. 1308	2 " Rebecca A	23	Wife	21	F	I.W.			
7940	3 " Charles	7	Son	4	M	1/16	1896	Sans Bois	2153
7941	4 " John	3	"	1	"	1/16			
7942	5 " Mary Melzona	1	Dau	4mo	F	1/16			
	6								
	7								
	8								
	9								
	10								
	11	ENROLLMENT							
	12	OF NOS. 2 HEREON							
	13	APPROVED BY THE SECRETARY OF INTERIOR MAR 14 1905							
	14								
	15	ENROLLMENT OF NOS. 1,3,4,5 HEREON							
	16	APPROVED BY THE SECRETARY OF INTERIOR JAN 17 1903							
	17								

TRIBAL ENROLLMENT OF PARENTS

	Name of Father	Year	County	Name of Mother	Year	County
1	Charley Cox	Dead	Non Citz	Letha Smith		Skullyville
2	J.D. Bush		" "	Rachel Bush		Non Citz
3	No1			No2		
4	No1			No2		
5	Nº1			Nº2		
6						
7						
8						
9	No1 on 1896 Roll as Joseph Cox					
10	No3 Affidavit of birth to be supplied					
11						
12	As to marriage, see testimony of					
13	No1 and David Folsom					
14	Nº5 Born April 26, 1902 enrolled Sept. 10, 1902					
	Evidence of marriage between Nᵒˢ 1and2 rec'd and filed Jan'y 31-1903					
15						
16				Date of Application for Enrollment. June 15/99		
17	Panther I.T.			No2 enrolled June 19/99		

20

Choctaw By Blood Enrollment Cards 1898-1914

RESIDENCE:	Sans Bois	COUNTY.		CARD NO.	
POST OFFICE:	Panther, I.T.	**Choctaw Nation**	Choctaw Roll (Not Including Freedmen)	FIELD NO.	2721

Dawes' Roll No.	NAME		Relationship to Person First Named	AGE	SEX	BLOOD	TRIBAL ENROLLMENT		
							Year	County	No.
7943	1 Choate, John	28	First Named	25	M	Full	1896	Sans Bois	2123
	2								
	3								
	4								
	5								
	6								
	7								
	8								
	9								
	10								
	11								
	12								
	13								
	14								
	15								
	16								
	17								

ENROLLMENT
OF NOS. 1 HEREON
APPROVED BY THE SECRETARY
OF INTERIOR JAN 17 1903

TRIBAL ENROLLMENT OF PARENTS

	Name of Father	Year	County	Name of Mother	Year	County
1	John Choate	Dead	Skullyville	Emily Choate	Dead	Sans Bois
2						
3						
4						
5						
6						
7						
8						
9						
10						
11						
12						
13						
14				Date of Application for Enrollment.		
15						
16				6/15/99		
17						

RESIDENCE:	Skullyville	COUNTY.	**Choctaw Nation**			**Choctaw Roll**	CARD No.	
POST OFFICE:	Bokoshe, I.T.					(Not Including Freedmen)	FIELD No.	2722

Dawes' Roll No.	NAME		Relationship to Person First Named	AGE	SEX	BLOOD	TRIBAL ENROLLMENT		
							Year	County	No.
DEAD.	1	McGinty, Joseph W	Named	36	M	I.W	1896	Skullyville	14854
14335	2	" Ida L	Wife	24	F	9/16	1896	Skullyville	9042
14336	3	" Lucretia	Dau	6	"	9/32	1896	"	9043
14337	4	" Burney W	Son	1½	M"F"	9/32			
14338	5	" Lois Lucile	Dau	4mo	F	9/32			
	6								
	7	⊕ 8/4/1916 Roll No. 14337, Sex changed from M to F per							
	8	Deptl. authority of July 18,1916 (See D-4804-1916)							
	9								
	10	ENROLLMENT OF NOS. 2 3 4 and 5 HEREON							
	11	APPROVED BY THE SECRETARY							
	12	OF INTERIOR APR 11 1903							
	13	No. 1 HEREON DISMISSED UNDER							
	14	ORDER OF THE COMMISSION TO THE FIVE							
	15	CIVILIZED TRIBES OF MARCH 31, 1905.							
	16								
	17								

TRIBAL ENROLLMENT OF PARENTS

	Name of Father	Year	County	Name of Mother	Year	County
1	Joseph McGinty	Dead	Non Citz	Mary McGinty	Dead	Non Citz
2	John Taylor	1896	Sans Bois	Lucretia Taylor	"	Skullyville
3	No1			No2		
4	No1			No2		
5	No.1			No.2		
6						
7						
8						
9						
10						
11	No1 on 1896 roll as Joseph McGinty.					
12	No.5 Enrolled June 23d, 1900					
13	No.1 Admitted as an intermarried citizen and Nos 2 and 3 as					
14	citizens by blood by Dawes Commission: Choctaw Case #347: No appeal					
15	No.1 died Oct. 9, 1900; Proof of death filed Dec 24 1902			Date of Application for Enrollment.		
16	For child of No.2 see NB (Mar 3-05) #581			6/15/99		
17						

Choctaw By Blood Enrollment Cards 1898-1914

RESIDENCE:	Sans Bois	COUNTY.	**Choctaw Nation**			**Choctaw Roll**		CARD NO.	
POST OFFICE:	Tamaha, I.T					*(Not Including Freedmen)*		FIELD NO. 2723	

Dawes' Roll No.	NAME		Relationship to Person First Named	AGE	SEX	BLOOD	TRIBAL ENROLLMENT		
							Year	County	No.
I.W 150	1 Norman, Isaac M	44	First Named	41	M	I.W			
7944	2 " Laura B	9	Dau	6	F	1/8	1896	Sans Bois	9540
	3								
	4								
	5								
	6								
	7								
	8								
	9								
	10								
	11								
	12								
	13								
	14								
	15								
	16								
	17								

ENROLLMENT
OF NOS. 2 HEREON
APPROVED BY THE SECRETARY
OF INTERIOR JAN 17 1903

ENROLLMENT
OF NOS. 1 HEREON
APPROVED BY THE SECRETARY
OF INTERIOR JUN 13 1903

TRIBAL ENROLLMENT OF PARENTS

Name of Father	Year	County	Name of Mother	Year	County
1 Richard Norman	Dead	Non Citz	Cilpha Norman	Dead	Non Citz
2 No1			Ara B Norman	"	Sans Bois
3					
4					
5					
6 No1 Further action in connection with allotment to No1 suspended under protest					
7 of Attorneys for Choctaw and Chickasaw Nation, Jan 23 1904					
8 Protest overruled by Dept March 3/19/04					
9					
10 No1 was admitted by Dawes Commission as an					
11 Intermarried Citizen, Case No 1143 No appeal					
12					
13					
14					
15				Date of Application for Enrollment.	
16				6/14/99	
17 Stigler I.T. 12/15/02					

23

Choctaw By Blood Enrollment Cards 1898-1914

Dawes' Roll No.	NAME	Relationship to Person First Named	AGE	SEX	BLOOD	TRIBAL ENROLLMENT Year	TRIBAL ENROLLMENT County	TRIBAL ENROLLMENT No.
7945	1 Evans, Lee ⁴⁰	First Named	37	M	1/16	1896	Skullyville	3680
7946	2 " Lizzie ³⁷	Wife	34	F	1/16	1896	"	3681
7947	3 " Edmond ¹⁵	Son	12	M	1/16	1896	"	3682
7948	4 " Jesse ¹³	Son	10	M	1/16	1896	"	3683
7949	5 " Rufus ⁹	"	6	"	1/16	1896	"	3684
7950	6 " Simpson ⁸	"	5	"	1/16	1896	"	3685
7951	7 " Tandy ¹	"	8mo	"	1/16			
	8							
	9							
	10							
	11							
	12							
	13							
	14							
	15	ENROLLMENT						
	16	OF NOS. 1,2,3,4,5,6,7 HEREON APPROVED BY THE SECRETARY						
	17	OF INTERIOR JAN 17 1903						

TRIBAL ENROLLMENT OF PARENTS

	Name of Father	Year	County	Name of Mother	Year	County
1	Harve Evans	Dead	Non Citz	Harriet Evans	Dead	Skullyville
2	John Parrish	"	Sans Bois	Bethena Parrish	"	Non Citz
3	No 1			No 2		
4	No 1			No 2		
5	No 1			No 2		
6	No 1			No 2		
7	No 1			No 2		
8						
9	No3 Name changed from Edna to Edmond under Departmental					
10	letter of November 30, 1903 (D.C. #33544-1903) Change of sex also authorized					
11	No4 on 1896 roll as Jessee Evans					
12	No3 " 1896 " " Edmund "					
13	Evidence of marriage of parents of No2 to be supplied. See Card of Cyrus B. Ward No 2695					
14						
15	Nº3 is a male correct name is Edmond. See testimony of Nº2 taken					
16	Aug 5, 1903			Date of Application for Enrollment.	6/15/99	
17						

24

Choctaw By Blood Enrollment Cards 1898-1914

RESIDENCE:	Skullyville	COUNTY.	**Choctaw Nation**				**Choctaw Roll** *(Not Including Freedmen)*	CARD NO.	
POST OFFICE:	Fort Smith, Ark							FIELD NO.	2725

Dawes' Roll No.		NAME	Relationship to Person First Named	AGE	SEX	BLOOD	TRIBAL ENROLLMENT		
							Year	County	No.
I.W. 728	1	Kayser, Elizabeth H	First Named	32	F	IW	1896	Skullyville	14716
	2								
	3								
	4								
	5								
	6	ENROLLMENT OF NOS. ~~~ 1 ~~~ HEREON APPROVED BY THE SECRETARY OF INTERIOR MAY -7 1904							
	7								
	8								
	9								
	10								
	11								
	12								
	13								
	14								
	15								
	16								
	17								

TRIBAL ENROLLMENT OF PARENTS

	Name of Father	Year	County	Name of Mother	Year	County
1	Thos Heard	Dead	Non Citz	Martha Heard	Dead	Non Citz
2						
3						
4						
5						
6						
7	No1 Wife of H.J. Kayser (now deceased) '96 Skullyville Co No 7463					
8	No1 See Decision of March 2 '04					
9	On 1896 roll as Elizabeth Kayser					
10	As to residence, see her testimony					
11						
12						
13						
14					Date of Application for Enrollment.	
15						
16					6/15/99	
17						

Choctaw By Blood Enrollment Cards 1898-1914

RESIDENCE: Skullyville COUNTY.	POST OFFICE: Brazil, I.T

Choctaw Nation   **Choctaw Roll** (Not Including Freedmen)

CARD No. FIELD No. 2726

Dawes' Roll No.	NAME		Relationship to Person First Named	AGE	SEX	BLOOD	TRIBAL ENROLLMENT		
							Year	County	No.
7952	1 James, Noel	54	First Named	51	M	Full	1896	Skullyville	6437
7953	2 " Malissa	69	Wife	66	F	"	1896	"	6438
	3								
	4								
	5								
	6								
	7								
	8								
	9								
	10								
	11								
	12								
	13								
	14								
	15								
	16								
	17								

ENROLLMENT
OF NOS. 1 and 2 HEREON
APPROVED BY THE SECRETARY
OF INTERIOR JAN 17 1903

TRIBAL ENROLLMENT OF PARENTS

	Name of Father	Year	County	Name of Mother	Year	County
1	Charles James	Dead	Skullyville	Sallie James	Dead	Sugar Loaf
2	Cornelius McCann	"	"			Skullyville
3						
4						
5						
6						.
7						
8			No2 on 1896 roll as Malissie James			
9						
10						
11						
12						
13						
14						
15						
16				Date of Application for Enrollment.	6/15/99	
17						

26

Choctaw By Blood Enrollment Cards 1898-1914

RESIDENCE: Skullyville COUNTY. **Choctaw Nation** **Choctaw Roll** CARD No. 2727
POST OFFICE: Wall, I.T. *(Not Including Freedmen)* FIELD NO. 2727

Dawes' Roll No.	NAME		Relationship to Person First Named	AGE	SEX	BLOOD	TRIBAL ENROLLMENT		
							Year	County	No.
7954	1 Dixon, Billy	48	First Named	45	M	Full	1896	Skullyville	3185
7955	2 DIED PRIOR TO SEPTEMBER 25 1902 " Betsy	38	Wife	35	F	"	1896	"	3186
7956	3 " Lilly	15	Dau	12	"	"	1896	"	3187
7957	4 " Mamie	12	"	9	"	"	1896	"	3188
7958	5 " Joseph	8	Son	5	M	"	1896	"	3189
7959	6 " Susan	5	Dau	1	F	"			
	7								
	8								
	9								
	10								
	11								
	12								
	13								
	14								
	15 ENROLLMENT OF NOS. HEREON								
	16 APPROVED BY THE SECRETARY OF INTERIOR								
	17								

TRIBAL ENROLLMENT OF PARENTS

	Name of Father	Year	County	Name of Mother	Year	County
1	Hopson Dixon	Dead	Gaines	Pisa-ho-tema	Dead	Gaines
2	Cass				"	"
3	No1			No2		
4	No1			No2		
5	No1			No2		
6	No1			No2		
7						
8						
9	No2 Died January 17" 1900: Proof of death filed December 23 1902					
10						
11	No5 on 1896 Lily Dixon					
	No2 died Jan. 17, 1900: Enrollment cancelled by Department July 9, 1904					
12						
13						
14						
15					Date of Application for Enrollment.	
16					6/15/99	
17	Lodi I.T. 12/18/02					

27

RESIDENCE:	Sans Bois	COUNTY.	**Choctaw Nation**	**Choctaw Roll**	CARD NO.	
POST OFFICE:	Stigler, I.T.			(Not Including Freedmen)	FIELD NO.	2728

Dawes' Roll No.	NAME		Relationship to Person First Named	AGE	SEX	BLOOD	TRIBAL ENROLLMENT		
							Year	County	No.
7960	₁ Jackson, Ben	38	First Named	35	M	Full	1896	Sans Bois	6378
DEAD.	₂ " Sicany		Wife	38	F	"	1896	" "	6424
	₃								
	₄ No. 2 HEREON DISMISSED UNDER								
	₅ ORDER OF THE COMMISSION TO THE FIVE CIVILIZED TRIBES OF MARCH 31, 1905.								
	₆								
	₇								
	₈								
	₉								
	10								
	11								
	12								
	13								
	14								
	15 ENROLLMENT OF NOS. 1 HEREON								
	16 APPROVED BY THE SECRETARY OF INTERIOR JAN 17 1903								
	17								

TRIBAL ENROLLMENT OF PARENTS

	Name of Father	Year	County	Name of Mother	Year	County
₁	E-ma-spa-subbee	Dead	Sans Bois		Dead	Sans Bois
₂	George James	"	" "	Ish-to-ma-hoke	"	Towson
₃						
₄						
₅						
₆	No.2 on 1896 roll as Sykney James					
₇	N⁰2 Died Feby 6, 1900. See note filed this day signed by N⁰1 Sept 25, 1902					
₈	N⁰1 is now husband of Louina Martin on Choctaw card #2628 Sept 25, 1902					
₉	N⁰2 Proof of death Feby 6, 1900, filed Nov 4, 1902					
	For child of No.1 see NB (March 3, 1905) #1103					
10						
11						
12						
13						
14						
15				Date of Application for Enrollment.		
16				6/15/99		
17						

Choctaw By Blood Enrollment Cards 1898-1914

RESIDENCE: Sans Bois COUNTY.	POST OFFICE: Iron Bridge, I.T

Choctaw Nation

Choctaw Roll *(Not Including Freedmen)*

CARD NO. FIELD NO. 2729

Dawes' Roll No.	NAME	Relationship to Person First Named	AGE	SEX	BLOOD	TRIBAL ENROLLMENT		
						Year	County	No.
7961	1 Jones, Mike	First Named	22	M	Full	1893	Sans Bois	277
	2							
	3							
	4							
	5							
	6							
	7							
	8							
	9							
	10							
	11							
	12							
	13							
	14							
	15							
	16							
	17							

ENROLLMENT
OF NOS. 1 HEREON
APPROVED BY THE SECRETARY
OF INTERIOR JAN 17 1903

TRIBAL ENROLLMENT OF PARENTS

Name of Father	Year	County	Name of Mother	Year	County
1 Julius Jones	Dead	Sans Bois	Julia Jones	Dead	Sans Bois
2					
3					
4					
5					
6					
7					
8 On 1893 Pay roll, Page 28, No 277, Sans Bois Co					
9 No 1 is now the husband of Emma Cass on Choctaw Card #2831 Aug 2, 1901					
10 Evidence of marriage filed Aug 12, 1901 with papers on Choctaw Card #2831. For child of No.1 see NB (March 3,1905) #686 683[sic]					
11					
12					
13					
14					
15				Date of Application for Enrollment.	
16				6/15/99	
17					

OFFICE: Brazil, I.T   **Choctaw Nation**   Choctaw Roll *(Not Including Freedmen)*   FIELD N

es' No.	NAME		Relationship to Person First Named	AGE	SEX	BLOOD	TRIBAL ENROLLMENT Year	County	No.
32	1 James, Ben	40	First Named	37	M	Full	1896	Skullyville	6453
33	2 " Rhoda	33	Wife	30	F	"	1896	"	10107
34	3 " Susan	17	Dau	14	"	"	1896	"	6454
35	4 " Louisa	2	"	1½	"	"			
36	5 Kincade, Levina	10	S.Dau	7	"	"	1896	Skullyville	7448
37	6 James, Jane	1	Dau	5mo	F	"			
	7								
	8								
	9								
	10								
	11								
	12								
	13								
	14								
	15								
	16								
	17								

ENROLLMENT
OF NOS. 1,2,3,4,5,6 HEREON
APPROVED BY THE SECRETARY
OF INTERIOR JAN 17 1903

TRIBAL ENROLLMENT OF PARENTS

	Name of Father	Year	County	Name of Mother	Year	C
1	Charles James	Dead	Skullyville	Sallie James	"	Sugar
2	Boland Perry	"	"	Emily Perry	"	Skully
3	No1			Elizabeth Harkins	"	
4	No1			No2		
5	Robert Kincade	1896	Sans Bois	No2		
6	No1			No2		
7						
8						
9	No2 on 1896 roll as Rhodie Perry					
10	No5 " 1896 " " Lavina Kingcade					
11	No.6 Enrolled Sept 4, 1901					
12	For child of Nos 1&2 see NB (Mar 3, 1905) #623					
13						
14						
15					#1 to 5 inc	
16				Date of Application for Enrollment.	6/15/99	
17						

RESIDENCE: Sans Bois COUNTY. **Choctaw Nation** Choctaw Roll CARD No.
POST OFFICE: Whitefield, I.T *(Not Including Freedmen)* FIELD No. 2731

Dawes' Roll No.	NAME	Relationship to Person First Named	AGE	SEX	BLOOD	TRIBAL ENROLLMENT		
						Year	County	No.
7968	1 Surratt, Jefferson D *DIED PRIOR TO SEPTEMBER 25, 1902*		39	M	1/2	1896	Sans Bois	11106
7969	2 " Fena 36	Wife	33	F	1/2	1896	" "	11107
	3 McKinney, Sampson	Ward	18	M	Full	1896	" "	9001
7970	4 McKinney Richard 18	"	15	"	"	1896	" "	9002
7971	5 Harrison, Benjamin 13	Ward	10	"	"	1896	" "	5069
	6							
	7							
	8							
	9							
	10							
	11							
	12							
	13 Nos 4 and 5 not living							
	14 with No2.							
	15 ENROLLMENT							
	OF NOS. 1,2, 4,5 HEREON							
	16 APPROVED BY THE SECRETARY							
	OF INTERIOR JAN 17 1903							
	17							

TRIBAL ENROLLMENT OF PARENTS

	Name of Father	Year	County	Name of Mother	Year	County
1	Henry Surratt	Dead	Non Citz	Lucy Surratt	Dead	Sans Bois
2	Jenett McDaniel	1896	Sugar Loaf	Ethie McDaniel	1896	Non Citz
3	Philip McKinney	Dead	Sans Bois	Pollie McKinney	Dead	Sans Bois
4	" "	"	" "	" "	"	" "
5	Mitchell Harrison	"	" "	Emma L Harrison	"	Non Citz
6						
7						
8						
9	No1 on 1896 roll as J.D. Surratt			No.3 transferred to		
10	No2 " 1896 " " Fona "			Choctaw card #5329		
11	No5 " 1896 " " Ben Harrison				May 28, 1900	
12	As to marriage of parents of No2, see testimony					
13	of G. W. Dukes					
14	Evidence of marriage of parents of No5					
15	to be supplied					
16	No1 Died Dec 4, 1900; Proof of death filed Nov. 4, 1902.			Date of Application for Enrollment.	6/15/99	
17	P.O. Graham I.T					

Choctaw By Blood Enrollment Cards 1898-1914

RESIDENCE: Skullyville   COUNTY. **Choctaw Nation**   **Choctaw Roll**   CARD NO.
POST OFFICE: Tucker, I.T.   (Not Including Freedmen)   FIELD NO.   2732

Dawes' Roll No.	NAME		Relationship to Person	AGE	SEX	BLOOD	TRIBAL ENROLLMENT		
							Year	County	
7972	1 Collins, Andrew	29	First Named	26	M	1/4	1896	Skullyville	2173
I.W. 965	2 " Claudie L	24	Wife	20	F	I.W.	1896	"	14575
7973	3 " Claudie C	6	Dau	2	"	1/8			
7974	4 " Andrew L	4	Son	2mo	M	1/8			
7975	5 " Nellie	10	Dau	7	F	1/8	1893	Chick Dist	134
7976	6 " Thomas Hugh	1	Son	2mo	M	1/8			
	7								
	8								
	9								
	10								
	11	ENROLLMENT							
	12	OF NOS. ~ 2 ~ HEREON APPROVED BY THE SECRETARY							
	13	OF INTERIOR SEP 22 1904							
	14								
	15	ENROLLMENT							
	16	OF NOS. 1,3,4,5,6 HEREON APPROVED BY THE SECRETARY							
	17	OF INTERIOR JAN 17 1903							

TRIBAL ENROLLMENT OF PARENTS

	Name of Father	Year	County	Name of Mother	Year	County
	Mike Collins	1896	Non Citz	Mary Collins	Dead	Skullyville
	Samuel Kersh	Dead	" "	Alice Kersh	1896	Non Citz
3	No1			No2		
4	No1			No2		
5	No1			Nannie Duncan	1896	Non Citz
6	No1			No2		
7	No2 See Decision of June 21 '04					
8	See affidavit of B.F. Kemp relative to divorce proceedings between					
9	N° 1 and former wife, filed July 6, 1903					
10	No2 on 1896 roll as Claudie L Collin					
11	No1 " 1896 " " Andrew J Collins					
12	Nos 3-4 Evidence of marriage to be supplied. Recd 6/22/99					
13	No5 On 1893 Pay Roll, Chickasaw District, Page 13,					
14	No 134, as Nettie Collins					
15	As to marriage of parents of No5, see testimony of E.J. Johnson			#1 to 5	Date of Application for Enrollment.	
16	No6 Enrolled March 16, 1901 Date of application for enrollment 6/15/99					
17						

Choctaw By Blood Enrollment Cards 1898-1914

RESIDENCE: Skullyville   COUNTY.   **Choctaw Nation**   Choctaw Roll   CARD No.
POST OFFICE: Brazil, I.T.   (Not Including Freedmen)   FIELD No. 2733

Dawes' Roll No.	NAME	Relationship to Person First Named	AGE	SEX	BLOOD	TRIBAL ENROLLMENT Year	County	No.
7977	1 Terrell, Solomon 44	First Named	41	M	Full	1896	Skullyville	11886
7978	2 " Emiline 51	Wife	48	F	"	1896	"	11887
7979	3 " Daniel 13	Son	10	M	"	1896	"	11889
7980	4 " Sillen 10	Dau	7	F	"	1896	"	11890
7981	5 Tarby, William 20	S.Son	17	M	"	1896	"	11888
7982	6 Williams, Ida 14	Ward	8	F	"	1896	"	12871
7983	7 " Melvina 10	"	7	"	"	1896	"	12872
7984	8 " Mary 8	"	5	"	"	1896	"	12873
7985	9 Betsy DIED PRIOR TO SEPTEMBER 25, 1902	"	1	"	"			
	10							
	11 ENROLLMENT							
	12 OF NOS. 1,2,3,4,5,6,7,8,9 HEREON APPROVED BY THE SECRETARY							
	13 OF INTERIOR JAN 17 1903							
	14 No9 died Aug – 1900; Proof of							
	15 death filed Dec 20 1902							
	16 No.9 died Aug-1900; Enrollment cancelled by Department July 8, 1904							
	17							

TRIBAL ENROLLMENT OF PARENTS

	Name of Father	Year	County	Name of Mother	Year	County
1	George Terrell	Dead	Skullyville	Mutsey Terrell	Dead	Skullyville
2	A-ha-yo-tubbee	"	"	E-la-ho-tema	"	"
3	No1			No2		
4	No1			No2		
5	William Tarby	Dead	Skullyville	No2		
6	Stephen Williams	"	Sugar Loaf	Easter Williams	Dead	Sugar Loaf
7	" "	"	" "	" "	"	" "
8	" "	"	" "	" "	"	" "
9	" "	"	" "	" "	"	" "
10						
11						
12	No4 on 1896 roll as Silen Terrel					
13	No7 " 1896 " " Fannie Williams					
14	No6 " 1896 " " Ida					
	No8 " 1896 " " Mary "					
15	No9 " 1896 " " Betsy "		No9 not on 1896 roll			
16	Surnames of first four appear on 1896			Date of Application for Enrollment.	6/15/99	
17	roll as Terrel					

33

Choctaw By Blood Enrollment Cards 1898-1914

RESIDENCE: Skullyville COUNTY. **Choctaw Nation** Choctaw Roll CARD NO.
POST OFFICE: Cameron I.T. (Not Including Freedmen) FIELD NO. 2734

Dawes' Roll No.	NAME		Relationship to Person First Named	AGE	SEX	BLOOD	TRIBAL ENROLLMENT		
							Year	County	No.
7986	1 Lewis Frank	22	First Named	19	M	1/32	1896	Skullyville	7718
7987	2 " Belle	20	Sist	17	F	1/32	1896	"	7719
DEAD.	3 " May	18	"	15	F	1/32	1896	"	7721
7988	4 " Annie	16	"	13	F	1/32	1896	"	7720
7989	5 " Curtis	11	Bro	8	M	1/32	1896	"	7723
7990	6 " Alice	9	Sis	6	F	1/32	1896	"	7724
7991	7 " Winnie	7	"	4	F	1/32	1896	"	7725
7992	8 " Wallis G	1	Bro	18mo	M	1/32		"	
	9								
	10 No 3 HEREON DISMISSED UNDER								
	11 ORDER OF THE COMMISSION TO THE FIVE								
	CIVILIZED TRIBES OF MARCH 31, 1905.								
	12								
	13								
	14								
	15 ENROLLMENT								
	OF NOS. 1,2,4,5,6,7,8 HEREON								
	16 APPROVED BY THE SECRETARY								
	OF INTERIOR JAN 17 1903								
	17								

TRIBAL ENROLLMENT OF PARENTS

	Name of Father	Year	County	Name of Mother	Year	County
1	William A Lewis	1896	Non Citz	Bettie A Lewis	Dead	Skullyville
2	" " "	"	" "	" " "	"	"
3	" " "	"	" "	" " "	"	"
4	" " "	"	" "	" " "	"	"
5	" " "	"	" "	" " "	"	"
6	" " "	"	" "	" " "	"	"
7	" " "	"	" "	" " "	"	"
8	" " "	"	" "	" " "	"	"
9						
10						
11	The following of the above named children were admitted by Act					
12	of Council approved Nov. 6, 1896, viz: Frank and Belle as Bettie,					
13	May as Mary, Annie, Curtis, Alice, Winnie. Bettie A, the mother of all these and baby Wallis G. was also admitted					
14	She is dead					
15	No3 died Nov 13, 1900; Proof of death filed Dec 20 1902					
16	For child of No.2 see NB (March 3, 1905) #742		Date of Application for Enrollment.			6/15/99
17	No2 PO Shady Point IT 4/6/05					

34

Choctaw By Blood Enrollment Cards 1898-1914

RESIDENCE:	Sans Bois	COUNTY.					Choctaw Roll	CARD NO.	
POST OFFICE:	Iron Bridge I.T.	**Choctaw Nation**					(Not Including Freedmen)	FIELD NO. 2735	

Dawes' Roll No.	NAME	Relationship to Person First Named	AGE	SEX	BLOOD	TRIBAL ENROLLMENT Year	County	No.
7993	₁ Franklin Ben 45	First Named	42	M	Full	1896	Sans Bois	3898
7994	₂ DIED PRIOR TO SEPTEMBER 25 1902 Sarah	Dau	14	F	"	1896	" "	3900
7995	₃ " John W 10	Son	7	M	"	1896	" "	3901
	4							
	5							
	6							
	7							
	8							
	9							
	10							
	11							
	12							
	13							
	14							
	15 ENROLLMENT OF NOS. 1, 2, 3 HEREON							
	16 APPROVED BY THE SECRETARY OF INTERIOR JAN 17 1903							
	17							

TRIBAL ENROLLMENT OF PARENTS

	Name of Father	Year	County	Name of Mother	Year	County
₁	Ta-nap-a-ya	Dead	Red River		Dead	Red River
₂	No 1			Ta-mis-se Franklin	"	Sans Bois
₃	No 1			" "	"	" "
₄						
₅						
₆						
₇						
₈	No3 On 1896 roll as Jno. W. Franklin					
₉	Nº2 died Aug. 11, 1902. Proof of death filed Dec 20 1902 filed Nov. 11, 1902					
₁₀	No2 died Aug 11 1902; Enrollment cancelled by Department July 8, 1904					
₁₁						
₁₂						
₁₃						
₁₄						
₁₅						
₁₆					Date of Application for Enrollment.	6/15/99
₁₇						

35

RESIDENCE:	Sans Bois	COUNTY.	**Choctaw Nation**		**Choctaw Roll**	CARD NO.	
POST OFFICE:	Stigler I.T.				*(Not Including Freedmen)*	FIELD NO.	2736

Dawes' Roll No.	NAME		Relationship to Person First Named	AGE	SEX	BLOOD	TRIBAL ENROLLMENT		
							Year	County	No.
7996	1 James Warren	40	First Named	37	M	Full	1896	Sans Bois	6384
7997	2 " Emiline	41	Wife	38	F	"	1896	" "	6385
7998	3 " Selina	11	Dau	8	F	"	1896	" "	6386
7999	4 " Jackson	7	Son	4	M	"	1896	" "	6387
8000	5 " Ella	2	Dau	17mo	F	"		" "	
8001	6 Folsom Ida	21	S.Dau	18	F	"	1896	" "	3890
8002	7 " Charlotte	16	S Dau	13	F	"	1896	" "	3891
8003	8 " Israel	13	S.Son	10	M	"	1896	" "	3892
8004	9 James, George	3	Son	1½yr	M	"			
15956	10 Jones, Annie		Dau of No 6	1	F	"			
	11								
	12								
	13								
	14								
	15								
	16								
	17								

ENROLLMENT OF NOS. ----10---- HEREON APPROVED BY THE SECRETARY OF INTERIOR NOV 27 1905

ENROLLMENT OF NOS. 1,2,3,4,5,6,7,8,9 HEREON APPROVED BY THE SECRETARY OF INTERIOR JAN 17 1903

TRIBAL ENROLLMENT OF PARENTS

	Name of Father	Year	County	Name of Mother	Year	County
1	George James	Dead	Sans Bois	Ish-te-ma-hoke	Dead	Towson
2	Boland Perry	"	Skullyville	Nancy Perry	"	Towson
3	No 1			No 2		
4	No 1			No 2		
5	No 1			No 2		
6	Billy Folsom	Dead	Sans Bois	No 2		
7	" "	"	" "	No 2		
8	" "	"	" "	No 2		
9	No 1			No 2		
10	Willie Jones		Choctaw #3108	No 6		
11						
12	No1 On 1896 roll as Warlin James					
13	Nos 6-7 and 8 on 1896 roll as Folsom					
	No 9 Enrolled August 2, 1901					
14						
15	Application for enrollment of No10 received under act of					
16	Congress approved March 3, 1905. Her name placed hereon Oct 9, 1905				Date of Application for Enrollment.	6/15/99
	For child of No.6 see NB (March 3, 1905) #1328					
17	" " " No.7 " " " " #1430					1 to 8

36

Choctaw By Blood Enrollment Cards 1898-1914

RESIDENCE: Sans Bois	COUNTY. **Choctaw Nation**		Choctaw Roll (Not Including Free...)	CARD NO.	
POST OFFICE: Iron Bridge				FIELD NO. 2737	

Dawes' Roll No.	NAME		Relationship to Person First Named	AGE	SEX	BLOOD	TRIBAL ENROLLMENT			
							Year	County		No.
DEAD.	1 Byington Philip			38	M	Full	1896	Sans Bois		629
8005	2 " Wycie	63	Wife	60	F	"	1896	" "		630
8006	3 " Henry	15	Son	12	M	"	1896	" "		631
8007	4 " Lizzie	12	Dau	9	F	"	1896	" "		632
	5									
	6									
	7 No. 1 HEREON DISMISSED UNDER									
	ORDER OF THE COMMISSION TO THE FIVE									
	8 CIVILIZED TRIBES OF MARCH 31, 1905.									
	9									
	10									
	11									
	12									
	13									
	14									
	15 ENROLLMENT OF NOS. 2,3,4 HEREON									
	16 APPROVED BY THE SECRETARY OF INTERIOR JAN 17 1903									
	17									

TRIBAL ENROLLMENT OF PARENTS

	Name of Father	Year	County	Name of Mother	Year	County
1	Silas Byington	Dead	Skullyville		Dead	Skullyville
2	Wa-ka-ta-bi	"	Sans Bois	Fe-le-ma	"	Sans Bois
3	No 1			No 2		
4	No 1			No 2		
5						
6						
7						
8						
9	No2 On 1896 roll as Vicy Byington					
10						
11	Nº1 Died Jany 16, 1902; Proof of death filed Nov. 11,1902					
12						
13						
14						
15					Date of Application for Enrollment.	
16					6/15/99	
17						

Choctaw By Blood Enrollment Cards 1898-1914

RESIDENCE: Sans Bois POST OFFICE: Milton I.T.	COUNTY. **Choctaw Nation**	**Choctaw Roll** *(Not Including Freedmen)*	CARD NO. FIELD NO. 2738

Dawes' Roll No.	NAME	Relationship to Person First Named	AGE	SEX	BLOOD	TRIBAL ENROLLMENT		
						Year	County	No.
8008	1 Wallen Sim 24	Named	21	M	Full	1896	Sans Bois	12678
8009	2 Sophia DIED PRIOR TO SEPTEMBER 25, 1902	Wife	19	F	"	1896	" "	11858
	3							
	4							
	5							
	6							
	7							
	8							
	9							
	10							
	11							
	12							
	13							
	14							
	15	ENROLLMENT OF NOS. 1 and 2 HEREON APPROVED BY THE SECRETARY OF INTERIOR JAN 17 1903						
	16							
	17							

	TRIBAL ENROLLMENT OF PARENTS						
Name of Father	Year	County	Name of Mother	Year	County		
1 Thompson Wallen	1896	Sans Bois	Incy Tok-fo-a-ta	Dead	Sans Bois		
2 Loman Thomas	1896	" "	Sacia Thomas	1896	" "		
3							
4							
5							
6							
7		No2 On 1896 roll as Sophia Thomas					
8							
9		No1 also on 1896 roll, Page 332, No 12657, as Sam Wallen.					
10		No2 died Aug 12, 1900; Enrollment cancelled by Department July 8, 1904					
11		For child of No.1 see NB (Mar 3, 1905) #672					
12							
13							
14							
15						Date of Application for Enrollment.	
16						6/15/99	
17							

38

Choctaw By Blood Enrollment Cards 1898-1914

RESIDENCE: Skullyville COUNTY. **Choctaw Nation** **Choctaw Roll** *(Not Including Freedmen)* CARD NO. FIELD NO. 2739
POST OFFICE: Brazil I.T.

Dawes' Roll No.	NAME		Relationship to Person First Named	AGE	SEX	BLOOD	TRIBAL ENROLLMENT		
							Year	County	No.
8010	1 James Adam	48	First Named	45	M	Full	1896	Skullyville	6441
8011	2 " Ticey	50	Wife	47	F	"	1896	"	6442
8012	3 " Isaac	26	Son	23	M	"	1896	"	6443
8013	4 " Frank	24	"	21	M	"	1896	"	6444
8014	5 " Emily	21	Dau	18	F	"	1896	"	6445
8015	6 DIED PRIOR TO SEPTEMBER 25 1902 " Eliza 20		"	17	F	"	1896	"	6446
8016	7 " Allen	16	Son	13	M	"	1896	"	6447
8017	8 " Jesse	13	"	10	M	"	1896	"	6448
	9								
	10								
	11								
	12								
	13								
	14								
	15								
	16								
	17								

ENROLLMENT
OF NOS. 1,2,3,4,5,6,7,8 HEREON
APPROVED BY THE SECRETARY
OF INTERIOR JAN 17 1903

TRIBAL ENROLLMENT OF PARENTS

	Name of Father	Year	County	Name of Mother	Year	County
1	Charles James	Dead	Skullyville	Siley James	Dead	Sugar Loaf
2	Simon Peter	1896	Sugar Loaf	Yum-mi-ho-ma	"	Skullyville
3	No 1			No 2		
4	No 1			No 2		
5	No 1			No 2		
6	No 1			No 2		
7	No 1			No 2		
8	No 1			No 2		
9						
10						
11			No8 On 1896 roll as Jessie James			
12						
13						
14			No6 died March 3, 1902: Proof of death filed Dec 20 1902			
15			No3 is the husband of Mary Harkins Choctaw card #2444			Date of Application for Enrollment.
16						6/15/99
17						

39

Choctaw By Blood Enrollment Cards 1898-1914

RESIDENCE: Skullyville	COUNTY.	**Choctaw Nation**				**Choctaw Roll** (Not Including Freedmen)	CARD No.	
POST OFFICE: Spiro I.T.							FIELD No. 2740	

Dawes' Roll No.	NAME	Relationship to Person First Named	AGE	SEX	BLOOD	TRIBAL ENROLLMENT		
						Year	County	No.
8018 ₁	Russell Robert ²⁷	Named	24	M	1/8	1896	Skullyville	10712
8019 ₂	" Eva	Dau	4days	F	1/16			
I.W. 1111 ₃	" Dora ²³	Wife	20	F	I.W.			
₄								
₅								
₆								
₇								
₈								
₉								
₁₀								
₁₁								
₁₂								
₁₃								
₁₄								
₁₅								
₁₆								
₁₇								

ENROLLMENT OF NOS. 3 HEREON APPROVED BY THE SECRETARY OF INTERIOR NOV 16 1904

ENROLLMENT OF NOS. 1 and 2 HEREON APPROVED BY THE SECRETARY OF INTERIOR JAN 17 1903

TRIBAL ENROLLMENT OF PARENTS

Name of Father	Year	County	Name of Mother	Year	County
₁ Jacob Russell	Dead	Non Citz	Elmira Russell	Dead	Skullyville
₂ N°1			Dora Russell		intermarried
₃ Walker Harris	dead	White – man	Sarah A Harris		White woman
₄					
₅					
₆					
₇	No 1 is the husband of Dora Russell on Choctaw card #D.640				
₈	Evidence of marriage filed with Choctaw #D.640				
₉	N°2 Born Sept 15, 1902, enrolled Sept 19, 1902				
₁₀	For child of Nos 1&3 see NB (Mar 3 '05) #551				
₁₁					
₁₂	No.3 transferred from Choctaw card #D-640 Oct 31, 1904: See decision of Oct 15, 1904				
₁₃					
₁₄					
₁₅				Date of Application for Enrollment.	
₁₆				6/15/99	
₁₇					

Choctaw By Blood Enrollment Cards 1898-1914

RESIDENCE: Skullyville   COUNTY. **Choctaw Nation**   **Choctaw Roll** CARD NO.
POST OFFICE: Brazil I.T.   *(Not Including Freedmen)*   FIELD NO. 2741

Dawes' Roll No.	NAME		Relationship to Person	AGE	SEX	BLOOD	TRIBAL ENROLLMENT		
							Year	County	No.
8020	1 Whistler Martin	28	First Named	25	M	Full	1896	Sugar Loaf	12863
8021	2 " Nancy	25	Wife	22	F	"	1896	" "	12864
8022	3 " Etna	1	Dau	6wks	F	"			
	4								
	5								
	6								
	7								
	8								
	9								
	10								
	11								
	12								
	13								
	14								
	15	ENROLLMENT OF NOS. 1, 2, 3 HEREON APPROVED BY THE SECRETARY OF INTERIOR JAN 17 1903							
	16								
	17								

TRIBAL ENROLLMENT OF PARENTS

	Name of Father	Year	County	Name of Mother	Year	County
1	Johnson Tach-bon-ta	Dead	Skullyville	Siney Wright	1896	Skullyville
2	Charles Fisher	"	Sugar Loaf	Nicey Fisher	Dead	Sugar Loaf
3	No 1			No 2		
4						
5						
6						
7			No3 Born Sept 14, 1901; Enrolled Nov. 2, 1901			
8			For child of Nos 1&2 see NB (Mar 3, 1905) #675			
9						
10						
11						
12						
13						
14						
15					#1 to 2 inc	
16				Date of Application for Enrollment.	6/15/99	
17	P.O. Sulter IT 4/4/05					

Choctaw By Blood Enrollment Cards 1898-1914

RESIDENCE:	Skullyville	COUNTY.	**Choctaw Nation**		Choctaw Roll	CARD No.		
POST OFFICE:	Oak Lodge I.T.				(Not Including Freedmen)	FIELD No.		2742

Dawes' Roll No.	NAME		Relationship to Person	AGE	SEX	BLOOD	TRIBAL ENROLLMENT		
							Year	County	No.
8023	1 LeFlore F Greenwood	30	First Named	27	M	1/8	1896	Skullyville	7727
8024	2 " Leona A	27	Wife	24	F	1/4	1896	"	8441
8025	3 " Florence L	4	Dau	1	F	3/16		"	
14771	4 " Greenwood	1	Son	2mo	M	3/16			
	5								
	6								
	7								
	8								
	9								
	10								
	11								
	12								
	13								
	14								
	15								
	16								
	17								

ENROLLMENT
OF NOS. 1, 2, 3 HEREON
APPROVED BY THE SECRETARY
OF INTERIOR JAN 17 1903

ENROLLMENT
OF NOS. 4 HEREON
APPROVED BY THE SECRETARY
OF INTERIOR MAY 20 1903

TRIBAL ENROLLMENT OF PARENTS

	Name of Father	Year	County	Name of Mother	Year	County
1	Greenwood LeFlore	Dead	Skullyville	Harriet LeFlore	1896	Non Citz
2	Wm P. Merryman	"	Non Citz	Caroline Merryman	1896	Skullyville
3	No 1			No 2		
4	No. 1			No. 2		
5						
6						
7						
8	No1 On 1896 roll as Greenwood LeFlore					
9	No2 On " " " Sumner Merryman					
10	No1 As to marriage of father and mother see card of Louis T LeFlore					
11	For child of Nos 1and2 see N.B. (Apr. 26-06) No. 575					
	" " " " " " " (Mar 3-05) " 185					
12						
13						
14						
15						
16				Date of Application for Enrollment.	6/15/99	
17				No.4 Enrolled May 24, 1900.		

Choctaw By Blood Enrollment Cards 1898-1914

RESIDENCE: Skullyville COUNTY. **Choctaw Nation**   **Choctaw Roll** CARD No.
POST OFFICE: Oak Lodge I.T.   *(Not Including Freedmen)* FIELD No. 2743

Dawes' Roll No.	NAME	Relationship to Person First Named	AGE	SEX	BLOOD	TRIBAL ENROLLMENT Year	TRIBAL ENROLLMENT County	TRIBAL ENROLLMENT No.
8026	1 Cartwright Hannah 45	First Named	42	F	1/4	1896	Skullyville	3190
8027	2 DeLoach Annie 19	Dau	16	F	1/8	1896	"	3192
8028	3 " " William 13	Son	10	M	1/8	1896	"	3193
8029	4 " " Josie 9	Dau	6	F	1/8	1896	"	3194
	5							
	6							
	7							
	8							
	9							
	10							
	11							
	12							
	13							
	14							
	15	ENROLLMENT OF NOS. 1, 2, 3, 4 HEREON APPROVED BY THE SECRETARY OF INTERIOR JAN 17 1903						
	16							
	17							

TRIBAL ENROLLMENT OF PARENTS

	Name of Father	Year	County	Name of Mother	Year	County
1	William Trahern	Dead	Miss.	Rebecca Trahern	Dead	Skullyville
2	Joseph DeLoach	"	Non Citz	No 1		
3	" " "	"	" "	No 1		
4	" " "	"	" "	No 1		
5						
6						
7						
8						
9		No1 On 1896 roll as Hannah DeLoach				
10		No3 " 1896 " Wm " "				
11		No4 " 1896 " Jossie " "				
12						
13						
14						
15					Date of Application for Enrollment.	
16					6/15/99	
17	P.O. Non IT 3/3/06					

43

Choctaw By Blood Enrollment Cards 1898-1914

RESIDENCE: Skullyville COUNTY.
POST OFFICE: Oak Lodge I.T.

Choctaw Nation

Choctaw Roll
(Not Including Freedmen)

CARD NO.
FIELD NO. 2744

Dawes' Roll No.	NAME		Relationship to Person First Named	AGE	SEX	BLOOD	TRIBAL ENROLLMENT		
							Year	County	No.
8030	1 Johnson Maud	21	First Named	18	F	1/8	1896	Skullyville	3191
8031	" Ola	4	Dau	13mo	F	1/16		"	
8032	" Sarah	2	Dau	2mo	F	1/16			
	4								
	5								
	6								
	7								
	8								
	9								
	10								
	11								
	12								
	13								
	14								
	15	ENROLLMENT OF NOS. 1, 2, 3 HEREON APPROVED BY THE SECRETARY OF INTERIOR JAN 17 1903							
	16								
	17								

TRIBAL ENROLLMENT OF PARENTS

	Name of Father	Year	County	Name of Mother	Year	County
1	Joseph DeLoach	Dead	Non Citz	Hannah Cartwright	1896	Skullyville
2	Jep Johnson	1896	" "	No 1		
3	J. P. Johnson		" "	No.1		
4						
5						
6						
7						
8	No1 On 1896 roll as Mollie DeLoach					
9	No2 Affidavits of birth to be supplied. Recd June 16/99					
10	No.3 Enrolled April 24, 1901					
	For child of No.1 see NB (March 3,1905) #1237					
11						
12						
13						
14					#1&2	
15				Date of Application for Enrollment.		
16				6/15/99		
17						

44

Choctaw By Blood Enrollment Cards 1898-1914

RESIDENCE: Sans Bois   COUNTY. **Choctaw Nation**   **Choctaw Roll** (Not Including Freedmen)   CARD No.
POST OFFICE: Starr I.T.   FIELD NO. 2745

Dawes' Roll No.	NAME		Relationship to Person First Named	AGE	SEX	BLOOD	TRIBAL ENROLLMENT		
							Year	County	No.
8033	1 Tom Ebenezer	36	First Named	33	M	3/4	1896	Sans Bois	11867
8034	2 " Bicy	10	Dau	7	F	7/8	1896	" "	11870
8035	3 " Elsie	8	Dau	5	F	7/8	1896	" "	11871
8036	4 " John	7	Son	4	M	7/8	1896	" "	11872
	5								
	6								
	7								
	8								
	9								
	10								
	11								
	12								
	13								
	14								
	15								
	16								
	17								

ENROLLMENT
OF NOS. 1,2,3,4
APPROVED BY THE SECRETARY HEREON
OF INTERIOR JAN 17 1903

TRIBAL ENROLLMENT OF PARENTS

	Name of Father	Year	County	Name of Mother	Year	County
1	Wilson Tom	Dead	Skullyville	Phoebe Scott	1896	Sans Bois
2	No 1			Sarah Tom	Dead	Sans Bois
3	No 1			Eliza Tom	"	" "
4	No 1			" "	"	" "
5						
6						
7						
8			No1 On 1896 roll as Ebeneezer Tom			
9						
10						
11						
12						
13						
14						
15						Date of Application for Enrollment.
16						6/15/99
17						

45

RESIDENCE: Sans Bois	COUNTY.
POST OFFICE: Starr I.T.	

Choctaw Nation

Choctaw Roll *(Not Including Freedmen)*

CARD NO.
FIELD NO. 2746

Dawes' Roll No.	NAME		Relationship to Person First Named	AGE	SEX	BLOOD	TRIBAL ENROLLMENT		
							Year	County	No.
8037	1 Tom Simeon	43	First Named	40	M	3/4	1896	Sans Bois	11840
DEAD.	2 " Isabelle DEAD		Wife	32	F	Full	1896	" "	11845
8038	3 " Mandy	21	Dau	18	F	7/8	1896	" "	11842
8039	4 " Levi	12	Son	9	M	7/8	1896	" "	11869
8040	5 " Albert	16	"	13	M	7/8	1896	" "	11846
8041	6 " Benjamin	13	"	10	M	7/8	1896	" "	11847
8042	7 " Elias	11	"	8	M	7/8	1896	" "	11848
8043	8 " Wilson	6	"	3	M	7/8	1896	" "	11849
8044	9 " Esias	4	"	11mo	M	7/8			
8045	10 " Gency	2	Dau	2mo	F	7/8			
14772	11 Harkins Adam	1	Son	1¾yrs	M	15/16			
	12 No. 2 HEREON DISMISSED UNDER ORDER OF THE COMMISSION TO THE FIVE								
	13 CIVILIZED TRIBES OF MARCH 31, 1905.								
	14								
	15 ENROLLMENT OF NOS. 13,4,5,6,7,8,9,10, HEREON APPROVED BY THE SECRETARY						ENROLLMENT OF NOS. 1 HEREON APPROVED BY THE SECRETARY		
	16 OF INTERIOR Jan 17 1903						OF INTERIOR MAY 20 1903		
	17								

TRIBAL ENROLLMENT OF PARENTS

	Name of Father	Year	County	Name of Mother	Year	County
1	Wilson Tom	Dead	Skullyville	Phoebe Scott	1896	Sans Bois
2	Hampton			Hampton	Dead	Gaines
3	No 1			Abilena Tom	Dead	Skullyville
4	No 1			Eliza Tom	"	Sans Bois
5	Aaron Tom	Dead	Sans Bois	No 2		
6	" "	"	" "	No 2		
7	" "	"	" "	No 2		
8	" "	"	" "	No 2		
9	" "	"	" "	No 2		
10	No 1			No 2		
11	Edward Harkins	1896	Skullyville	No.3		
12	No1 On 1896 roll as Simon Tom					
13	No6 " " " " Benny Tom					
14	No10 Enrolled May 23, 1901					
15	No.2 died April 4, 1901: Proof of death filed June 6, 1901				#1 to 9 inc	
16	Evidence of birth of No.9 received and filed March 4, 1902			Date of Application for Enrollment.	6/15/99	
17	Nº11 Born March 19, 1901 enrolled Dec 24, 1902					

RESIDENCE: Sans Bois COUNTY. **Choctaw Nation** **Choctaw Roll** CARD NO.
POST OFFICE: Garland I.T. 4/5/05 *(Not Including Freedmen)* FIELD NO. 2747

Dawes' Roll No.	NAME	Relationship to Person First Named	AGE	SEX	BLOOD	TRIBAL ENROLLMENT Year	County	No.
8046	1 Rockman Lizzie 27	First Named	24	F	1/4	1896	Sans Bois	12687
8047	2 " William H 6	Son	2	M	1/8		" "	
8048	3 Brown Tecumseh 11	"	8	M	1/8	1896	" "	636
8049	4 " Robert 9	"	6	M	1/8	1896	" "	637
8050	5 " Shorty 7	"	4	M	1/8	1896	" "	638
8051	6 Rockman Leona May 3	Dau	9mo	F	1/8			
	7							
	8							
	9							
	10							
	11							
	12							
	13							
	14							
	15 ENROLLMENT OF NOS. 1,2,3,4,5,6 HEREON APPROVED BY THE SECRETARY							
	16 OF INTERIOR JAN 17 1903							
	17							

TRIBAL ENROLLMENT OF PARENTS

	Name of Father	Year	County	Name of Mother	Year	County
1	George Folsom	Dead	Skullyville	Levicey Folsom	1896	Sans Bois
2	Joseph Rockman	1896	Non Citz	No 1		
3	Robert Brown	Dead	" "	No 1		
4	" "	"	" "	No 1		
5	" "	"	" "	No 1		
6	Joseph Rockman		" "	No 1		
7						
8	No2 Affidavit of birth to be supplied. Recd July 27/99					
9	For child of No1 see NB (Apr 26-06) Card #625					
10	" " " " 1 " " (March 3,1905) " #754					
11						
12	No.6 Enrolled May 24, 1900.					
13						
14					#1 to 5	
15					Date of Application for Enrollment.	
16					6/15/99	
17	P.O. Quinton I.T.					

Choctaw By Blood Enrollment Cards 1898-1914

RESIDENCE: Skullyville	COUNTY:	**Choctaw Nation**	Choctaw Roll	CARD No.	
POST OFFICE: Farmer I.T.			(Not Including Freedmen)	FIELD No. 2748	

Dawes' Roll No.	NAME	Relationship to Person First Named	AGE	SEX	BLOOD	TRIBAL ENROLLMENT Year	County	No.
8052	1 Williams Senora W ³⁵	First Named	32	M	1/4	1896	Sans Bois	12665
I.W. 913	2 " Sarah E ²⁰	Wife	16	F	IW			
8053	3 ~~DIED PRIOR TO SEPTEMBER 25, 1902~~ Albert J	Son	7mo	M	1/8			
	4							
	5							
	6							
	7	ENROLLMENT						
	8	OF NOS. 2 HEREON						
	9	~~APPROVED BY THE SECRETARY~~ OF INTERIOR AUG 3 1904						
	10							
	11							
	12							
	13							
	14	ENROLLMENT						
	15	~~OF NOS. 1 and 3 HEREON~~						
	16	APPROVED BY THE SECRETARY OF INTERIOR JAN 17 1903						
	17							

TRIBAL ENROLLMENT OF PARENTS

	Name of Father	Year	County	Name of Mother	Year	County
1	Williams	Dead	Non Citz	Amanda Williams	Dead	Skullyville
2	John W. Carter	1896	" "	Beckey Carter	"	Non Citz
3	~~No 1~~			~~No 2~~		
4						
5	No1 On 1896 roll as S.W. Williams					
6	No3 Affidavit of birth to be supplied. Recd Aug 9/99					
7						
8	No3 died October – 1899; Proof of death filed Dec 20 1902					
9	Evidence of divorce between S.W. and Emma Williams filed Jany 19, 1903					
10	No.3 died Oct – 1899 Enrollment cancelled by Department July 8, 1904					
11						
12	For child of Nos 1&2 see NB (Apr 26 '06) Card #825					
13	" " " " " " (March 3,1905) " #727					
14					Date of Application for Enrollment.	
15						
16					6/15/99	
17	P.O. Cowlington I.T.					

P.O. Panama I.T. 2/3/04

Choctaw By Blood Enrollment Cards 1898-1914

RESIDENCE: Skullyville COUNTY. **Choctaw Nation**   **Choctaw Roll** CARD NO.
POST OFFICE: Shady Point I.T.   *(Not Including Freedmen)* FIELD NO. 2749

Dawes' Roll No.	NAME	Relationship to Person First Named	AGE	SEX	BLOOD	TRIBAL ENROLLMENT Year	County	No.
8054	1 Terrell Houston 25	First Named	22	M	Full	1896	Wade	12048
	2							
	3							
	4							
	5							
	6							
	7							
	8							
	9							
	10							
	11							
	12							
	13							
	14							
	15							
	16							
	17							

ENROLLMENT
OF NOS. 1 HEREON
APPROVED BY THE SECRETARY
OF INTERIOR JAN 17 1903

TRIBAL ENROLLMENT OF PARENTS

Name of Father	Year	County	Name of Mother	Year	County
1 Solomon Terrell	1896	Skullyville	Rhoda Terrell	Dead	Skullyville
2					
3					
4					
5					
6		For child of No.1 see NB (March 3, 1905) #1253			
7					
8					
9					
10					
11					
12					
13					
14					
15				Date of Application for Enrollment.	
16				6/15/99	
17					

Choctaw By Blood Enrollment Cards 1898-1914

RESIDENCE: Skullyville	COUNTY. **Choctaw Nation**		**Choctaw Roll**	CARD NO.	
POST OFFICE: Bokoshe I.T.			(Not Including Freedmen)	FIELD NO. 2750	

Dawes' Roll No.	NAME	Relationship to Person First Named	AGE	SEX	BLOOD	TRIBAL ENROLLMENT Year	County	No.
8055	1 Moore David A 46	First Named	43	M	1/8	1896	Skullyville	8438
I.W. 120	2 " Dora M 22	Wife	19	F	IW	1896	"	14797
8056	3 " Stacy 13	Son	10	M	3/16	1896	"	8439
8057	4 " Thomas 11	"	8	M	3/16	1896	"	8440
8058	5 " Cecil 6	"	2	M	1/16		"	
8059	6 " Ola May 4	Dau	9mo	F	1/16			
	7							
	8							
	9							
	10							
	11							
	12	ENROLLMENT OF NOS. 2 HEREON APPROVED BY THE SECRETARY						
	13	OF INTERIOR JUN 13 1903						
	14							
	15	ENROLLMENT OF NOS. 1,3,4,5,6 HEREON						
	16	APPROVED BY THE SECRETARY OF INTERIOR JAN 17 1903						
	17							

TRIBAL ENROLLMENT OF PARENTS

	Name of Father	Year	County	Name of Mother	Year	County
1	Jeptha N Moore	Dead	Skullyville	Milberry J Moore	Dead	Non Citz
2	Thomas Rabern	1896	Non Citz	Mary J Rabern	1896	Non Citz
3	No 1			Clara Moore	Dead	Skullyville
4	No 1			" "	"	"
5	No 1			No 2		
6	No 1			No 2		
7						
8	No2 Admitted by Dawes Com as intermarried citizen					
9	Case #393					
10	No5 White mother admitted by Dawes Com which settles proof of marriage					
11						
12	No1 Admitted by Sup Court Choc Nation April term 1874					
13	For children of Nos 1&2 see NB (Mar 3 '05) #642					
14						
15					Date of Application for Enrollment.	
16					6/15/99	
17						

Choctaw By Blood Enrollment Cards 1898-1914

RESIDENCE: Creek Nation COUNTY. **Choctaw Nation** **Choctaw Roll** *(Not Including Freedmen)* CARD NO.
POST OFFICE: Muskogee, I.T. FIELD NO. 2751

Dawes' Roll No.	NAME		Relationship to Person	AGE	SEX	BLOOD	TRIBAL ENROLLMENT		
							Year	County	No.
8060	1 Gouger, Estelle	21	First Named	18	F	1/2	1896	Sans Bois	2149
8061	2 " Frank	3	Son	6mo	M	1/4			
8062	3 " Julia	1	Dau	3mo	F	1/4			
	4								
	5								
	6								
	7								
	8								
	9								
	10								
	11								
	12								
	13								
	14								
	15	ENROLLMENT OF NOS. 1, 2, 3 HEREON APPROVED BY THE SECRETARY OF INTERIOR JAN 17 1903							
	16								
	17								

TRIBAL ENROLLMENT OF PARENTS

	Name of Father	Year	County	Name of Mother	Year	County
1	Sam Cooper	Dead	Non Citz	Susan Shropshire	1896	Sans Bois
2	J.J. Gouger			No. 1		
3	" " "			No 1		
4						
5						
6						
7	Proper surname if Gouger; see letter Oct 30, 1901 #15540					
8						
9	On 1896 roll as Estella Cooper					
10	For child of No 1 see NB (Mar 3-1905) Card #231					
11						
12						
13						
14						
15		No2 Enrolled May 24, 1900.		Date of Application for Enrollment. #1		
16		No3 Enrolled Oct 4, 1901.		6/15/99		
17		Stigler I.T.				

P.O. [Illegible] IT 5/10/04   12/17/02

51

Choctaw By Blood Enrollment Cards 1898-1914

RESIDENCE: Sans Bois COUNTY.								

Choctaw Nation — Choctaw Roll (Not Including Freedmen)

RESIDENCE: Sans Bois COUNTY.
POST OFFICE: Iron Bridge, I.T.
CARD NO.
FIELD NO. 2752

Dawes' Roll No.	NAME	Relationship to Person First Named	AGE	SEX	BLOOD	TRIBAL ENROLLMENT Year	County	No.
Dead	1 Perry, Milton	Named	36	M	Full	1896	Sans Bois	10080
8063	2 " Wicy 22	Wife	19	F	"	1896	" "	10081
8064	3 " Edna 13	Dau	10	"	"	1896	" "	10082
8065	4 " Jonas 6	Son	2	M	"			
8066	5 " Gilbert 3	"	2mo	"	"			
8067	6 " Albert 1	Son	2mo	M	"			
	7							
	8 No. 1 HEREON DISMISSED UNDER ORDER OF THE COMMISSION TO THE FIVE							
	9 CIVILIZED TRIBES OF MARCH 31, 1905.							
	10							
	11							
	12							
	13							
	14							
	15 ENROLLMENT OF NOS. 2,3,4,5,6 HEREON							
	16 APPROVED BY THE SECRETARY OF INTERIOR JAN 17 1903							
	17							

TRIBAL ENROLLMENT OF PARENTS

Name of Father	Year	County	Name of Mother	Year	County
1 Gilbert Perry	Dead	Sugar Loaf		Dead	Sugar Loaf
2 John Tom	"	Skullyville	Phoebe Tom	1896	Sans Bois
3 No1			Fanny Perry	Dead	" "
4 No1			No2		
5 No1			No2		
6 Phillip Byington	1896	Sans Bois	Nº2		
7					
8					
9		No2 on 1896 roll as Vicey Perry			
10		No1 Died October 12, 1899. Evidence of death filed May 23, 1901			
11		Nº6 Born Aug. 21, 1902, enrolled Oct. 23, 1902			
12		Nº6 is illegitimate			
13					
14					
15					
16					
17					

Choctaw By Blood Enrollment Cards 1898-1914

RESIDENCE: Sans Bois COUNTY. POST OFFICE: Iron Bridge I.T.	**Choctaw Nation**	Choctaw Roll (Not Including Freedmen)	CARD NO. FIELD NO. 2753

Dawes' Roll No.	NAME	Relationship to Person First Named	AGE	SEX	BLOOD	TRIBAL ENROLLMENT Year	County	No.
8068	1 Tom Thomas ²⁸		25	M	Full	1896	Sans Bois	11843
	2							
	3							
	4							
	5							
	6							
	7							
	8							
	9							
	10							
	11							
	12							
	13	ENROLLMENT						
	14	OF NOS. 1 HEREON APPROVED BY THE SECRETARY						
	15	OF INTERIOR JAN 17 1903						
	16							
	17							

TRIBAL ENROLLMENT OF PARENTS

	Name of Father	Year	County	Name of Mother	Year	County
1	Wilson Tom	Dead	Skullyville	Phoebe Tom	1896	Sans Bois
2						
3						
4						
5						
6			On 1896 roll as Tommy Tom			
7						
8						
9						
10						
11						
12						
13						
14						
15				DATE OF APPLICATION FOR ENROLLMENT.		6/15/99
16						
17						

Choctaw By Blood Enrollment Cards 1898-1914

RESIDENCE: Skullyville	COUNTY.	Choctaw Nation	Choctaw Roll	CARD NO.
POST OFFICE: Poteau I.T.			(Not Including Freedmen)	FIELD NO. 2754

Dawes' Roll No.	NAME	Relationship to Person First Named	AGE	SEX	BLOOD	TRIBAL ENROLLMENT Year	County	No.
8069	1 Bohanan James W 27	First Named	24	M	7/8	1896	Skullyville	712
I.W. 1309	2 " Annie 21	Wife	21	F	IW			
8070	3 " Elmer Wear 3	Son	9mo	M	7/16			
	4							
	5							
	6							
	7							
	8							
	9							
	10							
	11	See testimony in allotment jacket #8070						
	12							
	13							
	14							

ENROLLMENT
OF NOS. 1 and 3 HEREON
APPROVED BY THE SECRETARY
OF INTERIOR JAN 17 1903

ENROLLMENT
OF NOS. 2 HEREON
APPROVED BY THE SECRETARY
OF INTERIOR MAR 14 1905

TRIBAL ENROLLMENT OF PARENTS

	Name of Father	Year	County	Name of Mother	Year	County
1	Lyman Bohanan	Dead	Skullyville	Celia Bohanan	Dead	Skullyville
2	Jack Trammel	1896	Non Citz		1896	Non Citz
3	No.1			No.2		
4						
5						
6						
7	No1 On 1896 roll as James Bohanan					
8	No3 Enrolled April 6, 1901					
9	Nos 1 and 2 have separated. See testimony of No1 taken 12/18/02					
10						
11						
12						
13						
14						
15					#1&2	
16				Date of Application for Enrollment.	6/15/99	
17						

Choctaw By Blood Enrollment Cards 1898-1914

RESIDENCE: Skullyville COUNTY. **Choctaw Nation** Choctaw Roll *(Not Including Freedmen)* CARD NO.
POST OFFICE: Brazil I.T. FIELD NO. 2755

Dawes' Roll No.	NAME	Relationship to Person First Named	AGE	SEX	BLOOD	TRIBAL ENROLLMENT		
						Year	County	No.
8074	1 Trahern James DIED PRIOR TO SEPTEMBER 25, 1902		45	M	1/2	1896	Skullyville	11937
	2							
	3							
	4							
	5							
	6							
	7							
	8							
	9							
	10							
	11							
	12							
	13							
	14							
	15	ENROLLMENT OF NOS. 1 HEREON APPROVED BY THE SECRETARY OF INTERIOR JAN 17 1903						
	16							
	17							

TRIBAL ENROLLMENT OF PARENTS

Name of Father	Year	County	Name of Mother	Year	County
1 James Trahern	Dead	Skullyville	Sarah Trahern	Dead	Skullyville
2					
3					
4					
5					
6					
7	No1 died Aug 18, 1900; Proof of death filed Dec 20 1902				
8	Is not this James the husband of Virginia P Trahern on Choctaw card 2756				
9	No.1 died Aug 18, 1900; Enrollment cancelled by Department July 8, 1904				
10					
11					
12					
13					
14					
15					Date of Application for Enrollment.
16					6/15/99
17					

RESIDENCE:	Skullyville	COUNTY.	**Choctaw Nation**		**Choctaw Roll**	CARD No.	
POST OFFICE:	Brazil I.T.				*(Not Including Freedmen)*	FIELD No.	2756

Dawes' Roll No.	NAME		Relationship to Person First Named	AGE	SEX	BLOOD	TRIBAL ENROLLMENT		
							Year	County	No.
I.W. 122	1 Trahern Virginia P	43	Named	40	F	I.W.	1896	Skullyville	15092
8072	2 " Docia	21	Dau	18	F	1/4	1896	"	11939
	3								
	4								
	5								
	6								
	7								
	8								
	9								
	10								
	11	ENROLLMENT OF NOS. 1 ~~~~~ HEREON APPROVED BY THE SECRETARY							
	12								
	13	OF INTERIOR JUN 13 1903							
	14								
	15	ENROLLMENT OF NOS. 2 HEREON APPROVED BY THE SECRETARY							
	16								
	17	OF INTERIOR JAN 17 1903							

	TRIBAL ENROLLMENT OF PARENTS					
Name of Father	Year	County	Name of Mother	Year	County	
1 John Closson	Dead	Non Citza	Christina Closson	Dead	Non Citz	
2 James N Trahern	"	Skullyville	No 1			
3						
4						
5						
6	No 1 Certificate of marriage exhibited, dated Aug. 11, 1879 of James					
7	N. Trahern and V. P. Closson, with certificate of record en-					
8	dorsed thereon.					
9	~~No. 1 admitted as an intermarried citizen by~~					
	Dawes Commission: Choctaw Case #53: No appeal.					
10	For child of No. 2 see NB (March 3, 1905) #1385					
11						
12						
13						
14					Date of Application for Enrollment.	
15					6/15/99	
16						
17						

Choctaw By Blood Enrollment Cards 1898-1914

RESIDENCE: Skullyville COUNTY, **Choctaw Nation** **Choctaw Roll** CARD No.
POST OFFICE: Poteau I.T. *(Not Including Freedmen)* FIELD No. 2757

Dawes' Roll No.	NAME		Relationship to Person First Named	AGE	SEX	BLOOD	TRIBAL ENROLLMENT		
							Year	County	No.
8073	1 James Etha M	19	First Named	16	F	1/2	1896	Sugar Loaf	6558
8074	2 " Walton D	17	Bro	14	M	1/2	1896	" "	6559
8075	3 " Davis	14	"	11	M	1/2	1896	" "	6560
8076	4 " Dennis	14	"	11	M	1/2	1896	" "	6561
I.W. 1310	5 Davis, Mollie J	42	Mother	42	F	I.W.	1885	Skullyville	596
	6								
	7								
	8								
	9								
	10								
	11	ENROLLMENT							
	12	OF NOS. 5 HEREON APPROVED BY THE SECRETARY							
	13	OF INTERIOR MAR 14 1905							
	14								
	15	ENROLLMENT OF NOS. 1,2,3,4 HEREON							
	16	APPROVED BY THE SECRETARY							
	17	OF INTERIOR JAN 17 1903							

TRIBAL ENROLLMENT OF PARENTS

	Name of Father	Year	County	Name of Mother	Year	County
1	Davis James	Dead	Sugar Loaf	Mollie J Davis	1896	Non Citz
2	" "	"	" "	" " "	"	" " "
3	" "	"	" "	" " "	"	" " "
4	" "	"	" "	" " "	"	" " "
5	James McKinney	dead	Non Citz	Elizabeth McKinney	dead	Non Citz
6						
7						
8						
9						
10	No1 On 1896 roll as Ettier James					
	No2 " " " " Walton "					
11	Mother enrolled on W.C.D. 245					
12	No.5 former husband, Davis James, 1885 Skullyville, No.595, died in 1889					
13	Nos 3 and 4 twins					
	No.5 Married Davis James a Choctaw, in 1881, lived with him until his					
14	death, married a white non citz in 1890. See her testimony.					
15	No5 on 1885 Choctaw Census Roll, Skullyville Co #596 as Mary James					
16	No.5 originally listed for enrollment on Choctaw card D-245. Transferred					
	to this card Jan. 30, 1905. See decision of Jan. 14, 1905.					
17	PO No1 is Sutter, I.T. For child of No.1 see NB (Mar 3,1905) #643					

57

Choctaw By Blood Enrollment Cards 1898-1914

RESIDENCE: Skullyville COUNTY. **Choctaw Nation** **Choctaw Roll** CARD NO.
POST OFFICE: Ward I.T. (Not Including Freedmen) FIELD NO. 2758

Dawes' Roll No.	NAME	Relationship to Person First Named	AGE	SEX	BLOOD	TRIBAL ENROLLMENT		
						Year	County	No.
8077	1 Derryberry Emma R ³¹	First Named	28	F	1/16	1896	Skullyville	3239
8078	2 " Brandon B ⁶	Son	3	M	1/32	1896	"	3240
I.W. 49	3 " Garrison W	Husband	33	M	I.W.			
	4							
	5							
	6							
	7							
	8							
	9							
	10							
	11							
	12							
	13							
	14							
	15							
	16							
	17							

ENROLLMENT
OF NOS. 1 and 2 HEREON
APPROVED BY THE SECRETARY
OF INTERIOR JAN 17 1903

ENROLLMENT
OF NOS. ~~ 3 ~~ HEREON
APPROVED BY THE SECRETARY
OF INTERIOR JUN 13 1903

TRIBAL ENROLLMENT OF PARENTS

	Name of Father	Year	County	Name of Mother	Year	County
1	Jacob Russell	Dead	Non Citz	Almira Russell	Dead	Skullyville
2	Garrison W Derryberry	1896	" "	No 1		
3	John W Derryberry		" "	Clementine Derryberry	Dead	Noncitizen
4						
5						
6						
7			No2 On 1896 roll as Brandon Derryberry			
8						
9			No3 transferred from Choctaw D #246 – March 20, 1903. See decision of March 4, 1903			
10						
11						
12						
13						
14						#1&2
15						Date of Application for Enrollment.
16						6/15/99
17						

Choctaw By Blood Enrollment Cards 1898-1914

RESIDENCE: Skullyville	COUNTY.						Choctaw Roll	CARD NO.	
POST OFFICE: Pocola I.T.		**Choctaw Nation**					*(Not Including Freedmen)*	FIELD NO. 2759	

Dawes' Roll No.	NAME	Relationship to Person First Named	AGE	SEX	BLOOD	TRIBAL ENROLLMENT		
						Year	County	No.
✓	1 Brake[sic] Amanda I		21	F	1/8			
DEAD.	2 " Mary	Dau	11mo	F	1/16			
DEAD.	3 " James Duval	Son	4mo	M	1/16			
DP	4 " Kully	Son	2mo	M	1/16			
	5							
	6							
	7 #4 DISMISSED MAY 27 1904							
	8							
	9							
	10							
	11 No. 2 and 3 HEREON DISMISSED UNDER							
	12 ORDER OF THE COMMISSION TO THE FIVE							
	13 CIVILIZED TRIBES OF MARCH 31, 1905.							
	14							
	15 DENIED CITIZENSHIP BY THE CHOCTAW AND							
	16 CHICKASAW CITIZENSHIP COURT							
	17							

	TRIBAL ENROLLMENT OF PARENTS						
	Name of Father	Year	County	Name of Mother	Year	County	
1	Wm Vandergrif	1896	Non Citz	Hazey Ann Vandergrif	1896	Skullyville	
2	Fletcher Blake	1896	" "	No 1			
3	" "		" "	No. 1			
4	" "		" "	No.1			
5							
6	No1 Denied in 96 Case #916						
7	No1 Admitted by U.S. Court at So McAlester Sept 11-1897 #62 as						
8	Amanda I. Vandergrift						
	As to residence and birth of child see her testimony						
9	No2 Born June 23, 1898						
10	No.4 born Dec 15, 1901: Enrolled Feby 17, 1902						
11	No2 Died May 17" 1900: Proof of death filed Dec' 23" 1902						
	No3 Died Jan 9" 1901: Proof of death filed Dec' 23" 1902						
12	Judgement[sic] of U/S Court admitting No1 vacated and set aside by Decree of Choctaw Chickasaw Cit Court Dec' 17'02						
13	No1 now in C.C.C.C Case #65						
14	No.3 Enrolled May 24, 1900						
15	For child of No1 see (Act Apr 26 '06) NB #1051					Date of Application for Enrollment.	
16	Duplicate record 7-4-575					6/15/99	
17	See Petition #C-132						

RESIDENCE:	Sans Bois	COUNTY.	**Choctaw Nation**		**Choctaw Roll**	CARD NO.	
POST OFFICE:	Cartersville, I.T.				*(Not Including Freedmen)*	FIELD NO.	2760

Dawes' Roll No.	NAME		Relationship to Person	AGE	SEX	BLOOD	TRIBAL ENROLLMENT		
							Year	County	No.
8079	1 Moore, Andrew J	42	First Named	39	M	1/4	1896	Sans Bois	8426
8080	2 " Laura	30	Wife	27	F	1/4	1896	" "	8427
8081	3 Rabon, Ora	19	Dau	16	"	1/4	1896	" "	8428
8082	4 Moore, Gertrude	13	"	10	"	1/4	1896	" "	8429
8083	5 " Beuna	8	"	5	"	1/4	1896	" "	8431
I.W. 7649	6 Rabon William T	21	Hus of No3	21	M	IW			
	7								
	8	ENROLLMENT OF NOS. 6 APPROVED BY THE SECRETARY OF INTERIOR MAR 26 1904							
	9								
	10								
	11								
	12								
	13								
	14								
	15	ENROLLMENT OF NOS. 1,2,3,4,5 HEREON APPROVED BY THE SECRETARY OF INTERIOR JAN 17 1903							
	16								
	17								

TRIBAL ENROLLMENT OF PARENTS

	Name of Father	Year	County	Name of Mother	Year	County
1	Jeptha N Moore	Dead	Skullyville	Milberry Moore	Dead	Non Citz
2	Wm Overstreet	"	Non Citz	Lutitia Overstreet	1896	Skullyville
3	No1			Ada Moore	Dead	"
4	No1			No2		
5	No1			No2		
6	Richard A Rabon		noncitizen	Loucila Rabon		noncitizen
7						
8						
9	No2 admitted by act of Council of Oct. 15, 1879					
10	No1 on 1896 roll as Jackson Moore, Admitted to citizenship					
11	by Supreme Court of Choctaw Nation April Term 1874					
12	Duly verified Copy of Admission exhibited but not in condition to be filed.					
13	No.3 is now the wife of William T. Rabon on Choctaw card #D.735: June 27, 1902					
14	No.6 transferred from Choctaw card D735 January 24,1905. See decision of January 7,1904 For child of No's 3&6, see N.B. (Apr 26, 1906) Card No. 53				Date of Application for Enrollment.	
15	" " " " " " (Mar 3-1905) " " 230					
16					6/15/99	
17	Nos 2 and 6 PO Bokoshe, I.L 3/24/05					

Choctaw By Blood Enrollment Cards 1898-1914

RESIDENCE: Skullyville **COUNTY.** **Choctaw Nation** **Choctaw Roll** *(Not Including Freedmen)* **CARD No.**
POST OFFICE: Spiro, I.T. **FIELD No.** 2761

Dawes' Roll No.	NAME	Relationship to Person First Named	AGE	SEX	BLOOD	TRIBAL ENROLLMENT Year	County	No.
8081[sic]	1 Thornton, Johnnie A ⁴¹	First Named	38	F	1/16	1896	Skullyville	11902
8085	2 Folsom, Annie ²¹	Dau	18	"	9/32	1896	"	3942
8086	3 Thornton, Paralee ¹⁶	"	13	"	1/32	1896	"	11903
8087	4 " John V ¹⁴	Son	11	M	1/32	1896	"	11904
8088	5 " Beulah ¹¹	Dau	8	F	1/32	1896	"	11905
8089	6 " Maud ⁹	"	6	"	1/32	1896	"	11906
8090	7 " Frederick ⁷	Son	4	M	1/32			
8091	8 " Eureka ⁵	Dau	2	F	1/32			
8092	9 " Jesse W ⁴	"	3mo	"	1/32			
8093	10 ~~DIED PRIOR TO SEPTEMBER 25, 1902~~ ~~Mabell~~	~~Dau~~	~~4mo~~	~~F~~	~~1/32~~			
	11							
	12							
	13 Nº 10 Born July 25, 1901; enrolled Nov 14, 1901.							
	14 No10 Died Jan 29" 1902: Proof of death filed Decʳ 23 1902							
	15 ENROLLMENT							
	16 OF NOS. 1,2,3,4,5,6,7,8,9,10 HEREON APPROVED BY THE SECRETARY							
	17 OF INTERIOR JAN 17 1903							

TRIBAL ENROLLMENT OF PARENTS

Name of Father	Year	County	Name of Mother	Year	County
1 John W Lyles	Dead	Skullyville	Mary Lyles	1896	Non Citz
2 Edwar[sic] Folsom	"	"	No1		
3 John V Thornton	1896	Non Citz	No1		
4 " " "	1896	" "	No1		
5 " " "	1896	" "	No1		
6 " " "	1896	" "	No1		
7 " " "	1896	" "	No1		
8 " " "	1896	" "	No1		
9 " " "	1896	" "	No1		
10 ~~T. V. Thornton~~		~~" "~~	~~Nº1~~		
11					
12 No3 on 1896 roll as Parlea Thornton					
13 No4 " 1896 " " Jno V "					
14 Nos 8-9 Affidavits of birth to be supplied. Recd 6/22/99				#1 to 9 inc	
15 As to marriage of parents of No2, see				Date of Application for Enrollment.	
16 Card of Mary Harlow, nee Lyles				6/15/99	
17 No.10 died Jan. 29 1902: Enrollment cancelled by Department July 8, 1904					

RESIDENCE: Sans Bois COUNTY.					Choctaw Roll (Not Including Freedmen)	CARD No.	
POST OFFICE: Cowlington, I.T. **Choctaw Nation**						FIELD NO. 2762	

Dawes' Roll No.	NAME	Relationship to Person First Named	AGE	SEX	BLOOD	TRIBAL ENROLLMENT		
						Year	County	No.
8094	1 Folsom, Walker 56		53	M	1/4	1896	Sans Bois	3879
I.W. 123	2 " Jane 57	Wife	54	F	IW	1896	" "	14510
	3							
	4							
	5							
	6							
	7							
	8							
	9							
	10							
	11 ENROLLMENT							
	12 OF NOS. 2 ~~~~ HEREON APPROVED BY THE SECRETARY							
	13 OF INTERIOR JUN 13 1903							
	14							
	15 ENROLLMENT OF NOS. 1 HEREON							
	16 APPROVED BY THE SECRETARY OF INTERIOR JAN 17 1903							
	17							

TRIBAL ENROLLMENT OF PARENTS

Name of Father	Year	County	Name of Mother	Year	County
1 Nathaniel Folsom	Dead	Sans Bois	Lucy Folsom	Dead	Sans Bois
2 Isaac Cannon	"	Non Citz	Elizabeth Cannon	"	Non Citz
3					
4					
5					
6		No1 on 1896 roll as Walker Folsum			
7					
8					
9					
10					
11					
12					
13					
14				Date of Application for Enrollment.	
15					
16				6/15/99	
17					

Choctaw By Blood Enrollment Cards 1898-1914

Dawes' Roll No.	NAME	Relationship to Person First Named	AGE	SEX	BLOOD	TRIBAL ENROLLMENT		
						Year	County	No.
8095	1 Boatright, Joseph 34		31	M	1/8	1896	Sans Bois	655
8096	2 " Ruth I 11	Dau	8	F	1/16	1896	" "	656
8097	3 " Viola M 9	"	6	"	1/16	1896	" "	657
8098	4 " Eva J 7	"	4	"	1/16	1896	" "	658
8099	5 " Robert E W 5	Son	2	M	1/16			
8100	6 " Martha Louzena 2	Dau	6mo	F	1/16			
I.W. 50	7 " Lou E	Wife	27	F	I.W.			
	8							

For child of Nos 1&7 see NB (Mar 3-05) Card #164

ENROLLMENT
OF NOS. ~~~ 7 ~~~ HEREON
APPROVED BY THE SECRETARY
OF INTERIOR JUN 13 1903

ENROLLMENT
OF NOS. 1,2,3,4,5,6 HEREON
APPROVED BY THE SECRETARY
OF INTERIOR JAN 17 1903

TRIBAL ENROLLMENT OF PARENTS

	Name of Father	Year	County	Name of Mother	Year	County
1	Elias Boatright	Dead	Non Citz	Ruth A Boatright		Tobucksy
2	No1			Lou E Boatright		white woman
3	No1			" " "		" "
4	No1			" " "		" "
5	No1			" " "		" "
6	No1			" " "		" "
7	John M. Mosbey		Noncitizen	Martha Mosbey		Noncitizen
8						
9	No2 on 1896 roll as Ruth Boatright					
10	No3 " 1896 " " Viola "					
11	No4 " 1896 " " Eva "					
	Surnames on 1896 roll as Boatright					
12	No5 Affidavit of birth to be supplied:- Recd 6/22/99					
13						
	Wife of No1 on Card D244					
14	No.6 Enrolled June 20, 1901					
15	No7 transferred from Choctaw card D #244 March 20, 1903 See				Date of Application for Enrollment.	
16	decision of March 4, 1903				June 15/99	
17	12/24/02 P.O. McCurtain I.T					

Choctaw By Blood Enrollment Cards 1898-1914

RESIDENCE:	Sans Bois	COUNTY.	**Choctaw Nation**	**Choctaw Roll**	CARD No.	
POST OFFICE:	Hoyt, Ind. Ter.			(Not Including Freedmen)	FIELD No.	2764

Dawes' Roll No.	NAME		Relationship to Person First Named	AGE	SEX	BLOOD	TRIBAL ENROLLMENT		
							Year	County	No.
I.W. 124	1 Russell, Campbell	38	First Named	35	M	I.W.	1896	Sans Bois	14958
8101	2 " Mary A	29	Wife	26	F	1/16	1896	" "	10700
8102	3 " Mary	6	Dau	2	"	1/32			
8103	4 " Margaret	4	"	1	"	1/32			
	5								
	6								
	7								
	8								
	9								
	10								
	11								
	12								
	13								
	14			ENROLLMENT OF NOS. 1 HEREON APPROVED BY THE SECRETARY					
	15	ENROLLMENT OF NOS. 2,3,4 HEREON APPROVED BY THE SECRETARY OF INTERIOR JAN 17 1903	OF INTERIOR JUN 13 1903						
	16								
	17			Bennett, I.T.					

TRIBAL ENROLLMENT OF PARENTS   12/19/02

	Name of Father	Year	County	Name of Mother	Year	County
1	Thos. D. Russell	Dead	Non Citz	Margaret Russell	Dead	Non Citz
2	Thos Overstreet	1896	" "	Margaret Constreet	"	Skullyville
3	No 1			No 2		
4	No 1			No 2		
5						
6						
7	No2 on 1896 roll as Mamie Russell					
8						
9	Nos 3-4 Affidavits of birth to be supplied: Recd June 22/99					
10						
11	For child of Nos 1&2 see NB (Mar 3-05) Card #165					
12						
13				Date of Application for Enrollment.		
14						
15						
16				6/15/99		
17						

Choctaw By Blood Enrollment Cards 1898-1914

RESIDENCE: Sans Bois	COUNTY. **Choctaw Nation**	**Choctaw Roll** *(Not Including Freedmen)*	CARD NO.
POST OFFICE: Stigler, I.T.			FIELD NO. 2765

Dawes' Roll No.	NAME		Relationship to Person First Named	AGE	SEX	BLOOD	TRIBAL ENROLLMENT		
							Year	County	No.
I.W. 125	1 Harrison Addell	26	First Named	23	F	I.W.	1896	Sans Bois	14591
8104	2 " Golden	4	Dau	1	"	1/4			
	3								
	4								
	5								
	6								
	7								
	8								
	9								
	10								
	11								
	12								
	13								
	14								
	15	ENROLLMENT OF NOS. 2 HEREON APPROVED BY THE SECRETARY OF INTERIOR JAN 17 1903		ENROLLMENT OF NOS. 1 HEREON APPROVED BY THE SECRETARY OF INTERIOR JUN 13 1903					
	16								
	17								

TRIBAL ENROLLMENT OF PARENTS

	Name of Father	Year	County	Name of Mother	Year	County
1	William Fenton	1896	Non Citz	Laura Fenton	1896	Non Citz
2	Henry Harrison	Dead	Sans Bois	No1		
3						
4						
5						
6						
7						
8		No1 on 1896 roll as Addell Harris				
9						
10		No2 Affidavit of birth to be supplied				
11		Recd Oct 6/99				
12						
13						
14					Date of Application for Enrollment.	
15						
16					6/15/99	
17						

Choctaw By Blood Enrollment Cards 1898-1914

RESIDENCE:	Sans Bois	COUNTY.	Choctaw Nation		Choctaw Roll	CARD NO.	
POST OFFICE:	Stigler, I.T.				(Not Including Freedmen)	FIELD NO.	2766

Dawes' Roll No.	NAME		Relationship to Person First Named	AGE	SEX	BLOOD	TRIBAL ENROLLMENT		
							Year	County	No.
I.W.823	1 Shropshire, Joseph J	46	First Named	43	M	I.W	1896	Sans Bois	15016
8105	2 " Susan	54	Wife	51	F	1/4	1896	" "	11120
8106	3 " Adolph	11	Son	8	M	1/8	1896	" "	11121
8107	4 Robertson, Irene	22	S.Dau	19	F	1/8	1896	" "	2151
8108	5 Cooper, Frank DIED DECEMBER 25, 1902		S.Son	16	M	1/8	1896	" "	2150
8109	6 Montague, Lottie Marie		Dau of No.4	4mo	F	1/16			
I.W.729	7 Robertson, David	44	HUSBAND OF NO.4	44	M	I.W.			
	8								
	9	ENROLLMENT OF NOS. 1 HEREON							
	10	APPROVED BY THE SECRETARY OF INTERIOR MAY 21 1904							
	11								
	12	ENROLLMENT OF NOS. ~~~ 7 ~~~ HEREON							
	13	APPROVED BY THE SECRETARY OF INTERIOR MAY -7 1904							
	14								
	15	ENROLLMENT OF NOS. 2,3,4,5,6 HEREON							
	16	APPROVED BY THE SECRETARY OF INTERIOR JAN 17 1903							
	17								

TRIBAL ENROLLMENT OF PARENTS

	Name of Father	Year	County	Name of Mother	Year	County
1	Jackson Shropshire	Dead	Non Citz	Levina Shropshire	Dead	Non Citz
2	Thos Lanier	"	" "	Susan P Lanier	"	Skullyville
3	No 1			No 2		
4	Sam Cooper	Dead	Non Citz	No 2		
5	" "	"	" "	No 2		
6	Joe Montague		" "	No.4		
7	George Robertson	dead	non-citizen	Susan Robertson	dead	non-citizen
8	No.7 transferred from Choctaw card #D.714: see decision of Feby 27, 1904					
9	No4 on 1896 roll as Irena Cooper					
10	No1 " 1896 " " J.J. Shropshire For child of Nos4&7 see NB (Mar 3 '05) #1380					
11	No.6 Enrolled June 23d, 1900, and is the illegitimate child of Irene Cooper.					
12	Nº4 is now the wife of David Robertson on Choctaw card #D714.					
13	No5 died Ded 25, 1900, Proof of death filed Dec 20 1902.					
14	Certified copy of divorce proceedings between Sue E and Samuel Cooper received and filed Feby 5, 1903					#1 to 5 inc
15					Date of Application for Enrollment.	
16					6/15/99	
17	No. 5 died Dec. 25, 1900; Enrollment cancelled by Department July 8, 1904					

Choctaw By Blood Enrollment Cards 1898-1914

| RESIDENCE: Skullyville | COUNTY. | **Choctaw Nation** | | **Choctaw Roll** (Not Including Freedmen) | CARD NO. FIELD NO. 2767 |
| POST OFFICE: Milton, I.T. | | | | | |

Dawes' Roll No.	NAME		Relationship to Person First Named	AGE	SEX	BLOOD	TRIBAL ENROLLMENT		
							Year	County	No.
8110	1 Daniels, Green	28		25	M	1/2	1896	Skullyville	3235
8111	2 DIED PRIOR TO SEPTEMBER 25 1902 Minnie		Wife	21	F	1/4	1896	"	11938
8112	3 " Thelma	3	Dau	4mos	F	3/8			
	4								
	5								
	6								
	7								
	8								
	9								
	10								
	11								
	12								
	13								
	14								
	15	ENROLLMENT OF NOS. 1, 2, 3, HEREON APPROVED BY THE SECRETARY OF INTERIOR JAN 17 1903							
	16								
	17								

TRIBAL ENROLLMENT OF PARENTS

	Name of Father	Year	County	Name of Mother	Year	County
1	Turner Daniels	1896	Skullyville	Susan Daniels	Dead	Skullyville
2	James Trahern	Dead	"	Virginia Trahern	1896	white woman
3	No.1			No.2		
4						
5						
6						
7						
8						
9	No2 on 1896 roll as Minnie Trahern					
10						
11	No2 Certificate of marriage of parents exhibited					
12	dated August 11, 1879 with certificate of record thereon. Names of contracting parties					
13	James N. Trahern and V.P. Closson					
14						
15	No. 3 Enrolled May 24, 1900				Date of Application for Enrollment,	
16	No2 died December 8, 1900; Proof of death filed Dec 20 1902				6/15/99	
17	No2 died Dec 8, 1900. Enrollment cancelled by Department July 8, 1904					

RESIDENCE: Skullyville	COUNTY.	Choctaw Nation	Choctaw Roll	CARD No.
POST OFFICE: Poteau, I.T.			(Not Including Freedmen)	FIELD No. 2768

Dawes' Roll No.	NAME	Relationship to Person First Named	AGE	SEX	BLOOD	TRIBAL ENROLLMENT Year	TRIBAL ENROLLMENT County	TRIBAL ENROLLMENT No.
DEAD.	1 Burties, James DEAD		38	M	Full	1896	Sugar Loaf	815
8113	2 " Rhoda 31	Wife	28	F	"	1893	Skullyville	487
DEAD,	3 Leonard DIED PRIOR TO SEPTEMBER 25, 1902	Son	6mo	M	"			
8114	4 Harris, Moses DIED PRIOR TO SEPTEMBER 25, 1902	S.Son	5	"	"			
	5							
	6 No. 1 HEREON DISMISSED UNDER ORDER OF THE COMMISSION TO THE FIVE CIVILIZED TRIBES OF MARCH 31, 1905.							
	7							
	8							
	9 No. 3 HEREON DISMISSED UNDER ORDER OF THE COMMISSIONER TO THE FIVE CIVILIZED TRIBES OF JULY 18, 1905.							
	10							
	11							
	12							
	13							
	14							
	15 ENROLLMENT OF NOS. 2 and 4 HEREON APPROVED BY THE SECRETARY OF INTERIOR JAN 17 1903							
	16							
	17							

TRIBAL ENROLLMENT OF PARENTS

	Name of Father	Year	County	Name of Mother	Year	County
1	Burties	Dead	in Mississippi	Sallie	Dead	in Mississippi
2	James Polk	"	Skullyville	Betsy Polk	"	Skullyville
3	No 1			No 2		
4	Demon Harris	Dead	Sugar Loaf	No 2		
5						
6	No 3 died in August 1897: Proof of death filed Dec 20 1902					
7	No4 died before Sept 25, 1902. Enrollment cancelled by Department July 8, 1904					
8	No 1 Died January 21" 1901. Proof of death filed Dec 23 1902					
9	No 2 on 1896 roll as Rhoda Harris					
10	" 2 " 1893 " " Rhoda Polk					
11	Nos 3-4 Affidavits of birth to be supplied. Recd July 27/99					
12						
13	No 3 has died since enrollment. See statement on blank affidavit hereto attached.					
14						
15						
16				Date of Application for Enrollment.	6/15/99	
17						

Choctaw By Blood Enrollment Cards 1898-1914

RESIDENCE: Skullyville	COUNTY.								

RESIDENCE: Skullyville COUNTY. **Choctaw Nation** (Not Including Freedmen) **Choctaw Roll** CARD No.
POST OFFICE: Pocola, I.T FIELD No. 2769

Dawes' Roll No.	NAME	Relationship to Person First Named	AGE	SEX	BLOOD	TRIBAL ENROLLMENT		
						Year	County	No.
✓✓0 1	Brogdon, Sarah D	Named	34	F	1/8			
✓✓0 2	" Wesley H	Son	14	M	1/16			
✓✓0 3	" Jodie J	"	12	"	1/16			
✓✓0 4	" Allaminta	Dau	10	F	1/16			
Dead 0 5	" Riley	Son	8	M	1/16			
6								
7								
8								
9								
10								
11								
12								
13								
14								
15								
No1 2, 3 and 4 16								
17								

DENIED CITIZENSHIP BY THE CHOCTAW AND CHICKASAW CITIZENSHIP COURT

TRIBAL ENROLLMENT OF PARENTS

	Name of Father	Year	County	Name of Mother	Year	County
1	Frank Cogbill	Dead	Non Citz	Isabell Cogbill	Dead	Choctaw
2	James M Brogdon	1896	" "	No1		
3	" " "	1896	" "	No1		
4	" " "	1896	" "	No1		
5	" " "	1896	" "	No1		
6	No1 1 to 5 incl. Denied in 96 Case #916					
7	Admitted by U.S. Court, Central District,					
8	September 11/97. Case No 62.					
9	As to residence, see testimony of James M Brogdon					
10	Judgements of US Court admitting No 1 to 5 vacated and set aside by Decree of Choctaw Chickasaw Cit Court Decr 17/02					
11	No 1 to 5 incl now in C.C.C.C. Case #[illegible]					
12						
13	Duplicate record in Choctaw [remainder illegible]					
14						
15					Date of Application for Enrollment:	
16					6/15/99	
17						

69

RESIDENCE: Skullyville COUNTY. **Choctaw Nation** **Choctaw Roll** CARD NO.
POST OFFICE: Milton, I.T. *(Not Including Freedmen)* FIELD NO. 2770

Dawes' Roll No.	NAME		Relationship to Person	AGE	SEX	BLOOD	TRIBAL ENROLLMENT		
							Year	County	No.
8115	1 Folsom, Albert	34	First Named	31	M	1/4	1896	Skullyville	3922
8116	2 " Susie K	29	Wife	26	F	1/4	1896	"	3923
8117	3 " Claude C	12	Son	9	M	1/4	1896	"	3924
8118	4 " David W	10	"	7	"	1/4	1896	"	3925
8119	5 " Allie M	8	Dau	5	F	1/4	1896	"	3926
8120	6 " Ollie E	5	"	3	"	1/4	1896	"	3927
8121	7 " Joseph S	4	Son	1	M	1/4			
8122	8 " Susie Irene	1	Dau	1mo	F	1/4			
	9								
	10								
	11								
	12								
	13								
	14								
	15	ENROLLMENT OF NOS. 1,2,3,4,5,6,7,8 HEREON							
	16	APPROVED BY THE SECRETARY OF INTERIOR JAN 17 1903							
	17								

TRIBAL ENROLLMENT OF PARENTS

	Name of Father	Year	County	Name of Mother	Year	County
1	Albert Folsom	Dead	Skullyville	Lucinda Folsom	Dead	Skullyville
2	Turner Brashears	"	"	Katie Brashears	"	Non Citz
3	No1			No2		
4	No1			No2		
5	No1			No2		
6	No1			No2		
7	No1			No2		
8	Nº1			Nº2		
9						
10						
11						
12	For child of Nos1 and 2 see NB (Apr 26-06) No 565					
13	As to evidence of parents of No2, see					#1 to 7
14	Card of John W Wyers, No 2711				Date of Application for Enrollment.	
15	No7 Affidavit of birth to be supplied. Recd 6/22/99					
16	Nº8 Born Jany 27, 1902" enrolled Feby 20, 1902				6/15/99	
17						

70

Choctaw By Blood Enrollment Cards 1898-1914

<table>
<tr><td>RESIDENCE: Skullyville COUNTY.</td><td rowspan="2" style="text-align:center">Choctaw Nation</td><td>Choctaw Roll</td><td>CARD NO.</td></tr>
<tr><td>POST OFFICE: Spiro, I.T.</td><td>(Not Including Freedmen)</td><td>FIELD NO. 2771</td></tr>
</table>

Dawes' Roll No.	NAME	Relationship to Person First Named	AGE	SEX	BLOOD	TRIBAL ENROLLMENT		
						Year	County	No.
8123	1 Hartshorne, David C 27	Named	24	F	3/8	1896	Skullyville	5175
8124	2 " Edward D 5	Son	2	M	3/16			
8125	3 " Jane E 3	Dau	6wks	F	3/16			
I.W. 51	4 " George E	Hus.	34	M	IW	1896	Skullyville	14598
	5							
	6							
	7							
	8							
	9							
	10							
	11	ENROLLMENT						
	12	OF NOS. ~~~ 4 ~~~ HEREON APPROVED BY THE SECRETARY						
	13	OF INTERIOR JUN 13 1903						
	14							
	15	ENROLLMENT OF NOS. 1,2,3 HEREON						
	16	APPROVED BY THE SECRETARY						
	17	OF INTERIOR JAN 17 1903						

TRIBAL ENROLLMENT OF PARENTS

	Name of Father	Year	County	Name of Mother	Year	County
1	David McCurtain	Dead	Skullyville	Rebecca Lanier	1896	Skullyville
2	Geo S Hartshorne	1896	white man	No1		
3	" " "	1896	" "	No1		
4	Robt D Hartshorne	Dead	noncitizen	Margaret Hartshorne		noncitizen
5						
6						
7						
8						
9						
10						
11	No2 on 1896 roll as David Hartshorne					
12						
13	Husband, Geo E Hartshorne, on Card No D247					
14	Nos 2-3 Affidavits of birth to be supplied Recd June 16/99					
15	No4 transferred to this card from Choctaw card D#247. See decision			Date of Application for Enrollment.		
16	of March 4, 1903			6/15/99		
17	For child of Nos1&4 see NB (Mar 3-1905) Card #192			No4 Enrolled March 20, 1903		

71

Choctaw By Blood Enrollment Cards 1898-1914

RESIDENCE: Skullyville   COUNTY. **Choctaw Nation**   Choctaw Roll   CARD NO.

POST OFFICE: Spiro, I.T.   *(Not Including Freedmen)*   FIELD NO. 2772

Dawes' Roll No.	NAME	Relationship to Person First Named	AGE	SEX	BLOOD	TRIBAL ENROLLMENT		
						Year	County	No.
8126	1 Barbour, Hester A ²¹	First Named	18	F	1/8	1896	Skullyville	11941
8127	2 " James William²	Son	1mo	M	1/16			
8128	3 " David Preston ¹	Son	1mo	M	1/16			
	4							
	5							
	6							
	7							
	8							
	9							
	10							
	11							
	12							
	13							
	14							
	15	ENROLLMENT OF NOS. 1, 2, 3 HEREON						
	16	APPROVED BY THE SECRETARY OF INTERIOR JAN 17 1903						
	17							

TRIBAL ENROLLMENT OF PARENTS

	Name of Father	Year	County	Name of Mother	Year	County
1	James Taylor	1896	Skullyville	Martha J Taylor	1896	Non Citz
2	David P. Barber		Non-citizen	No.1		
3	" " "		" "	No.1		
4						
5						
6	On 1896 roll as Hester Taylor					
7						
8	As to marriage of parents, see judgment					
9	of Dawes Commission, admitting her					
10	mother Martha J. Taylor as an Intermarried Citizen, Case No 278					
11	No.2 Enrolled June 23d, 1900					
12	No.3 Born Feby 18, 1902; Enrolled March 17, 1902.					
13	For child of No1 see NB (Mar 3-1905) Card #193					
14	" " " " " (Apr 26 '06) " #1233					#1
15					Date of Application for Enrollment.	
16					6/15/99	
17	PO seems to be Tamaha I.T. 12/16/02					

72

Choctaw By Blood Enrollment Cards 1898-1914

RESIDENCE: Skullyville   COUNTY. **Choctaw Nation**   Choctaw Roll _(Not Including Freedmen)_   CARD NO.

POST OFFICE: Spiro I.T.   FIELD NO. 2773

Dawes' Roll No.	NAME	Relationship to Person First Named	AGE	SEX	BLOOD	TRIBAL ENROLLMENT		
						Year	County	No.
8129 29₁	Walker K. Tandy ³²	First Named	29	M	1/4	1896	Skullyville	12840
26 ₂	" Mattie ²⁷	Wife	24	F	I.W.	1896	"	15151
₃								
₄								
₅								
₆								
₇								
₈								
₉								
10								
11								
12								
13								
14								
15	ENROLLMENT OF NOS. 1 HEREON APPROVED BY THE SECRETARY OF INTERIOR JAN 17 1903		ENROLLMENT OF NOS. 2 HEREON APPROVED BY THE SECRETARY OF INTERIOR JUN 13 1903					
16								
17								

TRIBAL ENROLLMENT OF PARENTS

	Name of Father	Year	County	Name of Mother	Year	County
₁	Tandy Walker	Dead	Sans Bois	Sillin Walker	Dead	Sans Bois
₂	John Gill	1896	Non Citz	Henrietta Gill	"	Non Citz
₃						
₄						
₅						
₆						
₇	No1 On 1896 roll as Tandy Walker					
₈	Evidence of divorce between N°1 and his former					
₉	wife filed Jany 20, 1903					
	~~See also certified copy of divorce proceedings between N°1~~					
10	and Agnes Walker filed Jany 26, 1903					
11						
12						
13						
14						
15					Date of Application for Enrollment.	
16					6/15/99	
17						

Choctaw By Blood Enrollment Cards 1898-1914

RESIDENCE: Gaines COUNTY. **Choctaw Nation** **Choctaw Roll** CARD NO.
POST OFFICE: Hartshorne, I.T. *(Not Including Freedmen)* FIELD NO. 2774

Dawes' Roll No.	NAME	Relationship to Person First Named	AGE	SEX	BLOOD	TRIBAL ENROLLMENT		
						Year	County	No.
8130	1 Grady, Fannie E ⁵⁸	First Named	55	F	1/8	1896	Skullyville	5176
	2							
	3							
	4							
	5							
	6							
	7							
	8							
	9							
	10							
	11							
	12							
	13							
	14							
	15							
	16							
	17							

ENROLLMENT
OF NOS. 1 HEREON
APPROVED BY THE SECRETARY
OF INTERIOR JAN 17 1903

TRIBAL ENROLLMENT OF PARENTS

	Name of Father	Year	County	Name of Mother	Year	County
1	Henry Massey	Dead	Non Citz	Louisa Griffith		Gaines
2						
3						
4						
5						
6						
7	On 1896 Roll as Fannie Hendrickson					
8						
9	N° 1 was at one time wife of John M. Grady on					
10	Choctaw card #3159.					
11						
12						
13						
14						
15					Date of Application for Enrollment.	
16					June 15/99	
17						

Choctaw By Blood Enrollment Cards 1898-1914

RESIDENCE: Sans Bois   COUNTY. **Choctaw Nation**   **Choctaw Roll** *(Not Including Freedmen)*   CARD No.
POST OFFICE: Starr, I.T.   FIELD No. 2775

Dawes' Roll No.	NAME		Relationship to Person First Named	AGE	SEX	BLOOD	TRIBAL ENROLLMENT		
							Year	County	No.
8131	1 Allen, Callie	35	First Named	32	F	1/16	1896	Sans Bois	1
8132	2 " Maud	16	Dau	13	"	1/32	1896	" "	2
8133	3 " William	14	Son	11	M	1/32	1896	" "	3
8134	4 " David	12	"	9	"	1/32	1896	" "	4
8135	5 " May	10	Dau	7	F	1/32	1896	" "	5
8136	6 " Walter	8	Son	5	M	1/32	1896	" "	6
I.W. 1112	7 " Richard M	51	Husband	51	M	I.W.	1896	" "	14250
	8								
	9								
	10 No.7 was separated from No.1 in								
	11 March, 1901, and were subsequently								
	12 in 1902 divorced. Nov. 3, 1904								
	13								
	14 ENROLLMENT								
	15 OF NOS. 1,2,3,4,5,6 HEREON								
	16 APPROVED BY THE SECRETARY								
	17 OF INTERIOR JAN 17 1903								

ENROLLMENT
OF NOS. ~~~~ 7 ~~~~ HEREON
APPROVED BY THE SECRETARY
OF INTERIOR NOV 16 1904

TRIBAL ENROLLMENT OF PARENTS

	Name of Father	Year	County	Name of Mother	Year	County
1	Gaines Simcoe	Dead	Non Citz	Fannie Simcoe	1896	Gaines
2	Richard M Allen	1896	" "	No1		
3	" " "	1896	" "	No1		
4	" " "	1896	" "	No1		
5	" " "	1896	" "	No1		
6	" " "	1896	" "	No1		
7	Alex Allen	dead	" "	Spazzee Allen	dead	Non Citz
8						
9						
10						
11	Husband, Richard M. Allen, on Card D248					
12	No.5 on 1896 Choctaw roll as Mary Allen			father of		
13	Evidence of marriage between No1 and 2 filed Jany 26, 1903					
14	No.7 transferred from Choctaw card #D-248, Oct. 31, 1904: See decision of Oct. 15, 1904					
15	For child of No2 see NB (Apr 26 '06) Card #1179				Date of Application for Enrollment.	
16	" " " 2 " " (Mar 3 1905) " #763				6/15/99	
17						

Choctaw By Blood Enrollment Cards 1898-1914

RESIDENCE: Sans Bois	COUNTY.							CARD NO.	
POST OFFICE: Blaine, I.T.	**Choctaw Nation**					**Choctaw Roll** (Not Including Freedmen)		FIELD NO. 2776	

Dawes' Roll No.	NAME		Relationship to Person Named	AGE	SEX	BLOOD	TRIBAL ENROLLMENT		
							Year	County	No.
8137	1 Daggs, William W	25	First Named	22	M	1/8	1896	Sans Bois	3172
8138	2 " Leonidas	23	Bro	20	"	1/8	1896	" "	3173
8139	3 " John C	20	"	17	"	1/8	1893	Gaines	139
8140	4 " James W	18	"	15	"	1/8	1893	"	140
8141	5 " Sarah E	1	Dau	1wk	F	1/16			
I.W. 1113	6 " Mollie	22	Wife	22	F	I.W.			
I.W. 1114	7 " James M	55	Father	55	M	I.W.	1896	Sans Bois	14452
	8								
	9	ENROLLMENT							
	10	OF NOS. ~ 6 and 7 ~~ HEREON APPROVED BY THE SECRETARY							
	11	OF INTERIOR NOV 16 1904							
	12								
	13	For child of Nos1&6 see NB							
	14	(Apr 26-06) Card #528							
	15	ENROLLMENT							
	16	OF NOS. 1,2,3,4,5 HEREON APPROVED BY THE SECRETARY							
	17	OF INTERIOR JAN 17 1903							

TRIBAL ENROLLMENT OF PARENTS

	Name of Father	Year	County	Name of Mother	Year	County
1	Jas M Daggs	1896	Non Citz	Amanda Daggs	Dead	Skullyville
2	" " "	1896	" "	" "	"	"
3	" " "	1896	" "	" "	"	"
4	" " "	1896	" "	" "	"	"
5	Nº 1			Mollie Daggs		white woman
6	Baily[sic] Simpson	dead	non-citizen	Betty Simpson	dead	non-citizen
7				No. 6	Born Feb 3 – 06	

8	No1 on 1896 roll as W. W. Daggs
9	No3 on 1893 Pay Roll, Page 14, No 139, Gaines Co, as John Deggs
10	No4 " 1893 " " " 14 " 140 " " " James "
	No.1 is now the husband of Mollie Daggs on Choctaw card #D.678
11	No.3 on 1896 Choctaw census roll, page 52, No. 2154 as Nov. 11, 1901
12	John Crockett. For child of Nos 1&6 see NB (March 3, 1905) #1450
13	No.4 on 1896 Choctaw census roll, page 332, No. 12664 as
	James Walker No.1 on 1896 Choc census roll as J.M. Daggs
14	Nº5 Born April 19, 1902; enrolled April 26, 1902
15	No.6 transferred from Choctaw card #D-678 Oct 31, 1904: See decision of Oct. 15, 1904
16	No 7 " " " " #R-72 " 31, 1904: " " " 15, 1904
17		Date of Application for Enrollment. 6/15/99

No6 P.O. Ada, I.T. 11/11/02   No.7 P.O. Sailor I.T. 12/24/02

RESIDENCE: Sans Bois   COUNTY. **Choctaw Nation**   **Choctaw Roll** CARD No.

POST OFFICE: Blaine, I.T.   *(Not Including Freedmen)*   FIELD NO. 2777

Dawes' Roll No.	NAME		Relationship to Person First Named	AGE	SEX	BLOOD	TRIBAL ENROLLMENT		
							Year	County	No.
8142	1 Winters, Daisy L	22	First Named	19	F	1/8	1896	Sans Bois	12723
8143	2 " Walter B	6	Son	2	M	1/16	1896	" "	12724
8144	3 " Amanda	3	Dau	9mo	F	1/16			
NB 618	4 " Hazel V								
	5								
	6								
	7								
	8								
	9								
	10								
	11								
	12								
	13								
	14								
	15								
	16								
	17								

ENROLLMENT
OF NOS. 1, 2, 3 HEREON
APPROVED BY THE SECRETARY
OF INTERIOR JAN 17 1903

TRIBAL ENROLLMENT OF PARENTS

	Name of Father	Year	County	Name of Mother	Year	County
1	Jas M Daggs	1896	Non Citz	Amanda Daggs	Dead	Sans Bois
2	Frank Winters	1896	" "	No1		
3	" "	"	" "	No.1		
4	" "	"	" "	"	Born	Oct. 11 – 05
5						
6						
7	No1 on 1896 roll as Lizzie Winters					
8	No.3 Enrolled November 14th 1900					
9	For child of No1 see NB (Apr 26-06) Card No 618					
10	" " " " (Mar 3-1905) " 46					
11						
12						
13						
14					#1&2	
15					Date of Application for Enrollment.	
16					6/15/99	
17						

Choctaw By Blood Enrollment Cards 1898-1914

RESIDENCE:	Skullyville	COUNTY.							
POST OFFICE:	Oak Lodge I.T.								

Choctaw Nation — Choctaw Roll *(Not Including Freedmen)* CARD No. FIELD NO. **2778**

Dawes' Roll No.	NAME		Relationship to Person Named	AGE	SEX	BLOOD	TRIBAL ENROLLMENT		
							Year	County	No.
8145	1 Darneal Stephen	47	First Named	44	M	1/2	1896	Skullyville	3219
I.W. 127	2 " Mary	35	Wife	32	F	IW			
8146	3 " James	15	Son	12	M	1/4	1896	"	3220
8147	4 " Elias	12	"	9	M	1/4	1896	"	3221
8148	5 " William	9	"	6	M	1/4	1896	"	3222
8149	6 " Henry	6	"	3	M	1/4			
8150	7 " Fred S	2	Son	6mo	M	1/4			
	8								
	9								
	10								
	11								
	12	ENROLLMENT OF NOS. 2 HEREON APPROVED BY THE SECRETARY OF INTERIOR JUN 13 1903							
	13								
	14								
	15	ENROLLMENT OF NOS. 1,3,4,5,6,7 HEREON APPROVED BY THE SECRETARY OF INTERIOR JAN 17 1903							
	16								
	17								

TRIBAL ENROLLMENT OF PARENTS

	Name of Father	Year	County	Name of Mother	Year	County
1	Jim Darneal	1896	Skullyville	Caroline Darneal	Dead	Skullyville
2	Milt Long	Dead	Non Citz	Louisa Long	1896	Non Citz
3	No1			No2		
4	No1			No2		
5	No1			No2		
6	No1			No2		
7	No.1			No.2		
8						
9	No3 On 1896 roll as Jim Darneal					
10	No5 " " " " Willy "					
11	No2 As to marriage see testimony of Stephen Darneal and Polly Barnard					
12	No 7 Enrolled July 11, 1901					
13	Evidence of marriage between N⁰1 and 2 filed Jany. 26, 1903					
14	For child of Nos 1 & 2 see NB (March 3, 1905) #725			#1 to 6 inc		
15				Date of Application for Enrollment.		
16	P.O. Whitefield I.T.			6/15/99		
17		12/18/03				

Choctaw By Blood Enrollment Cards 1898-1914

RESIDENCE: Skullyville	COUNTY.					

RESIDENCE: Skullyville   **COUNTY.**   **Choctaw Nation**   **Choctaw Roll** *(Not Including Freedmen)*   **CARD NO.**
POST OFFICE: Oak Lodge, I.T.   **FIELD NO.** 2779

Dawes' Roll No.	NAME	Relationship to Person First Named	AGE	SEX	BLOOD	TRIBAL ENROLLMENT Year	County	No.
8151	1 Ainsworth, Jesse B ⁴⁸	First Named	45	M	1/4	1896	Skullyville	45
I.W. 151	2 " Margaret ⁴⁸	Wife	45	F	I.W.	1896	"	14252
8152	3 " Clifford ¹⁸	Son	15	M	1/8	1896	"	46
8153	4 " Chester ¹⁵	"	13	"	1/8	1896	"	47
8154	5 " Alice ⁹	Dau	6	F	1/8	1896	"	48
	6							
	7							
	8							
	9							
	10							
	11							
	12							
	13							
	14							
	15	ENROLLMENT OF NOS. 1,3,4,5 HEREON APPROVED BY THE SECRETARY OF INTERIOR JAN 17 1903		ENROLLMENT OF NOS. 2 HEREON APPROVED BY THE SECRETARY OF INTERIOR JUN 13 1903				
	16							
	17							

TRIBAL ENROLLMENT OF PARENTS

	Name of Father	Year	County	Name of Mother	Year	County
1	J. G. Ainsworth	Dead	Non Citz	Martha Ainsworth	Dead	Skullyville
2	D.S. Ainsworth	1896	" "	Nancy Ainsworth	"	Non Citz
3	No1			No2		
4	No1			No2		
5	No1			No2		
6						
7						
8						
9			No1 on 1896 roll as Jessie B Ainsworth			
10			No5 " 1896 " " Ally "			
11			As to marriage, see testimony of No1 and D.S. Ainsworth			
12						
13						
14						
15					Date of Application for Enrollment.	
16					6/15/99	
17						

79

RESIDENCE:	Skullyville	COUNTY.	**Choctaw Nation**		**Choctaw Roll**		CARD NO.	
POST OFFICE:	Oak Lodge, I.T.				*(Not Including Freedmen)*		FIELD NO.	2780

Dawes' Roll No.	NAME		Relationship to Person First Named	AGE	SEX	BLOOD	TRIBAL ENROLLMENT		
							Year	County	No.
I.W. 128	1 Fannin, Elijah W	46		43	M	I.W			
8155	2 " Johanna	44	Wife	41	F	1/4	1896	Skullyville	3935
8156	3 " Henry	22	Son	19	M	1/8	1896	"	3936
8157	4 " Pauline	20	Dau	17	F	1/8	1896	"	3937
8158	5 " Fredrica	17	"	14	"	1/8	1896	"	3938
8159	6 " Georgina	14	"	11	"	1/8	1896	"	3939
8160	7 " Myrtle I	12	"	9	"	1/8	1896	"	3940
8161	8 " Madaline F	8	"	5	"	1/8	1896	"	3941
8162	9 " Johanna F	5	"	1	"	1/8			
8163	10 " Mella Belle	1	Gr.Dau	5mo	F	1/16	ENROLLMENT OF NOS. ~~~ 12 ~~~ HEREON		
14773	11 " Allice	1	Dau	4mo	F	1/8	APPROVED BY THE SECRETARY OF INTERIOR MAY -7 1904		
I.W. 730	12 " Florence Loren	23	WIFE OF NO.3	23	F	I.W.			
	13		Nº11 Proof of birth rec'd 12/15/02						
	14		Parents of No.12: FATHER: W. D. Meroney, dead: MOTHER: Kate Meroney						
	15	ENROLLMENT OF NOS. 2,3,4,5,6,7,8,9,10 HEREON APPROVED BY THE SECRETARY OF INTERIOR	No11 Born August 3, 1902; Enrolled December 20, 1902						
	16								
	17		No12 transferred from Choctaw card #D.792: See decision of Feby 27, 1904						

	TRIBAL ENROLLMENT OF PARENTS					
	Name of Father	Year	County	Name of Mother	Year	County
1	Wᵐ H Fannin	1896	Non Citz	Adaline Fannin	1896	Non Citz
2	Jas. G. Ainsworth	Dead	" "	Martha Ainsworth	Dead	Skullyville
3	No1			No2		
4	No1			No2		
5	No1	ENROLLMENT OF NOS. ~~~~~~ HEREON		No2		
6	No1	APPROVED BY THE SECRETARY OF INTERIOR JUN 13 1903		No2		
7	No1			No2		
8	No1			No2	ENROLLMENT OF NOS. 11 HEREON	
9	No1			No2	APPROVED BY THE SECRETARY OF INTERIOR MAY 20 1903	
10	No1			No2		
11	Nº3			Florence Fannin		non-citizen
12	No 1			No 2		
13	No2 on 1896 roll as Joanna Fannin					
14	No5 " 1896 " " Freddie "					
15	No6 " 1896 " " Georgia "					
16	No7 " 1896 " " Kyle "				Date of Application #1 to 9	
17	No8 " 1896 " " Madaline "				for Enrollment. 6/15/99	
	Nº3 is now the husband of Florence Fannin-noncitizen: Evidence of marriage					
	filed Sept 8, 1902. Nº10 Born March 18, 1903; enrolled Sept 8, 1903					

Wife of No3 is Florence Lorell Fannin on Choctaw card #D792 Sept 16, 1902 Evidence of marriage now on file in 7D-792

Choctaw By Blood Enrollment Cards 1898-1914

RESIDENCE: Skullyville COUNTY. **Choctaw Nation** — Choctaw Roll *(Not Including Freedmen)* — CARD NO. FIELD NO. 2781
POST OFFICE: Ward, I.T.

Dawes' Roll No.		NAME		Relationship to Person First Named	AGE	SEX	BLOOD	TRIBAL ENROLLMENT		
								Year	County	No.
8164	1	Simpson, Nettie R	37	First Named	34	F	1/8	1896	Skullyville	11151
8165	2	" Edward R	12	Son	9	M	1/16	1896	"	11152
8166	3	" William N	10	"	7	"	1/16	1896	"	11153
8167	4	" Marion	8	Dau	5	F	1/16	1896	"	11154
	5									
	6									
	7									
	8									
	9									
	10									
	11									
	12									
	13									
	14									
	15									
	16									
	17									

ENROLLMENT
OF NOS. 1,2,3,4, HEREON
APPROVED BY THE SECRETARY
OF INTERIOR JAN 17 1903

TRIBAL ENROLLMENT OF PARENTS

	Name of Father	Year	County	Name of Mother	Year	County
1	Jacob Russell	Dead	Non Citz	Almira Russell	Dead	Skullyville
2	W. M. Simpson	1896	" "	No1		
3	" " "	1896	" "	No1		
4	" " "	1896	" "	No1		
5						
6						
7						
8		No2 on 1896 roll as Russel E. Simpson				
9		No3 " 1896 " " Wᵐ N. "				
10						
11						
12						
13						
14						
15				Date of Application for Enrollment.		
16				6/15/99		
17						

Choctaw By Blood Enrollment Cards 1898-1914

RESIDENCE: Skullyville COUNTY.	**Choctaw Nation**	**Choctaw Roll** (Not Including Freedmen)	CARD No.
POST OFFICE: Oak Lodge, I.T			FIELD No. 2782

Dawes' Roll No.	NAME	Relationship to Person Named	AGE	SEX	BLOOD	TRIBAL ENROLLMENT Year	County	No.
8168	1 Merryman, William B[30]	First Named	27	M	1/8	1896	Skullyville	8442
I.W. 270	2 " Florence A[30]	Wife	27	F	IW	1896	"	14798
8169	3 " William H[8]	Son	5	M	1/16	1896	"	8443
8170	4 " Frank S[5]	"	3	"	1/16	1896	"	8444
8171	5 " Nancy J[4]	Dau	9mo	F	1/16			
8172	6 " Ezra Ruben[1]	Son	7wks	M	1/16			
	7							
	8							
	9							
	10							

ENROLLMENT OF NOS. 2 HEREON APPROVED BY THE SECRETARY OF INTERIOR SEP 12 1903

ENROLLMENT OF NOS. 1,3,4,5,6 HEREON APPROVED BY THE SECRETARY OF INTERIOR JAN 17 1903

TRIBAL ENROLLMENT OF PARENTS

	Name of Father	Year	County	Name of Mother	Year	County
1	W. P. Merryman	Dead	Non Citz	Caroline Merryman	1896	Skullyville
2	Jas H Bowman	1896	" "	Sarah Bowman	Dead	Non Citz
3	No1			No2		
4	No1			No2		
5	No1			No2		
6	No1			No2		
7						
8						
9						
10	No1 on 1896 roll as Wm Merryman					
11	No3 " 1896 " " Wm " Jr					
12	No4 " 1896 " " Frank "					
13	No2 " 1896 " " Allie "					
	No2 was admitted by Dawes Com,					
14	as an Intermarried Citizen, Case				#1 to 5 inc	
15	No 622 as Allie Merryman				Date of Application for Enrollment.	
16	No.6 Enrolled July 29, 1901				6/15/99	
17	For child of Nos 1&2 see NB (Mar 3-1905) Card #194					

82

Choctaw By Blood Enrollment Cards 1898-1914

RESIDENCE: Skullyville COUNTY. **Choctaw Nation** Choctaw Roll CARD
POST OFFICE: Fort Smith, Ark (Not Including Freedmen) FIELD NO. 2783

Dawes' Roll No.	NAME	Relationship to Person First Named	AGE	SEX	BLOOD	TRIBAL ENROLLMENT		
						Year	County	No.
8173	1 LeFlore, Frank T 30	First Named	27	M	1/16	1896	Skullyville	7715
I.W. 1311	2 " Gertrude 19	Wife	19	F	I.W.			
	3							
	4							
	5							
	6							
	7	ENROLLMENT						
	8	OF NOS. 2 HEREON APPROVED BY THE SECRETARY						
	9	OF INTERIOR MAR 14 1905						
	10	No.2 is now named Gertrude May						
	11	PO address Rogers, Ark						
	12	See testimony of Nov 8, 1904						
	13							
	14							
	15	ENROLLMENT						
	16	OF NOS. 1 HEREON APPROVED BY THE SECRETARY						
	17	OF INTERIOR JAN 17 1903						

TRIBAL ENROLLMENT OF PARENTS

	Name of Father	Year	County	Name of Mother	Year	County
1	Campbell LeFlore	Dead	Skullyville	Ida L LeFlore now Foucar	1896	Non Citz
2	Wm F. May		non citizen	Mary J. May		non citizen
3						
4						
5						
6						
7						
8						
9	As [sic] marriage of parents, see Card of					
10	Louie LeFlore					
11						
12	On 1896 roll as Frank LeFlore					
13	Gertrude LeFlore, wife of No.1 on Choctaw card #D 622					
14	On Dec 27, 1900, No.2 married No.1 a recognized and enrolled citizen by blood of the Choctaw Nation.					
15	No.2 originally listed for enrollment on Choctaw card D-622 Feb. 28, 1901: transferred to this card Jan. 28, 1905.					
16	See decision of Jan. 12, 1905.		Date of Application for Enrollment.	6/15/99		
17						

RESIDENCE:	Sans Bois	COUNTY.	**Choctaw Nation**	**Choctaw Roll**	CARD NO.
POST OFFICE:	Sans Bois I.T.			*(Not Including Freedmen)*	FIELD NO. 2784

Dawes' Roll No.	NAME		Relationship to Person	AGE	SEX	BLOOD	TRIBAL ENROLLMENT		
							Year	County	No.
8174	1 Woods Susan	36	First Named	33	F	1/2	1896	Sans Bois	12716
8175	2 " George	11	Son	8	M	1/4	1896	" "	12717
8176	3 " Louis	9	"	6	M	1/4	1896	" "	12718
8177	4 Folsom Albert	16	"	13	M	3/8	1896	" "	3828
8178	5 Winlock Lavinia	18	Dau	15	F	1/2	1896	" "	12715
8179	6 " Charlotte	15	Niece	13	F	1/2	1896	" "	12713
I.W.1312	7 Woods, Lyons	42	Husband	42	M	I.W.			
	8								
	9								
	10								
	11	ENROLLMENT							
	12	OF NOS. 7 HEREON APPROVED BY THE SECRETARY							
	13	OF INTERIOR MAR 14 1905							
	14								
	15	ENROLLMENT OF NOS. 1,2,3,4,5,6, HEREON							
	16	APPROVED BY THE SECRETARY							
	17	OF INTERIOR JAN 17 1903							

TRIBAL ENROLLMENT OF PARENTS

	Name of Father	Year	County	Name of Mother	Year	County
1	Charley McGilberry	Dead	Sans Bois	Amsa McGilberry	Dead	Sans Bois
2	Lyons Woods	1896	Non Citz	No 1		
3	" "	"	" "	No 1		
4	Jerry Folsom	1896	Sugar Loaf	No 1		
5	Rufus Winlock	1896	Gaines	No 1		
6	Peter Winlock	Dead	Sans Bois	Polly Winlock	Dead	Sans Bois
7	James Woods	dead	non citz	Martha J Woods	dead	non citz
8						
9						
10	No4 On 1896 roll as Albert Folsum					
11	Husband of No1 on W.C. D253					
12	No.7 formerly the husband of Maggie Ward, Choctaw card No 2695 final roll number 7852 they lived together in said Nation					
13	for about a month when they separated and were afterwards divorced					
14	No.7 originally listed for enrollment on Choctaw card D-253 6/19/99;					
15	transferred to this card Jan. 28, 1905. See decision of Jan. 12, 1905		#1 to 6			
16				Date of Application for Enrollment. 6/15/99		
17				1 to 6		

Choctaw By Blood Enrollment Cards 1898-1914

RESIDENCE: Skullyville COUNTY.	**Choctaw Nation**	Choctaw Roll (Not Including Freedmen)	CARD NO.
POST OFFICE: Spiro I.T.			FIELD NO. 2785

Dawes' Roll No.	NAME		Relationship to Person	AGE	SEX	BLOOD	TRIBAL ENROLLMENT		
							Year	County	No.
8180	1 Folsom John	43	First Named	40	M	1/4	1896	Tobucksey[sic]	4064
	2								
	3								
	4								
	5								
	6								
	7								
	8								
	9								
	10								
	11								
	12								
	13								
	14								
	15	ENROLLMENT OF NOS. 1 HEREON APPROVED BY THE SECRETARY							
	16	OF INTERIOR JAN 17 1903							
	17								

TRIBAL ENROLLMENT OF PARENTS

	Name of Father	Year	County	Name of Mother	Year	County
1	Edmond Folsom	Dead	Sans Bois	Ann Folsom	Dead	Towson
2						
3						
4						
5						
6			On 1896 roll as John Fulsom			
7						
8						
9						
10						
11						
12						
13						
14						Date of Application for Enrollment.
15						
16	P.O. McAlister Ind Ter					6/15/99
17			12/20/02			

Choctaw By Blood Enrollment Cards 1898-1914

RESIDENCE: Skullyville	COUNTY.							
POST OFFICE: Ward I.T.		**Choctaw Nation**				**Choctaw Roll** (Not Including Freedmen)	CARD NO. FIELD NO. **2786**	

Dawes' Roll No.	NAME	Relationship to Person First Named	AGE	SEX	BLOOD	TRIBAL ENROLLMENT Year	County	No.
DEAD	1 Folsom David	DEAD	25	M	5/16	1896	Skullyville	3944
I.W. 271	2 McDaniel, Kate ²³	Wife	20	F	I.W.	1896	"	14516
VOID.	3 McDaniel Velma A	Dau of Nº2	1mo	F	1/16			
	4							
	5 No. 1 HEREON DISMISSED UNDER							
	6 ORDER OF THE COMMISSION TO THE FIVE							
	7 CIVILIZED TRIBES OF MARCH 31, 1905.							
	8							
	9							
	10							
	11							
	12							
	13							
	14							
	15 ENROLLMENT OF NOS. 2 HEREON							
	16 APPROVED BY THE SECRETARY OF INTERIOR SEP 12 1903							
	17							

TRIBAL ENROLLMENT OF PARENTS

Name of Father	Year	County	Name of Mother	Year	County
1 Isaac Folsom	Dead	Skullyville	Millie Folsom	Dead	Skullyville
2 Robert Norman	"	Non Citz	Maggie Norman	1896	Non Citz
3 Thomas McDaniel		Chickasaw	Nº2		
4					
5					
6 No.1 died Feby 4, 1900: Proof of death filed Feby 14, 1902					
7 No.2 is now the wife of Thomas McDaniel on Chickasaw card #638: March 7, 1902					
8					
9 Nº3 Born June 18, 1902; enrolled July 25, 1902					
10 " " transferred to Choctaw Card No 5394, with father, Oct 30, 1902					
11 For child of No.2 see NB (March 3, 1905) #1275					
12					
13					
14					
15				Date of Application for Enrollment.	
16				6/15/99	
17					

Choctaw By Blood Enrollment Cards 1898-1914

RESIDENCE: Skullyville COUNTY. **Choctaw Nation** Choctaw Roll CARD No.
POST OFFICE: Oak Lodge I.T. *(Not Including Freedmen)* FIELD No. 2787

Dawes' Roll No.	NAME	Relationship to Person First Named	AGE	SEX	BLOOD	TRIBAL ENROLLMENT		
						Year	County	No.
8181	1 Merryman Leonidas 26	First Named	23	M	1/8	1896	Skullyville	8445
I.W. 1403	2 " Sarah 27	Wife	22	F	I W	1896	"	14799
8182	3 " Daniel W. 5	Son	2	M	1/16		"	
8183	4 " Lee Roy 3	"	3mo	"	1/16			
8184	5 " Theodore 1	Son	2mo	M	1/16			
	6							
	7							
	8 ENROLLMENT							
	9 OF NOS. 2 HEREON APPROVED BY THE SECRETARY							
	10 OF INTERIOR JUN 12 1905							
	11							
	12							
	13							
	14							
	15 ENROLLMENT OF NOS. 1,3,4,5, HEREON							
	16 APPROVED BY THE SECRETARY							
	17 OF INTERIOR JAN 17 1903							

TRIBAL ENROLLMENT OF PARENTS

	Name of Father	Year	County	Name of Mother	Year	County
1	Wᵐ P. Merryman	Dead	Non Citz	Caroline Merryman	1896	Skullyville
2	Providence Chapman	1896	" "	Sarah Chapman	1896	Non Citz
3	No 1			No 2		
4	No 1			No 2		
5	Nº1			Nº2		
6						
7						
8	No.2 restored to roll by Departmental authority of January 19,1909 (File 5-51)					
9	No2 On 1896 roll as Sally Merryman					
10	No3 Affidavit of birth to be supplied Recd 6/22/99					
11	Enrollment of No.2 cancelled by order of Department March 4, 1907					
12	Dec 6/99. See if she was denied by Dawes Com in '96 Choctaw Cit Case # Commission in 1896					
13	No.2 Denied by Dawes Com in '96 Choctaw Cit Case # Commission in 1896 in Choctaw Case #345; No appeal.					
14	Nº5 Born Feby. 4 1902: enrolled March 26, 1902					
15	Evidence of marriage between Nᵒˢ 1 and 2 filed Jany. 3, 1903		#1 to 3 inc			
16	For child of Nos 172 see NB (Mar 3-05) #550	Date of Application for Enrollment	6/15/99			
17	PO Spiro I T	No4 enrolled Dec 14/99				

12/18/03

87

Choctaw By Blood Enrollment Cards 1898-1914

RESIDENCE:	Sans Bois	COUNTY.	**Choctaw Nation**		**Choctaw Roll**	CARD NO.	
POST OFFICE:	Garland, I.T.				*(Not Including Freedmen)*	FIELD NO.	2788

Dawes' Roll No.	NAME		Relationship to Person	AGE	SEX	BLOOD	TRIBAL ENROLLMENT		
							Year	County	No.
8185	₁ Folsom, Robert	29	First Named	26	M	1/2	1896	Sans Bois	3860
I.W. 129	₂ " Alice	29	Wife	26	F	I.W			
8186	₃ " Robbie	6	Dau	3	F	1/4	1896	Sans Bois	3861
8187	₄ " George D	3	Son	1	M	1/4			
	₅								
	₆								
	₇								
	₈								
	₉								
	10								
	11								
	12								
	13								
	14			ENROLLMENT					
	15	ENROLLMENT OF NOS. 1, 3, 4, HEREON APPROVED BY THE SECRETARY OF INTERIOR JAN 17 1903		OF NOS. 2 HEREON APPROVED BY THE SECRETARY OF INTERIOR JUN 13 1903					
	16								
	17								

TRIBAL ENROLLMENT OF PARENTS

	Name of Father	Year	County	Name of Mother	Year	County
₁	George Folsom	Dead	Skullyville	Levicey Folsom		Sans Bois
₂	Harkins	"	Non Citz	Prude Cox		Non Citz
₃	No1			No2		
₄	No1			No2		
₅						
₆						
₇						
₈						
₉						
10	For child of Nos 1 and 2 see NB (Apr 26-06) No 841					
11	No3 on 1896 Roll as Robt. Folsom Jr. No4 Affidavit of birth to be supplied: Recd July 1/99					
12						
13						
14	For child of Nos 1&2 see NB (Mar 3-1905) Card #195.					
15	No3 is a girl. Sex changed under Departmental instructions of Nov. 21, 1904 (D.C. #45426-1904)					
16				Date of Application for Enrollment.	June 15/99	
17						

Choctaw By Blood Enrollment Cards 1898-1914

RESIDENCE:	Sans Bois	COUNTY.							
POST OFFICE:	Garland I.T.								

Choctaw Nation

Choctaw Roll (Not Including Freedmen)

CARD No. FIELD No. 2789

Dawes' Roll No.	NAME		Relationship to Person First Named	AGE	SEX	BLOOD	TRIBAL ENROLLMENT		
							Year	County	No.
8188	Hulsey Louvisa	51	First Named	48	F	1/4	1896	Sans Bois	5100
8189	" May	17	Dau	14	F	1/8	1896	" "	5103
8190	" Henry	19	Son	16	M	1/8	1896	" "	5102
8191	" Walter	11	"	8	M	1/8	1896	" "	5104
5									
6									
7									
8									
9									
10									
11									
12									
13									
14									
15	ENROLLMENT OF NOS. 1, 2, 3, 4, HEREON APPROVED BY THE SECRETARY								
16	OF INTERIOR JAN 17 1903								
17									

TRIBAL ENROLLMENT OF PARENTS

	Name of Father	Year	County	Name of Mother	Year	County
1	Jim Harkins	Dead	Towson		Dead	
2	J. C. Hulsey	1896	Non Citz	No 1		
3	" " "	"	" "	No 1		
4	" " "	"	" "	No 1		
5						
6						
7						
8			No1 On 1896 roll as Lavica Hulsey			
9			For child of No.3 see NB (March 3 1905) #1198			
10						
11						
12						
13						
14						Date of Application for Enrollment.
15						
16						6/15/99
17						

Choctaw By Blood Enrollment Cards 1898-1914

RESIDENCE:	Sans Bois	COUNTY.	Choctaw Nation	Choctaw Roll	CARD NO.	
POST OFFICE:	Garland, I.T			(Not Including Freedmen)	FIELD NO.	2790

Dawes' Roll No.	NAME	Relationship to Person First Named	AGE	SEX	BLOOD	TRIBAL ENROLLMENT Year	County	No.
8192	1 Minton, Winnie DIED PRIOR TO SEPTEMBER 25 1902	First Named	21	F	1/2	1896	Sans Bois	8432
8193	2 Brown, Laut 5	Son	5	M	1/4			
8194	3 Minton, Barney 3	"	6wks	"	1/4			
	4							
	5							
	6							
	7							
	8							
	9							
	10							
	11							
	12							
	13							
	14							
	15	ENROLLMENT OF NOS. 1, 2, 3, HEREON APPROVED BY THE SECRETARY OF INTERIOR JAN 17 1903						
	16							
	17							

TRIBAL ENROLLMENT OF PARENTS

	Name of Father	Year	County	Name of Mother	Year	County
1	George Folsom	Dead	Sans Bois	Louvisa Harkins	1896	Sans Bois
2	Robert Brown	1896	Non Citz	No 1		
3	Robert Minton	Dead	" "	No 1		
4						
5						
6						
7	Nos 2-3 Affidavits of birth to be supplied. Recd 6/22/99					
8						
9	No1 died June 7, 1901; Proof of death filed Dec 20 1902					
10	No. 1 died June 7, 1901. Enrollment cancelled by Department July 8, 1904					
11						
12						
13						
14						
15						Date of Application for Enrollment.
16	P.O. Cowlington I T.					6/15/99
17						

Choctaw By Blood Enrollment Cards 1898-1914

RESIDENCE: Sans Bois COUNTY.
POST OFFICE: Blaine, I.T.

Choctaw Nation

Choctaw Roll
(Not Including Freedmen)

CARD No.
FIELD No. 2791

Dawes' Roll No.	NAME	Relationship to Person First Named	AGE	SEX	BLOOD	TRIBAL ENROLLMENT		
						Year	County	No.
8195	1 McMahan, Cornelia ²⁵	First Named	22	F	1/4	1896	Sans Bois	9028
	2							
	3							
	4							
	5							
	6							
	7							
	8							
	9							
	10							
	11							
	12							
	13							
	14							
	15	ENROLLMENT OF NOS. 1 HEREON APPROVED BY THE SECRETARY OF INTERIOR JAN 17 1903						
	16							
	17							

TRIBAL ENROLLMENT OF PARENTS

	Name of Father	Year	County	Name of Mother	Year	County
1	M. F. Taylor	Dead	Sans Bois	Lina Taylor	Dead	Non Citz
2						
3						
4						
5						
6			On 1896 roll as Cornelia McMahon			
7						
8			As to marriage of parents, see testimony of Mrs. Fannie Grady			
9			Mother said to be an Indian			
10						
11						
12						
13						
14						
15					Date of Application for Enrollment.	
16					6/15/99	
17						

RESIDENCE:	Skullyville	COUNTY.	**Choctaw Nation**		**Choctaw Roll**	CARD No.	
POST OFFICE:	Ward, I.T.				(Not Including Freedmen)	FIELD No.	2792

Dawes' Roll No.	NAME		Relationship to Person First Named	AGE	SEX	BLOOD	TRIBAL ENROLLMENT		
							Year	County	No.
8195	₁ Long, Jesse	23		20	M	1/2	1896	Skullyville	7726
I.W. 1313	₂ " Julia	34	Wife	34	F	I.W.			
	₃								
	₄								
	₅								
	₆								
	₇								
	₈								
	₉								
	10								
	11	ENROLLMENT							
	12	OF NOS. 2 HEREON APPROVED BY THE SECRETARY							
	13	OF INTERIOR MAR 14 1905							
	14								
	15	ENROLLMENT							
	16	OF NOS. 1 HEREON APPROVED BY THE SECRETARY							
	17	OF INTERIOR JAN 17 1903							

TRIBAL ENROLLMENT OF PARENTS

	Name of Father	Year	County	Name of Mother	Year	County
₁	Charley Long	Dead	Non Citz	Parma Long	Dead	Skullyville
₂	Caleb Cox	dead	non citizen	Sarah Pirtle		non citizen
₃						
₄						
₅						
₆	On 1896 roll as Jessie Long					
₇						
₈	No.1 is husband of Julia Long on Choctaw Card No. D-948. Evidence of					
₉	marriage filed December 16, 1902.					
10	Nos 1 and 2 were married Jan. 2, 1901. They are separated but not divorced					
11	No.2 originally listed for enrollment on Choctaw card D-948 Dec. 16, 1902: transferred to this card Jan. 29, 1905. See decision of Jan. 13, 1905					
12						
13	For child of Nos 1&2 see NB (Mar 3-1905) Card #128.					
14						
15				Date of Application for Enrollment.		
16				6/15/99		
17	No2 P.O. Poteau I.T. 11/20/04					

Choctaw By Blood Enrollment Cards 1898-1914

Dawes' Roll No.	NAME	Relationship to Person First Named	AGE	SEX	BLOOD	TRIBAL ENROLLMENT Year	County	No.
DEAD.	Tickness, John		52	M	Full	1896	Sans Bois	11877
8197	" Lizzie (DIED PRIOR TO SEPTEMBER 25th 1902)	Wife	43	F	"	1896	" "	11878
8198	" Tillian 13	Dau	10	"	"	1896	" "	11879
8199	" Frances 9	"	6	"	"	1896	" "	11880
8200	" Frank 6	Son	3	M	"	1896	" "	11881

No. 1 HEREON DISMISSED UNDER ORDER OF THE COMMISSION TO THE FIVE CIVILIZED TRIBES OF MARCH 31, 1905.

ENROLLMENT
OF NOS. 2,3,4,5, HEREON
APPROVED BY THE SECRETARY
OF INTERIOR JAN 17 1903

TRIBAL ENROLLMENT OF PARENTS

	Name of Father	Year	County	Name of Mother	Year	County
1	A-sha-lin-tubbee	Dead	Sans Bois		Dead	Sans Bois
2	Henry Scott	"	" "	I yo na	"	" "
3	No1			No2		
4	No1			No2		
5	No1			No2		

No2 died August ... 1901: Enrollment cancelled by Department May ... 190...

No3 on 1896 roll as Sillian Tickness

No1 died April 15, 1901: Proof of death filed Dec 11 1902

Date of Application for Enrollment.
6/15/99

Choctaw By Blood Enrollment Cards 1898-1914

RESIDENCE:	Sans Bois	COUNTY.	**Choctaw Nation**	Choctaw Roll	CARD NO.	
POST OFFICE:	Iron Bridge I.T.			(Not Including Freedmen)	FIELD NO.	2794

Dawes' Roll No.	NAME	Relationship to Person First Named	AGE	SEX	BLOOD	TRIBAL ENROLLMENT		
						Year	County	No.
8201	1 McCann Philip	27 First Named	24	M	Full	1896	Sans Bois	9017
	2							
	3							
	4							
	5							
	6							
	7							
	8							
	9							
	10							
	11							
	2							

ENROLLMENT
OF NOS. 1 HEREON
APPROVED BY THE SECRETARY
OF INTERIOR JAN 17 1903

TRIBAL ENROLLMENT OF PARENTS

	Name of Father	Year	County	Name of Mother	Year	County
1	Charley McCann	Dead	Sugar Loaf	Silway McCann	Dead	Skullyville
2						
3						
4						
5						
6						
7						
8						
9						
10						
11						
12						
13						
14						
15					Date of Application for Enrollment.	
16					6/15/99	
17						

Choctaw By Blood Enrollment Cards 1898-1914

RESIDENCE: Skullyville COUNTY.
POST OFFICE: Pocola, I.T.

Choctaw Nation

Choctaw Roll (Not Including Freedmen)

CARD No. FIELD No. 2795

Dawes' Roll No.	NAME	Relationship to Person First Named	AGE	SEX	BLOOD	TRIBAL ENROLLMENT Year	TRIBAL ENROLLMENT County	TRIBAL ENROLLMENT No.
I.W. 272	1 Nessmith, David		23	M	I.W.			
8202	2 " Mary V 23	Wife	20	F	1/4	1896	Skullyville	10098
8203	3 " Frank 4	Son	1	M	1/8			
8204	4 (X) Greyton, Lillith 8	S. Dau / S. Son	5	F	1/8	1896	Skullyville	4663
8205	5 Nessmith, Robert P 1	Son	2mo	M	1/8			
	6							
	7							
	8							
	9							
	10	ENROLLMENT OF NOS. 1 HEREON APPROVED BY THE SECRETARY OF INTERIOR SEP 12 1903						
	11							
	12							
	13							
	14							
	15	ENROLLMENT OF NOS. 2,3,4,5 HEREON APPROVED BY THE SECRETARY OF INTERIOR JAN 17 1903						
	16							
	17							

TRIBAL ENROLLMENT OF PARENTS

	Name of Father	Year	County	Name of Mother	Year	County
1	David Nessmith	Dead	Non Citz	Susan K Nessmith	Dead	Non Citz
2	Robt Page	1896	Skullyville	Ann Page	"	" "
3	No1			No2		
4	Jno. Greyton	1896	Non Citz	No2		
5	No.1			No.2		
6						
7	(X) Change of sex of No.8204 from "M" to "F" made by authority granted in Dept letter No 5594-1914					
8						
9						
10	No2 on 1896 roll as Mary Page					
11						
12	Evidence of marriage of parents of No2 to be supplied:					
13	No3 Affidavit of birth to be supplied: Recd Oct 6/99					
14	No.5 Enrolled June 4th, 1901					#1 to 4
15	For child of Nos 1&2 see NB (Mar 3-05) Care No 196				Date of Application for Enrollment.	
16	No4 Claims to be a female - See SFeb 613912-1911				5[sic]/15/99	
17						

Choctaw By Blood Enrollment Cards 1898-1914

RESIDENCE: Skullyville COUNTY. **Choctaw Nation** Choctaw Roll CARD NO.
POST OFFICE: Brazil, I.T. (Not Including Freedmen) FIELD NO. 2796

Dawes' Roll No.	NAME	Relationship to Person First Named	AGE	SEX	BLOOD	TRIBAL ENROLLMENT Year	County	No.
8206	1 James, Solomon 30	First Named	27	M	Full	1896	Skullyville	6439
	2							
	3							
	4							
	5							
	6							
	7							
	8							
	9							
	10							
	11							
	12							
	13							
	14							
	15							
	16							
	17							

ENROLLMENT
OF NOS. 1 HEREON
APPROVED BY THE SECRETARY
OF INTERIOR JAN 17 1903

TRIBAL ENROLLMENT OF PARENTS

	Name of Father	Year	County	Name of Mother	Year	County
1	Noel James	1896	Skullyville	Melissa McCann	1896	Skullyville
2						
3						
4						
5						
6						
7						
8						
9		No				
10						
11						
12						
13						
14						
15						
16				Date of Application for Enrollment.	6/16/99	
17						

Choctaw By Blood Enrollment Cards 1898-1914

RESIDENCE: Skullyville COUNTY.
POST OFFICE: Shady Point, I.T.

Choctaw Nation

Choctaw Roll
(Not Including Freedmen)

CARD No.
FIELD No. 2797

Dawes' Roll No.	NAME	Relationship to Person First Named	AGE	SEX	BLOOD	TRIBAL ENROLLMENT		
						Year	County	No.
8207	1 Jackson, Willis 24	First Named	21	M	Full	1896	Skullyville	6468
	2							
	3							
	4							
	5							
	6							
	7							
	8							
	9							
	10							
	11							
	12							
	13							
	14							
	15	ENROLLMENT OF NOS. 1 HEREON APPROVED BY THE SECRETARY OF INTERIOR JAN 17 1903						
	16							
	17							

TRIBAL ENROLLMENT OF PARENTS

Name of Father	Year	County	Name of Mother	Year	County
1 Robin Jackson	1896	Skullyville	Mollie Jackson	Dead	Skullyville
2					
3					
4					
5					
6					
7					
8					
9					
10					
11					
12					
13					
14					
15				Date of Application for Enrollment.	
16				6/16/99	
17					

Choctaw By Blood Enrollment Cards 1898-1914

RESIDENCE:	Skullyville	COUNTY.							
POST OFFICE:	Tucker I.T.								

Choctaw Nation *(Not Including Freedmen)* Choctaw Roll CARD NO. / FIELD NO. 2798

Dawes' Roll No.	NAME	Relationship to Person First Named	AGE	SEX	BLOOD	TRIBAL ENROLLMENT Year	County	No.
DEAD. 1	Burgevin John T	First Named	40	M	IW		Skullyville	
DEAD. 2	" Ella	Wife	25	F	3/16	1896	"	705
8208 3	" Francis H 10	Dau	7	F	3/32	1896	"	706
8209 4	" Edmond A 8	Son	5	M	3/32	1896	"	707
8210 5	" Henry A 6	"	2	M	3/32		"	
8211 6	" Julia G 2	Dau	4mo	F	3/32		"	
7								
8	No. 1 and 2 HEREON DISMISSED UNDER							
9	ORDER OF THE COMMISSION TO THE FIVE							
10	CIVILIZED TRIBES OF MARCH 31, 1905.							
11								
12								
13								
14								
15	ENROLLMENT OF NOS. 3,4,5,6 HEREON							
16	APPROVED BY THE SECRETARY OF INTERIOR JAN 17 1903							
17								

TRIBAL ENROLLMENT OF PARENTS

	Name of Father	Year	County	Name of Mother	Year	County
1	Edmond Burgevin	1896	Non Citz	Frances Burgevin	Dead	Non Citz
2	Reuben Williams	Dead	Atoka	Susanna Williams	"	Atoka
3	No 1			No 2		
4	No 1			No 2		
5	No 1			No 2		
6	No 1			No 2		
7						
8						
9			No1 Admitted by Dawes Com. as intermarried citizen Case No. 87 A John T. Burgevin			
10						
11			No3 On 1896 roll as Francis Burgevin			
12			No4 " " " " Edward "			
13			N°1 Died Feby 9, 1902; Proof of death filed Oct. 29, 1902			
14			N°2 Died Feby 14, 1902 Proof of death filed Oct. 29, 1902			
15				Date of Application for Enrollment.		
16				6/15/99		
17						

98

Choctaw By Blood Enrollment Cards 1898-1914

RESIDENCE: Skullyville   COUNTY.   **Choctaw Nation**   **Choctaw Roll** CARD No.
POST OFFICE: Cameron, I.T.   *(Not Including Freedmen)* FIELD No. **2799**

Dawes' Roll No.	NAME	Relationship to Person First Named	AGE	SEX	BLOOD	TRIBAL ENROLLMENT		
						Year	County	No.
8212	1 Krebbe[sic], Oscar 24	First Named	21	M	5/8	1896	Skullyville	7455
	2							
	3							
	4							
	5							
	6							
	7							
	8							
	9							
	10							
	11							
	12							
	13							
	14							
	15							
	16							
	17							

ENROLLMENT
OF NOS. 1 HEREON
APPROVED BY THE SECRETARY
OF INTERIOR **Jan 17, 1903**

TRIBAL ENROLLMENT OF PARENTS

	Name of Father	Year	County	Name of Mother	Year	County
1	Reuben Krebbs	Dead	Skullyville	Easter Krebbs	Dead	Skullyville
2						
3						
4						
5						
6						
7			On 1896 roll as Oscar Krebs			
8						
9						
10						
11						
12						
13						
14						
15					Date of Application for Enrollment.	
16					6/15/99	
17						

wes' Roll No.	NAME	Relationship to Person	AGE	SEX	BLOOD	TRIBAL ENROLLMENT		
						Year	County	No.

RESIDENCE: Skullyville COUNTY.
POST OFFICE: Cowlington, I.T.

Choctaw Nation

Choctaw Roll (Not Including Freedmen)

CARD NO. FIELD NO. 2800

wes' Roll No.	NAME	Relationship to Person	AGE	SEX	BLOOD	TRIBAL ENROLLMENT Year	County	No.
8213	1 Carney, Maud L [DIED PRIOR TO SEPTEMBER 25, 1902]	First Named	18	F	7/16	1896	Skullyville	2201
8214	2 John S P [DIED PRIOR TO SEPTEMBER 25, 1902]	Son	1	M	7/32			
8215	3 " William McK [2]	Son	1mo	M	7/32			
	4							
	5							
	6							
	7							
	8							
	9							
	10							
	11							
	12							
	13							
	14							
	15							
	16							
	17							

ENROLLMENT
OF NOS. 1,2,3, HEREON
APPROVED BY THE SECRETARY
OF INTERIOR JAN 17 1903

TRIBAL ENROLLMENT OF PARENTS

	Name of Father	Year	County	Name of Mother	Year	County
1	Ben Conway	Dead	Non Citz	Wesley A Conway	Dead	Skullyville
2	Frank W Carney		" "	No.1		
3	" "		" "	No.1		
4						
5			No1 on 1896 Roll as Maud Conaway			
6			No3 Enrolled January 2, 1901			
7			Husband of No.1 and father of Nos 2&3 on Choctaw D250.			
8						
9						
10			No1 died January 8 1902; proof of death filed Dec 20 1902			
11			No2 " March 8 1902; " " " " " " "			
12			No. 1 died Jan 8 1902; No. 2 died March 8 1902; Enrollment cancelled by Department July 8, 1904			
13						
14					#1&2	
15					DATE OF APPLICATION FOR ENROLLMENT	
16					June 15/99	
17						

RESIDENCE: Sans Bois	COUNTY.		CARD NO.
POST OFFICE: Garland, I.T.	**Choctaw Nation**	Choctaw Roll (Not Including Freedmen)	FIELD NO. **2801**

Dawes' Roll No.	NAME	Relationship to Person First Named	AGE	SEX	BLOOD	TRIBAL ENROLLMENT		
						Year	County	No.
1	Morgan, Wiley B	Named	73	M	I.W.			
2								
3								
4								
5	DISMISSED							
6	Sep. 20 1904							
7								
8								
9								
10								
11								
12								
13								
14								
15								
16								
17								

TRIBAL ENROLLMENT OF PARENTS

	Name of Father	Year	County	Name of Mother	Year	County
1	Armstead Morgan	Dead	Non Citz	Sibbie Morgan	Dead	Non Citz
2						
3						
4						
5						
6	No.1 admitted in 96 Case 360					
	Admitted by U.S. Court, Central District, Aug. 25/97					
7	Case 127, as an Intermarried Citizen as W.B. Morgan					
8	As to residence see his testimony					
9	No.1 is the husband of Susan Morgan, on Choctaw Card #D677, Nov. 9, 1901					
10	Judgement[sic] of U.S. Ct. admitting No. 1 vacated and set aside by Decree of Choctaw -					
	Chickasaw Citizenship Court Decr 17 '02					
11	No appeal to C.C.C.C.					
12						
13						
14						
15					Date of Application for Enrollment.	
16					6/16/99	
17						

Choctaw By Blood Enrollment Cards 1898-1914

RESIDENCE: Skullyville   COUNTY. **Choctaw Nation**   **Choctaw Roll**   CARD No.
POST OFFICE: Milton, I.T.   *(Not Including Freedmen)*   FIELD No. 280

Dawes' Roll No.	NAME		Relationship to Person	AGE	SEX	BLOOD	TRIBAL ENROLLMENT		
							Year	County	No.
8216	1 Trahern, Lysander	50	First Named	47	M	1/2	1896	Skullyville	11922
8217	2 McFerran, Isabelle	20	Dau	17	F	1/2	1896	"	11923
14937	3 Trahern, Walter	24	Son	21	M	1/2	1896	"	11924
I.W. **650**	4 McFerran, Walter	24	Hus of No2	24	M	I.W.			
NB 336	5 " Harry Deseveridge								
	6								
	7								
	8								
	9								
	10								
	11 ENROLLMENT OF NOS. 4 HEREON								
	12 APPROVED BY THE SECRETARY OF INTERIOR MAR 26 1904								
	13								
	14								
	15 ENROLLMENT OF NOS. 1 and 2 HEREON			ENROLLMENT OF NOS. ~~3~~ HEREON					
	16 APPROVED BY THE SECRETARY OF INTERIOR JAN 17 1903			APPROVED BY THE SECRETARY OF INTERIOR OCT 15 1903					
	17								

TRIBAL ENROLLMENT OF PARENTS

	Name of Father	Year	County	Name of Mother	Year	County
1	Jas Trahern	Dead	Skullyville	Sallie Trahern	Dead	Skullyville
2	No1			Annie Trahern	"	
3	No1			" "	"	
4	John McFerran		noncitizen	Ruthie McFerran		noncitizen
5	No. 4			No. 2	Born Jun	
6						
7	No4 transferred from Choctaw card D696 January 25,1904. See decision of January 8,					
8	No3 also on 1896 roll Page 311 No 12005,					
9	Gaines Co.					
	No.2 is now the wife of Walter McFerran on Choctaw card #D.696: Jany 23d, 1902					
10	No3 is in Phillipine[sic] island Jany 23, 1902					
11						
12	For child of Nos 2&4 see NB (Apr 26-06) card #336					
13	" " " " " " (Mar 3-05) " #738					
14						
15					Date of Application for Enrollment.	
16					6/16/00	
17	PO Walls IT 4/15/03					

Choctaw By Blood Enrollment Cards 1898-1914

RESIDENCE: Skullyville COUNTY. **Choctaw Nation** **Choctaw Roll** CARD NO.
POST OFFICE: Farmers, I.T. (Not Including Freedmen) FIELD NO. 2803

Dawes' Roll No.	NAME		Relationship to Person First Named	AGE	SEX	BLOOD	TRIBAL ENROLLMENT		
							Year	County	No.
8218	1 Victor, Alfred W	32	First Named	29	M	1/4	1896	Skullyville	12591
I.W 273	2 " Trudy May	35	Wife	30	F	I.W	1896	"	15133
8219	3 " Ether M	7	Dau	4	"	1/8	1896	"	12592
8220	4 " Ida E	5	"	1	"	1/8			
	5								
	6								
	7								
	8								
	9								
	10								
	11	ENROLLMENT							
	12	OF NOS. 2 HEREON APPROVED BY THE SECRETARY							
	13	OF INTERIOR SEP 12 1903							
	14	ENROLLMENT							
	15	OF NOS. 1, 3, 4, HEREON APPROVED BY THE SECRETARY							
	16	OF INTERIOR JAN 17 1903							
	17								

TRIBAL ENROLLMENT OF PARENTS

	Name of Father	Year	County	Name of Mother	Year	County
1	Penson Victor	Dead	Skullyville	Jane Victor	Dead	Non Citz
2	Thomas Bice	1896	Non Citz	Beckie Bice	1897	" "
3	No1			No2		
4	No1			No2		
5						
6						
7						
8	No1 on 1896 roll as Alfred Victor					
9	No2 " 1896 " " Mary "					
10	No3 " 1896 " Ether "					
11	No4 Affidavit of birth to be supplied. Recd June 22/99					
12	No1 As to marriage of parents, see testimony of Robert J. Ward					
13						
14				Date of Application for Enrollment.		
15						
16				6/16/99		
17						

Cameron 12/16/02

103

Choctaw By Blood Enrollment Cards 1898-1914

RESIDENCE: Skullyville   COUNTY.   **Choctaw Nation**   **Choctaw Roll**   CARD No.
POST OFFICE: Fort Smith Ark, Box 661   (Not Including Freedmen)   FIELD NO. 2804

Dawes' Roll No.	NAME	Relationship to Person First Named	AGE	SEX	BLOOD	TRIBAL ENROLLMENT		
						Year	County	No.
8221	1 Collins Miles S 31	First Named	28	M	1/8	1896	Skullyville	2180
I.W. 274	2 " Gracie 27	Wife	24	F	I.W.	1896	"	14377
8222	3 " Stella 8	Dau	5	F	1/16	1896	"	2181
8223	4 " Mary A 6	"	2	F	1/16		"	
8224	5 " Mamie A 4	"	1	F	1/16		"	
8225	6 " Miles Ricker 2	Son	2mo	M	1/16			
	7							
	8							
	9							
	10							
	11	ENROLLMENT OF NOS. 2 HEREON APPROVED BY THE SECRETARY OF INTERIOR SEP 12 1903						
	12							
	13							
	14	ENROLLMENT OF NOS. 1,3,4,5,6 HEREON APPROVED BY THE SECRETARY OF INTERIOR JAN 17 1903						
	15							
	16							
	17							

TRIBAL ENROLLMENT OF PARENTS

	Name of Father	Year	County	Name of Mother	Year	County
1	Mills Collins	1896	Non Citz	Mary Collins	Dead	Skullyville
2	J. R. Jones	1896	" "	Ann Jones	1896	Non Citz
3	No 1			No 2		
4	No 1			No 2		
5	No 1			No 2		
6	No.1			No.2		
7						
8			No1 On 1896 roll as Miles Collins			
9			No2 " " " " Gracie Collin[sic]			
10			Nos 4 and 5 Affidavits to be supplied. Recd June 22/99			
11			No.6 Enrolled May 17, 1901			
			For children of Nos 1&2 see NB (Mar. 3 1905) #622			
12						
13						
14						#1 to 5 inc
15						Date of Application for Enrollment.
16			Date of application for enrollment 6/15/99			
17	P.O. Stairs I.T. 3/15/					

104

Choctaw By Blood Enrollment Cards 1898-1914

RESIDENCE: Skullyville COUNTY. **Choctaw Nation** Choctaw Roll *(Not Including Freedmen)*

POST OFFICE: Oak Lodge I.T.

CARD NO.

FIELD NO. 2805

Dawes' Roll No.	NAME		Relationship to Person First Named	AGE	SEX	BLOOD	TRIBAL ENROLLMENT		
							Year	County	No.
8226	1 Smith Cora	21	First Named	18	F	1/4	1896	Skullyville	11137
8227	2 " Mary F	5	Dau	2	F	1/8		"	
8228	3 DIED PRIOR TO SEPTEMBER 25 1902 " Onie		"	1	F	1/8		"	
8229	4 " Robert F	1	Son	3wks	M	1/8			
	5								
	6								
	7								
	8								
	9								
	10								
	11								
	12								
	13								
	14	ENROLLMENT							
	15	OF NOS. 1,2,3,4 HEREON							
	16	APPROVED BY THE SECRETARY OF INTERIOR JAN 17 1903							
	17								

TRIBAL ENROLLMENT OF PARENTS

	Name of Father	Year	County	Name of Mother	Year	County
1	Robert J. Ward	1896	Skullyville	Addie L Ward	1896	Non Citz
2	Zach T Smith	1896	Non Citz	No 1		
3	" " "	1896	Non "	No 1		
4	" " "	1896	" "	Nº1		
5						
6			For child of No1 see NB (Apr 26-06) Card #687			
7			No1 As to evidence of marriage of father and mother see testi-			
8			mony in case of Robert J. Ward			
9			Nº4 Born Sept. 3, 1902, enrolled Sept. 19, 1902.			
10	No3 died July 25, 1901; Proof of death filed Dec 20 1902					
11	No3 died July 25, 1901: Enrollment cancelled by Department July 8, 1904					
12						
13						
14					Date of Application for Enrollment.	
15						
16					6/15/99	
17	Spiro I.T. 1/18/03					

105

Choctaw By Blood Enrollment Cards 1898-1914

RESIDENCE: Skullyville   COUNTY.   **Choctaw Nation**   **Choctaw Roll**   CARD NO.
POST OFFICE: Ft. Smith, Ark   *(Not Including Freedmen)*   FIELD NO. 2806

Dawes' Roll No.	NAME		Relationship to Person First Named	AGE	SEX	BLOOD	TRIBAL ENROLLMENT		
							Year	County	No.
8230	₁ Collins, John F	27	First Named	24	M	1/8	1896	Skullyville	2174
I.W. 731	₂ " Daisy	25	Wife	22	F	I.W.	1896	"	14376
8231	₃ " Foly D	7	Son	4	M	1/16	1896	"	2178
8232	₄ " Elijah A	6	"	2	"	1/16			
8233	₅ " Clara May	2	Dau	3mo	F	1/16			
8234	₆ DIED PRIOR TO SEPTEMBER 25, 1902 Clarence Cole		Son	3mo	M	1/16			
	7								
	8								
	9								
	10 DECISION PREPARED								
	11								
	12 No.6 died June 11, 190? Enrollment cancelled by Department July 8, 1904								
	13								
	14								
	15 ENROLLMENT OF NOS. 1,3,4,5,6 HEREON APPROVED BY THE SECRETARY OF INTERIOR JAN 17 1903			ENROLLMENT OF NOS. ~~~ 2 ~~~ HEREON APPROVED BY THE SECRETARY OF INTERIOR MAY -7 1904					
	16								
	17								

TRIBAL ENROLLMENT OF PARENTS

	Name of Father	Year	County	Name of Mother	Year	County
1	Miles S Collins	1896	Non Citz	Mary Collins	Dead	Skullyville
2	David Bishop	Dead	" "	Myrah Bishop	1896	Non Citz
3	No1			No2		
4	No1			No2		
5	No.1			No.2		
6	No.1			No.2		
7						
8						
9	No2 See Decision of March 2 '04					
10	No.6 Died June 11, 1901. Proof of death filed Dec 24 1902					
11	No1 on 1896 roll as John Collins					
	No3 " 1896 " " Tallia "					
12	No4 Affidavit of birth to be supplied: Recd 6/22/99					
13	No.5 Enrolled May 17, 1901					
14	No.6 Enrolled May 17, 1901					
	Nos 5 and 6 are twins					
15	For child of Nos 1&2 see NB (Mar 3-1905) Card #197.					
16				Date of Application for Enrollment	6/16/99	
17				➤ 1 to 4 inc		

Choctaw By Blood Enrollment Cards 1898-1914

RESIDENCE: Skullyville   COUNTY.   **Choctaw Nation**   **Choctaw Roll** (Not Including Freedmen)   CARD NO.

POST OFFICE: Spiro, I.T.   FIELD NO. 2807

Dawes' Roll No.	NAME	Relationship to Person First Named	AGE	SEX	BLOOD	TRIBAL ENROLLMENT Year	County	No.
8235	1 Merryman, John S [47]	First Named	44	M	1/4	1896	Skullyville	8453
I.W. 275	2 " Ellen [24]	Wife	21	F	I.W.			
8236	3 " Edgar B [DIED PRIOR TO SEPTEMBER 25 1902]	Son	17	M	1/4	1896	Skullyville	8456
8237	4 " Belva [17]	Dau	14	F	1/4	1896	"	8457
8238	5 " John Q [15]	Son	12	M	1/4	1896	"	8458
8239	6 " Roscoe C [13]	"	10	"	1/4	1896	"	8459
8240	7 " Ophelia [11]	Dau	8	F	1/4	1896	"	8460
8241	8 " Minnie I [8]	"	5	"	1/4	1896	"	8461
8242	9 " Erie V [4]	"	7mo	"	1/8			
8243	10 " Theodore Scott [1]	Son	4mo	M	1/8			
	11							
	12 No3 Died May 27, 1902: Proof of death filed Nov 24 1902							
	13 No.3 died May 27, 1902: Enrollment cancelled by Department July 8, 1904							
	14 No2 Decree of divorce from former husband							
	15 filed Dec 26, 1902							
	16							
	17							

ENROLLMENT
OF NOS. 2 HEREON
APPROVED BY THE SECRETARY
OF INTERIOR SEP 12 1903

ENROLLMENT
OF NOS. 1,3,4,5,6,7,8,9,10 HEREON
APPROVED BY THE SECRETARY
OF INTERIOR JAN 17 1903

TRIBAL ENROLLMENT OF PARENTS

	Name of Father	Year	County	Name of Mother	Year	County
1	W. P. Merryman	Dead	Non Citz	Anna Merryman	Dead	Skullyville
2	Jack Bailey	1896	" "	Rebecca Bailey	1896	Non Citz
3	No1			Joanna Merryman	Dead	Skullyville
4	No1			"	"	"
5	No1			"	"	
6	No1			"	"	
7	No1			"	"	
8	No1			"	"	
9	No1			No2		
10	Nº1			Nº2		
11	No1 on 1896 roll as John Merryman					
12	No5 " 1896 " " Jno Q. "					
13	No6 " 1896 " " Rosco " No8 " 1896 " " Ivy V. "					
14	No9 Affidavit of birth to be supplied. Recd 6/22/99					
15	No4 on 1896 roll as Beloa Merryman			Date of Application for Enrollment.		
16	Nº10 Born May 20, 1902. Enrolled Sept. 30, 1902			6/16/99		
17						

Choctaw By Blood Enrollment Cards 1898-1914

RESIDENCE: Skullyville   COUNTY.   **Choctaw Nation**   Choctaw Roll   CARD NO.
POST OFFICE: Shady Point I.T.   *(Not Including Freedmen)*   FIELD NO. 2808

Dawes' Roll No.	NAME	Relationship to Person First Named	AGE	SEX	BLOOD	TRIBAL ENROLLMENT		
						Year	County	No.
8244	1 Cricklin Jesse DIED PRIOR TO SEPTEMBER 25 1902		54	M	1/2	1896	Skullyville	2169
	2							
	3							
	4							
	5							
	6							
	7							
	8							
	9							
	10							
	11							
	12							
	13							
	14	ENROLLMENT						
	15	OF NOS. 1 HEREON						
	16	APPROVED BY THE SECRETARY OF INTERIOR JAN 17 1903						
	17							

TRIBAL ENROLLMENT OF PARENTS

	Name of Father	Year	County	Name of Mother	Year	County
1	John Cricklin	Dead	Non Citz	Shan-tay-o	Dead	Skullyville
2						
3						
4						
5						
6						
7	On 1896 roll as Jessie Cricklin					
8	No.1 died Aug 17, 1901: Proof of death filed Dec 24 1902					
9	No 1 died Aug 17, 1901: Enrollment cancelled by Department July 8, 1904					
10						
11						
12						
13						
14					Date of Application for Enrollment.	
15						
16					6/15/99	
17						

Choctaw By Blood Enrollment Cards 1898-1914

RESIDENCE: Skullyville   COUNTY. **Choctaw Nation**   **Choctaw Roll** *(Not Including Freedmen)*   CARD NO.

POST OFFICE: Brazil I.T.   FIELD NO. 28__

Dawes' Roll No.	NAME		Relationship to Person First Named	AGE	SEX	BLOOD	TRIBAL ENROLLMENT		
							Year	County	No.
8245	1 James Ellis	32	First Named	29	M	Full	1896	Skullyville	6449
8246	2 " Sealy	32	Wife	29	F	"	1896	"	6450
8247	3 " Amanda	8	Dau	5	F	"	1896	"	6451
8248	4 " Bennie	7	Son	4	M	"	1896	"	6452
8249	5 " Mary	6	Dau	2	F	"		"	
8250	6 " Selina	4	Dau	6mo	F	"		"	
8251	7 Freeman John	13	StepSon	10	M	"	1896	"	3931
8252	8 James Levi	1	Son	2mo	M	"			
	9								
	10								
	11								
	12								
	13								
	14								
	15								
	16								
	17								

ENROLLMENT
OF NOS. 1,2,3,4,5,6,7,8 HEREON
APPROVED BY THE SECRETARY
OF INTERIOR JAN 17 1903

TRIBAL ENROLLMENT OF PARENTS

	Name of Father	Year	County	Name of Mother	Year	County
1	Noel James	1896	Skullyville	Malina James	1896	Skullyville
2	Jerry Mackey	Dead	Sugar Loaf	Adaline Hoy-tea-be	Dead	Sugar Loaf
3	No 1			No 2		
4	No 1			No 2		
5	No 1			No 2		
6	No 1			No 2		
7	George Freeman	1896	Sugar Loaf	No 2		
8	Nº1			Nº2		
9						
10	No2 On 1896 roll as Sely James					
11	No7 child of Sealy aove					
12	Nº8 Born July 11, 1902: enrolled Sept. 4, 1902					
13	For child of Nos 1&2 see NB (Apr 26-06) Care #619					
14						
15					#1 to 7 inc	
16					Date of Application for Enrollment.	6/15/99
17						

Choctaw By Blood Enrollment Cards 1898-1914

RESIDENCE: Sans Bois
POST OFFICE: Stigler, I.T.

COUNTY. **Choctaw Nation**

Choctaw 1 (Not Including Freedmen)

CARD No.
FIELD No. 2810

Dawes' Roll No.	NAME		Relationship to Person	AGE	SEX	BLOOD	TRIBAL ENROLLMENT		
							Year	County	No.
8253	1 Cooper, Henry	28	First Named	25	M	1/16	1896	Sans Bois	2148
I.W. 276	2 " Mary	28	Wife	25	F	I.W.	1896	" "	14370
8254	3 " Maud S	5	Dau	1	"	1/32			
8255	4 " Willie Vera	1	Dau	7mo	F	1/32			
	5								
	6								
	7								
	8								
	9								
	10								
	11								
	12								
	13								
	14								
	15								
	16								
	17								

ENROLLMENT OF NOS. 2 HEREON APPROVED BY THE SECRETARY OF INTERIOR SEP 12 1903

ENROLLMENT OF NOS. 1,3,4, HEREON APPROVED BY THE SECRETARY OF INTERIOR JAN 17 1903

TRIBAL ENROLLMENT OF PARENTS

	Name of Father	Year	County	Name of Mother	Year	County
1	Samuel Cooper	Dead	Non Citz	Susan Cooper	1896	Sans Bois
2	Jas. W. Ray	1896	" "	Margaret Ray	1896	Non Citz
3	No1			No2		
4	Nº1			Nº2		
5						
6						
7						
8						
9						
10	Evidence of marriage to be supplied. Recd 6/22/99					
11	No3 Affidavit of birth to be supplied. Recd 6/22/99					
12	Nº4 Born Sept 28, 1901: enrolled April 28, 1902					
13	For child of Nos 1&2 See NB (Apr 26-1906) Card #602					
14					#1 to 3	
15					Date of Application for Enrollment.	
16					6/16/99	
17						

110

Choctaw By Blood Enrollment Cards 1898-1914

Choctaw Nation

Choctaw Roll (Not Including Freedmen)

CARD No. FIELD No. 2811

Dawes' Roll No.	NAME	Relationship to Person First Named	AGE	SEX	BLOOD	TRIBAL ENROLLMENT		
						Year	County	No.
8256	1 Sockey, William DIED RIVER TOWN SEPTEMBER 25 1902		42	M	Full	1896	Skullyville	11148
8257	2 " Lula 11	Dau	8	F	"	1896	"	11149
8258	3 " Salina 8	"	5	"	"	1896	"	11150
	4							
	5							
	6							
	7							
	8							
	9							
	10							
	11							
	12							
	13							
	14							
	15	ENROLLMENT OF NOS. 1, 2, 3 HEREON APPROVED BY THE SECRETARY OF INTERIOR JAN 17 1903						
	16							
	17							

TRIBAL ENROLLMENT OF PARENTS

	Name of Father	Year	County	Name of Mother	Year	County
1	Wallace Sockey	Dead	in Mississippi	Eliza Sockey	Dead	in Mississippi
2	No1			Elizabeth Sockey	"	Skullyville
3	No1			" "	"	"
4						
5						
6						
7	Surnames on 1896 roll as Sakki					
8	No1 died January 29, 1902; Proof of death filed Dec 20 1902					
9	No1 died Jan 29, 1902: Enrollment cancelled by					
10						
11						
12						
13						
14					Date of Application for Enrollment.	
15						
16					6/16/99	
17						

Choctaw By Blood Enrollment Cards 1898-1914

POST OFFICE: Spiro, I.T. **Choctaw Nation** *(Not Including Freedmen)* FIELD NO. 2812

Dawes' Roll No.	NAME	Relationship to Person First Named	AGE	SEX	BLOOD	TRIBAL ENROLLMENT		
						Year	County	No.
8259	1 Ford, William W 19		16	M	1/8	1896	Sans Bois	3910
8260	2 LeFlore, Arizona 9	Cousin	6	F	1/16	1896	Tobucksy	7883
	3							
	4							
	5							
	6							
	7							
	8							
	9							
	10							
	11							
	12							
	13							
	14							
	15							
	16							
	17							

ENROLLMENT OF NOS. 1 and 2 HEREON APPROVED BY THE SECRETARY OF INTERIOR JAN 17 1903

TRIBAL ENROLLMENT OF PARENTS

	Name of Father	Year	County	Name of Mother	Year	County
1	Zack Fork[sic]	1896	Non Citz	Victoria Ford	Dead	Sans Bois
2	Walter LeFlore	Dead	Gaines	Ann LeFlore		Non Citz
3						
4						
5						
6						
7	As to marriage of parents of No2					
8	see testimony of Zack Ford					
9						
10	No1 on 1896 roll as William Ford					
11						
12						
13						
14						
15	P.O. Blount I.T.					
16		12/17/02		Date of Application for Enrollment.	6/16/99	
17						

Choctaw By Blood Enrollment Cards 1898-1914

RESIDENCE: Skullyville   COUNTY. **Choctaw Nation**   **Choctaw Roll** (Not Including Freedmen)   CARD NO. FIELD NO. 2813
POST OFFICE: Braden, I.T.

Dawes' Roll No.	NAME		Relationship to Person First Named	AGE	SEX	BLOOD	TRIBAL ENROLLMENT		
							Year	County	No.
8261	1 Payton, Mary	22	First Named	19	F	Full	1896	Blue	10499
8261	2 " Philip	26	Bro	23	M	"	1896	"	10498
14774	3 Fryer, Ella	2	Dau	1½	F	3/4			
	4								
	5								
	6								
	7								
	8								
	9								
	10								
	11								
	12								
	13								
	14								
	15								
	16								
	17								

ENROLLMENT OF NOS. 3 HEREON APPROVED BY THE SECRETARY OF INTERIOR MAY 20 1903

ENROLLMENT OF NOS. 1 and 2 HEREON APPROVED BY THE SECRETARY OF INTERIOR JAN 17 1903

TRIBAL ENROLLMENT OF PARENTS

	Name of Father	Year	County	Name of Mother	Year	County
1	Daniel Payton		Blue	Sophie Payton	Dead	Blue
2	" "		"	" "	"	"
3	Elijah Fryer			No 1		
4						
5						
6						
7	No1 was the wife of Elijah Fry[sic] from whom she is now separated					
8					12/3/02	
9	No3 born March 13, 1901: enrolled Dec 6, 1902					
10						
11						
12						
13						
14					#1&2	
15					Date of Application for Enrollment.	
16					6/16/99	
17	PO Boswall[sic] IT 7/15/03					

113

Choctaw By Blood Enrollment Cards 1898-1914

Choctaw Nation

Choctaw Roll (Not Including Freedmen)

CARD NO. FIELD NO. 2814

	NAME	Relationship to Person First Named	AGE	SEX	BLOOD	TRIBAL ENROLLMENT		
						Year	County	No.
1	Webster, Thomas ⁶⁸	First Named	65	M	Full	1896	Sans Bois	12645
2	" Jincy DIED PRIOR TO SEPTEMBER 25, 1902	Wife	42	F	"	1896	" "	12646
3	" Albert ¹⁸	Son	15	M	"	1896	" "	12649
4	" Minnie ¹²	Dau	9	F	"	1896	" "	12651
5	Joe, Sophia ¹⁵	G.Dau	12	"	"	1893	" "	924
6	Perry, Caroline DIED PRIOR TO SEPTEMBER 25, 1902	"	10	"	"	1896	" "	10060
7	" Jennie ¹¹	"	8	"	"	1893	" "	699
8								
9								
10								
11								
12	No 2, died April 7, 1901, No 6 died May – 1900							
13	Enrollment cancelled by Department July 8, 1904							
14								
15	ENROLLMENT OF NOS. 1,2,3,4,5,6,7 HEREON APPROVED BY THE SECRETARY OF INTERIOR JAN 17 1903							
16								
17								

TRIBAL ENROLLMENT OF PARENTS

	Name of Father	Year	County	Name of Mother	Year	County
1	Tobley	Dead	Sans Bois		Dead	Sans Bois
2	Isom Wallace	"	" "	Nellie Wallace		" "
3	No1			No2		
4	No1			No2		
5	Adam Joe	1896	Tobucksy	Elizabeth Joe	Dead	Sans Bois
6	Lyman Perry	Dead	Sans Bois	Nancy Perry	"	" "
7	" "	"	" "	" "	"	" "
8						
9	For child of No5 – See NB (Apr 26-06) Card #622					
10	No5 on 1893 Pay Roll, Page 89, No 924, Sans Bois County as Sophie Joe					
11	No7 " 1893 " " " 68, " 699 " " " " Martha Perry					
12	No7 is now ward of Daniel Perry on Choctaw card #3198 Evidence thereof					
13	filed in this case Dec. 24, 1902					
14	Nº2 Died April 7, 1901, Proof of death filed Dec 24 1902					
15	Nº6 died in May 1900, Proof of death filed Dec 24 1902					
16				Date of Application for Enrollment.	6/16/99	
17						

Choctaw By Blood Enrollment Cards 1898-1914

RESIDENCE:	Skullyville	COUNTY.	**Choctaw Nation**		**Choctaw Roll**	CARD NO.	
POST OFFICE:	Walls, I.T.				*(Not Including Freedmen)*	FIELD NO.	2815

Dawes' Roll No.	NAME		Relationship to Person First Named	AGE	SEX	BLOOD	TRIBAL ENROLLMENT		
							Year	County	No.
8270	1 Wall, William W	27	First Named	24	M	1/2	1896	Skullyville	12733
8271	2 " Lillie D	25	Wife	22	F	1/4	1896	"	12734
8272	3 " Cz rena[sic] B	2	Dau	3mo	"	3/8			
8273	4 " Roena Estell	1	Dau	3mo	"	3/8			
	5								
	6								
	7								
	8								
	9								
	10								
	11								
	12								
	13								
	14								
	15	ENROLLMENT OF NOS. 1,2,3,4 HEREON APPROVED BY THE SECRETARY OF INTERIOR JAN 17 1903							
	16								
	17								

TRIBAL ENROLLMENT OF PARENTS

	Name of Father	Year	County	Name of Mother	Year	County
1	Benj Wall	1896	Skullyville	Abigail Wall	1896	Skullyville
2	Jesse Hardaway	1896	"	Margaret Hardaway	1896	Non Citz
3	No1			No2		
4	Nº1			Nº2		
5						
6						
7	No1 on 1896 roll as Willie W Walls					
8	No2 " 1896 " " Lillie "					
9	No3 Affidavit of birth to be supplied. Recd 6/22/99					
10	Evidence of marriage of parents of No2 to be supplied. See evidence filed					
11	with Card No 2841					
12	Nº4 Born Dec. 7, 1901, enrolled March 8, 1902.					
13						
14						
15				#1 to 3		
16				Date of Application for Enrollment.	6/16/99	
17						

115

Choctaw By Blood Enrollment Cards 1898-1914

RESIDENCE: Sans Bois	COUNTY.	**Choctaw Nation**	**Choctaw Roll** (Not Including Freedmen)	CARD N
POST OFFICE: Stigler, I.T				FIELD NO. 2816

Dawes' Roll No.	NAME		Relationship to Person First Named	AGE	SEX	BLOOD	TRIBAL ENROLLMENT		
							Year	County	No.
DEAD.	₁ Jones, John	DEAD.		28	M	Full	1896	Sans Bois	6364
8274	₂ Cooper Clara	28	Wife	25	F	"	1896	" "	6365
8275	₃ Jones Edward	7	Son	4	M	"	1896	" "	6366
8276	₄ Cooper, Douglas	1	Son of Nº2	1mo	M	"			
	₅								
	₆								
	₇ No. 1 HEREON DISMISSED UNDER								
	₈ ORDER OF THE COMMISSION TO THE FIVE								
	₉ CIVILIZED TRIBES OF MARCH 31, 1905								
	10								
	11								
	12								
	13								
	14								
	15 ENROLLMENT OF NOS. 2, 3, 4 HEREON								
	16 APPROVED BY THE SECRETARY OF INTERIOR JAN 17 1903								
	17								

TRIBAL ENROLLMENT OF PARENTS

Name of Father	Year	County	Name of Mother	Year	County
₁ Forbis Jones	Dead	Gaines	Eliza Jones	Dead	Gaines
₂ Allen McGilbery	"	Sugar Loaf	Pe-sa-le-ma	"	Sugar Loaf
₃ No 1			No 2		
₄ Abel Cooper	1896	Sans Bois	Nº2		
₅					
₆					
₇					
₈ Nº1 is dead. Died Dec. 27, 1900, Proof of death filed Oct 23, 1902					
₉ Nº2 is now the wife of Abel Cooper on Choctaw Card #2520. Evidence of					
10 marriage requested Oct. 9, 1902.					
11 Nº4 Born Sept. 10, 1902, enrolled Oct. 11, 1902					
12					
13					
14			Date of Application for Enrollment.	For Nos	
15				1-2&3	
16				6/16/99	
17					

Choctaw By Blood Enrollment Cards 1898-1914

RESIDENCE: **Sans Bois** COUNTY. **Choctaw Nation** **Choctaw Roll** CARD NO.
POST OFFICE: **Sans Bois, I.T.** (Not Including Freedmen) FIELD NO. **2817**

Dawes' Roll No.	NAME	Relationship to Person First Named	AGE	SEX	BLOOD	TRIBAL ENROLLMENT		
						Year	County	No.
8277	1 Taylor, John 22	First Named	19	M	1/4	1896	Sans Bois	11818
	2							
	3							
	4							
	5							
	6							
	7							
	8							
	9							
	10							
	11							
	12							
	13							
	14							
	15							
	16							
	17							

ENROLLMENT
OF NOS. 1 HEREON
APPROVED BY THE SECRETARY
OF INTERIOR Jan 17 1903

TRIBAL ENROLLMENT OF PARENTS

	Name of Father	Year	County	Name of Mother	Year	County
1	General Taylor	Dead	Sans Bois	Mary Taylor	Dead	Non Citz
2						
3						
4						
5						
6			As to marriage of parents, see			
7			testimony of John Hendricks.			
8			For child of No.1 see NB (March 3, 1905) #1377			
9						
10						
11						
12						
13						
14						
15					Date of Application for Enrollment.	
16					6/19/99	
17	P.O. Enterprise I.T. 11/5/05					

117

RESIDENCE:	Gaines	COUNTY.				Choctaw Roll		CARD No.	
POST OFFICE:	Wilburton, I.T.	**Choctaw Nation**				(Not Including Freedmen)		FIELD No.	2818

Dawes' Roll No.	NAME		Relationship to Person	AGE	SEX	BLOOD	TRIBAL ENROLLMENT		
							Year	County	No.
I.W. 130	1 Rabon, Rufus	32	First Named	29	M	I.W.	1896	Gaines	14966
8278	2 " Ethel M	26	Wife	23	F	1/32	1896	"	10747
8279	3 " Floyd	7	Son	4	M	1/64	1896	"	10748
8280	4 " Hazel	5	Dau	1	F	1/64			
8281	5 " Curtis	1	Son	2mo	M	1/64			
	6								
	7								
	8								
	9								
	10								
	11	ENROLLMENT OF NOS. 1 HEREON APPROVED BY THE SECRETARY OF INTERIOR JUN 13 1903							
	12								
	13								
	14								
	15	ENROLLMENT OF NOS. 2,3,4,5 HEREON APPROVED BY THE SECRETARY OF INTERIOR JAN 17 1903							
	16								
	17								

TRIBAL ENROLLMENT OF PARENTS

	Name of Father	Year	County	Name of Mother	Year	County
1	Thos. Rabon	1896	Non Citz	Mary Rabon	1896	Non Citz
2	William T. Ross	1896	Sans Bois	Lizzie Ross	1896	" "
3	No1			No2		
4	No1			No2		
5	No1			No2		
6						
7						
8	No1 was admitted by Dawes Com as an Intermarried					
9	citizen, Case No 677					
10	No3 was admitted by Dawes Com as Floyd Rabon, Case No 677					
11	No2 was admitted by Act of Choctaw Council, No 69; Approved					
12	November 7, 1898, as Ethen Ross, daughter of William T. Ross;					
13	mother Lizzie Ross, also admitted by same Act					
14	No4 Affidavit of birth to be supplied Recd 6/22/99					
15	No3 on 1896 roll as Frod Rabon					
	No5 Born May 22nd 1902; Enrolled July 21st 1902					
	For child of Nos 1&2 see NB (March 3, 1905) #1115			Date of Application for Enrollment.		
16				6/19/99		
17	PO Madill IT 4/3/05					

Choctaw By Blood Enrollment Cards 1898-1914

RESIDENCE: Sans Bois   COUNTY. **Choctaw Nation**   **Choctaw Roll** *(Not Including Freedmen)*   CARD NO. FIELD NO. 2819
POST OFFICE: Stigler, I.T.

Dawes' Roll No.		NAME	Relationship to Person First Named	AGE	SEX	BLOOD	TRIBAL ENROLLMENT		
							Year	County	No.
8282	1	King, Ellen DIED PRIOR TO SEPTEMBER 25 1902	First Named	34	F	Full	1896	Sans Bois	5083
	2								
	3								
	4								
	5								
	6								
	7								
	8								
	9								
	10								
	11								
	12								
	13								
	14								
	15								
	16								
	17								

ENROLLMENT
OF NOS. 1 HEREON
APPROVED BY THE SECRETARY
OF INTERIOR JAN 17 1903

TRIBAL ENROLLMENT OF PARENTS

	Name of Father	Year	County	Name of Mother	Year	County
1	Mickie King	Dead	Sans Bois	Susan King	Dead	Sans Bois
2						
3						
4						
5						
6						
7						
8	On 1896 roll as Ellen Homer					
9	No.1 Died March 5, 1902. Proof of death received and filed Dec 30 1902					
10	No. 1 died March 5, 1902				July 8, 1904	
11						
12						
13						
14						
15					Date of Application for Enrollment.	
16					6/19/99	
17						

Choctaw By Blood Enrollment Cards 1898-1914

RESIDENCE:	Sans Bois	COUNTY:					CARD NO.		
POST OFFICE:	Whitefield, I.T.	**Choctaw Nation**				Choctaw Roll *(Not Including Freedmen)*	FIELD NO.	2820	

Dawes' Roll No.	NAME	Relationship to Person First Named	AGE	SEX	BLOOD	TRIBAL ENROLLMENT		
						Year	County	No.
15665	1 Hendricks, John 58	First Named	55	M	1/4	1896	Sans Bois	5161
I.W. 1195	2 " Martha M 52	Wife	49	F	I.W.			
	3							
	4 DECISION PREPARED							
	5							
	6							
	7							
	8							
	9							
	10							
	11	ENROLLMENT						
	12	OF NOS. ~~~ 1 ~~~ HEREON						
	13	APPROVED BY THE SECRETARY OF INTERIOR DEC -2 1904						
	14							
	15	ENROLLMENT OF NOS ~~~ 2 ~~~ HEREON						
	16	APPROVED BY THE SECRETARY OF INTERIOR NOV 16 1904						
	17							

TRIBAL ENROLLMENT OF PARENTS

	Name of Father	Year	County	Name of Mother	Year	County
1	Jesse Hendricks	Dead	Non Citz	Nancy Hendricks	Dead	Non Citz
2	Balaan Strawn	"	" "	Mary L Strawn	"	" "
3						
4						
5						
6						
7						
8						
9	No1 was admitted by Dawes Com, Case No 429					
10	See whether by blood or intermarriage. Says					
11	he does not know whether father was a Choctaw or not but thinks he was. His mother Nancy was					
12	an intermarried citizen, so he says.					
13	No1 was also recognized as a Choctaw Citizen by					
14	the Supreme Court of that Nation, at the April Term A.D. 1883 Instrument ehibited[sic] not in			Date of Application for Enrollment.		
15	a condition to be filed.					
16	No1 admitted as a citizen by blood by Dawes Commission			6/19/99		
17	in 1896, Choctaw Case #429. No appeal.					

120

Choctaw By Blood Enrollment Cards 1898-1914

RESIDENCE: Sans Bois   COUNTY. **Choctaw Nation**   **Choctaw Roll** (Not Including Freedmen)   CARD No.

POST OFFICE: Sans Bois, I.T.   FIELD No. 2821

Dawes' Roll No.	NAME	Relationship to Person First Named	AGE	SEX	BLOOD	TRIBAL ENROLLMENT Year	County	No.
8283	1 Thompson, James 60	First Named	57	M	Full	1896	Sans Bois	11823
8284	2 DIED PRIOR TO SEPTEMBER 25, 1902 Ishtahoma	Wife	57	F	"	1896	" "	11824
	3							
	4							
	5							
	6							
	7							
	8							
	9							
	10							
	11							
	12							
	13							
	14							
	15	ENROLLMENT OF NOS. 1 and 2 HEREON						
	16	APPROVED BY THE SECRETARY OF INTERIOR JAN 17 1903						
	17							

TRIBAL ENROLLMENT OF PARENTS

Name of Father	Year	County	Name of Mother	Year	County
1 Tach-kah-ka	Dead	Sans Bois	E-la-che-ho-na	Dead	Sans Bois
2 Ka-ne-o-tubbee	"	Gaines		"	" "
3					
4					
5					
6					
7	No2 on 1896 roll as Ishtohena Thompson				
8	No 2 died Nov — 1901 Enrollment cancelled by Department July 8, 1903				
9					
10					
11					
12					
13					
14					
15				Date of Application for Enrollment.	
16				6/19/99	
17					

Choctaw By Blood Enrollment Cards 1898-1914

| RESIDENCE POST OFFICE | COUNTY. Choctaw Nation | | | | Choctaw Roll (Not Including Freedmen) | CARD NO. FIELD NO. 2822 |

Dawes' Roll No.	NAME		Relationship to Person	AGE	SEX	BLOOD	TRIBAL ENROLLMENT		
							Year	County	No.
8285	1 Battles, Mattie E.	32	First Named	29	F	1/2	1896	Gaines	854
8286	2 Denton, Ada	10	Dau	7	"	1/4	1896	"	3283
8287	3 " John	8	Son	5	M	1/4	1896	"	3284
8288	4 " Emma	7	Dau	4	F	1/4	1896	"	3283
8289	5 " James L	19	S.Son	16	M	1/8	1896	"	3280
8290	6 " Nancy I	22	S.Dau	19	F	1/8	1896	"	3279
	7								
	8								
	9								
	10								
	11								
	12								
	13								
	14								
	15								
	16								
	17								

ENROLLMENT
OF NOS. 1,2,3,4,5,6 HEREON
APPROVED BY THE SECRETARY
OF INTERIOR JAN 17 1903

TRIBAL ENROLLMENT OF PARENTS

	Name of Father	Year	County	Name of Mother	Year	County
1	Stephen Cooper	Death	Gaines	Sarah Cooper	1896	Sans Bois
2	John Denton	"	Non Citz	No 1		
3	" "	"	" "	No 1		
4	" "	"	" "	No 1		
5	" "	"	" "	Johnnie Denton	Dead	Gaines
6	" "	"	" "	" "	"	"
7						
8	No1 on 1896 roll as Mattie D Battles					
9	No3 " 1896 " " Johnny Denton					
10	No5 " 1896 " " Jas. L. "					
11						
12	No1 is now divorced from Wᵐ Battles by decree of Choctaw Court. She appeared as plaintiff					
13						
14	For child of No6 see NB (Mar 3-1905) Card #198					
15	" " " " " " (Apr 26-1906) " #1238					
16	" " " No1 " " (Mar 3-1905) " #1372			Date of Application for Enrollment.	6/19/99	
17	No6 P.O. Canadian I.T. 12/11/02					

122

Choctaw By Blood Enrollment Cards 1898-1914

RESIDENCE: Sans Bois   COUNTY. **Choctaw Nation**   **Choctaw Roll** *(Not Including Freedmen)*   CARD No.
POST OFFICE: Sans Bois, I.T.   FIELD No. 2823

Dawes' Roll No.	NAME		Relationship to Person First Named	AGE	SEX	BLOOD	TRIBAL ENROLLMENT		
							Year	County	No.
8291	1 Cooper, Sarah ~~DIED PRIOR TO SEPTEMBER 25 1902~~		First Named	63	F	1/2	1896	Sans Bois	2099
8292	2 " Charles	25	Son	22	M	1/2	1896	Gaines	2301
8293	3 " Joseph C	14	G.Son	11	"	1/4	1896	Sans Bois	2082
8294	4 " Maggie Jane	1	Dau of No2	8mo	F	1/4			
I.W. 1530	5 " Margaret Jane		Wife of No2	20	F	I.W.			
	6								
	7								
	8								
	9								
	10								
	11								
	12								
	13								
	14								
	15								
	16								
	17 For child of Nos 2&5 see NB (Apr 26-06) Card #520								

ENROLLMENT
OF NOS. ~~5~~ HEREON
APPROVED BY THE SECRETARY
OF INTERIOR MAR 14 1906

ENROLLMENT
OF NOS. 1,2,3,4 HEREON
APPROVED BY THE SECRETARY
OF INTERIOR JAN 17 1903

TRIBAL ENROLLMENT OF PARENTS

	Name of Father	Year	County	Name of Mother	Year	County
1	~~Jack Riddle~~	~~Dead~~	~~Gaines~~		~~Dead~~	~~Gaines~~
2	Stephen Cooper	"	"	No1		
3	Douglas Cooper	"	"	Liza Cooper	1896	Non Citz
4	No2			Margaret J Cooper		Non Citz
5	Wm F Gammel	dead	noncitizen	Sarah J Gammel		noncitizen
6						
7						
8	No5 transferred to this card from D-853 Nov 22, 1905: see decision of Nov 6, 1905					
9	No2 on 1896 roll as Charley Cooper					
10	No2 Now Husband of Margaret J Cooper, non citz: Evidence of marriage filed June 20th 1902					
11	~~As to marriage of parents of No3 see testimony of Annie Cooper~~					
12	~~No1 died Sept – 1899. Enrollment cancelled by Department July 8, 1904~~ As to evidence of marriage of father and mother of No.3, see enrollment of					
13	Sarah E. Wilson. No.3 should read Joseph S. Cooper/ ~~No.4 Born October 30th 1901. Enrolled June 20th 1902~~					
14	No.1 Died in Sept. 1899. Proof of death filed Dec 30 1902					
15				#1 to 3		9/15/99
16				Date of Application for Enrollment.	6/19/99	
17						

123

Choctaw By Blood Enrollment Cards 1898-1914

RESIDENCE: Skullyville COUNTY.
POST OFFICE: Milton, I.T.

Choctaw Nation

Choctaw Roll (Not Including Freedmen)

CARD No.
FIELD No. 2824

Dawes' Roll No.	NAME		Relationship to Person First Named	AGE	SEX	BLOOD	TRIBAL ENROLLMENT		
							Year	County	No.
8295	1 Davis, Maggie	22	First Named	19	F	1/2	1896	Skullyville	3228
8296	2 " Letha	6	Dau	3	"	1/4	1896	"	3238
8297	3 " Lennie	4	"	1	"	1/4			
8298	4 " Bertie Lorena	2	Dau	4mo	F	1/4			
8299	5 " Eva	1	"	1mo	F	1/4			
	6								
	7								
	8								
	9								
	10								
	11								
	12								
	13								
	14								
	15	ENROLLMENT OF NOS. 1,2,3,4,5, HEREON APPROVED BY THE SECRETARY OF INTERIOR JAN 17 1903							
	16								
	17								

TRIBAL ENROLLMENT OF PARENTS

Name of Father	Year	County	Name of Mother	Year	County
1 Charley Cox	Dead	Non Citz	Letha Smith	1896	Skullyville
2 Dave E. Davis	1896	" "	No1		
3 " " "	1896	" "	No1		
4 " " "		" "	No.1		
5 " " "		" "	No1		
6					
7					
8		No2 on 1896 roll ax Laithey Davis			
9		No.4 Enrolled April 12, 1901			
10		No5 Born March 16, 1901: enrolled April 23, 1902			
11		For child of No1 see NB (Apr 26-06) Card #502			
12		" " " " " " (Mar 3-05) " #199			
13					
14					
15			#1 to 5		
16			Date of Application for Enrollment.	6/19/99	
17					

124

Choctaw By Blood Enrollment Cards 1898-1914

RESIDENCE: Sugar Loaf COUNTY. **Choctaw Nation** **Choctaw Roll** *(Not Including Freedmen)* CARD No.
POST OFFICE: Red Oak, Ind. Ter FIELD No. 2825

Dawes' Roll No.	NAME		Relationship to Person	AGE	SEX	BLOOD	TRIBAL ENROLLMENT		
							Year	County	No.
8300	1 Coley, Anderson	45	First Named	42	M	Full	1893	Sugar Loaf	131
8301	2 " Biney	31	Wife	29	F	"	1893	" "	132
8302	3 " Wilburn	22	Son	19	M	"	1893	" "	133
8303	4 " Edward	10	"	7	"	"	1893	" "	134
8304	5 " Edmond	5	"	2	"	"			
8305	6 " Johnson	24	Nephew	21	"	"	1893	Gaines	114
8306	7 " Caldwell	22	"	19	"	"	1896	Sans Bois	2163
8307	8 " Ella	2	Dau	1	F	"			
	9								
	10								
	11								
	12								
	13								
	14								
	15								
	16								
	17								

ENROLLMENT
OF NOS. 1,2,3,4,5,6,7,8 HEREON
APPROVED BY THE SECRETARY
OF INTERIOR JAN 17 1903

TRIBAL ENROLLMENT OF PARENTS

	Name of Father	Year	County	Name of Mother	Year	County
1	Ith-ko-chee	Dead	Sans Bois	O-ke-ma	Dead	Sans Bois
2	Loma Wade	"	Sugar Loaf	Le-man-lo-na	"	Sugar Loaf
3	No1			Pe-sa-to-na	"	Skullyville
4	No1			No2		
5	No1			No2		
6	Jacob Coley	Dead	Sans Bois	Sema Coley	Dead	Skullyville
7	" "	"	" "	" "	"	"
8	No.1			No.2		
9						
10	No1 on 1893 Pay Roll, Sugar Loaf Co, Page 13, No 131					
11	No2 " 1893 " " " " " 13, No 132					
12	No3 " 1893 " " " " " 13, No 133					
	No4 " 1893 " " " " " 13, No 134					
13	No6 " 1893 " " Gaines Co " 12, No 114					
14	No.8 Enrolled April 25, 1901				#1 to 7 inc	
15	For child of Nos 1&2 see NB (March 3, 1905) #720				Date of Application for Enrollment.	
16	" " " No 6 " " " " " #1009				6/19/99	
17						

Choctaw By Blood Enrollment Cards 1898-1914

RESIDENCE: Sans Bois	COUNTY.	Choctaw Nation		Choctaw Roll (Not Including Freedmen)	CARD NO.	
OFFICE: Sans Bois, I.T.					FIELD NO. 2826	

Dawes' Roll No.	NAME	Relationship to Person First Named	AGE	SEX	BLOOD	TRIBAL ENROLLMENT		
						Year	County	No.
08	1 Wilkin, Sealy DIED PRIOR TO SEPTEMBER 25 1902		42	F	Full	1893	Sans Bois	869
09	2 Byington, Joseph 25	Son	22	M	"	1893	" "	870
10	3 Thompson, Bicey 18	Dau	15	F	"	1896	" "	11831
	4							
	5							
	6							
	7							
	8							
	9							
	10							
	11							
	12							
	13							
	14							

ENROLLMENT
OF NOS. 1, 2, 3,   HEREON
APPROVED BY THE SECRETARY
OF INTERIOR JAN 17 1903

TRIBAL ENROLLMENT OF PARENTS

	Name of Father	Year	County	Name of Mother	Year	County
1	Pe-sun-tubbee	Dead	Skullyville	Melissa	Dead	Skullyville
2	Philip Byington	1896	"	No1		
3	Billy Thompson	1896	Sans Bois	No1		
4						
5						
6						
7						
8	No1 on 1893 Pay Roll, Sans Bois Co, Page 84, No 869 as Cely Wilkin					
9	No2 " 1893 " " " " " " 84 " 870					
10	No 1 died April 1 1902. Enrollment cancelled by Department May 2, 1906. For child of No. 3 see NB (March 3, 1905) #1434					
11						
12						
13						
14						
15					Date of Application for Enrollment.	
16					6/19/99	
17						

Choctaw By Blood Enrollment Cards 1898-1914

RESIDENCE: Sans Bois	COUNTY.								

RESIDENCE: Sans Bois   **COUNTY.**   **Choctaw Nation**   **Choctaw Roll** *(Not Including Freedmen)*   CARD NO.
POST OFFICE: Stigler, I.T.   FIELD NO. **2827**

Dawes' Roll No.	NAME		Relationship to Person First Named	AGE	SEX	BLOOD	TRIBAL ENROLLMENT		
							Year	County	No.
8311	1 Perry, Stephen	29	First Named	26	M	Full	1896	Sans Bois	10061
	2								
	3								
	4								
	5								
	6								
	7								
	8								
	9								
	10								
	11								
	12								
	13								
	14								
	15								
	16								
	17								

ENROLLMENT
OF NOS. 1 HEREON
APPROVED BY THE SECRETARY
OF INTERIOR JAN 17 1903

TRIBAL ENROLLMENT OF PARENTS

	Name of Father	Year	County	Name of Mother	Year	County
1	Jefferson Perry	Dead	Sans Bois	Rachel Perry	Dead	Sans Bois
2						
3						
4						
5						
6						
7	No1 Husband of Siney Perry Choctaw Card #2438					
8						
9						
10						
11						
12						
13						
14						
15					Date of Application for Enrollment.	
16					6/19/99	
17						

Choctaw By Blood Enrollment Cards 1898-1914

RESIDENCE: Sans Bois   COUNTY. **Choctaw Nation**   **Choctaw Roll**   CARD NO.
POST OFFICE: Stigler, I.T.   *(Not Including Freedmen)*   FIELD NO. **2828**

Dawes' Roll No.	NAME	Relationship to Person First Named	AGE	SEX	BLOOD	TRIBAL ENROLLMENT		
						Year	County	No.
8312	₁ McCann, Joseph ³⁰	First Named	27	M	Full	1896	Sans Bois	9032
8313	₂ " Betsy ³⁹	Wife	36	F	"	1896	" "	9033
8314	₃ Nail, Jeff ¹⁸	S.Son	15	M	"	1896	" "	9562
8315	₄ McCann, Alexander ³	Son	5mo	M	"			
	₅							
	₆							
	₇							
	₈							
	₉							
	₁₀							
	₁₁							
	₁₂							
	₁₃							
	₁₄							
	₁₅							
	₁₆							
	₁₇							

ENROLLMENT
OF NOS. 1, 2, 3, 4   HEREON
APPROVED BY THE SECRETARY
OF INTERIOR   JAN 17 1903

TRIBAL ENROLLMENT OF PARENTS

	Name of Father	Year	County	Name of Mother	Year	County
₁	Alex McCann	Dead	Sans Bois	Ho-ya-ho-ke	dead	Sans Bois
₂	Fulton Knight	"	Gaines	Liza Knight	"	Gaines
₃	Morris Nail			No2		
₄	No.1			No.2		
₅						
₆						
₇						
₈	No.4 Enrolled March 10th, 1900					
₉	No.3 died Feb 17 - 1905, Proof rec'd Jan 29 – 08					
₁₀						
₁₁						
₁₂						
₁₃						
₁₄						
₁₅				#1 to 3 inc		
₁₆				Date of Application for Enrollment.	6/19/99	
₁₇						

RESIDENCE:	Skullyville	COUNTY.	**Choctaw Nation**		**Choctaw Roll**	CARD	
POST OFFICE:	Lodi, I.T.				*(Not Including Freedmen)*	FIELD NO.	2829

Dawes' Roll No.	NAME		Relationship to Person First Named	AGE	SEX	BLOOD	TRIBAL ENROLLMENT		
							Year	County	No.
8316	1 Bell, Sweeny		DIED PRIOR TO SEPTEMBER 25 1902	31	M	Full	1896	Skullyville	744
8317	2 " Alice	39	Wife	36	F	"	1896	"	745
8318	3 " Amon	7	Son	4	M	"	1896	"	747
8319	4 " Agnes	4	Dau	1	F	"			
8320	5 Bascom, Oscar	17	S.Son	14	M	"	1896	Skullyville	746
8321	6 Merryman, Frances	25	Sister	22	F	"	1896	"	8477
	7								
	8								
	9								
	10								
	11								
	12								
	13								
	14								
	15	ENROLLMENT OF NOS. 1,2,3,4,5,6 HEREON APPROVED BY THE SECRETARY OF INTERIOR JAN 17 1903								
	16								
	17								

TRIBAL ENROLLMENT OF PARENTS

	Name of Father	Year	County	Name of Mother	Year	County
1	Daniel Bell	1896	Tobucksy	Lucy Henry	Dead	Skullyville
2	Tandy Folsom	Dead	Skullyville	Artimissie Folsom	"	Sans Bois
3	No1			No2		
4	No1			No2		
5	Joe Bascom	Dead	Skullyville	No2		
6	John Merryman	"	"	Lucy Henry	Dead	Skullyville
7						
8						
9	No1 on 1896 roll as Sweeny Belle					
10	No2 " 1896 " Alice "					
11	No3 " 1896 " Baby "					
	No6 is an imbecile					
12	No 1 dies Aug. 19, 1901: Enrollment cancelled by Department July 8, 1904					
13						
14						
15					Date of Application for Enrollment	
16					6/19/99	
17						

Choctaw By Blood Enrollment Cards 1898-1914

	NAME		Relationship to Person	AGE	SEX	BLOOD	TRIBAL ENROLLMENT		
							Year	County	No.
1	Sexton, Mary	26	First Named	23	F	1/2	1896	Sans Bois	11098
2	" David	13	Son	10	M	1/4	1896	" "	11099
3	" Cora	12	Dau	9	F	1/4	1896	" "	11100
4	" Gilbert	7	Son	4	M	1/4	1896	" "	11101
5	" Claracy	5	Dau	1	F	1/4			
6	~~Elisabeth~~ DIED PRIOR TO SEPTEMBER 25, 1902		Dau	9mo	F	1/4			
7									
8									
9									
10									
11									
12									
13									
14									
15									
16									
17									

E: Sans Bois   COUNTY.   **Choctaw Nation**   Choctaw Roll (Not Including Freedmen)   CARD NO.
CE: Enterprise, I.T.   FIELD NO. 2830

ENROLLMENT
OF NOS. 1,2,3,4,5,6 HEREON
APPROVED BY THE SECRETARY
OF INTERIOR   JAN 17 1903

TRIBAL ENROLLMENT OF PARENTS

	Name of Father	Year	County	Name of Mother	Year	County
1	Jack Riddle	1896	Colored	Ho-ke-ma	Dead	Sans Bois
2	James Sexton	1896	"	No1		
3	" "	1896	"	No1		
4	" "	1896	"	No1		
5	" "	1896	"	No1		
6	~~" "~~	~~1896~~	~~Choc. freedman~~	~~No1~~		
7						
8	No.1 is the wife of James Sexton, a Choctaw freedman: see Choctaw freedman card #770					
9	No2 on 1896 roll as Dave Sexton					
10	~~No5 Affidavit of birth to be supplied: Recd Aug 9/99~~					
11	No.6 Enrolled June 6, 1901					
12	No.6 Died Dec 23, 1901. Proof of death filed Dec 30 1902					
13	~~No.6 died Dec 23, 1901. Enrollment cancelled by Department July 8, 1904~~ #1 to 5 inc					
14	For child of No1 see NB (Apr 26 '06) Card #1167					
15	" " " " 3 " " (Mar 3 '05) " #666					
16	" " " No1 " " " " " #1064 Date of Application for Enrollment 6/19/99					
17	Winton I.T. 12/22/03					

130

Choctaw By Blood Enrollment Cards 1898-1914

RESIDENCE: Sans Bois COUNTY. **Choctaw Nation** Choctaw Roll CARD No.
POST OFFICE: Iron Bridge, I.T. *(Not Including Freedmen)* FIELD No. 2831

Dawes' Roll No.	NAME	Relationship to Person First Named	AGE	SEX	BLOOD	TRIBAL ENROLLMENT		
						Year	County	No.
DEAD.	₁ Cass, Adam DEAD.		23	M	Full	1896	Sans Bois	2122
8328	₂ Jones, Emma ²³	Wife	20	F	"	1896	" "	9561
8329	₃ Cass, Lewis ²	Son	1yr	M				
	4							
	5							
	6							
	7 No. 1 HEREON DISMISSED UNDER							
	8 ORDER OF THE COMMISSION TO THE FIVE							
	9 CIVILIZED TRIBES OF MARCH 31, 1905.							
	10							
	11							
	12							
	13							
	14							
	15 ENROLLMENT OF NOS. 2 and 3 HEREON							
	16 APPROVED BY THE SECRETARY							
	17 OF INTERIOR JAN 13 1903							

TRIBAL ENROLLMENT OF PARENTS

	Name of Father	Year	County	Name of Mother	Year	County
1	Ben Crop	1896	Tobucksy	Mollie Jackson	Dead	Skullyville
2	Morris Nail	Dead	Gaines	Betsy McCann	1896	Sans Bois
3	No.1			No.2		
4						
5						
6	No2 on 1896 roll as Emma Nail					
7	No3 Enrolled August 2, 1901					
8	No1 is dead. Proof of death filed Aug 12, 1901					
9	No2 is now the wife of Mike Joneson[sic] Choctaw Card #2729. Evidence of marriage requested Aug 2, 1901. Filed Aug 12, 1901					
10	For child o No.2 see NB (March 3, 1905) #685					
11						
12						
13						
14						
15					Date of Application for Enrollment.	
16					6/19/99	
17						

131

Choctaw By Blood Enrollment Cards 1898-1914

RESIDENCE: Sugar Loaf COUNTY.	**Choctaw Nation**	Choctaw Roll (Not Including Freedmen)	CARD NO.
POST OFFICE: Summerfield, I.T.			FIELD NO. 2832

Dawes' Roll No.	NAME		Relationship to Person First Named	AGE	SEX	BLOOD	TRIBAL ENROLLMENT		
							Year	County	No.
8330	1 Holson, Noel J.	51	First Named	48	M	Full	1896	Sugar Loaf	5199
8331	2 " Lizzie	49	Wife	46	F	"	1896	" "	5200
8332	3 " Ada	18	Dau	15	"	"	1896	" "	5201
8333	4 " Boyd	16	Son	13	M	"	1896	" "	5202
8334	5 " Clara A	13	Dau	10	F	"	1896	" "	5203
8335	6 Lomby, Lucy	16	Ward	13	"	"	1896	Skullyville	7766
	7								
	8								
	9								
	10								
	11								
	12								
	13								
	14								
	15	ENROLLMENT OF NOS. 1,2,3,4,5,6 HEREON APPROVED BY THE SECRETARY							
	16	OF INTERIOR JAN 17 1903							
	17								

TRIBAL ENROLLMENT OF PARENTS

	Name of Father	Year	County	Name of Mother	Year	County
1	Stephen Holson	Dead	Sugar Loaf	Beckie Holson	Dead	Sugar Loaf
2	Wallace LeFlore	"	" "	Jude LeFlore	"	" "
3	No1			No2		
4	No1			No2		
5	No1			No2		
6	John Lomby	Dead	Sugar Loaf	Hannah Lomby	Dead	Skullyville
7						
8	No1 is guardian of estate of Sweeney F Holson, deceased, on Choctaw card #2856					
9						
10	No6 on 1896 roll as Lucy Lumber					
11						
12						
13	No2 is guardian of No6 Letters of guardianship filed Dec 26, 1902					
14	No2 is guardian of Mary Bond on Choctaw card #3068. Letters of guardianship filed Dec 26, 1902.					
15					Date of Application for Enrollment.	
16					6/19/99	
17	Page I.T. 11/1/04					

132

Choctaw By Blood Enrollment Cards 1898-1914

Dawes' Roll No.	NAME		Relationship to Person	AGE	SEX	BLOOD	TRIBAL ENROLLMENT		
							Year	County	No.
15666	1 Farrell, Theodosia	23	First Named	20	F	1/8	1896	Sans Bois	5163
15667	2 " Gertrude	6	Dau	2	"	1/16			
15668	3 " Eunice	4	"	4mo	"	1/16			
15669	4 " John Raymond	2	Son	7wk	M	1/16			
	5								
	6								
	7								
	8								
	9								
	10								
	11								
	12								
	13								
	14								
	15	ENROLLMENT OF NOS. 1, 2, 3 and 4 HEREON APPROVED BY THE SECRETARY OF INTERIOR DEC -2 1904							
	16								
	17								

TRIBAL ENROLLMENT OF PARENTS

	Name of Father	Year	County	Name of Mother	Year	County
1	John Hendricks	1896	Sans Bois	Ann Hendricks	Dead	Non Citz
2	Walter Farrell	1896	Non Citz	No1		
3	" "	1896	" "	No1		
4	" "			No1		
5						
6						
7	See decision in Choctaw jacket #2820					
8	No1 on 1896 roll as Theodosia Hendricks			No4 Enrolled Feby 18, 1901		
9				For child of No1 see NB (Mar 3'05)#523		
10	As to marriage of parents of No1, see					
11	testimony of her father, John Hendricks,					
12	and Arnold Folsom, also see Card of					
13	John Hendricks No 2820 as to additional information concerning degree of blood etc.					
14	No.1 admitted by Dawes Commission in 1896 in					
15	Choctaw case #429: no appeal.					
16	Admitted as Theodosia A. Ferrill			Date of Application for Enrollment.	6/19/99	
17						

133

Choctaw By Blood Enrollment Cards 1898-1914

NAME: Sans Bois
RESIDENCE: Sans Bois, I.T.

(Not Including Freedmen) FIELD NO. 2834

NAME	Relationship to Person First Named	AGE	SEX	BLOOD	TRIBAL ENROLLMENT		
					Year	County	No.
15670 1 Hall, Daisy C 29	Person First Named	26	F	1/8	1896	Sans Bois	5067
15671 2 Harrison, Mitchell 9	Son	6	M	5/16	1896	" "	5070
15672 3 " Milo H 5	"	2	"	5/16			
4 Hall, Leo Bennett 1	"	1mo	M	1/16			
5							
6							
7							
8							
9 For child of No1 see NB (Mar 3-05) Card #200.							
10							
11							
12							
13							
14							
15							
16							
17							

ENROLLMENT
OF NOS. 1 2 3 and 4 HEREON
APPROVED BY THE SECRETARY
OF INTERIOR DEC 2 1904

TRIBAL ENROLLMENT OF PARENTS

Name of Father	Year	County	Name of Mother	Year	County
1 John Hendricks	1896	Sans Bois	Ann Hendricks	Dead	Non Citz
2 Mitchell Harrison	Dead	" "	No1		
3 " "	"	" "	No1		
4 William S. Hall		" "	No1		
5					
6					
7					
8 See decision in Choctaw Jacket #2820					
9 No1 originally enrolled on this Card as Daisy Harrison, changed to Hall Aug 10-04					
10 No1 on 1896 roll as Mrs. D.C. Harrison					
11 No2 " 1896 " " Mitchell "					
12 No3 Affidavit of birth to be supplied: Recd 7/1/99					
13 As to marriage of father and mother of					
14 No2, see testimony of Theodosia Farrell,					
also Card of her father, John Hendricks					
as to degree of blood and other information					
15 No.1 is the wife of William S. Hall on Choc Card 2653. Evidence of marriage filed 11/2/02					
16 No.4 Born Oct 6, 1901: Enrolled Nov. 2, 1901. Date of application for enrollment 6/19/99					
No1 admitted by Dawes Commission in 1896 in Choctaw					
17 P.O. Case No 429: No appeal					

1 to 3 Date of Application for Enrollment.

Whitefield, I.T.

12/18/02

134

Choctaw By Blood Enrollment Cards 1898-1914

RESIDENCE: Skullyville COUNTY. **Choctaw Nation** Choctaw Roll CARD No.
POST OFFICE: Lodi, I.T. (Not Including Freedmen) FIELD No. 2835

Dawes' Roll No.	NAME	Relationship to Person First Named	AGE	SEX	BLOOD	TRIBAL ENROLLMENT Year	County	No.
8336	1 Jefferson, Stephen 29	First Named	26	M	3/4	1896	Skullyville	6465
8337	2 DIED PRIOR TO SEPTEMBER 25, 1902 Jennie	Wife	32	F	Full	1896	"	5184
8338	3 " Layson 4	Son	9mo	M	7/8			
8339	4 Harrison, Albert 11	S.Son	8	"	Full	1896	Skullyville	5185
	5							
	6							
	7							
	8							
	9							
	10							
	11							
	12							
	13							
	14							
	15 ENROLLMENT OF NOS. 1,2,3,4 HEREON APPROVED BY THE SECRETARY							
	16 OF INTERIOR JAN 17 1903							
	17							

TRIBAL ENROLLMENT OF PARENTS

	Name of Father	Year	County	Name of Mother	Year	County
1	Jas. Jefferson	Dead	Skullyville	Mary Jefferson	Dead	Gaines
2	William Jackson	"	"		"	Skullyville
3	No1			No2		
4	Chas. Harrison	1896	Skullyville	No2		
5						
6						
7	No2 on 1896 roll as Jane Harrison					
8	No2 Died Decr 18" 1901: Proof of death filed Decr 23rd 1902					
9	No1 is husband of Siney Colbert, Choctaw card #2840					
10	No 2 died Dec 18, 1901: Enrollment cancelled by Department July 8, 1904					
11						
12						
13						
14						
15						
16				Date of Application for Enrollment	6/19/99	
17						

Choctaw By Blood Enrollment Cards 1898-1914

RESIDENCE: Sans Bois	COUNTY.	**Choctaw Nation**	**Choctaw Roll**	CARD No.
POST OFFICE: Sans Bois, I.T.			*(Not Including Freedmen)*	FIELD No. 2836

Dawes' Roll No.	NAME	Relationship to Person First Named	AGE	SEX	BLOOD	TRIBAL ENROLLMENT		
						Year	County	No.
8340	1 James, Eli 11	First Named	8	M	1/4	1896	Sans Bois	6422
8341	2 " Lena 9	Sister	6	F	1/4	1896	" "	6423
	3							
	4							
	5							
	6							
	7							
	8							
	9							
	10							
	11							
	12							
	13							
	14							
	15							
	16							
	17							

ENROLLMENT
OF NOS. 1 and 2 HEREON
APPROVED BY THE SECRETARY
OF INTERIOR JAN 17 1903

TRIBAL ENROLLMENT OF PARENTS

	Name of Father	Year	County	Name of Mother	Year	County
1	Isaac James	1896	Non Citz	Winnie James	Dead	Sans Bois
2	" "	1896	" "	" "	"	" "
3						
4						
5						
6						
7						
8		These children are now living with				
9		Scott Sheppard (colored) P.O. Webers Falls, I.T.				
10			8/30/02			
11						
12						
13						
14					Date of Application for Enrollment.	
15						
16					6/19/99	
17						

Choctaw By Blood Enrollment Cards 1898-1914

RESIDENCE: Sans Bois COUNTY. **Choctaw Nation** Choctaw Roll CARD NO.
POST OFFICE: Sans Bois, I.T (Not Including Freedmen) FIELD NO. 2837

Dawes' Roll No.	NAME	Relationship to Person First Named	AGE	SEX	BLOOD	TRIBAL ENROLLMENT		
						Year	County	No.
8342	1 Scott, Alice 23	First Named	20	F	1/2	1896	Sans Bois	11196
8343	2 DIED PRIOR TO SEPTEMBER 25, 1902 Emma	Dau	2	"	1/4			
8344	3 " Clifford B. 3	Son	4mo	M	1/4			
	4							
	5							
	6							
	7							
	8							
	9							
	10							
	11							
	12							
	13							
	14							
	15 ENROLLMENT OF NOS. 1, 2, 3, HEREON							
	16 APPROVED BY THE SECRETARY							
	17 OF INTERIOR JAN 17 1903							

TRIBAL ENROLLMENT OF PARENTS

Name of Father	Year	County	Name of Mother	Year	County
1 Green McCurtain	1896	Sans Bois	Kittie McCurtain	1896	Sans Bois
2 George Scott	1896	Chickasaw	No 1		
3 " "	1896	"	No 1		
4					
5					
6					
7 Husband on Chickasaw Card No 679					
8					
9 No2 Affidavit of birth to be supplied. Recd 6/22/99					
10 No2 Died Oct. 11, 1900, Proof of death filed Feby 3, 1903 No 2 died Oct. 11, 1900 enrollment cancelled by Department July 3, 1904					
11 For child of No.1 see N.B. (Apr. 26-06) No. 801					
12					
13					
14					
15			#1&2		
16			Date of Application for Enrollment.	6/19/99	
17			No3 enrolled Nov 1/99		

137

Choctaw By Blood Enrollment Cards 1898-1914

RESIDENCE: Sans Bois   COUNTY.   **Choctaw Nation**   **Choctaw Roll**   CARD NO.
POST OFFICE: Sans Bois, I.T.   *(Not Including Freedmen)*   FIELD NO.   2838

Dawes' Roll No.	NAME	Relationship to Person First Named	AGE	SEX	BLOOD	TRIBAL ENROLLMENT		
						Year	County	No.
8345	1 Bohanan, Joseph 23	First Named	20	M	1/2	1896	Sans Bois	585
	2							
	3							
	4							
	5							
	6							
	7							
	8							
	9							
	10							
	11							
	12							
	13							
	14							
	15							
	16							
	17							

ENROLLMENT
OF NOS. 1 HEREON
APPROVED BY THE SECRETARY
OF INTERIOR JAN 17 1903

		TRIBAL ENROLLMENT OF PARENTS				
Name of Father	Year	County	Name of Mother	Year	County	
1 Sy Bohanan	Dead	Chickasaw	Rachel Bohanan	Dead	Sans Bois	
2						
3						
4						
5						
6						
7	No.1 is the husband of Mary Cooper on Chickasaw card #644					
8	For child of No.1 see NB (March 3, 1905) #1426					
9						
10						
11						
12						
13						
14						
15					Date of Application for Enrollment.	
16					6/19/99	
17						

138

Choctaw By Blood Enrollment Cards 1898-1914

RESIDENCE: Sans Bois   COUNTY. **Choctaw Nation**   **Choctaw Roll**   CARD NO.
POST OFFICE: Panther, I.T.   *(Not Including Freedmen)*   FIELD NO. 2839

Dawes' Roll No.	NAME		Relationship to Person First Named	AGE	SEX	BLOOD	TRIBAL ENROLLMENT		
							Year	County	No.
8346	1 Thompson, Jonas	54	First Named	51	M	Full	1896	Sans Bois	11873
8347	2 " Elizabeth	42	Wife	39	F	"	1896	" "	11874
	3								
	4								
	5								
	6								
	7								
	8								
	9								
	10								
	11								
	12								
	13								
	14								
	15								
	16								
	17								

ENROLLMENT
OF NOS. 1 and 2 HEREON
APPROVED BY THE SECRETARY
OF INTERIOR JAN 17 1903

TRIBAL ENROLLMENT OF PARENTS

	Name of Father	Year	County	Name of Mother	Year	County
1	Henry Thompson	Dead	Sugar Loaf	Tona Thompson	Dead	Skullyville
2	Thos. Colbert	"	Sans Bois	Cha-fa-ho-ke	"	Sans Bois
3						
4						
5						
6						
7						
8						
9						
10						
11						
12						
13						
14						
15				Date of Application for Enrollment.		
16				6/19/99		
17						

139

RESIDENCE:	Skullyville	COUNTY.	Choctaw Nation		Choctaw Roll	CARD No.	
POST OFFICE:	Lodi, I.T.				(Not Including Freedmen)	FIELD No.	2840

Dawes' Roll No.	NAME		Relationship to Person	AGE	SEX	BLOOD	TRIBAL ENROLLMENT		
							Year	County	No.
8348	1 Colbert, Siney	42	First Named	39	F	Full	1896	Skullyville	2196
8349	2 " Edward	19	Son	16	M	3/4	1896	"	2197
	3								
	4								
	5								
	6								
	7								
	8								
	9								
	10								
	11								
	12								
	13								
	14								
	15	ENROLLMENT OF NOS. 1 and 2 HEREON APPROVED BY THE SECRETARY OF INTERIOR JAN 17 1903							
	16								
	17								

TRIBAL ENROLLMENT OF PARENTS

Name of Father	Year	County	Name of Mother	Year	County
1 Ok-sak-nip-ku	Dead		Ah-le-he-ma	Dead	Gaines
2 Willie Colbert	"	Skullyville	No1		
3					
4					
5					
6					
7	N°2 is husband of Lena Lewis No2 on Choctaw card #306				
8			12/17/02		
9	For child of No2 see NB (Mar 3-05) Card #205				
10					
11					
12					
13					
14					
15					
16			Date of Application for Enrollment.	6/19/99	
17					

140

Choctaw By Blood Enrollment Cards 1898-1914

RESIDENCE:	Sans Bois	COUNTY.								
POST OFFICE:	Stigler, I.T.	**Choctaw Nation**					**Choctaw Roll** *(Not Including Freedmen)*	CARD NO. FIELD NO.	2841	

Dawes' Roll No.	NAME		Relationship to Person First Named	AGE	SEX	BLOOD	TRIBAL ENROLLMENT		
							Year	County	No.
8350	1 Colbert, Thomas	42	First Named	39	M	Full	1896	Sans Bois	2083
8351	2 " Cornelia	44	Wife	41	F	"	1896	" "	2084
	3								
	4								
	5								
	6								
	7								
	8								
	9								
	10								
	11								
	12								
	13								
	14								
	15								
	16								
	17								

ENROLLMENT
OF NOS. 1 and 2 HEREON
APPROVED BY THE SECRETARY
OF INTERIOR JAN 17 1903

TRIBAL ENROLLMENT OF PARENTS

Name of Father	Year	County	Name of Mother	Year	County
1 Thos. Colbert	Dead	Sans Bois	Cha-fa-ho-ke	Dead	Sans Bois
2 Ya-mo-tan-tubbee	"	" "		"	" " "
3					
4					
5					
6					
7					
8					
9					
10					
11					
12					
13					
14					
15				Date of Application for Enrollment.		
16				6/19/99		
17 No2 P.O. Vinton I.T. 9/3/07						

141

Choctaw By Blood Enrollment Cards 1898-1914

RESIDENCE:	Skullyville COUNTY.		Choctaw Nation			Choctaw Roll		CARD No.	
POST OFFICE:	Walls, I.T.					*(Not Including Freedmen)*		FIELD No.	2842

Dawes' Roll No.	NAME		Relationship to Person First Named	AGE	SEX	BLOOD	TRIBAL ENROLLMENT		
							Year	County	No.
DEAD.	Wall, Benjamin F DEAD	1		31	M	1/4	1896	Skullyville	12727
I.W. 277	" Octavia	32	Wife	29	F	I.W.	1896	"	15148
DEAD.	" Benjamin H DEAD	3	Son	11	M	1/8	1896	"	12728
8352	" Walter T	12	"	9	"	1/8	1896	"	12729
8353	" Jesse E	10	"	7	"	1/8	1896	"	12730
8354	" Ellis W	8	"	5	"	1/8	1896	"	12731
8355	" Cervera M	4	Dau	1	F				
8356	Drake, John E	21	Ward	18	M	1/4	1896	Skullyville	3154
	" Canzada	19	"	16	F	1/4	1896	"	3155
10	No. 1 HEREON DISMISSED UNDER								
11	ORDER OF THE COMMISSION TO THE FIVE						ENROLLMENT		
12	CIVILIZED TRIBES OF MARCH 31, 1905.						OF NOS. 2 HEREON		
							APPROVED BY THE SECRETARY		
13	As to marriage, see testimony						OF INTERIOR SEP 12 1903		
14	of No1 and C.C. Dunlap						ENROLLMENT		
15	No7 Affidavit of birth to be						OF NOS. 4,5,6,7,8 HEREON		
16	supplied. Filed Nov 1/99						APPROVED BY THE SECRETARY OF INTERIOR JAN 17 1903		
17									

	TRIBAL ENROLLMENT OF PARENTS							
	Name of Father	Year	County	Name of Mother		Year	County	
1	Ben F Wall	1896	Skullyville	Abbie E Wall		1896	Skullyville	
2	Tom Smith	Dead	Non Citz	Bettie Smith		Dead	Non Citz	
3	No1			No2				
4	No1			No2				
5	No1			No2				
6	No1			No2				
7	No1			No2				
8	John Drake	Dead	Non Citz	Palmer Drake		Dead	Sans Bois	
9	" "	"	" "	" "		"	" "	
10	No1 on 1896 roll as Ben F Walls			No8 on 1896 roll as John Drake				
11	No2 " 1896 " " Octave "			No9 " 1896 " " Cansada "				
12	No3 " 1896 " " Ben H. " No4 " 1896 " " Walter F "			No3 died April 3, 1900, Proof of death filed Dec 20 1902				
13	No5 " 1896 " " Jessie E "							
14	No6 " 1896 " " Ellis W. "							
15	No1 Died March 12, 1900: proof [sic] death filed March 8, 1902					Date of Application for Enrollment.	For Nos 1 to 6 inc	
16						6/19/99		
17								

142

Choctaw By Blood Enrollment Cards 1898-1914

RESIDENCE: Skullyville COUNTY.
POST OFFICE: Walls, I.T.

Choctaw Nation

Choctaw Roll
(Not Including Freedmen)

CARD No.
FIELD NO. 2843

Dawes' Roll No.	NAME	Relationship to Person First Named	AGE	SEX	BLOOD	TRIBAL ENROLLMENT		
						Year	County	No.
8357	1 Wall, Benjamin F ⁶⁰	First Named	57	M	1/2	1896	Skullyville	12828
8358	2 " Abigail E ⁵⁹	Wife	56	F	1/2	1896	"	12829
	3							
	4							
	5							
	6							
	7							
	8							
	9							
	10							
	11							
	12							
	13							
	14							
	15							
	16							
	17							

ENROLLMENT
OF NOS. 1 and 2 HEREON
APPROVED BY THE SECRETARY
OF INTERIOR JAN 17 1903

TRIBAL ENROLLMENT OF PARENTS

	Name of Father	Year	County	Name of Mother	Year	County
1	Tom Wall	Dead	Skullyville	Katie Wall	Dead	Skullyville
2	Ward Folsom	"	"	Bettie Folsom	"	"
3						
4						
5						
6						
7						
8			No1 on 1896 roll as Ben F Walls			
9			No2 " 1896 " " Abigail E "			
10						
11						
12						
13						
14						
15						
16				Date of Application for Enrollment.	6/19/99	
17						

143

Choctaw By Blood Enrollment Cards 1898-1914

RESIDENCE: Sans Bois	COUNTY.	**Choctaw Nation**	Choctaw Roll	CARD NO.	
POST OFFICE: Stigler, I.T.			*(Not Including Freedmen)*	FIELD NO.	2844

Dawes' Roll No.	NAME		Relationship to Person First Named	AGE	SEX	BLOOD	TRIBAL ENROLLMENT		
							Year	County	No.
8359	1 Nail, Richard	44	First Named	41	M	1/2	1896	Sans Bois	9548
8360	2 " Nelson	19	Son	16	"	3/4	1896	" "	9550
8361	3 " Greenwood	17	"	14	"	3/4	1896	" "	9551
8362	4 ~~Elizabeth~~ DIED PRIOR TO SEPTEMBER 25, 1902		Dau	10	F	3/4	1896	" "	9552
8363	5 " William	12	Son	9	M	1/2	1896	" "	9553
8364	6 " Maggie	9	Dau	6	F	1/2	1896	" "	9554
	7								
	8								
	9								
	10								
	11								
	12								
	13								
	14								
	15	ENROLLMENT OF NOS. 1,2,3,4,5,6 HEREON APPROVED BY THE SECRETARY OF INTERIOR JAN 17 1903							
	16								
	17								

TRIBAL ENROLLMENT OF PARENTS

	Name of Father	Year	County	Name of Mother	Year	County
1	Greenwood Nail	Dead	Sans Bois	Manda Nail	Dead	Tobucksy
2	No 1			Empsy Nail	"	"
3	No 1			" "	"	"
4	No 1			" "	"	"
5	No 1			Cillen Nail	"	Sans Bois
6	No 1			" "	"	" " "
7						
8						
9	No 1 is the husband of Saline Nail on Choctaw Card #4851. See letter filed in that case Oct 5, 1901					
10	No 4 died March 17,1902. Proof of death received and filed Dec 30 1902					
11	No.4 died March 17, 1902. Enrollment cancelled by Department July 2, 1902					
11	For child of No.1 see NB (Apr 26, 1906) card No. 213					
12	" " " " " " (Mar 3, 1905) " " 1352					
13						
14						
15						
16				Date of Application for Enrollment.	6/19/99	
17						

144

Choctaw By Blood Enrollment Cards 1898-1914

RESIDENCE:	Skullyville	COUNTY.							CARD No.	
POST OFFICE:	Walls I.T.								FIELD No.	2845

RESIDENCE: Skullyville COUNTY. **Choctaw Nation** Choctaw Roll *(Not Including Freedmen)*
POST OFFICE: Walls I.T. CARD No. / FIELD No. 2845

Dawes' Roll No.	NAME		Relationship to Person First Named	AGE	SEX	BLOOD	TRIBAL ENROLLMENT		
							Year	County	No.
8365	1 Henry Amos	54	First Named	51	M	Full	1896	Skullyville	5191
8366	2 " Arian	28	Wife	25	F	"	1896	"	5192
8367	3 " Wilburn	21	Son	18	M	"	1896	"	5193
8368	4 " Alexander	2	"	10mo	M	"			
DEAD.	5 " Susan DEAD.		Dau	7w	F	"			
8369	6 " Roosevelt	4	Son	2½ mo	M	"			
	7								
	8 No. 5 HEREON DISMISSED UNDER								
	9 ORDER OF THE COMMISSION TO THE FIVE CIVILIZED TRIBES OF MARCH 31, 1905.								
	10								
	11								
	12								
	13								
	14								
	15 ENROLLMENT OF NOS. 1,2,3,4 and 6 HEREON APPROVED BY THE SECRETARY OF INTERIOR JAN 17 1903								
	16								
	17								

TRIBAL ENROLLMENT OF PARENTS

	Name of Father	Year	County	Name of Mother	Year	County
1	A-tom-be	Dead	Sans Bois	Nancy A-tom-be	Dead	Sans Bois
2	Alex Burns	1896	" "	Martha Burns	"	" " "
3	No1			Lucy Henry	"	Skullyville
4	No1			No2		
5	No1			No2		
6	Nº1			Nº2		
7						
8						
9						
10						
11		No5 Enrolled January 29, 1901				
12		Nº6 Born June 25, 1902, enrolled Sept 4, 1902				
13		Nº5 Died April 2, 1902, Proof of death filed Oct. 6, 1902				
14		Nº3 is husband of No4 on Choctaw card #2870 12/15/02				
15		For child of Nos 1&2 see NB (March 3, 1905) #784 #1 to 4				
16				Date of Application for Enrollment.	6/19/99	
17						

RESIDENCE: Skullyville COUNTY.						Choctaw Roll	CARD NO.	
POST OFFICE: Shady Point I.T.	**Choctaw Nation**					(Not Including Freedmen)	FIELD NO. 2846	

Dawes' Roll No.	NAME	Relationship to Person First Named	AGE	SEX	BLOOD	TRIBAL ENROLLMENT		
						Year	County	No.
I.W. 131	1 Hickman James H ⁴⁴	First Named	41	M	I.W.	1896	Skullyville	14597
8370	2 " Minnie ³¹	Wife	28	F	1/8	1896	"	5172
8371	3 " Jesse J ⁹	Son	6	M	1/16	1896	"	5173
	4							
	5							
	6							
	7							
	8							
	9							
	10							
	11							
	12							
	13							
	14							
	15	ENROLLMENT OF NOS. 2 and 3 HEREON APPROVED BY THE SECRETARY OF INTERIOR JAN 17 1903				ENROLLMENT OF NOS. 1 ~~~~~ HEREON APPROVED BY THE SECRETARY OF INTERIOR JUN 13 1903		
	16							
	17							

TRIBAL ENROLLMENT OF PARENTS

Name of Father	Year	County	Name of Mother	Year	County
1 W.A. Hickman	Dead	Non Citz	Sarah Hickman	Dead	Non Citz
2 Jesse Hardaway	1896	Skullyville	Margaret Hardaway	1896	Skullyville
3	No 1		No 2		
4					
5					
6					
7	No1 On 1896 roll as James Hickman				
8	No3 " " " " Jessie J. Hickman				
9	No2 Evidence of marriage of father and mother to be				
10	supplied Received June 19, 1899				
11	No1 admitted as an intermarried citizen by Dawes Commission in 1896: Choctaw Case #402: No appeal				
12					
13					
14					
15				Date of Application for Enrollment.	
16				6/19/99	
17	Panama I.T. 12/18/02				

146

Choctaw By Blood Enrollment Cards 1898-1914

RESIDENCE: Sugar Loaf	COUNTY.			**Choctaw Nation**			Choctaw Roll	CARD No.
POST OFFICE: Wister I.T.						(Not Including Freedmen)	FIELD No. 2847

Dawes' Roll No.	NAME		Relationship to Person First Named	AGE	SEX	BLOOD	TRIBAL ENROLLMENT		
							Year	County	No.
8372	1 Rose Wilmon	27	First Named	24	M	Full	1896	Sugar Loaf	10720
8374	2 " Jincy	19	Wife	16	F	"	1896	" "	10721
8375	3 DIED PRIOR TO SEPTEMBER 25, 1902 " Lewis		Son	4	M	"	1896	" "	10722
8377	4 DIED PRIOR TO SEPTEMBER 25, 1902 " Sampson		"	1	M	"			
8376	5 " John	2	"	14m	M	"			
8377	6 " Martha	1	Dau	7wks	F	"			
	7								
	8								
	9								
	10								
	11								
	12								
	13								
	14								
	15	ENROLLMENT OF NOS. 1,2,3,4,5,6 HEREON APPROVED BY THE SECRETARY OF INTERIOR JAN 17 1903							
	16								
	17								

TRIBAL ENROLLMENT OF PARENTS

	Name of Father	Year	County	Name of Mother	Year	County
1	He-ke-an-ta-be	Dead	Sugar Loaf	Amy He-ke-an-ta-be	Dead	Sugar Loaf
2	Sampson Lorin	"	" "	A-tob-bi	"	" "
3	No 1			No 2		
4	No 1			No 2		
5	No 1			No 2		
6	No 1			No 2		
7						
8						
9			No2 On 1896 roll as Jensy Rose			
10			No5 Born April 3rd 1901 Enrolled June 26" 1902 No6 Born May 6th 1902 Enrolled June 26th 1902			
11			No3 died December 2, 1900; proof of death filed Dec 20 1902			
12			No4 died December – 1900; " " " " " " "			
13						
14	No3 died Dec.2,1900; No.4 died Dec - 1900: Enrollment cancelled by Department July 8, 1904					
15					#1 to 4 inc	
16				Date of Application for Enrollment.	6/19/99	
17						

Choctaw By Blood Enrollment Cards 1898-1914

Dawes' Roll No.	NAME	Relationship to Person First Named	AGE	SEX	BLOOD	TRIBAL ENROLLMENT Year	County	No.
I.W. 1496	1 Rabon Robert L 28		24	M	IW	1896	Sans Bois	14955
8378	2 " Cora E 24	Wife	21	F	1/32	P R 1893	" "	738
8379	3 DIED PRIOR TO SEPTEMBER 25, 1902 Wallace	Son	2	M	1/64			
8380	4 " Eunice	Dau	6mo	F	1/64			
8381	5 " Lee Ora 1	Dau	1mo	F	1/64			
	6							
	7							
	8	ENROLLMENT OF NOS. 1 HEREON APPROVED BY THE SECRETARY OF INTERIOR JUN 12 1905						
	9							
	10							
	11	No3 died October 16, 1900; Proof of death filed Dec 20 1902						
	12							
	13	No.3 died Oct. 16, 1900: Enrollment cancelled by Department July 6, 1904						
	14							
	15	ENROLLMENT OF NOS. 2,3,4,5 HEREON APPROVED BY THE SECRETARY OF INTERIOR JAN 17 1903						
	16							
	17							

TRIBAL ENROLLMENT OF PARENTS

	Name of Father	Year	County	Name of Mother	Year	County
1	Thomas Rabon	1896	Non Citz	Mary Jane Rabon	1896	Non Citz
2	W. T. Ross	1896	Sans Bois	Lizzie Ross	1896	" "
3	No 1			No 2		
4	No 1			No 2		
5	No. 1			No. 2		
6						
7	No 1 restored to roll by Department authority of January 19, 1909 [remainder illegible]					
8	Enrollment of No 1 cancelled by order of Department March 4, 1904					
9	No1 On 1896 roll as R.L. Rabon			For child of Nos1 & 2 see NB (Mar 3 '05)		
10	No2 " P 72 #738 – 1893 P.R. Sans Bois Co #565					
11	" 2 As Cora E. Ross. Admitted by act of Council No 69 approved					
12	Nov. 7, 1888 as Cora Ross daughter of William T. Ross					
13	Mother Lizzie also admitted in same act.					
13	In 1896 an application was made by R.L. Rabon, as an intermarried Choctaw:					
14	in Choctaw case #1017: said case is briefed and docket "L.W. James vs.				1 to 3	
15	Choctaw Nation": no appeal.				Date of Application for Enrollment.	
16	L.W. James as a party to an affidavit submitted in support of such application No5 born Oct. 25, 1901: Enrolled Nov 30, 1901				6/19/99	
17	Sans Bois I.T. 12/30/03 Affidavit of B.B. Woodward as to marriage of Nos 1 and2 filed March 21, 1903					

Kingston IT 6/12/03

Choctaw By Blood Enrollment Cards 1898-1914

| | RESIDENCE: Sans Bois — POST OFFICE: Sans Bois I.T. | COUNTY. | **Choctaw Nation** | | | | Choctaw Roll (Not Including Freedmen) | | CARD NO. FIELD NO. 2849 | |

Dawes' Roll No.		NAME		Relationship to Person First Named	AGE	SEX	BLOOD	TRIBAL ENROLLMENT		
								Year	County	No.
8382	1	Cooper Andrew J	35	First Named	32	M	1/2	1896	Sans Bois	2060
I.W. 278	2	" Eliza A	32	Wife	29	F	I W	1896	" "	14369
8383	3	" Mattie	14	Dau	11	F	1/4	1896	" "	2061
8384	4	" Stephen	8	Son	5	M	1/4	1896	" "	2062
8385	5	" Austin Albro	1	Son	5mo	M	1/4			
	6									
	7									
	8									
	9									
	10									
	11	ENROLLMENT OF NOS. 2 HEREON APPROVED BY THE SECRETARY OF INTERIOR SEP 12 1903								
	12									
	13									
	14									
	15	ENROLLMENT OF NOS. 1,3,4,5, HEREON APPROVED BY THE SECRETARY OF INTERIOR JAN 17 1903								
	16									
	17									

TRIBAL ENROLLMENT OF PARENTS

	Name of Father	Year	County	Name of Mother	Year	County
1	Stephen Cooper	Dead	Gaines	Sarah Cooper	1896	Sans Bois
2	Caleb Wilson	"	Non Citz	Sarah Wilson	1896	Non Citz
3	No 1			No 2		
4	No 1			No 2		
5	No 1			No 2		
6						
7						
8		No2 On 1896 roll as Annie Cooper. As to marriage see testimony				
9		of Mattie E Battles and of herself.				
10		No3 On 1896 roll as Mattee Cooper				
11		No1 " 1896 " " A. J. "				
12		No.5 Born May 3, 1901 and enrolled October 23, 1901.				
13		Affidavit relative to the marriage of N°s 1&2 received and filed Jan. 31, 1903.				
14		For child of No3 see NB (Apr 26 '06) #1282				
15					1 to 4 inc	
16				Date of Application for Enrollment	6/19/99	
17						

Stigler I.T.

149

Choctaw By Blood Enrollment Cards 1898-1914

RESIDENCE:	Sans Bois	COUNTY.								

RESIDENCE: Sans Bois COUNTY. **Choctaw Nation** **Choctaw Roll** CARD NO.
POST OFFICE: Sans Bois I.T. (Not Including Freedmen) FIELD NO. 2850

Dawes' Roll No.	NAME	Relationship to Person First Named	AGE	SEX	BLOOD	TRIBAL ENROLLMENT		
						Year	County	No.
8386	1 Holmes Betsy 45		42	F	Full	1896	Sans Bois	5126
8387	2 DIED PRIOR TO SEPTEMBER 25, 1902 Morris	Son	18	M	"	1896	" "	5127
8388	3 DIED PRIOR TO SEPTEMBER 25 1902 Charles	"	13	M	"	1896	" "	5128
	4							
	5							
	6							
	7							
	8							
	9							
	10							
	11							
	12							
	13							
	14							
	15	ENROLLMENT OF NOS. 1,2,3, HEREON						
	16	APPROVED BY THE SECRETARY OF INTERIOR JAN 17 1903						
	17							

TRIBAL ENROLLMENT OF PARENTS

Name of Father	Year	County	Name of Mother	Year	County
1 Jesse Jones	Dead	Sans Bois	He-ke-ma	Dead	Sans Bois
2 Robinson Holmes	"	" "	No 1		
3 " "	"	" "	No 1		
4					
5					
6					
7					
8					
9					
10					
11					
12					
13					
14					
15					
16			Date of Application for Enrollment.	6/19/99	
17					

Choctaw By Blood Enrollment Cards 1898-1914

RESIDENCE: Sans Bois COUNTY. **Choctaw Nation** **Choctaw Roll** CARD NO.
POST OFFICE: Sans Bois I.T. *(Not Including Freedmen)* FIELD NO. 2851

Dawes' Roll No.	NAME	Relationship to Person First Named	AGE	SEX	BLOOD	TRIBAL ENROLLMENT		
						Year	County	No.
8389	1 Thompson Jimpson 56		53	M	Full	1896	Sans Bois	11828
8390	2 DIED PRIOR TO SEPTEMBER 25, 1902 Lucy	Wife	54	F	"	1896	" "	11829
	3							
	4							
	5							
	6							
	7							
	8							
	9							
	10							
	11							
	12							
	13							
	14							
	15	ENROLLMENT OF NOS. 1 and 2 HEREON						
	16	APPROVED BY THE SECRETARY OF INTERIOR JAN 17 1903						
	17							

TRIBAL ENROLLMENT OF PARENTS

Name of Father	Year	County	Name of Mother	Year	County
1 Tash-kah-ke	Dead	Sans Bois	E-la-chi-ho-na	Dead	Sans Bois
2 John Cooper	"	" "		"	" "
3					
4					
5					
6					
7					
8					
9	No2 died Nov - 1900; Proof of death filed Dec 12 1902				
10	No.2 died Nov - 1900; Enrollment cancelled by Department July 8, 1904				
11					
12					
13					
14					
15					Date of Application for Enrollment.
16					6/19/99
17					

Choctaw By Blood Enrollment Cards 1898-1914

RESIDENCE: Sans Bois	COUNTY. **Choctaw Nation**	**Choctaw Roll** (Not Including Freedmen)	CARD NO. 2852
POST OFFICE: Red Oak I.T.			FIELD NO.

Dawes' Roll No.	NAME	Relationship to Person First Named	AGE	SEX	BLOOD	TRIBAL ENROLLMENT		
						Year	County	No.
8391	1 McCurtain Winnie 37	First Named	34	F	Full	1896	Gaines	9166
8392	2 " Mitchell 22	Neph	19	M	1/2	1896	"	9167
8393	3 " Osborne 17	"	14	M	1/2	1896	"	9168
14775	4 " Cornelius 13	"	10	M	1/2	1896	"	9169
	5							
	6							
	7							
	8							
	9							
	10							
	11							
	12							
	13							
	14							
	15	ENROLLMENT OF NOS. 1, 2, 3 HEREON APPROVED BY THE SECRETARY OF INTERIOR JAN 17 1903			ENROLLMENT OF NOS. 4 HEREON APPROVED BY THE SECRETARY OF INTERIOR MAY 20 1903			
	16							
	17							

TRIBAL ENROLLMENT OF PARENTS

	Name of Father	Year	County	Name of Mother	Year	County
1	John Dixon	Dead	Sans Bois	Julia Dixon	Dead	Sans Bois
2	George McCurtain	"	Sugar Loaf	Sillen McCurtain	"	Gaines
3	" "	"	" "	" "	"	"
4	" "	"	" "	" "	"	"
5						
6						
7	No1 Husband on Chickasaw card No 1450 7-5575					
8	No3 On 1896 roll as Osborn McCurtain					
9	No3 also " 1896 " " " "					
10	Page 228, No 9079, Sugar Loaf Co.					
	No1 and Sampson McCurtain separated					
11						
12						
13						
14						
15					Date of Application for Enrollment.	6/19/99
16						
17						

Choctaw By Blood Enrollment Cards 1898-1914

RESIDENCE:	Gaines	COUNTY.	Choctaw Nation		Choctaw Roll	CARD No.	
POST OFFICE:	Wilburton I.T.				(Not Including Freedmen)	FIELD No.	2853

Dawes' Roll No.	NAME		Relationship to Person First Named	AGE	SEX	BLOOD	TRIBAL ENROLLMENT		
							Year	County	No.
DEAD ✓ ✗	1	Langford William		36	M	1/8			
✓ ✗	2	" Calvin	Son	15	M	1/16			
✓ ✗	3	" Leberry	"	13	M	1/16			
✓ ✗	4	" Benjamin	"	10	M	1/16			
	5								
	6								
	7								
	8	No. 1 HEREON DISMISSED UNDER ORDER OF THE COMMISSION TO THE FIVE							
	9	CIVILIZED TRIBES OF MARCH 31, 1905.							
	10								
	11								
	12								
	13								
	14								
	15								
	16								
	17								

TRIBAL ENROLLMENT OF PARENTS

	Name of Father	Year	County	Name of Mother	Year	County
1	Henry Langford	Dead	Non Citz	Rachel Langford	1896	Gaines
2	No 1			Nettie Langford	Dead	Non Citz
3	No 1			" "	"	" "
4	No 1			Mary Ann Langford	"	" "
5						
6	Nos 1 to 4 incl. denied by the Dawes Com in 96 by Choc Crt Case #598					
7	All admitted by U.S. Court at So. McAlester Aug 24, 1897 Leberry as Lex = Case No 94					
8	As to residence see testimony of William Langford above					
9	No.1 Died July 7, 1900. Evidence of death filed April 15, 1901					
10	Judgement[sic] of U.S. Court C.D. admitting Nos 1,2,3 and 4 vacated and set aside by Decree of Choctaw Chickasaw Cit Court Decr 17ᵗʰ 02					
11	No 1 to 4 admitted by Choctaw-Chickasaw Citizenship Court Feb 1ˢᵗ 04 Case #79					
12						
13						
14					Date of Application for Enrollment.	
15						
16					6/19/99	
17						

Choctaw By Blood Enrollment Cards 1898-1914

RESIDENCE: Sans Bois COUNTY. **Choctaw Nation** **Choctaw Roll** CARD NO.
POST OFFICE: Sans Bois I.T. *(Not Including Freedmen)* FIELD NO. 2854

Dawes' Roll No.	NAME	Relationship to Person	AGE	SEX	BLOOD	TRIBAL ENROLLMENT		
						Year	County	No.
8394	1 Garland Joel 58	First Named	55	M	1/8	1896	Sans Bois	4601
	2							
	3							
	4							
	5							
	6							
	7							
	8							
	9							
	10							
	11							
	12							
	13							
	14							
	15							
	16							
	17							

ENROLLMENT
OF NOS. 1 HEREON
APPROVED BY THE SECRETARY
OF INTERIOR JAN 17 1903

TRIBAL ENROLLMENT OF PARENTS

Name of Father	Year	County	Name of Mother	Year	County
1 James Garland	Dead	Sans Bois	Peggy Garland	Dead	Sans Bois
2					
3					
4					
5					
6					
7		Wife and children on Chick. Card No 1451			
8		" now on Choctaw card #5586			
9					
10					
11					
12					
13					
14					
15					
16			DATE OF APPLICATION FOR ENROLLMENT.	6/19/99	
17					

154

Choctaw By Blood Enrollment Cards 1898-1914

RESIDENCE: Gaines COUNTY. **Choctaw Nation** Choctaw Roll (Not Including Freedmen) FIELD NO. 2855

POST OFFICE: Ola I.T.

Dawes' Roll No.	NAME	Relationship to Person First Named	AGE	SEX	BLOOD	TRIBAL ENROLLMENT		
						Year	County	No.
* 1	Kinsey Charles		31	M	1/8			
* 2	" Callie	Wife	24	F	I W			
* 3	" Samuel	Son	7	M	1/16			
4	" James H	"	1mo	"	1/16			
5	" Amison J	Son	2mo	M	1/16			
6								
7								
8	Nos 4 and 5 DISMISSED							
9								
10	MAY 24 1904							
11								
12								
13								
14								
15	DENIED CITIZENSHIP BY THE CHOCTAW AND							
16	Nos 1-2&3 CHICKASAW CITIZENSHIP COURT							
17								

TRIBAL ENROLLMENT OF PARENTS

Name of Father	Year	County	Name of Mother	Year	County
1 Andrew J Kinsey	Dead	Non Citz	Sarah Ann Kinsey	1896	Skullyville
2 James Massey	"	" "	Mattie Massey	Dead	Non Citz
3 No 1			Charlotta Kinsey	"	Non Citz
4 No 1			No 2		
5 N°1			N°2		
6					
7	Nos 1,2 and 3 Denied by Dawes Com in '96 Choctaw Cit Case # 598				
8	No1 and No2 Admitted by U.S. Court at So McAlester Aug. 24/97				
9	Case No 94 Callie Kinsey as Callie Kinsie intermarried				
10	No1 As to residence see his testimony				
11	N°5 Born July 18, 1902 – enrolled Sept 24, 1902				
12	Judgement[sic] of U.S. Court admitting Nos 1,2 and 3 vacated and set aside by Decree of Choctaw Chickasaw Cit Court Dec 17/02				
13				Date of Application for Enrollment.	
14				6/19/99	
15				No4 enrolled Oct 6/99	
16					
17					

155

RESIDENCE:	Sugar Loaf	COUNTY.						CARD No.	
POST OFFICE:	Summerfield I.T.	**Choctaw Nation**				**Choctaw Roll** (Not Including Freedmen)		FIELD No.	2856

Dawes' Roll No.	NAME	Relationship to Person First Named	AGE	SEX	BLOOD	TRIBAL ENROLLMENT		
						Year	County	No.
8395	1 Holson Sweeney	DIED PRIOR TO SEPTEMBER 25, 1902 First Named	46	M	Full	1896	Sugar Loaf	5211
8396	2 " Amanda 42	Wife	39	F	"	1896	Wade	962
8397	3 Sockey, Josephine 19	Dau	16	F	"	1896	Sugar Loaf	5214
8398	4 Holson, Rebecca 16	Dau	13	F	"	1896	" "	5216
DEAD.	5 " Stephen	Son	11	M	"	1896	" "	5217
DEAD.	6 " Shony	"	7	M	"	1896	" "	5218
8399	7 " Minnie DIED PRIOR TO SEPTEMBER 25, 1902	Dau	4	F	"	1896	" "	5219
8400	8 Bacon Mollie 22	Step Dau	19	F	"	1896	Wade	963
8401	9 " Reuben J 8	" Son	5	M	"	1896	"	966
DEAD.	10 Durant, Sallie 3	G.Dau	3mo	F				
8401	11 Sockey, Emmit 1	Gr Son	6mo	M	7/8			
	12							
	13							
	14 Father of No 11 is William Sakki on 1896 Choctaw census roll #11325, Wade Co.							
	15 Mother of No 11 is No 3 hereon							
	16 No 1 N.J. Holson now guardian of estate, Choctaw card #2832.							

No. 5 Card 1 HEREON DISMISSED UNDER ORDER OF THE COMMISSION TO THE FIVE CIVILIZED TRIBES OF MARCH 31, 1905.

No 11 Born Aug 28, 1906 (sic) on this card.
Enrollment cancelled by Department Jan.2

	TRIBAL ENROLLMENT OF PARENTS					
	Name of Father	Year	County	Name of Mother	Year	County
1	Stephen Holson	Dead	Sugar Loaf	Rebecca Holson	Dead	Sugar Loaf
2	Joseph Anderson	"	Jack's Fork	Juliana Anderson	"	Jack's Fork
3	No 1			Sukey Holson	"	Sugar Loaf
4	No 1			" "	"	" "
5	No 1			" "	"	" "
6	No 1			" "	"	" "
7	No 1			" "	"	" "
8	Reuben Bacon	Dead	Wade	Amanda Holson	1896	Sugar Loaf
9	" "	"	"	" "	1896	" "
10	Alfohns Durant		Choctaw	No 3		
11	No 1 On 1896 roll as Sweeny Holson			For child of No 3 see NB (Mar 3-1907[sic]) #1219		
12	No 2 " 1896 " " Amanda Bacon			No 5 died in 1900; Proof of death filed Dec 12 1902		
	No 3 " 1896 " " Joseph Holson					
13	No 9 " 1896 " " Reuben Bacon Jr			No 10 " Nov 1901 " " " " " "		
14	No 3 is now the wife of William Sakki on Choctaw card #2119. See affidavits					
	of Gibson Battise, Oscar and Mary Davis as to marriage filed Sept 9, 1902					
15	No 11 Born Feby 28, 1902. enrolled Sept 9, 1902					#1 to 9
16	No 1 died April 1901; Proof of death filed Dec 12 1902				DATE OF APPLICATION FOR ENROLLMENT.	6/19/99
17	No 6 died Aug 1899. proof of death filed Dec 12 1902				No 10 enrolled Dec 14/99	
	No 7 " Sept 1900 " " " " " " "					

ENROLLMENT OF NOS 1,2,3,4,7,8,9,11 HEREON APPROVED BY THE SECRETARY OF INTERIOR JAN 17 1903

Choctaw By Blood Enrollment Cards 1898-1914

RESIDENCE: Sans Bois COUNTY. **Choctaw Nation** Choctaw Roll CARD NO.
POST OFFICE: Sans Bois I.T.   (Not Including Freedmen) FIELD NO. 2857

Dawes' Roll No.		NAME		Relationship to Person	AGE	SEX	BLOOD	TRIBAL ENROLLMENT		
								Year	County	No.
8403	1	Patterson Walton	51	First Named	48	M	1/8	1896	Sans Bois	10034
I.W. 732	2	" Martha J	33	Wife	30	F	IW	1896	" "	149[?]3
8404	3	" Maggie	16	Dau	13	F	1/16	1896	" "	10035
8405	4	" Green	13	Son	10	M	1/16	1896	" "	10036
8406	5	" Pearl A	7	Dau	4	F	1/16	1896	" "	10037
8407	6	" Kittie J	5	"	1	F	1/16			
8408	7	" Ethel	1	Dau	1mo	F	1/16			
	8									
	9									
	10									
	11									
	12									
	13									
	14									
	15									
	16									
	17									

ENROLLMENT
OF NOS. ~~~ 2 ~~~ HEREON
APPROVED BY THE SECRETARY
OF INTERIOR MAY -7 1904

ENROLLMENT
OF NOS. 1,3,4,5,6,7 HEREON
APPROVED BY THE SECRETARY
OF INTERIOR JAN 17 1903

TRIBAL ENROLLMENT OF PARENTS

	Name of Father	Year	County	Name of Mother	Year	County
1	J. M. Patterson	1896	Non Citz	Sarah Patterson	Dead	Miss
2	Wm Anderson	1896	" "	Martha Anderson	"	Non Citz
3	No 1			No 2		
4	No 1			No 2		
5	No 1			No 2		
6	No 1			No 2		
7	No.1			No.2		
8			No2 See Decision of March 2 '04			
9			No2 On 1896 roll as Martha Patterson. Also admitted by Council			
10			Act No 50 approved Nov 6th 1884 as Martha Jane Patterson wife of Walton Patterson, white woman			
11			No5 On 1896 roll as Pearl O. Patterson			
12			No.7 born Dec 27, 1901: Enrolled Jany 14, 1902			
13			Evidence of birth of No6 received and filed Feby 8, 1902			
14			Certified copy of act of Council of 1884 admitting Nos 1-2 to citizenship in the Choctaw Nation			
15			For child of Nos 1&2 see NB (Apr 27[sic]-06) Card #363			Date of Application for Enrollment.
16			" " " " " " " (Mar 3-05) " #[illegible]			6/19/99
17			PO Terral[sic] IT 10/22/02			

PO Ryan IT 8/22/02

Choctaw By Blood Enrollment Cards 1898-1914

RESIDENCE: Sugar Loaf   COUNTY. **Choctaw Nation**   Choctaw Roll   CARD NO.
POST OFFICE: Le Flore I.T.   (Not Including Freedmen)   FIELD NO. **2858**

Dawes' Roll No.	NAME		Relationship to Person First Named	AGE	SEX	BLOOD	TRIBAL ENROLLMENT		
							Year	County	No.
8409	1 Battiest Gibson	67		64	M	Full	1896	Sugar Loaf	782
8410	2 " Eliza	39	Wife	36	F	"	1896	" "	783
8411	3 " Andrew	9	Son	6	M	"	1896	" "	785
8412	4 Wesley Harris	13	Step Son	10	M	"	1896	" "	784
	5								
	6								
	7								
	8								
	9								
	10								
	11								
	12								
	13								
	14								
	15	ENROLLMENT OF NOS. 1,2,3,4 HEREON APPROVED BY THE SECRETARY OF INTERIOR JAN 17 1903							
	16								
	17								

TRIBAL ENROLLMENT OF PARENTS

	Name of Father	Year	County	Name of Mother	Year	County
1	Nak-in-to-la	Dead	Sugar Loaf	E-la-to-ba	Dead	Red River
2	Me-sha-fih-na-be	"	Red River	Me-he-le	"	Sugar Loaf
3	No 1			No 2		
4	Noel Wesley	Dead	Sugar Loaf	No 2		
5						
6						
7						
8	No2 On 1896 roll as Liza Battiest					
9	No4 " " " " Harris Battiest					
10						
11						
12						
13						
14					Date of Application for Enrollment.	
15						
16					6/19/99	
17						

Choctaw By Blood Enrollment Cards 1898-1914

RESIDENCE: Sans Bois COUNTY. **Choctaw Nation** **Choctaw Roll** CARD No.
POST OFFICE: Garland I.T. (Not Including Freedmen) FIELD No

Dawes' Roll No.	NAME		Relationship to Person First Named	AGE	SEX	BLOOD	TRIBAL ENROLLMENT		
							Year	County	No.
8413	1 Folsom James W	10		7	M	1/4	1896	Sans Bois	3864
8414	2 " Ara D	13	Sister	10	F	1/4	1896	" "	3863
	3								
	4								
	5								
	6								
	7								
	8								
	9								
	10								
	11								
	12								
	13								
	14								
	15								
	16								
	17								

ENROLLMENT
OF NOS. 1 and 2 HEREON
APPROVED BY THE SECRETARY
OF INTERIOR JAN 17 1903

TRIBAL ENROLLMENT OF PARENTS

	Name of Father	Year	County	Name of Mother	Year	County
1	James Folsom	Dead	Sans Bois	Laura Folsom	1896	Non Citz
2	" "	"	" " "	" "	1896	" "
3						
4						
5						
6						
7						
8	No1 On 1896 roll as Jas. W. Folsum					
9	No2 " " " " Ara B. "					
10						
11	For child of No2 see NB (Apr 26-06) Card #689					
12	" " " " " " (Mar 3-05) " #1075					
13						
14						
15					Date of Application for Enrollment	
16						6/19/99
17						

159

RESIDENCE: Sans Bois COUNTY.
POST OFFICE: Whitefield, I.T.

Choctaw Nation
Choctaw Roll (Not Including Freedmen)

CARD NO.
FIELD NO. 2860

Dawes' Roll No.	NAME	Relationship to Person Named	AGE	SEX	BLOOD	TRIBAL ENROLLMENT		
						Year	County	No.
15674	1 Farrill, Harriet 27	First Named	24	F	1/8	1896	Sans Bois	5162
DEAD.	2 " Anna	Dau	2	"	1/16			
15675	3 Farrill, Zelma Lee 2	Dau	2mo	F	1/16			
	4							
	5 No2 DISMISSED							
	6							
	7 OCT 14 1904							
	8							
	9							
	10							
	11							
	12							
	13							
	14							
	15 ENROLLMENT OF NOS. 1 and 3 HEREON							
	16 APPROVED BY THE SECRETARY OF INTERIOR DEC -2 1904							
	17							

TRIBAL ENROLLMENT OF PARENTS

	Name of Father	Year	County	Name of Mother	Year	County
1	John Hendricks		Sans Bois	Anna Hendricks	Dead	Non Citz
2	Emry Farrill		Non Citz	No1		
3	" "		" "	No.1		
4						
5						
6						
7	For child of No1 see NB (Mar 3, 1905) card #524					
8	For child of No1 see NB (Apr 26, 1906) Card No 48					
9	No1 on 1896 Roll as Harriet Hendricks.					
10	See decision in Choctaw jacket #2820					
11	As to marriage of parents of No2					
12	see testimony in case of Theodosia Farrill					
13	Also see card o her father, John Hendricks, No 2820, as to additional information concerning degree of blood, etc.					
14	No.1 admitted by Dawes Commission in 1896:					
15	Choctaw case #429: no appeal: admitted Harriett Ferrill				Date of Application for Enrollment.	
16	No.3 Enrolled Feby 9th, 1901					
17	Nº2 Died Sept 18, 1900, Proof of death filed Nov. 4, 1902				June 19/99	

Choctaw By Blood Enrollment Cards 1898-1914

RESIDENCE:	Sans Bois	COUNTY.				CARD No.	
POST OFFICE:	Enterprise I.T.	**Choctaw Nation**		Choctaw Roll *(Not Including Freedmen)*		FIELD No.	2861

Dawes' Roll No.	NAME	Relationship to Person First Named	AGE	SEX	BLOOD	TRIBAL ENROLLMENT		
						Year	County	No.
I.W. 914	1 Egbert, Elizabeth 68		60	F	IW	1896	Sans Bois	14512
2								
3						1885	Sans Bois	136
4								
5								
6	ENROLLMENT							
7	OF NOS. 1 HEREON APPROVED BY THE SECRETARY							
8	OF INTERIOR AUG 3 1904							
9	Originally enrolled as Lizzie Frazier							
10								
11								
12								
13								
14								
15								
16								
17								

TRIBAL ENROLLMENT OF PARENTS

	Name of Father	Year	County	Name of Mother	Year	County
1	Baker					
2						
3						
4						
5	Choctaw Husband Kelly Frazier died about year 1872					
6						
7						
8						
9						
10						
11						
12						
13						
14						
15						
16				Date of Application for Enrollment.	6/19/99	
17						

161

RESIDENCE:	Sans Bois	COUNTY.					CARD NO.	
POST OFFICE:	Enterprise I.T.		**Choctaw Nation**			**Choctaw Roll** (Not Including Freedmen)	FIELD NO.	2862

Dawes' Roll No.	NAME		Relationship to Person	AGE	SEX	BLOOD	TRIBAL ENROLLMENT		
							Year	County	No.
8415	1 Taylor Leitha	33	First Named	30	F	3/8	1896	Sans Bois	11851
8416	2 " Tishy	5	Dau	17mo	F	3/16		" "	
8417	3 " Mamie	20	Step Dau	17	F	1/4	1896	" "	11852
8418	4 Foreman Fannie	13	Dau	10	F	3/16	1896	" "	3882
~~8419~~	5 ~~DIED PRIOR TO SEPTEMBER 25, 1902~~ ~~Mattie~~		~~"~~	~~8~~	~~F~~	~~3/16~~	~~1896~~	~~" "~~	~~3883~~
8420	6 " Josephine	10	"	7	F	3/16	1896	" "	3884
8421	7 " Ben G	9	Son	6	M	3/16	1896	" "	3885
I.W. 52	8 Taylor Green		Husband of No1	40	M	IW	1896	Sans Bois	15086
	9								
	10 No.5 died July 16, 1900: Enrollment								
	11 cancelled by Department July 8, 1904								
	12 ENROLLMENT OF NOS. 8 HEREON								
	13 APPROVED BY THE SECRETARY OF INTERIOR JUN 13 1903								
	14								
	15 ENROLLMENT OF NOS. 1,2,3,4,5,6,7 HEREON								
	16 APPROVED BY THE SECRETARY OF INTERIOR JAN 17 1903								
	17								

TRIBAL ENROLLMENT OF PARENTS

	Name of Father	Year	County	Name of Mother	Year	County
1	Kelly Frazier	Dead	Gaines	Elizabeth Frazier	1896	Non Citz
2	Green Taylor	1896	Non Citz	No 1		
3	" "	1896	" "	Sallie Taylor	Dead	Sans Bois
4	Ben Foreman	Dead	" "	No 1		
5	" "	" "	" "	~~No 1~~		
6	" "	" "	" "	No 1		
7	" "	" "	" "	No 1		
8	Newton Taylor	Dead	Non Citz	Pamelia Taylor	Dead	Non Citz
9	No1 On 1896 roll as Leathy Taylor. Certificate of marriage of					
10	Kelly Frazier and Elizabeth Baker dated June 14-1864 cere-					
11	mony performed by Willis F. Folsom Minister of the Gospel					
	exhibited and left in possession of family. Filed with Card No 2861					
12	No3 On 1896 roll as Mamie Taylor					
13	Husband enrolled on Choctaw Card D252					
	No.5 Died July 16, 1900: Proof of death filed Dec 30 1902					
14	No7 transferred from Choctaw card #D252 March 39, 1903					Date of Application for Enrollment.
15	See decision of March 13 1903 For child of No3 See NB (Apr 26 06) Card #494					
16	" " " " " NB (Mar 3-05) " "1272					6/19/99
17	P.O. Quinton 12/22/02					

Choctaw By Blood Enrollment Cards 1898-1914

RESIDENCE: Sans Bois COUNTY. **Choctaw Nation** Choctaw Roll CARD NO.
POST OFFICE: Sans Bois I.T. (Not Including Freedmen) FIELD NO. 2863

Dawes' Roll No.	NAME		Relationship to Person	AGE	SEX	BLOOD	TRIBAL ENROLLMENT		
							Year	County	No.
8422	1	Harris Emily	26	First Named	23	F	3/4	1896	Sans Bois	5080
8423	2	" Rose B	6	Dau	3	F	3/8	1896	" "	5081
8424	3	" Daniel	4	Son	1	M	3/8			
8425	4	DIED PRIOR TO SEPTEMBER 25, 1902 Benjamin		Son	2mo	M	3/8			
	5									
	6									
	7									
	8									
	9									
	10									
	11									
	12									
	13									
	14									
	15	ENROLLMENT OF NOS. 1,2,3,4, HEREON								
	16	APPROVED BY THE SECRETARY OF INTERIOR JAN 17 1903								
	17									

TRIBAL ENROLLMENT OF PARENTS

	Name of Father	Year	County	Name of Mother	Year	County
1	Jack Riddle	1896	Sans Bois	Ho-ke-ma	Dead	Sans Bois
2	Battiest Harris	1896	Non Citz	No 1		
3	" "	1896	" "	No 1		
4	" "	1896	On Choctaw Freedmen Card #773	No.1		
5						
6						
7						
8	No1 Wife of Battice Harris on Choctaw Freedmen Card #773					
9	No2 on 1896 roll as Rosa B. Harris					
10	No3 Affidavit of birth to be					
11	supplied: Recd July 27/99					
12	No4 Born April 16" 1902: Enrolled June 28" 1902					
13	No4 Proof of death filed Dec 30 1902 requested 12/17/03					
14	For child of No.1 see NB (Mar 3,1905) #519					
15						Date of Application for Enrollment.
16					For Nos 1 to 3	6/19/99
17	P.O. Kinta I.T. 2/2/05					

Choctaw By Blood Enrollment Cards 1898-1914

RESIDENCE:	Sans Bois	COUNTY.							
POST OFFICE:	Sans Bois I.T.	**Choctaw Nation**				**Choctaw Roll** (Not Including Freedmen)	CARD No. FIELD No.	**2864**	

Dawes' Roll No.	NAME		Relationship to Person First Named	AGE	SEX	BLOOD	TRIBAL ENROLLMENT		
							Year	County	No.
8426	1 James Harris	53	First Named	50	M	Full	1896	Sans Bois	6357
8427	2 " Cornelia	63	Wife	60	F	"	1896	" "	6358
8428	3 " Louisa	14	Dau	11	F	"	1896	" "	6359
8429	4 " Clarissa	12	"	9	F	"	1896	" "	6360
	5								
	6								
	7								
	8								
	9								
	10								
	11								
	12								
	13								
	14								
	15	ENROLLMENT OF NOS. 1, 2, 3, 4, HEREON APPROVED BY THE SECRETARY OF INTERIOR JAN 17 1903							
	16								
	17								

TRIBAL ENROLLMENT OF PARENTS

	Name of Father	Year	County	Name of Mother	Year	County
1	A-he-lat-am-be	Dead	Skullyville	Eliza	Dead	Sans Bois
2	A-chuk-mat-he-ket-a-be	Dead	"	Ta-lo-at-e-ma	"	Skullyville
3	No 1			No 2		
4	No 1			No 2		
5						
6						
7						
8	For child of No.3 see NB (Marc 3 1905) #1253					
9						
10						
11						
12						
13						
14						
15						Date of Application for Enrollment.
16						6/19/99
17						

Choctaw By Blood Enrollment Cards 1898-1914

RESIDENCE: Gaines COUNTY. **Choctaw Nation** **Choctaw Roll** CARD No.
POST OFFICE: Wilburton I.T. *(Not Including Freedmen)* FIELD No. 2865

Dawes' Roll No.	NAME	Relationship to Person First Named	AGE	SEX	BLOOD	TRIBAL ENROLLMENT		
						Year	County	No.
1	Sorrels Sarah	Named	39	F	1/8			
2	" Mollie	Dau	18	F	1/16			
3	" Martha	"	8	F	1/16			
4	" John	Son	5	M	1/16			
5	" Maud	Dau	2mo	F	1/16			
6								
7								
8								
9								
10								
11								
12								
13								
14								
15								
16								
17								

DISMISSED
MAY 24 1904

DENIED CITIZENSHIP BY THE CHOCTAW AND CHICKASAW CITIZENSHIP COURT

TRIBAL ENROLLMENT OF PARENTS

	Name of Father	Year	County	Name of Mother	Year	County
1	Henry Langford	Dead	Non Citz	Rachel Langford	1896	Gaines
2	Newton Sorrels	1896	" "	No 1		
3	" "	1896	" "	No 1		
4	" "	1896	" "	No 1		
5	" "	1896	" "	No 1		
6						
7	Nos1,2,3 and 4 Denied by Dawes Com in '96 Choc Cit Case #598					
8	Nos 1-2-3 and 4 Admitted by U.S. Court at So MᶜAlester Aug 24, 1897					
9	Case No. 94. As to residence and date of birth of Maud see her testimony.					
10	Judgement ag of U.S. Court admitting Nos 1,2,3 and 4 vacated and set aside by Decree of Choctaw Chickasaw Cit Court Decr 17 02					
11	Nos1,2,3 and 4 admitted by Choctaw-Chickasaw Citizenship Court Feb 1, 1904 Case #13					
12						
13						
14						
15						Date of Application for Enrollment.
16						6/19/99
17						

165

Choctaw By Blood Enrollment Cards 1898-1914

RESIDENCE: Skullyville   COUNTY. **Choctaw Nation**   **Choctaw Roll** CARD No.
POST OFFICE: Walls I.T.   *(Not Including Freedmen)*   FIELD NO. 2866

Dawes' Roll No.	NAME		Relationship to Person First Named	AGE	SEX	BLOOD	TRIBAL ENROLLMENT		
							Year	County	No.
8430	1 Hardaway Jesse H	52	First Named	49	M	1/8	1896	Skullyville	5186
I.W. 651	2 " Margaret	52	Wife	49	F	I.W.	1896	"	14600
8431	3 " John R	21	Son	18	M	1/16	1896	"	5187
8432	4 " Julia	19	Dau	16	F	1/16	1896	"	5188
8433	5 " Julius	19	Son	16	M	1/16	1896	"	5189
8434	6 " Edgar	13	"	10	M	1/16	1896	"	5190
	7								
	8								
	9								
	10								
	11	ENROLLMENT							
	12	OF NOS. 2 HEREON							
		APPROVED BY THE SECRETARY							
	13	OF INTERIOR MAR 26 1904							
	14								
	15	ENROLLMENT							
		OF NOS. 1,3,4,5,6 HEREON							
	16	APPROVED BY THE SECRETARY							
		OF INTERIOR JAN 17 1903							
	17								

TRIBAL ENROLLMENT OF PARENTS

	Name of Father	Year	County	Name of Mother	Year	County	
1	John Hardaway	Dead	Skullyville	Sarah Ann Hardaway	Dead	Non Citz	
2	Gore Pitts	"	Non Citz	Martha Pitts	"	"	"
3	No 1			No 2			
4	No 1			No 2			
5	No 1			No 2			
6	No 1			No 2			
7							
8			No1 On 1896 roll as Jesse Hardaway				
9			No2 Certificate of marriage filed with card of Minnie Hickman				
			wife of J.H. Hickman Card No 2846				
10			No3 On 1896 roll as Jno. R. Hardaway				
11			No1 As to marriage of father and mother, see testimony of				
12			Green McCurtain				
13			Nos 4 and 5 twins				
			For child of No.4 see NB (Mar 3, 1905) #493				
14							
15						Date of Application for Enrollment.	
16						6/19/99	
17							

Choctaw By Blood Enrollment Cards 1898-1914

Dawes' Roll No.	NAME	Relationship to Person First Named	AGE	SEX	BLOOD	TRIBAL ENROLLMENT		
						Year	County	No.

RESIDENCE: Gaines COUNTY. **Choctaw Nation** **Choctaw Roll** *(Not Including Freedmen)* CARD No. FIELD NO. 2867

POST OFFICE: Wilburton I.T.

Dawes' Roll No.	NAME	Relationship to Person First Named	AGE	SEX	BLOOD	Year	County	No.
8435	1 Wheeler, Louisa 21	First Named	18	F	1/4	1896	Gaines	7836
8436	2 Wheeler, Rhoda 1	Dau	2mo	F	1/8			
	3							
	4							
	5							
	6							
	7							
	8							
	9							
	10							
	11							
	12							
	13							
	14							
	15	ENROLLMENT OF NOS. 1 and 2 HEREON						
	16	APPROVED BY THE SECRETARY						
	17	OF INTERIOR JAN 17 1903						

TRIBAL ENROLLMENT OF PARENTS

Name of Father	Year	County	Name of Mother	Year	County
1 Benjamin Lewis	Dead	Non Citz	Mary Lewis	Dead	Tobucksy
2 Wᵐ P. Wheeler		non-citizen	No.1		
3					
4					
5					
6					
7 No.1 is now the wife of Wᵐ P Wheeler, a non-citizen white man: Feby 14, 1902.					
8					
9 No.1 On 1896 roll as Luisa Lewis					
10 No.2 born Dec. 25, 1901: Enrolled Feby 14, 1901.					
11 For child of No.1 see NB (March 2, 1905) #1286					
12					
13					
14					
15				#1	
16			Date of Application for Enrollment.	6/19/99	
17 Heavener I.T. 1/12/08					

RESIDENCE:	Sans Bois	COUNTY.	**Choctaw Nation**	**Choctaw Roll**	CARD No.	
POST OFFICE:	Penther I.T.			*(Not Including Freedmen)*	FIELD No.	2868

Dawes' Roll No.	NAME	Relationship to Person First Named	AGE	SEX	BLOOD	TRIBAL ENROLLMENT		
						Year	County	No.
DEAD 1	Franklin Tolena ⁶⁴	First Named	61	F	Full	P.R. 1893	Sans Bois	295
2								
3								
4								
5	No.__1___ HEREON DISMISSED UNDER							
6	ORDER OF THE COMMISSION TO THE FIVE CIVILIZED TRIBES OF MARCH 31, 1905.							
7								
8								
9								
10								
11								
12								
13								
14	ENROLLMENT OF NOS........................							
15	APPROVED BY THE SECRETARY HEREON OF INTERIOR.							
16								
17								

TRIBAL ENROLLMENT OF PARENTS

	Name of Father	Year	County	Name of Mother	Year	County
1		Dead			Dead	
2						
3						
4						
5						
6	On page 29 No 295, 1893 Pay Roll Sans Bois Co as					
7	Louvinia Franklin					
8	N⁰1 died about Jany 31, 1902, proof of death filed Jany 21, 1903					
9						
10						
11						
12						
13						
14					Date of Application for Enrollment.	
15						
16					6/19/99	
17						

Choctaw By Blood Enrollment Cards 1898-1914

| RESIDENCE: Sans Bois COUNTY, | POST OFFICE: Iron Bridge, I.T. |

Choctaw Nation

Choctaw Roll *(Not Including Freedmen)*   CARD NO. FIELD NO. **2869**

Dawes' Roll No.	NAME	Relationship to Person First Named	AGE	SEX	BLOOD	TRIBAL ENROLLMENT Year	County	No.
DEAD.	1 Loving, Milton		30	M	1/2	1896	Sans Bois	7688
8437	2 " Sampson ⁹	Son	6	M	3/4	1896	" "	7690
	3							
	4							
	5 No. 1 HEREON DISMISSED UNDER							
	6 ORDER OF THE COMMISSION TO THE FIVE							
	7 CIVILIZED TRIBES OF MARCH 31, 1905.							
	8							
	9							
	10							
	11							
	12							
	13							
	14							
	15 ENROLLMENT OF NOS. 2 HEREON							
	16 APPROVED BY THE SECRETARY							
	17 OF INTERIOR JAN 17 1903							

TRIBAL ENROLLMENT OF PARENTS

Name of Father	Year	County	Name of Mother	Year	County
1 Jackson Loving	Dead	San[sic] Bois	Lucinda Loving	Dead	Skullyville
2 No.1		" "	Silsy Loving	"	San
3					
4					
5					
6					
7 Nº 1 Died Aug 10, 1899, proof of death filed March 30, 1903					
8					
9					
10					
11					
12					
13					
14					
15				Date of Application for Enrollment.	
16					6/19/99
17					

169

Choctaw By Blood Enrollment Cards 1898-1914

Dawes' Roll No.	NAME		Relationship to Person First Named	AGE	SEX	BLOOD	TRIBAL ENROLLMENT		
							Year	County	No.
8438	1 Williams, Forrest	26	First Named	23	M.	Full	1896	Skullyville	12812
8439	2 " Jincy	41	Wife	38	F.	"	1896	"	12813
8440	3 " Leona	5	Dau.	1	F.	"			
8441	4 Thompson, Joanna	25	St. "	22	F.	"	1896	Skullyville	11926
8442	5 " Julia	20	St. "	17	F.	"	1896	"	11927
8443	6 Williams Freeman	1	Son	15mo	M	"			
	7								
	8								
	9								
	10								
	11								
	12								
	13								
	14								
	15								
	16								
	17								

ENROLLMENT
OF NOS. 1,2,3,4,5,6 HEREON
APPROVED BY THE SECRETARY
OF INTERIOR JAN 17 1903

TRIBAL ENROLLMENT OF PARENTS

	Name of Father	Year	County	Name of Mother	Year	County
1	Iyaktubbe	Dd.	Skullyville	Mary Jefferson	1896	Skullyville
2	Nicholas Jefferson	1896	San[sic] Bois	Elas Jefferson	Dd.	San[sic] Bois
3	No.1			No.2		
4	Isham Thomson	Dd.	San Bois	No.2		
5	" "	"	" "	No.2		
6	Nº1			Nº2		
7						
8						
9						
10	No 4 also on 1896 roll Sans Bois Co;					
11	Page 307, No 1182 as Johana Thompson					
12	No 5 also on 1896 roll, Sans Bois Co.,					
13	Page 307, No 11883					
14	Nº6 Born May 19, 1901: enrolled Aug 26, 1902					
15	For child of No.5 see NB (March 3, 1905) #1009					
16				No 2 on roll as Jensie Williams	Date of Application for Enrollment.	
17	No5 PO Lodi IT 4/12/05				6/19/99	

170

Choctaw By Blood Enrollment Cards 1898-1914

	RESIDENCE: Sugar Loaf	COUNTY.							CARD No.	
	POST OFFICE: Red Oak, I.T.	Choctaw Nation				Choctaw Roll (Not Including Freedmen)			FIELD No. 2871	

Dawes' Roll No.	NAME	Relationship to Person	AGE	SEX	BLOOD	TRIBAL ENROLLMENT		
						Year	County	No.
8444	1 Jefferson, Mary 53	First Named	50	F	Full	1896	Skullyville	6472
	2							
	3							
	4							
	5							
	6							
	7							
	8							
	9							
	10							
	11							
	12							
	13	ENROLLMENT OF NOS. 1 HEREON APPROVED BY THE SECRETARY OF INTERIOR JAN 17 1903						
	14							
	15							
	16							
	17							

TRIBAL ENROLLMENT OF PARENTS

	Name of Father	Year	County	Name of Mother	Year	County
1	Unknown			Elas Jefferson	Dd	Sans Bois
2						
3						
4						
5						
6						
7						
8						
9						
10						
11						
12						
13						
14						
15						
16				Date of Application for Enrollment.	6/19/99	
17						

Choctaw By Blood Enrollment Cards 1898-1914

RESIDENCE: Sugar Loaf	COUNTY.	Choctaw Nation	Choctaw Roll	CARD NO.
POST OFFICE: Fanshaw, I.T.			(Not Including Freedmen)	FIELD NO. 2872

Dawes' Roll No.	NAME		Relationship to Person	AGE	SEX	BLOOD	TRIBAL ENROLLMENT		
							Year	County	No.
8445	1 Tobley, Sam	31	First Named	28	M	Full	1896	Sans Bois	11834
	2								
	3								
	4								
	5								
	6								
	7								
	8								
	9								
	10								
	11								
	12								
	13								
	14								
	15	ENROLLMENT OF NOS. 1 HEREON							
	16	APPROVED BY THE SECRETARY OF INTERIOR JAN 17 1903							
	17								

TRIBAL ENROLLMENT OF PARENTS

Name of Father	Year	County	Name of Mother	Year	County
1 Willis Tobley	1896	Towson	Ellen Tobley		Atoka
2					
3					
4					
5					
6					
7					
8					
9					
10	On 1896 roll as Sam Tobly				
11	For child of No1 see NB (Apr 26 '06) Card No 1198				
12					
13					
14					Date of Application for Enrollment.
15					
16	P.O. Iron Bridge, I.T.			6/19/99	
17	12/16/03				

172

Choctaw By Blood Enrollment Cards 1898-1914

RESIDENCE: Skullyville   COUNTY.   **Choctaw Nation**   Choctaw Roll   CARD No.

POST OFFICE: Lodi, I.T.   *(Not Including Freedmen)*   FIELD NO.   2873

Dawes' Roll No.	NAME	Relationship to Person First Named	AGE	SEX	BLOOD	TRIBAL ENROLLMENT Year	County	No.
1	Bobo, Josephine	First Named	33	F	1/4			
2	" Ethel B	Dau	12	"	1/8			
3	" Mary E	"	10	"	1/8			
4	" Arrena	"	7	"	1/8			
5	" Estilla	"	5	"	1/8			
6	" William	Son	3	M	1/8			
7	" James P	"	6mo	"	1/8			
8	" Ola Odessa	Dau	7mo	F	1/8			
9								
10								
11	Judgement[sic] of U.S. Court CD admitting Nos 1 to 8 vacated							
12	and set aside by Decree of Choctaw Chickasaw Cit Court Decr 17 02							
13	Nos 1 to 8 denied by Choctaw-Chickasaw Citizenship Court Feb 1" 04 Case #13							
14								
15	ENROLLMENT OF NOS	HEREON						
16	APPROVED BY THE SECRETARY OF INTERIOR							
17								

TRIBAL ENROLLMENT OF PARENTS

	Name of Father	Year	County	Name of Mother	Year	County
1	James Biddie	Dead	Choctaw	Elizabeth Biddie	Dead	Non Citz
2	James P. Bobo	1896	Non Citz	No 1		
3	" " "	1896	" "	No 1		
4	" " "	1896	" "	No 1		
5	" " "	1896	" "	No 1		
6	" " "	1896	" "	No 1		
7	" " "	1896	" "	No 1		
8	" " "	1896	" "	No 1		
9						
10	Nos1 to 5 incl Denied by Dawes Com in '96 Choc Cit case #598					
11	Admitted by the U.S. Court, Central District, Aug 24/97 Case No 94					
12	No2 was admitted as Ethel P Bobo					
13	As to residence, see testimony of No1					
14						
15	No 6-7 Affidavits of birth to be supplied Recd 7/1/99				Date of Application for Enrollment.	
16	No8 Born March 14, 1901 and enrolled October 29, 1901					
17	Post office address is now Hallaman, I.T. Oct. 29, 1901			6/19/99		

Choctaw By Blood Enrollment Cards 1898-1914

Choctaw Nation

Choctaw Roll
(Not Including Freedmen)

POST OFFICE: Sans Bois, I.T.

CARD NO.

FIELD NO. 2874

Dawes' Roll No.	NAME	Relationship to Person	AGE	SEX	BLOOD	TRIBAL ENROLLMENT		
						Year	County	No.
8446	1 Meshemahtubbee, Semelian 69	First Named	66	F	Full	1893	Sugar Loaf	507
	2							
	3							
	4							
	5							
	6							
	7							
	8							
	9							
	10							
	11							
	12							
	13							
	14							
	15							
	16							
	17							

ENROLLMENT
OF NOS. 1 HEREON
APPROVED BY THE SECRETARY
OF INTERIOR JAN 17 1903

TRIBAL ENROLLMENT OF PARENTS

	Name of Father	Year	County	Name of Mother	Year	County
1	Ak-kos-to-nechi	Dead	in Mississippi	Ah-pe-la	Dead	Sugar Loaf
2						
3						
4						
5						
6						
7			On 1893 Pay Roll Sugar Loaf County, Page 54, No 507 as			
8			Semmie Meshemahtubbee			
9						
10						
11						
12						
13						
14						
15						
16				Date of Application for Enrollment.	6/19/99	
17						

Choctaw By Blood Enrollment Cards 1898-1914

RESIDENCE:	Gaines	COUNTY.							CARD NO.	
POST OFFICE:	Wilburton, I.T		**Choctaw Nation**				Choctaw Roll *(Not Including Freedmen)*		FIELD NO.	2875

Dawes' Roll No.	NAME		Relationship to Person	AGE	SEX	BLOOD	TRIBAL ENROLLMENT		
							Year	County	No.
I.W. 733	1 Hall, Robert H	(34)	First Named	30	M	I.W	1896	Tobucksy	14618
8447	2 " Susan	DIED PRIOR TO SEPTEMBER 25 1902	Wife	28	F	3/4	1896	Tobucksy	5383
8448	3 " George B	9	Son	6	M	3/8	1896	"	5384
8449	4 " Ada V	7	Dau	4	F	3/8	1896	"	5385
	5								
	6								
	7								
	8								
	9								
	10	ENROLLMENT							
	11	OF NOS. ~~ 1 ~~ HEREON							
	12	APPROVED BY THE SECRETARY OF INTERIOR MAY -7 1904							
	13								
	14								
	15	ENROLLMENT OF NOS. 2, 3, 4, HEREON							
	16	APPROVED BY THE SECRETARY							
	17	OF INTERIOR JAN 17 1903							

TRIBAL ENROLLMENT OF PARENTS

	Name of Father	Year	County	Name of Mother	Year	County
1	John Hall	Dead	Non Citz	Ann Hall	1896	Non Citz
2	George Riddle	1896	Gaines	Isabelle Riddle	Dead	Gaines
3	No1					
4	No1					
5						
6						
7	No1 See Decision of March 2 '04					
8	No1 was admitted by Dawes Commission as an					
9	Intermarried Citizen; as R. H. Hall, Case No 1371					
	No4 on 1896 roll as Ada B Hall					
10	No1 on 1896 " " Robt. H "					
11	No.2 died April 11, 1901: Proof of death filed Dec 23 1902					
12	No.2 died April 11, 1901: Enrollment cancelled by Department July 2, 1904					
13						
14						
15						
16	P.O.			Date of Application for Enrollment	6/19/99	
17	Ashland IT.					

12/17/02

Choctaw By Blood Enrollment Cards 1898-1914

RESIDENCE: Sans Bois   COUNTY. **Choctaw Nation**   **Choctaw Roll** (Not Including Freedmen)   CARD NO.

POST OFFICE: Sans Bois, I.T   FIELD NO. 2876

Dawes' Roll No.	NAME	Relationship to Person First Named	AGE	SEX	BLOOD	TRIBAL ENROLLMENT		
						Year	County	No.
8450	1 Byington, Joseph ²⁰		17	M	Full	1896	Sans Bois	586
8451	2 ~~DIED PRIOR TO SEPTEMBER 25 1902~~ Malinda	Wife	20	F	"	1896	~~Sugar Loaf~~	~~11200~~
	3							
	4							
	5							
	6							
	7							
	8							
	9							
	10							
	11							
	12							
	13							
	14							
	15	ENROLLMENT OF NOS. 1 and 2 HEREON APPROVED BY THE SECRETARY OF INTERIOR JAN 17 1903						
	16							
	17							

TRIBAL ENROLLMENT OF PARENTS

	Name of Father	Year	County	Name of Mother	Year	County
1	Philip Byington	1896	Sans Bois	Sealy Byington	1896	Sans Bois
2	~~Noel Sage~~	~~Dead~~	~~Sugar Loaf~~	~~Wincy Sage~~	~~1896~~	" "
3						
4						
5						
6						
7		No2 on 1896 roll as Malinda Sage				
8						
9						
10						
11						
12						
13						
14					Date of Application for Enrollment.	
15						
16					6/19/99	
17						

Choctaw By Blood Enrollment Cards 1898-1914

RESIDENCE: Sugar Loaf   COUNTY. **Choctaw Nation**   **Choctaw Roll**   CARD No.
POST OFFICE: Summerfield, I.T.   *(Not Including Freedmen)*   FIELD No.   2877

Dawes' Roll No.	NAME	Relationship to Person First Named	AGE	SEX	BLOOD	TRIBAL ENROLLMENT		
						Year	County	No.
8452	1 Tolbert, Washington 33	First Named	30	M	Full	1896	Sugar Loaf	11971
8453	2 Elizabeth DIED PRIOR TO SEPTEMBER 25, 1902	Wife	20	F	"	1896	" "	57
	3							
	4							
	5							
	6							
	7							
	8							
	9							
	10							
	11							
	12							
	13							
	14							
	15	ENROLLMENT OF NOS. 1 and 2 HEREON APPROVED BY THE SECRETARY OF INTERIOR JAN 17 1903						
	16							
	17							

TRIBAL ENROLLMENT OF PARENTS

	Name of Father	Year	County	Name of Mother	Year	County
1	John Tolbert	Dead	Sugar Loaf	Nellie Tolbert	Dead	Sugar Loaf
2	John Adams	"	" "	Seal Adams	"	" "
3						
4						
5						
6	No2 on 1896 roll as Elizabeth Adams					
7	No2 died Dec 1900. Proof of death filed Dec 30 1902					
8	No2 died Dec 1900. Enrollment cancelled by Department Sept 16, 1904					
9						
10						
11						
12						
13						
14						
15						
16			Date of Application for Enrollment.	6/19/99		
17						

177

Choctaw By Blood Enrollment Cards 1898-1914

RESIDENCE:	Sans Bois	COUNTY.	**Choctaw Nation**	**Choctaw Roll**	CARD NO.	
POST OFFICE:	Panther, I.T			*(Not Including Freedmen)*	FIELD NO.	2878

Dawes' Roll No.	NAME	Relationship to Person First Named	AGE	SEX	BLOOD	TRIBAL ENROLLMENT Year	TRIBAL ENROLLMENT County	TRIBAL ENROLLMENT No.
DEAD.	₁ Brandy, James		50	M	Full	1896	Sans Bois	649
8454	₂ " Betsy ⁶⁵	Wife	62	F	"	1896	" "	650
	₃							
	₄							
	₅							
	₆ No. 1 HEREON DISMISSED UNDER							
	₇ ORDER OF THE COMMISSION TO THE FIVE CIVILIZED TRIBES OF MARCH 31, 1905.							
	₈							
	₉							
	10							
	11							
	12							
	13							
	14							
	15 ENROLLMENT OF NOS. 2 HEREON							
	16 APPROVED BY THE SECRETARY OF INTERIOR JAN 17 1903							
	17							

TRIBAL ENROLLMENT OF PARENTS

Name of Father	Year	County	Name of Mother	Year	County
₁ Jacob Brandy	Dead	Sans Bois	E-che-ka-huna	Dead	Sans Bois
₂ To-ka-halle	"	Red River	Ho-ba-chee	"	in Mississippi
₃					
₄					
₅					
₆					
₇ No1 died January 17, 1902. Affidavits of No.2 filed					
₈ Dec 26, 1902; further evidence requested			12/2/02		
₉					
10					
11					
12					
13					
14					
15					
16			DATE OF APPLICATION FOR ENROLLMENT.	6/19/99	
17 PO McCurtain, I.T					

12/22/03

178

Choctaw By Blood Enrollment Cards 1898-1914

RESIDENCE: Sugar Loaf   COUNTY.
POST OFFICE: Bengal, I.T

Choctaw Nation

Choctaw Roll
(Not Including Freedmen)

CARD No.
FIELD No. 2879

Dawes' Roll No.	NAME	Relationship to Person First Named	AGE	SEX	BLOOD	TRIBAL ENROLLMENT Year	County	No.
8455 ₁	Merryman, David C ⁴⁹	First Named	46	M	1/8	1896	Sugar Loaf	8517
I.W.915 ₂	" Cordelia E ⁴⁵	Wife	38	F	IW	1896	" "	14806
8456 ₃	" Abraham ¹⁸	Son	15	M	1/16	1896	" "	8519
8457 ₄	" Mary J. F ¹⁶	Dau	13	F	1/16	1896	" "	8520
8458 ₅	" William H ¹⁴	Son	11	M	1/16	1896	" "	8521
8459 ₆	" Leo E ¹¹	Dau	8	F	1/16	1896	" "	8522
I.W.1314 ₇	" Ora ¹⁶	Wife of No.3	16	F	I.W.			
₈								
₉								
₁₀	ENROLLMENT OF NOS. 2 HEREON APPROVED BY THE SECRETARY OF INTERIOR AUG 3 1904							
₁₁								
₁₂								
₁₃								
₁₄	ENROLLMENT OF NOS. 1,3,4,5,6 HEREON APPROVED BY THE SECRETARY OF INTERIOR JAN 17 1903					ENROLLMENT OF NOS. 7 HEREON APPROVED BY THE SECRETARY OF INTERIOR MAR 14 1905		
₁₅								
₁₆								
₁₇								

TRIBAL ENROLLMENT OF PARENTS

	Name of Father	Year	County	Name of Mother	Year	County
₁	W.P. Merryman	Dead	Non Citz	Annie Merryman	Dead	Skullyville
₂	John W. Blair	"	" "	Mary Revard	1896	Non Citz
₃	No1			No2		
₄	No1			No2		
₅	No1			No2		
₆	No1			No2		
₇	John Graham		non citizen	Orminda Graham		non citizen
₈	Record as to enrollment of No 7 forwarded Department Mar 14, 1906					
₉	No2 on 1896 roll as Cordelia Merryman. Record returned. See opinion of Assistant Attorney					
₁₀	No4 " 1896 " " Mary " al of March 15, 1906 in case of Omer R Nicholson No5 " 1896 " " Wᵐ H. "					
₁₁	Nº3 is now the husband of Ora Merryman on Choctaw Card #D807, Sept 24, 1902					
₁₂	On Aug 10, 1902 No.7 was married to No.3					
₁₃	No.7 originally listed for enrollment on Choctaw card D-807 Sept 24, 1902: transferred to this card Feb. 1, 1905. See decision of Jan. 16, 1905.					
₁₄						#1 to 6
₁₅	For child of Nos 3&7 see NB (Mar 3-05) Card #137				Date of Application for Enrollment.	
₁₆	" " " No 4 " " " " " #589				6/19/99	
₁₇						

RESIDENCE: Sugar Loaf	COUNTY.	**Choctaw Nation**	Choctaw Roll	CARD NO.
POST OFFICE: Bengal, I.T.			(Not Including Freedmen)	FIELD NO. 2880

Dawes' Roll No.	NAME	Relationship to Person First Named	AGE	SEX	BLOOD	TRIBAL ENROLLMENT		
						Year	County	No.
8460	1 Merryman, Walter G ²⁶	First Named	23	M	1/16	1896	Sugar Loaf	8523
DEAD.	2 " Lula DEAD	Wife	21	F	I.W	1896	" "	14807
8461	3 " John D ⁷	Son	4	M	1/32	1896	" "	8524
8462	4 " Zado C ⁵	Dau	1½	F	1/32			
8563	5 " Izora Lula ³	Dau	4mo	F	1/32			
8464	6 " Gabe ²	Son	3mo	M	1/32			
I.W 824	7 " Mary ²⁹	Wife	29	F	I.W.			
	8 No. 2 HEREON DISMISSED UNDER							
	9 ORDER OF THE COMMISSION TO THE FIVE CIVILIZED TRIBES OF MARCH 31, 1905.							
	10 No.1 is now married to Mrs Mary Lewis a							
	11 non-citizen January 25,1900. Evidence of							
	12 marriage filed APR 21 1901							
	13 ✓ No.6 Enrolled April 24, 1901 For child of No7 see NB 980 - (Act Apr 26-06)					ENROLLMENT		
	14 PO Leflore IT 3/30/05					OF NOS. 7 HEREON		
	15 No.5 Enrolled May 24, 1900					APPROVED BY THE SECRETARY		
	16 ENROLLMENT OF NOS. 1,3,4,5,6 HEREON					OF INTERIOR MAY 21 1904		
	17 APPROVED BY THE SECRETARY OF INTERIOR JAN 17 1903							

TRIBAL ENROLLMENT OF PARENTS

	Name of Father	Year	County	Name of Mother	Year	County
1	David C Merryman	1896	Sugar Loaf	Cordelia Merryman	1896	white woman
2	Joe Poteet	1896	Non-Citz	Tishie Poteet	1896	Non-Citz
3	No1			No2		
4	No1			No2		
5	No.1			No.2		
6	No.1			Mary Merryman		white woman
7	John Willis		noncitizen	Ruth Willis		noncitizen
8	✓No3 on 1896 roll as Jno D Merryman					
9						
10	✓As to marriage of parents of No1 see Card of David C Merryman No 2879					
11						
12	✓No4 Affidavit of birth to be supplied: Recd 7/1/99					
13	No7 transferred from Choctaw card D947 April 15, 1904. See decision of March 15, 1904					
14	See affidavit attached to birth affidavit of Izora Lula Merryman for evidence of death of No.2 Feby 1st, 1900					
15	Nº2 Died Jan 18,1900. Proof of death filed Nov 14, 1901				Date of Application for Enrollment.	
16	Wife of Nº1 is Mary Merryman, Choctaw card #D947				6/19/99	
17	For child of Nos 1&7 see NB (Mar 3 '05) Card No. 186					

Choctaw By Blood Enrollment Cards 1898-1914

RESIDENCE: Sugar Loaf   COUNTY.
POST OFFICE: Wister, I.T

Choctaw Nation

Choctaw Roll (Not Including Freedmen)

CARD No.
FIELD No. 2881

Dawes' Roll No.	NAME	Relationship to Person First Named	AGE	SEX	BLOOD	TRIBAL ENROLLMENT Year	County	No.
8465	1 Lee, Rizzie — DIED PRIOR TO SEPTEMBER 25, 1902		32	F	Full	1896	Sugar Loaf	7815
8466	2 Jefferson, Mary 15	Dau	12	"	"	1896	" "	6563
8467	3 " Mollie 13	"	10	"	"	1896	" "	6564
	4							
	5							
	6							
	7							
	8							
	9							
	10							
	11							
	12							
	13							
	14							
	15	ENROLLMENT OF NOS. 1, 2, 3 HEREON APPROVED BY THE SECRETARY OF INTERIOR JAN 17 1903						
	16							
	17							

TRIBAL ENROLLMENT OF PARENTS

	Name of Father	Year	County	Name of Mother	Year	County
1	Forbis Williams	Dead	Sugar Loaf	Melcanna Williams	1896	Sugar Loaf
2	Watson Jefferson	"	" "	No1		
3	" "	"	" "	No1		
4						
5						
6						
7	No1 died March, 1902; proof of death filed Dec 16 1902					
8	No.1 died March, 1902; Enrollment cancelled by Department July 8, 1904					
9						
10						
11						
12						
13						
14						Date of Application for Enrollment.
15						
16						6/19/99
17						

Choctaw By Blood Enrollment Cards 1898-1914

RESIDENCE:	Sans Bois	COUNTY.	**Choctaw Nation**	**Choctaw Roll**	CARD No.	
POST OFFICE:	Panther, I.T.			*(Not Including Freedmen)*	FIELD No.	2882

Dawes' Roll No.	NAME		Relationship to Person First Named	AGE	SEX	BLOOD	TRIBAL ENROLLMENT		
							Year	County	No.
468	1 Kanehta, Morris	58	First Named	55	M	Full	1896	Sans Bois	7416
469	2 " David	18	Son	15	"	"	1896	" "	7417
470	3 " Annette	13	Dau	10	F	"	1896	" "	7418
471	4 DIED PRIOR TO SEPTEMBER 25, 1902 Joseph		Son	8	M	"	1896	" "	7419
	5								
	6								
	7								
	8								
	9								
	10								
	11								
	12								
	13								
	14								
	15	ENROLLMENT OF NOS. 1,2,3,4 HEREON APPROVED BY THE SECRETARY							
	16	OF INTERIOR JAN 17 1903							
	17								

TRIBAL ENROLLMENT OF PARENTS

	Name of Father	Year	County	Name of Mother	Year	County	
1	Ka-neh-ta	Dead	Sans Bois		Dead	Sans Bois	
2	No1			Lola Kanehta	"	" " "	
3	No1			Rhoda Kanehta	"	" " "	
4	No1			" "	"	" " "	
5							
6							
7	No2 on 1896 roll as Dave Kanehta						
8	No3 " 1896 " " Arnetta "						
9	No4 Died April 6" 1901; Proof of death filed Dec 22 1902						
10	No4 died April 6, 1901. Enrollment cancelled by Department July 8, 1904						
	For child of No3 see NB (March 3, 1905) #924						
11							
12							
13							
14				Date of Application for Enrollment.			
15							
16				6/19/99			
17	PO Sans Bois I T						

12/23/03

Choctaw By Blood Enrollment Cards 1898-1914

RESIDENCE:	Sans Bois	COUNTY.							
POST OFFICE:	Stigler, I.T.								

Choctaw Nation

Choctaw Roll (Not Including Freedmen)

CARD No. FIELD NO. 2883

Dawes' Roll No.	NAME	Relationship to Person First Named	AGE	SEX	BLOOD	TRIBAL ENROLLMENT		
						Year	County	No.
8472	1 Wade, Sampson 29	First Named	26	M	Full	1896	Sans Bois	12662
8473	2 " Phoebe 29	Wife	26	F	"	1896	" "	12663
8474	3 Pearson, Joseph 16	S.Son	13	M	1/2	1896	" "	10086
8475	4 Wilson, Allington 12	Ward	9	"	Full	1896	" "	12710
	5							
	6							
	7							
	8							
	9							
	10							
	11							
	12							
	13							
	14							
	15							
	16							
	17							

ENROLLMENT
OF NOS. 1, 2, 3, 4 HEREON
APPROVED BY THE SECRETARY
OF INTERIOR JAN 17 1903

TRIBAL ENROLLMENT OF PARENTS

	Name of Father	Year	County	Name of Mother	Year	County
1	Connickey Wade	Dead	Sans Bois	Sarah Boyd	Dead	Sans Bois
2	Ah-hubbee	"	" "	Mollie	"	Skullyville
3	Jonas Pearson	"	Chickasaw	No2		
4	Cornelius Wilson	"	Skullyville	Cillen Wilson	Dead	Sans Bois
5						
6						
7						
8						
9						
10						
11						
12						
13						
14						
15					Date of Application for Enrollment.	
16					6/19/99	
17						

RESIDENCE:	Sans Bois	COUNTY.	**Choctaw Nation**	**Choctaw Roll**	CARD No.	
POST OFFICE:	Red Oak, I.T.			*(Not Including Freedmen)*	FIELD NO.	2884

Dawes' Roll No.	NAME		Relationship to Person First Named	AGE	SEX	BLOOD	TRIBAL ENROLLMENT		
							Year	County	No.
8476	1 Jefferson, Alfred	33	Named	30	M	1/2	1896	Sans Bois	6398
8477	2 DIED PRIOR TO SEPTEMBER 25 1902 Siney		Wife	29	F	Full	1896	" "	6399
8478	3 " Benjamin	4	Son	1	M	3/4			
8479	4 Hischa, Houston	15	S.Son	12	"	1/2	1896	Sans Bois	5159
8480	5 " Lillie	10	S.Dau	7	F	1/2	1896	" "	5138
	6								
	7								
	8								
	9								
	10								
	11								
	12								
	13								
	14								
	15 ENROLLMENT OF NOS. 1,2,3,4,5 HEREON								
	16 APPROVED BY THE SECRETARY OF INTERIOR JAN 17 1903								
	17								

TRIBAL ENROLLMENT OF PARENTS

	Name of Father	Year	County	Name of Mother	Year	County
1	Nicholas Jefferson	1896	Sans Bois	Elis Jefferson	Dead	Sans Bois
2	Jonas Thompson	1896	" "	Artimissie Collins	1896	Sugar Loaf
3	No1			No2		
4	Davis Hischa	Dead	Chickasaw	No2		
5	" "	"	" "	No2		
6						
7						
8	No4 on 1896 roll as Houston Hecha					
9	No5 " 1896 " " Lily Hacha					
10	No2 died February – 1900; proof of death filed Dec 20 1902					
11	No2 died Feb – 1920; Enrollment cancelled by Department July 3, 1904					
12						
13						
14						
15				Date of Application for Enrollment.		
16				6/19/99		
17						

Choctaw By Blood Enrollment Cards 1898-1914

RESIDENCE: Skullyville   COUNTY. **Choctaw Nation**   **Choctaw Roll** *(Not Including Freedmen)*   CARD No.

POST OFFICE: Lodi, I.T.   FIELD NO. 2885

Dawes' Roll No.	NAME		Relationship to Person First Named	AGE	SEX	BLOOD	TRIBAL ENROLLMENT		
							Year	County	No.
8481	1 Johnson, Arbin	31	First Named	29	M	Full	1896	Skullyville	6478
8482	2 " Lula	26	Wife	23	F	"	1896	"	6479
8484	3 " Lizzie	6	Dau	3	"	"	1896	"	6480
8484	4 " Susan	4	"	1	"	"			
13363	5 " Leolena	1	"	1½	"	"			
	6								
	7								
	8								
	9								
	10								
	11								
	12								
	13								
	14								
	15								
	16								
	17								

ENROLLMENT OF NOS. 1,2,3,4 HEREON APPROVED BY THE SECRETARY OF INTERIOR JAN 17 1903

ENROLLMENT OF NOS. ~ 5 ~ HEREON APPROVED BY THE SECRETARY OF INTERIOR MAR 19 1903

TRIBAL ENROLLMENT OF PARENTS

	Name of Father	Year	County	Name of Mother	Year	County
1	Wᵐ Johnson	Dead	Sans Bois	Susan Johnson	Dead	Sans Bois
2	Willie Gage	"	Skullyville	Betsy Gage	"	Skullyville
3	No1			No2		
4	No1			No2		
5	No. 1			No. 2		
6						
7			No1 on 1896 roll as Albin Johnson			
8			No2 " 1896 " " Lulu "			
9			No3 " 1896 " " Lizer "			
10			No.5 born May 5, 1901. Application made Dec 24, 1902. Proof of birth filed Jan 30, 1903. For child of Nos 1&2 see NB (Mar 3' 05) #656			
11						
12						
13						
14						
15				#1 to 4		
16				Date of Application for Enrollment.	6/19/99	
17	P.O. McCurtain I.T.					

Choctaw By Blood Enrollment Cards 1898-1914

RESIDENCE:	Gaines	COUNTY.						
POST OFFICE:	Wilburton, I.T.						CARD NO. FIELD NO. 2886	

Choctaw Nation **Choctaw Roll** (Not Including Freedmen)

Dawes' Roll No.	NAME	Relationship to Person First Named	AGE	SEX	BLOOD	TRIBAL ENROLLMENT		
						Year	County	No.
1	Kinsey, Francis		29	M	1/8			
2	" Emily	Wife	19	F	I.W.			
3	" Gertrude	Dau	9mo	F	1/16			
4								
5								
6								
7								
8								
9								
10	Nº3 DISMISSED							
11	MAY 24 1904							
12								
13								
14								
15	DENIED CITIZENSHIP BY THE CHOCTAW AND							
16	CHICKASAW CITIZENSHIP COURT							
17								

TRIBAL ENROLLMENT OF PARENTS

	Name of Father	Year	County	Name of Mother	Year	County
1	Andrew J Kinsey	Dead	Non Citz	Sarah A. Kinsey		Skullyville
2	Andrew Freeney	"	" "	Mary Freeney	Dead	Non Citz
3	No.1			No.2		
4						
5						
6	Nos 1&2 Denied by Dawes Com in '96 Choc Cit Case #598					
7	Admitted by U.S. Court, Central District, August 24, 1897, Case No 94					
8	As to residence, see his testimony No.3 Enrolled April 18, 1901					
9	Judgement(s) of U.S. Court C.D. admitting No vacated and set aside by Decree of Choctaw Chickasaw Citizenship Court Dec' 17'02					
10	No1&2 Denied by Choctaw-Chickasaw Citizenship Court Feb 1 '04 Case #13					
11	For children of Nos 1&2 see NB 984 (Act Apr 26-06)					
12						
13						
14						
15				Date of Application for Enrollment.		
16				June 19/99		
17				No2 enrolled Aug. 3/99		

186

Choctaw By Blood Enrollment Cards 1898-1914

RESIDENCE:	Sugar Loaf	COUNTY.	**Choctaw Nation**		**Choctaw Roll**	CARD NO.
POST OFFICE:	Fanshaw I.T.				*(Not Including Freedmen)*	FIELD NO. 2887

Dawes' Roll No.	NAME		Relationship to Person First Named	AGE	SEX	BLOOD	TRIBAL ENROLLMENT		
							Year	County	No.
8485	1 McCurtain Thomas	21	First Named	18	M	1/2	1896	Sugar Loaf	9119
8486	2 " Minnie	17	Sister	14	F	1/2	1896	" "	9120
	3								
	4								
	5								
	6								
	7								
	8								
	9								
	10								
	11								
	12								
	13								
	14								
	15	ENROLLMENT OF NOS. 1, 2, HEREON APPROVED BY THE SECRETARY							
	16	OF INTERIOR JAN 17 1903							
	17								

TRIBAL ENROLLMENT OF PARENTS

	Name of Father	Year	County	Name of Mother	Year	County
1	Joshua McCurtain	1896	Sugar Loaf	Jane McCurtain	Dead	Sugar Loaf
2	" "	1896	" "	" "	"	" "
3						
4						
5						
6	No2 On 1896 roll as Miney McCurtain					
7	Father on Chickasaw Card No 1454					
8						
9						
10	is 18 years of age N°2 ∧was married to John Williams in July 1902. See testimony					
11	of May 21, 1903.					
12						
13	For child of No2 see NB (Mar 3-05) Card #1413					
14	" " " " " " (Apr 26-06) " #473					Date of Application for Enrollment.
15						
16	No2 P.O. Nashoba IT 4/26/05					6/19/99
17	P.O. Hughes Ind. Ter.					

PO LeFlora[sic] IT 1/28/05

Choctaw By Blood Enrollment Cards 1898-1914

Choctaw Nation (Not Including Freedmen)

Choctaw Roll

CARD No.
FIELD No. 2888

Dawes' Roll No.	NAME	Relationship to Person First Named	AGE	SEX	BLOOD	TRIBAL ENROLLMENT Year	County	No.
8487	1 BAKER HOUSTON		47	M	Full	1896	Skullyville	730
8488	2 " ELIZABETH	Wife	45	F	"	1896	"	731
8489	3 " ELUM	Son	21	M	"	1896	"	732
8490	4 " LOUIS	"	16	M	"	1896	"	733
8491	5 " ROBERT	"	10	M	"	1896	"	734
8492	6 " MILAN	Dau.	8	F	"	1896	"	735
8493	7 " EMELINE	Dau.	5	F	"	1896	"	736
	8							
	9							
	10							
	11							
	12							
	13							
	14							
	15							
	16							
	17							

ENROLLMENT
OF NOS. 1,2,3,4,5,6,7 HEREON
APPROVED BY THE SECRETARY
OF INTERIOR Jan. 17, 1903

TRIBAL ENROLLMENT OF PARENTS

Name of Father	Year	County	Name of Mother	Year	County
1 Lewis Baker	dead	Sugar Loaf	Ma-ka-ho-te-ma	dead	Skullyville
2 Hom-ma	"	Skullyville	Susan Johnson	"	Sans Bois
3	No. 1		No.2		
4	No. 1		No.2		
5	No. 1		No.2		
6	No. 1		No.2		
7	No. 1		No.2		
8					
9	No. 6 On 1896 roll as Millin Baker				
10	No. 3 is now the husband of Sillin Slaughter on Choctaw Card #2991, May 8,				
11	1901 and Evidence of marriage filed in Choctaw Case #2991				
12	Date of application for enrollment 6/19/99			Date of Application for Enrollment.	
13					
14				6/19/99	
15					
16					
17					

188

Choctaw By Blood Enrollment Cards 1898-1914

RESIDENCE: Sugar Loaf COUNTY. **Choctaw Nation** **Choctaw Roll** CARD No.
POST OFFICE: Red Oak I.T. *(Not Including Freedmen)* FIELD No. 2889

Dawes' Roll No.		NAME		Relationship to Person	AGE	SEX	BLOOD	TRIBAL ENROLLMENT		
								Year	County	No.
8494	1	Green Morris	53	First Named	50	M	1/4	1896	Sugar Loaf	4672
8495	2	" Daniel	13	Son	11	M	1/4	1896	" "	4673
8496	3	" Sophie	12	Dau	9	F	1/4	1896	" "	4674
	4									
	5									
	6									
	7									
	8									
	9									
	10									
	11									
	12									
	13									
	14									
	15	ENROLLMENT OF NOS. 1, 2, 3 HEREON								
	16	APPROVED BY THE SECRETARY								
	17	OF INTERIOR JAN 17 1903								

TRIBAL ENROLLMENT OF PARENTS

	Name of Father	Year	County	Name of Mother	Year	County
1	Lewis Green	Dead	Non Citz	Nellie Green	Dead	Gaines
2	No 1			Edmona Green	"	Sugar Loaf
3	No 1			" "	"	" " "
4						
5						
6						
7						
8	Nº1 is husband of Ida Green on Chickasaw card #1400 and					
9	father of Robert Green thereon.					
10						
11						
12						
13						
14						
15						
16				Date of Application for Enrollment	6/19/99	
17						

Choctaw By Blood Enrollment Cards 1898-1914

RESIDENCE:	Sans Bois	COUNTY.							CARD NO.	
POST OFFICE:	Red Oak I.T.	**Choctaw Nation**			**Choctaw Roll** *(Not Including Freedmen)*				FIELD NO.	2890

Dawes' Roll No.	NAME		Relationship to Person	AGE	SEX	BLOOD	TRIBAL ENROLLMENT		
							Year	County	No.
8497	1 Luke Emma	63	First Named	60	F	Full	1896	Sans Bois	7695
	2								
	3								
	4								
	5								
	6								
	7								
	8								
	9								
	10								
	11								
	12								
	13								
	14								
	15								
	16								
	17								

ENROLLMENT
OF NOS. 1 HEREON
APPROVED BY THE SECRETARY
OF INTERIOR JAN 17 1903

TRIBAL ENROLLMENT OF PARENTS

	Name of Father	Year	County	Name of Mother	Year	County
1	To-kah-li	Dead	Sugar Loaf	Au-i-chi	Dead	Sugar Loaf
2						
3						
4						
5						
6						
7						
8			Husband on Chickasaw card No 1456			
9						
10						
11						
12						
13						
14						
15						
16				Date of Application for Enrollment.	6/19/99	
17						

190

Choctaw By Blood Enrollment Cards 1898-1914

RESIDENCE: Sugar Loaf   COUNTY.   **Choctaw Nation**   **Choctaw Roll**   CARD NO.
POST OFFICE: Red Oak I.T.   *(Not Including Freedmen)*   FIELD NO. 2891

Dawes' Roll No.	NAME	Relationship to Person First Named	AGE	SEX	BLOOD	TRIBAL ENROLLMENT Year	County	No.
8498	1 Jefferson Thomas 33	First Named	30	M	Full	1896	Sans Bois	6401
8499	2 " Bicey 27	Wife	24	F	"	1896	" "	6402
8500	3 " Lena 12	Dau	9	F	"	1896	" "	6403
8501	4 " Ada 9	"	6	F	"	1896	" "	6404
8502	5 " Benjamin 6	Son	3	M	"	1896	" "	6405
~~8503~~	~~6 Calvin~~ DIED PRIOR TO SEPTEMBER 25, 1902	~~Son~~	~~5mo~~	~~M~~	"		" "	
8504	7 " Allen 1	Son	9mo	M	"			
	8							
	9							
	10							
	11							
	12							
	13							
	14							
	15	ENROLLMENT OF NOS. 1,2,3,4,5,6,7 HEREON						
	16	APPROVED BY THE SECRETARY OF INTERIOR JAN 17 1903						
	17							

TRIBAL ENROLLMENT OF PARENTS

	Name of Father	Year	County	Name of Mother	Year	County
1	Nicholas Jefferson	1896	Sans Bois	Arian Jefferson	Dead	Sans Bois
2	Charleson Wesley	1896	Sugar Loaf	Rhoda Wesley	"	Gaines
3	No 1			No 2		
4	No 1			No 2		
5	No 1			No 2		
6	~~No 1~~			~~No 2~~		
7	N°1			N°2		
8						
9	No3 On 1896 roll as Lina Jefferson					
10	No5 " 1896 " " Dixon Jefferson					
11	N°7 Born Aug. 27, 1901: enrolled May 13, 1902 ~~No6 died July 1899; proof of death filed Dec 20 1902~~					
12	No6 died July - 1899: Enrollment cancelled by Department July 8,					
13	For child of Nos 1&2 see N.B (Apr 26, 1906) Card No 126					
14	" " " " " " " " (March 3 1905) " 72					#1 to 6 inc
15						Date of Application for Enrollment.
16						6/19/99
17						

Choctaw By Blood Enrollment Cards 1898-1914

RESIDENCE: Skullyville	COUNTY.							
POST OFFICE: Lodi I.T.	Choctaw Nation			Choctaw Roll (Not Including Freedmen)		CARD NO.		
						FIELD NO. 2892		

Dawes' Roll No.	NAME	Relationship to Person First Named	AGE	SEX	BLOOD	TRIBAL ENROLLMENT		
						Year	County	No.
8505 ₁	Adams James ⁵⁹	First Named	56	M	Full	1896	Skullyville	25
8506 ₂	Eliza ⁴⁹ DIED PRIOR TO SEPTEMBER 25, 1902	Wife	39	F	"	1896	"	26
8507 ₃	" Reuben ¹⁸	Son	15	M	"	1896	"	28
8508 ₄	" Louina ¹⁷	Dau	14	F	"	1896	"	29
8509 ₅	" Selin ¹⁵	"	12	F	"	1896	"	30
8510 ₆	" Jonas ¹¹	Son	8	M	"	1896	"	31
8511 ₇	" Rhoda ⁷	Dau	4	F	"	1896	"	32

ENROLLMENT
OF NOS. 1,2,3,4,5,6,7 HEREON
APPROVED BY THE SECRETARY
OF INTERIOR JAN 17 1903

TRIBAL ENROLLMENT OF PARENTS						
Name of Father	Year	County	Name of Mother	Year	County	
₁ John Williams	Dead	Skullyville	Chi-ma-ho-ke	Dead	Skullyville	
₂ John Tallapoch	"	"	Mary Tallapoch	"	"	
₃	No 1		No 2			
₄	No 1		No 2			
₅	No 1		No 2			
₆	No 1		No 2			
₇	No 1		No 2			

No2 Died in October 1900: Proof of death filed Dec[r] 23" 1902
No4 On 1896 roll as Lawrence Adams
No5 " 1896 " " Sebonn Adams
No6 " 1896 " " Lony "
For child of No.3 see NB (March 3, 1905) #472
" " " No.4 " " " " " #1180
N[o]7 said to be dead. Evidence of death to be supplied
12/18/02

Date of Application for Enrollment. 6/19/99

₁₇ PO LeFlore 4/21/05

192

Choctaw By Blood Enrollment Cards 1898-1914

RESIDENCE: Skullyville   COUNTY. **Choctaw Nation**   **Choctaw Roll** (Not Including Freedmen)   CARD NO.

POST OFFICE: Lodi I.T.   FIELD NO. 2893

Dawes' Roll No.	NAME		Relationship to Person	AGE	SEX	BLOOD	TRIBAL ENROLLMENT		
							Year	County	No.
8512	1 Adams Davis	43	First Named	40	M	Full	1896	Skullyville	33
	2								
	3								
	4								
	5								
	6								
	7								
	8								
	9								
	10								
	11								
	12								
	13								
	14								
	15	ENROLLMENT OF NOS. 1 HEREON APPROVED BY THE SECRETARY OF INTERIOR JAN 17 1903							
	16								
	17								

TRIBAL ENROLLMENT OF PARENTS

	Name of Father	Year	County	Name of Mother	Year	County
1	John Williams	Dead	Skullyville	Chi-ma-he-ke	Dead	Skullyville
2						
3						
4						
5						
6						
7						
8						
9						
10						
11						
12						
13						
14						
15	P.O. Red Oak IT					Date of Application for Enrollment.
16		12/16/03				6/19/99
17						

193

Choctaw By Blood Enrollment Cards 1898-1914

RESIDENCE:	Sugar Load	COUNTY.	Choctaw Nation		Choctaw Roll	CARD No.	
POST OFFICE:	Bengal, I.T				(Not Including Freedmen)	FIELD No.	2894

Dawes' Roll No.	NAME	Relationship to Person First Named	AGE	SEX	BLOOD	TRIBAL ENROLLMENT		
						Year	County	No.
8513	1 Merryman, Gipson V 24		21	M	1/16	1896	Sugar Loaf	8518
I.W. 734	2 " Pairlee ㉗	Wife	24	F	I.W.			
8514	3 " Agnes 3	Dau	3mo	F	I/32			
	4							
	5							
	6							
	7							
	8	ENROLLMENT OF NOS. ～～ 2 ～～ HEREON						
	9	APPROVED BY THE SECRETARY OF INTERIOR MAY -7 1904						
	10							
	11							
	12							
	13							
	14							
	15	ENROLLMENT OF NOS. 1 and 3 HEREON						
	16	APPROVED BY THE SECRETARY OF INTERIOR JAN 17 1903						
	17							

TRIBAL ENROLLMENT OF PARENTS

Name of Father	Year	County	Name of Mother	Year	County
1 David C Merryman	1896	Sugar Loaf	Cadelia Merryman	1896	white man[sic]
2 E.J. Norris	1896	Non Citz	Neoma Norris	1896	Non Citz
3 No.1			No.2		
4					
5					
6					
7					
8	As to marriage of parents of No1, see				
9	Card of David C. Merryman				
10	For children of Nos 1 and 2 see NB (March 3,1905) #1260				
11					
12					
13					
14					
15					
16			Date of Application for Enrollment.	6/19/99	
17	P.O. Wilburton I.T	No.3 Enrolled May 24, 1900			

12/5/02

194

Choctaw By Blood Enrollment Cards 1898-1914

Dawes' Roll No.	NAME	Relationship to Person	AGE	SEX	BLOOD	TRIBAL ENROLLMENT		
						Year	County	No.
8515	1 King, Abel 25	First Named	22	M	Full	1896	Sugar Loaf	7471
	2							
	3							
	4							
	5							
	6							
	7							
	8							
	9							
	10							
	11							
	12							
	13							
	14							
	15	ENROLLMENT OF NOS. 1 HEREON APPROVED BY THE SECRETARY OF INTERIOR JAN 17 1903						
	16							
	17							

TRIBAL ENROLLMENT OF PARENTS

	Name of Father	Year	County	Name of Mother	Year	County
1	Harris King	Dead	Sugar Loaf	Sammie King	Dead	Sugar Loaf
2						
3						
4						
5						
6						
7			No1 is now husband of Emiline Taylor			
8			on Choctaw card #2296			
9			Dec 18/02			
10						
11						
12						
13						
14						
15						
16				Date of Application for Enrollment. 6/19/99		
17						

Choctaw By Blood Enrollment Cards 1898-1914

RESIDENCE: Skullyville COUNTY.								
CE: Milton, I.T. **Choctaw Nation**			Choctaw Roll (Not Including Freedmen)			CARD No. FIELD No. 2896		

NAME	Relationship to Person First Named	AGE	SEX	BLOOD	TRIBAL ENROLLMENT		
					Year	County	No.
8216 1 Thomas, Elias 42		39	M	Full	1896	Skullyville	11917
2 " Alice 31	Wife	28	F	"	1896	"	11918
3 " Minnie 13	S.Dau	10	"	"	1896	"	11919
4 " Stephen 11	S.Son	8	M	"	1896	"	11920
5 " Wilson 8	"	5	"	"	1896	"	11921
6							
7							
8							
9							
10							
11							
12							
13							
14							
15							
16							
17							

ENROLLMENT
OF NOS. 1,2,3,4,5, HEREON
APPROVED BY THE SECRETARY
OF INTERIOR JAN 17 1903

TRIBAL ENROLLMENT OF PARENTS

Name of Father	Year	County	Name of Mother	Year	County
1 Shi-konney	Dead	Skullyville	Celey Tallipoose	Dead	Skullyville
2 Ah-no-la-tubbee	"	Nashoba	Bessie	"	Eagle
3 Jame[sic] Nohic	1896	Sans Bois	No2		
4 No1			No2		
5 No1			No2		
6					
7					
8					
9					
10					
11					
12					
13					
14					
15				Date of Application for Enrollment.	
16				6/19/99	
17					

196

Choctaw By Blood Enrollment Cards 1898-1914

RESIDENCE: Sugar Loaf COUNTY. **Choctaw Nation** **Choctaw Roll** CARD NO.
POST OFFICE: Red Oak, I.T *(Not Including Freedmen)* FIELD NO. 2897

Dawes' Roll No.	NAME	Relationship to Person First Named	AGE	SEX	BLOOD	TRIBAL ENROLLMENT		
						Year	County	No.
DEAD.	1 Anderson, Davis		27	M	Full	1896	Sugar Loaf	79
8521	2 " Lucy A 33	Wife	30	F	"	1896	" "	81
8522	3 DIED PRIOR TO SEPTEMBER 25, 1902 " Andee	Son	2	M	"			
8523	4 DIED PRIOR TO SEPTEMBER 25, 1902 Wilson, Martha	S.Dau	11	F	"	1896	Sugar Loaf	9578
8524	5 " Jonas 12	S.Son	9	M	"	1896	" "	9579
8525	6 " Daniel 11	"	8	"	"	1896	" "	9580
	7							
	8 No. 1 HEREON DISMISSED UNDER							
	9 ORDER OF THE COMMISSION TO THE FIVE CIVILIZED TRIBES OF MARCH 31, 1905.							
	10							
	11 No3 died Aug - 1901; No4 died							
	12 Aug 9, 1901; Enrollment cancelled							
	13 by Department July 8, 1904							
	14							
	15 ENROLLMENT							
	16 OF NOS. 2,3,4,5,6 HEREON APPROVED BY THE SECRETARY							
	17 OF INTERIOR JAN 17 1903							

TRIBAL ENROLLMENT OF PARENTS

Name of Father	Year	County	Name of Mother	Year	County
1 Richard Anderson	Dead	Sugar Loaf	Jincey Anderson	Dead	Sugar Loaf
2 Pataley McCurtain	"	Skullyville	Te-le-mah	"	" "
3 No1			No2		
4 Smallwood Nelson	Dead	Sugar Loaf	No2		
5 " "	"	" "	No2		
6 " "	"	" "	No2		
7					
8					
9					
10					
11 No2 on 1896 roll as Lucy Ann Anderson					
12 No5 " 1896 " " Jon Nelson					
13 No6 " 1896 " " Dannil "					
No1 died October — 1899; Proof of death filed Dec 30 1902					
14 No3 " August - 1901; " " " " " " "					
15 No4 " August 9-1901; " " " " " " "			Date of Application for Enrollment.		
16				6/19/99	
17					

Choctaw By Blood Enrollment Cards 1898-1914

RESIDENCE:	Sans Bois	COUNTY.							
POST OFFICE:	Red Oak I.T.		**Choctaw Nation**			**Choctaw Roll** *(Not Including Freedmen)*		CARD NO. FIELD NO.	2898

Dawes' Roll No.	NAME		Relationship to Person First Named	AGE	SEX	BLOOD	TRIBAL ENROLLMENT		
							Year	County	No.
8526	1 Hancock Betsy	58	First Named	55	F	Full	1896	Sans Bois	5143
8527	2 " Clayton	16	GrandSon	13	M	"	1896	" "	5145
8528	3 Williams George	12	GrandSon	9	M	"	1896	" "	12641
	4								
	5								
	6								
	7								
	8								
	9								
	10								
	11								
	12								
	13								
	14								
	15	ENROLLMENT OF NOS. 1, 2, 3 HEREON APPROVED BY THE SECRETARY							
	16	OF INTERIOR JAN 17 1903							
	17								

TRIBAL ENROLLMENT OF PARENTS

	Name of Father	Year	County	Name of Mother	Year	County
1	Chi-li-ta	Dead	Sans Bois	E-la-ho-na	Dead	Jack's Fork
2	Willis Hancock	1896	" "	Nicey Jefferson	"	Gaines
3	Coleman Williams	Dead	Sans Bois	Sophy Williams	"	Sugar Loaf
4						
5						
6						
7						
8						
9						
10						
11						
12						
13						
14					Date of Application for Enrollment.	
15						
16					6/19/99	
17						

Choctaw By Blood Enrollment Cards 1898-1914

RESIDENCE: Skullyville   COUNTY. **Choctaw Nation**   **Choctaw Roll** (Not Including Freedmen)   CARD NO.

POST OFFICE: Lodi I.T.   FIELD NO. 2899

Dawes' Roll No.	NAME		Relationship to Person	AGE	SEX	BLOOD	TRIBAL ENROLLMENT		
							Year	County	No.
8529	1 Williams Joel	36	First Named	33	M	Full	1896	Skullyville	12814
8530	2 " Phoebe	37	Wife	34	F	3/4	1896	"	12815
8531	3 " Hickman	16	Son	13	M	7/8	1896	"	12816
8532	4 " Emeline	9	Dau	6	F	7/8	1896	"	12817
8533	5 " Mattie B	7	"	4	F	7/8	1896	"	12818
8534	6 " Mollie	4	"	1	F	"			
	7								
	8								
	9								
	10								
	11								
	12								
	13								
	14								
	15	ENROLLMENT OF NOS. 1,2,3,4,5,6 HEREON APPROVED BY THE SECRETARY OF INTERIOR JAN 17 1903							
	16								
	17								

TRIBAL ENROLLMENT OF PARENTS

	Name of Father	Year	County	Name of Mother	Year	County
1	Ya-kan-ta-be	Dead	Skullyville	Mary Jefferson	1896	Skullyville
2	Thomas Jefferson	1896	"	Betsy Jefferson	Dead	Gaines
3	No 1			No 2		
4	No 1			No 2		
5	No 1			No 2		
6	No 1			No 2		
7						
8						
9			No5 On 1896 roll as Mattie Williams			
10						
11						
12						
13						
14						
15						
16				Date of Application for Enrollment.	6/19/99	
17						

Choctaw By Blood Enrollment Cards 1898-1914

RESIDENCE: Sugar Loaf   COUNTY. **Choctaw Nation**   **Choctaw Roll**   CARD NO.
POST OFFICE: Red Oak I.T.   (Not Including Freedmen)   FIELD NO. 2900

Dawes' Roll No.	NAME		Relationship to Person First Named	AGE	SEX	BLOOD	TRIBAL ENROLLMENT		
							Year	County	No.
I.W. 652	1 Moon Joseph J.	50	First Named	46	M	IW	1896	Sugar Loaf	14805
14915	2 " Mattie	38	Wife	35	F	1/4	1896	" "	8511
14916	3 " Levi L	16	Son	13	M	1/8	1896	" "	8512
14917	4 " Joe J	14	"	11	M	1/8	1896	" "	8513
14918	5 " Susie O	13	Dau	10	F	1/8	1896	" "	8514
	6								
	7								
	8								
	9								
	10								
	11								
	12								
	13								
	14								
	15								
	16								
	17								

ENROLLMENT
OF NOS. 2,3,4 and 5 HEREON
APPROVED BY THE SECRETARY
OF INTERIOR MAY 21 1903

ENROLLMENT
OF NOS. 1 HEREON
APPROVED BY THE SECRETARY
OF INTERIOR MAR 26 1904

TRIBAL ENROLLMENT OF PARENTS

	Name of Father	Year	County	Name of Mother	Year	County
1	Levi Moon	Dead	Non Citz	Ann Moon	1896	Non Citz
2	Turner Brashears	"	Skullyville	Kate Brashears	Dead	Non Citz
3	No 1			No 2		
4	No 1			No 2		
5	No 1			No 2		
6						
7						
8						

9   No1 Admitted by Dawes Com as intermarried citizen Case

10   No. 383 as Joe J Moore, On 1896 roll as J. J. Moore

11   No2 As to marriage of father and mother see testimony
of S.E. Lewis

12   Nos 2,3,4 and 5 admitted by Dawes Commission in 1896 as citizens by blood;

13   Choctaw case #383. No appeal

14   See affidavits of C.I. Dalton, R.L. Reagan, W.T. Maddix, and W.W. Allen as
to residence of persons on this card filed March 14, 1903

15

16

Date of Application for Enrollment.
6/20/99

17   P.O. Fort Smith Ark.
3/11/03 P.O. [Illegible] I.T.

Choctaw By Blood Enrollment Cards 1898-1914

POST OFFICE: ans Bois / Sans Bois Ind. Ter.   COUNTY. **Choctaw Nation**   Choctaw Roll *(Not Including Freedmen)*   CARD No. FIELD No. 2901

Dawes' Roll No.	NAME		Relationship to Person First Named	AGE	SEX	BLOOD	TRIBAL ENROLLMENT Year	County	No.
8535	1 McCurtain Green	53	First Named	50	M	3/4	1896	Sans Bois	8984
8536	2 " Katie	47	Wife	44	F	1/2	1896	" "	8985
8537	3 " Lena	20	Dau	17	F	5/8	1896	" "	8986
8538	4 " Cora	16	"	13	F	5/8	1896	" "	8987
8539	5 " Bertha	12	"	9	F	5/8	1896	" "	8988
8540	6 " Lester	9	Son	6	M	5/8	1896	" "	8989
8541	7 Cooper Kirby	15	Ward	12	m	11/16	1896	" "	2055
8542	8 " Dora	13	Ward	10	F	11/16	1896	" "	2056
8543	9 Fennel, Louisa	20	Niece	17	F	11/16	1896	Gaines	10191
I.W. 735	10 " Jack (31)		Hus of No9	32	M	I.W.			
	11								
	12	ENROLLMENT OF NOS. ~~~ 10 ~~~ HEREON APPROVED BY THE SECRETARY OF INTERIOR MAY 7 1904							
	13								
	14								
	15	ENROLLMENT OF NOS. 1,2,3,4,5,6,7,8,9 HEREON APPROVED BY THE SECRETARY OF INTERIOR JAN 17 1903							
	16								
	17								

TRIBAL ENROLLMENT OF PARENTS

	Name of Father	Year	County	Name of Mother	Year	County
1	Cornelius McCurtain	Dead	Sugar Loaf	Amy McCurtain	Dead	Skullyville
2	John Spring	"	Wade	Sally Spring	"	Wade
3	No 1			No 2		
4	No 1			No 2		
5	No 1			No 2		
6	No 1			No 2		
7	Thompson Cooper	Dead	Sans Bois	Katie Cooper	Dead	Sans Bois
8	" "	"	" "	" "	"	" "
9	Joseph Pitchlyn	"	Gaines	Becky Pitchlyn	"	Gaines
10	Samuel Fennel		non citz	Ann Fennel	dead	non citz
11	No1 On 1896 roll as Green McCurtain (Gov)					
12	No.9 is now the wife of Jack Fennel on Choctaw Care #D647. Evidence					
13	of marriage filed with papers in Choctaw Case #647 Aug 20, 1902. No10 transferred from Choctaw card #D647. See decision of Feby 29, 1904.					
14						
15						Date of Application for Enrollment. #1 to 9
16	For child of No3 see NB (Mar 3-1905) Card #219					6/20/99
17	" " " Nos9&10 " " " " #1344					

201

Choctaw By Blood Enrollment Cards 1898-1914

RESIDENCE:	Sans Bois	COUNTY.						
POST OFFICE:	Brooken, I.T.	**Choctaw Nation**				**Choctaw Roll** (Not Including Freedmen)	CARD No. FIELD No. 2902	

Dawes' Roll No.	NAME		Relationship to Person First Named	AGE	SEX	BLOOD	TRIBAL ENROLLMENT		
							Year	County	No.
I.W. 1211	1 Sanders, John A	54	First Named	51	M	I.W	1896	Sans Bois	15013
8544	2 " Nona	14	Dau	11	F	1/16	1896	" "	11089
8545	3 " Newton	17	Son	14	M	1/16	1896	" "	11088
	4								
	5								
	6								
	7								
	8								
	9								
	10	ENROLLMENT							
	11	OF NOS. ~ 1 ~ HEREON							
	12	APPROVED BY THE SECRETARY OF INTERIOR DEC 13 1904							
	13								
	14	ENROLLMENT							
	15	OF NOS. 2 and 3 HEREON							
	16	APPROVED BY THE SECRETARY OF INTERIOR JAN 17 1903							
	17								

TRIBAL ENROLLMENT OF PARENTS

	Name of Father	Year	County	Name of Mother	Year	County
1	Robt Sanders	Dead	Non Citz	Lizzie Sanders	Dead	Non Citz
2	No1			Leona Sanders	"	Sans Bois
3	No1			" "	"	" " "
4						
5						
6	No1 on 1896 roll as Jno. A. Sanders					
7	No2 " 1896 " " Norma "					
8	No3 " 1896 " " Newt. "					
9	As to marriage, see testimony of					
10	No1 and S.E. Lewis					
11	No.1 formerly husband of Leona Sanders, a recognized Choctaw by blood, who died in about the year 1896					
12	For child of No1 see NB (Apr 26-06) #1239					
13	" " " No2 " " " " 1304					
14						
15					Date of Application for Enrollment.	
16					6/20/99	
17						

202

Choctaw By Blood Enrollment Cards 1898-1914

RESIDENCE: Sans Bois   COUNTY. **Choctaw Nation**   **Choctaw Roll**   CARD NO.
POST OFFICE: Brooken, I.T   *(Not Including Freedmen)*   FIELD NO. 2903

Dawes' Roll No.	NAME		Relationship to Person First Named	AGE	SEX	BLOOD	TRIBAL ENROLLMENT		
							Year	County	No.
I.W. 1315	1 Walker, Robert L	37	First Named	33	M	I.W	1896	Sans Bois	15138
8546	2 " Oscar W	11	Son	8	"	1/4	1896	" "	12720
8547	3 " D. Clifton	9	"	6	"	1/4	1896	" "	12721
8548	4 " Jesse A	7	"	4	"	1/4	1896	" "	12722
8549	5 Burs, Isaac	16	S.Son	13	"	1/4	1896	" "	659
	6								
	7								
	8								
	9								
	10								
	11								
	12								
	13								
	14								
	15								
	16								
	17								

ENROLLMENT
OF NOS. 1 HEREON
APPROVED BY THE SECRETARY
OF INTERIOR MAR 14 1905

ENROLLMENT
OF NOS 2,3,4,5 HEREON
APPROVED BY THE SECRETARY
OF INTERIOR JAN 17 1903

TRIBAL ENROLLMENT OF PARENTS

	Name of Father	Year	County	Name of Mother	Year	County
1	John W. Walker	Dead	Non Citz	Lucinda Walker	Dead	Non Citz
2	No1			Kizzie Walker	"	Sans Bois
3	No1			" "	"	" " "
4	No1			" "	"	" " "
5	Sidney Burs	1896	Chickasaw	" "	"	" " "
6						
7	No1 formerly husband of Cassie Walker (formerly Burris)					
8	1896 Choctaw Census Roll, Sans Bois County, No 12719, who died in 1898					
9	No4 on 1896 roll as Jesse Allen Walker					
10	No5 " 1896 " " Isaac Burris					
	No1 " 1896 " " R. L. Walker					
11						
12	No1 is father of children on Choctaw card D #1005					
13	For children of No1 see NB (Apr 26 '06) #1242					
	P.O. Midland I.T.					
14						
15						
16				Date of Application for Enrollment.	6/20/99	
17						

Choctaw By Blood Enrollment Cards 1898-1914

RESIDENCE: Sans Bois COUNTY.					**Choctaw Nation**			CARD NO.	
POST OFFICE: Red Oak, I.T.					*(Not Including Freedmen)* Choctaw Roll			FIELD NO. 2904	

Dawes' Roll No.	NAME	Relationship to Person	AGE	SEX	BLOOD	TRIBAL ENROLLMENT		
						Year	County	No.
8550	1 Jefferson, Sackey 37	First Named	34	F	Full	1896	Sans Bois	6407
8551	2 " Sampson 12	Son	9	M	3/4	1896	" "	6408
8552	3 " Eli 10	"	7	"	3/4	1896	" "	6409
8553	4 " Joseph 5	"	2	"	3/4			
13122	5 " Sarah 3	Dau	2 3/4	F	3/4			
13123	6 " Bessie 1	"	3½mo	"	3/4			
	7							
	8							
	9							
	10 ENROLLMENT							
	11 OF NOS. 5 & 6 HEREON APPROVED BY THE SECRETARY							
	12 OF INTERIOR MAR 19 1903							
	13							
	14 ENROLLMENT							
	15 OF NOS. 1,2,3,4 HEREON							
	16 APPROVED BY THE SECRETARY OF INTERIOR JAN 17 1903							
	17							

TRIBAL ENROLLMENT OF PARENTS

	Name of Father	Year	County	Name of Mother	Year	County
1	Morris Nail	Dead	Gaines	Louisa Nail	Dead	Gaines
2	Wallace Jefferson	1896	Chickasaw	No1		
3	" "	1896	"	No1		
4	" "	1896	"	No1		
5	" "		"	No.1		
6	" "		"	No.1		
7						
8						
9	No1 on 1896 roll as Siley Jefferson					
10						
11	Husband on Chickasaw Card No1457					
12	No5 Born March 11, 1900. Proof of birth received and filed Dec 24, 1902					
13	No6 Born Sept 12, 1902. Proof of birth received and filed Dec 24, 1902					
14	For child of No.1 see NB (March 3 1905) #807			#1 to 4		
15				Date of Application for Enrollment.		
16				6/20/99		
17						

Choctaw By Blood Enrollment Cards 1898-1914

RESIDENCE: Sans Bois COUNTY. **Choctaw Nation**   Choctaw Roll   CARD NO.
POST OFFICE: Red Oak, I.T.   *(Not Including Freedmen)* FIELD NO. 2905

Dawes' Roll No.	NAME	Relationship to Person First Named	AGE	SEX	BLOOD	TRIBAL ENROLLMENT		
						Year	County	No.
8554	1 Hancock, Willis ³²	Named	29	M	Full	1896	Sans Bois	5157
	2							
	3							
	4							
	5							
	6							
	7							
	8							
	9							
	10							
	11							
	12							
	13							
	14	ENROLLMENT						
	15	OF NOS. 1 HEREON						
	16	APPROVED BY THE SECRETARY						
	17	OF INTERIOR JAN 17 1903						

TRIBAL ENROLLMENT OF PARENTS

Name of Father	Year	County	Name of Mother	Year	County
1 Cornelius Hancock	Dead	Sans Bois	Betsy Hancock	1896	Sans Bois
2					
3					
4					
5					
6 Wife and children on Chickasaw Card No 1459					
7					
8					
9 Wife and children now on Choctaw card #5557					
10 For child of No1 see NB (Mar 3-05) card #549					
11					
12					
13					
14					
15					
16				6/20/99	
17					

Choctaw By Blood Enrollment Cards 1898-1914

RESIDENCE: Sans Bois   COUNTY. **Choctaw Nation**   **Choctaw Roll**   CARD No.
POST OFFICE: Iron Bridge, I.T.   (Not Including Freedmen)   FIELD No. 2906

Dawes' Roll No.	NAME	Relationship to Person First Named	AGE	SEX	BLOOD	TRIBAL ENROLLMENT Year	County	No.
8555	₁ Billy, Dixon ⁴⁴		41	M	Full	1896	Sans Bois	641
8556	₂ " Lita ³⁴	Wife	31	F	"	1896	" "	642
8557	₃ " Bicy ⁷	Dau	4	"	"	1896	" "	646
8558	₄ " Cephus ⁶	Son	3	M	"	1896	" "	647
8559	₅ " Eliza ⁵	Dau	1	F	"			
8560	₆ Smith, Milton ¹³	S.Son	10	M	"	1893	Sans Bois	645
8561	₇ Billy, Jennie ¹²	Niece	9	F	"	1893	" "	40
	₈							
	₉							
	10							
	11							
	12							
	13							
	14	ENROLLMENT						
	15	OF NOS. 1,2,3,4,5,6,7 HEREON						
	16	APPROVED BY THE SECRETARY OF INTERIOR JAN 17 1903						
	17							

TRIBAL ENROLLMENT OF PARENTS

	Name of Father	Year	County	Name of Mother	Year	County
₁	Sodie Billy	Dead	Skullyville		Dead	Skullyville
₂	He-kin-tubbee	"	"		"	Cedar
₃	No1			No2		
₄	No1			No2		
₅	No1			No2		
₆	Layman Smith	Dead	Sans Bois	No2		
₇	John Billy	"	" "	Nicey Billy	Dead	Sans Bois
₈						
₉						
10						
11			No2 on 1896 roll as Lida Billy			
12			No6 " 1896 " " Milton "			
13						
14						
15					Date of Application for Enrollment.	
16					6/20/99	
17						

Choctaw By Blood Enrollment Cards 1898-1914

RESIDENCE: Skullyville   COUNTY. **Choctaw Nation**   **Choctaw Roll**   CARD NO.
POST OFFICE: Lodi, I.T.   *(Not Including Freedmen)*   FIELD NO. 2907

Dawes' Roll No.	NAME	Relationship to Person First Named	AGE	SEX	BLOOD	TRIBAL ENROLLMENT		
						Year	County	No.
8562	1 Jefferson, Eastman ²⁰		17	M	Full	1896	Gaines	6608
	2							
	3							
	4							
	5							
	6							
	7							
	8							
	9							
	10							
	11							
	12							
	13							
	14	ENROLLMENT						
	15	OF NOS. 1 HEREON						
	16	APPROVED BY THE SECRETARY OF INTERIOR JAN 17 1903						
	17							

TRIBAL ENROLLMENT OF PARENTS

	Name of Father	Year	County	Name of Mother	Year	County
1	Jas Jefferson	Dead	Skullyville	Nicey Jefferson	Dead	Gaines
2						
3						
4						
5						
6						
7						
8						
9						
10						
11						
12						
13						
14						
15						
16				Date of Application for Enrollment.	6/20/99	
17	Wilburton I.T. 3/23/07					

Choctaw By Blood Enrollment Cards 1898-1914

RESIDENCE: Sugar Loaf   COUNTY. **Choctaw Nation**   **Choctaw Roll** *(Not Including Freedmen)*   CARD NO.
POST OFFICE: Le Flore, I.T.   FIELD NO. 2908

Dawes' Roll No.	NAME		Relationship to Person First Named	AGE	SEX	BLOOD	TRIBAL ENROLLMENT		
							Year	County	No.
8563	1 LeFlore, Selina	33	First Named	30	F	Full	1896	Sugar Loaf	7787
8564	2 " McAlester	12	Son	9	M	3/4	1896	" "	7788
8565	3 " Joseph Jr	10	"	7	"	3/4	1896	" "	7789
8566	4 " Minerva	8	Dau	5	F	3/4	1896	" "	7790
8567	5 " Polina	6	"	3	"	3/4	1896	" "	7791
	6								
	7								
	8								
	9								
	10								
	11								
	12								
	13								
	14	ENROLLMENT							
	15	OF NOS. 1,2,3,4,5 HEREON							
	16	APPROVED BY THE SECRETARY OF INTERIOR JAN 17 1903							
	17								

TRIBAL ENROLLMENT OF PARENTS

	Name of Father	Year	County	Name of Mother	Year	County
1	Thos. Moore	Dead	Sugar Loaf	Phoebe Moore	Dead	Sugar Loaf
2	Jos. LeFlore	1896	Chick Roll	No 1		
3	" "	1896	" "	No 1		
4	" "	1896	" "	No 1		
5	" "	1896	" "	No 1		
6						
7						
8			No3 on 1896 roll as Joseph LeFlore			
9			No4 " 1896 " " Maniva "			
10			No5 " 1896 " " [Illegible] "			
11			Husband, Jos LeFlore, on Chickasaw			
12			Card No 1463			
13			For child of No1 see NB (Apr 26-06) Card #409			
14			" " " " (Mar 3 '05) " #220			
15					Date of Application for Enrollment	
16					6/20/99	
17						

208

Choctaw By Blood Enrollment Cards 1898-1914

RESIDENCE: Sans Bois	COUNTY. **Choctaw Nation**			**Choctaw Roll** (Not Including Freedmen)		CARD No. FIELD No. 2909
POST OFFICE: Brooken, I.T.						

Dawes' Roll No.	NAME	Relationship to Person	AGE	SEX	BLOOD	TRIBAL ENROLLMENT		
						Year	County	No.
8568	1 Spann, Freeman R 28	First Named	25	M	1/16	1896	Sans Bois	11090
	2							
	3							
	4							
	5							
	6							
	7							
	8							
	9							
	10							
	11							
	12							
	13							
	14	ENROLLMENT						
	15	OF NOS. 1 HEREON						
	16	APPROVED BY THE SECRETARY OF INTERIOR JAN 17 1903						
	17							

TRIBAL ENROLLMENT OF PARENTS

Name of Father	Year	County	Name of Mother	Year	County
1 John H Spann	Dead	Non Citz	Leona Spann	Dead	Sans Bois
2					
3					
4					
5					
6					
7		On 1896 roll as Freeman Spann			
8					
9		Admitted by Act of Council in October 1874			
10		Copy of which is to be presented or supplied:			
11					
12					
13					
14					
15			Date of Application for Enrollment. 6/20/99		
16					
17					

209

Choctaw By Blood Enrollment Cards 1898-1914

RESIDENCE: Sans Bois COUNTY.

POST OFFICE: Brooken, I.T.

Choctaw Nation

Choctaw Roll

(Not Including Freedmen) FIELD NO. 2910

Dawes' Roll No.	NAME		Relationship to Person First Named	AGE	SEX	BLOOD	TRIBAL ENROLLMENT		
							Year	County	No.
8569	1 Spann, John H	26	First Named	23	M	1/16	1896	Sans Bois	11091
I.W. 1316	2 " Katie A	22	Wife	19	F	I.W.			
8570	3 " Claud E	2	Son	2½m	M	1/32			
8571	4 " Carrel M	1	Son	4mo	M	1/32			
	5								
	6								
	7								
	8								
	9								
	10								
	11	ENROLLMENT							
	12	OF NOS. 2 HEREON APPROVED BY THE SECRETARY							
	13	OF INTERIOR MAR 14 1905							
	14	ENROLLMENT							
	15	OF NOS. 1, 3, 4 HEREON							
	16	APPROVED BY THE SECRETARY OF INTERIOR JAN 17 1903							
	17								

TRIBAL ENROLLMENT OF PARENTS

	Name of Father	Year	County	Name of Mother	Year	County
1	John H Spann	Dead	Non Citz	Leona Spann	Dead	Sans Bois
2	W. C. Seabolt	1896	" "	Annie Seabolt	1896	Non Citz
3	No.1			No.2		
4	No 1			No 2		
5						
6						
7						
8						
9						
10	No1 on 1896 roll as J H. Spann					
11						
12	No1 admitted by an Act of Council in October					
13	1874. Same to be presented or supplied.					
14	No.3 Enrolled Dec. 8th 1900.				#1&2	
15	No5 Born Feb 23rd 1902: Enrolled June 28th 1902:			DATE OF APPLICATION FOR ENROLLMENT		
16	For child of Nos1&2 see NB (Mar 3-1905) Card #129			6/20/99		
17		P.O. Ruff Ind Ter				

210

Choctaw By Blood Enrollment Cards 1898-1914

RESIDENCE: Sugar Loaf	COUNTY:	**Choctaw Nation**	Choctaw Roll	CARD NO.
POST OFFICE: Red Oak, I.T.			(Not Including Freedmen)	FIELD NO. 2911

Dawes' Roll No.	NAME	Relationship to Person First Named	AGE	SEX	BLOOD	TRIBAL ENROLLMENT Year	County	No.
8572	1 Hicker, Edward	25	22	M	3/8	1896	Gaines	5322
8573	2 DIED PRIOR TO SEPTEMBER 25 1902 Minnie	Wife	19	F	3/4	1896	Sugar Loaf	7781
8574	3 DIED PRIOR TO SEPTEMBER 25, 1902 John Little	Son	2mo	M	9/16			
8575	4 DIED PRIOR TO SEPTEMBER 25 1902 Jonas	Son	6mo	M	9/16			
	5							
	6							
	7							
	8							
	9							
	10							
	11							
	12							
	13							
	14							
	15	ENROLLMENT OF NOS. 1,2,3,4 HEREON APPROVED BY THE SECRETARY OF INTERIOR JAN 17 1903						
	16							
	17							

TRIBAL ENROLLMENT OF PARENTS

Name of Father	Year	County	Name of Mother	Year	County
1 Simon Hicker	Dead	Chick Roll	Lucinda Hicker	1896	Sugar Loaf
2 Reuben Lewis	1896	Sugar Loaf	Sincy Lewis	Dead	" "
3 No1			No2		
4 No 1			No 2		
5					
6					
7					
8	No1 on 1896 roll as Eddie Hicker				
9	No2 " 1896 " " Minnie Lewis				
10	No.4 Born June 3, 1901: Enrolled Nov. 12, 1901				
	No2 died February 15, 1901; proof of death filed Dec 20 1902				
11	No3 " April 10, 1900; " " " " " " "				
12	No4 " January 9, 1902; " " " " " " "				
13	No2 died Feb 15, 1902: No3 died April 10, 1900: No4 Jan 9, 1902: Enrollment cancelled by Department July 8, 1904				
14	For child of No1 see NB (Mar 3 1905) #202				
15					
16				Date of Application for Enrollment.	6/20/99
17					

Choctaw By Blood Enrollment Cards 1898-1914

RESIDENCE: Sans Bois COUNTY.
POST OFFICE: Brooken, I.T.

Choctaw Nation

Choctaw Roll (Not Including Freedmen)

CARD NO. FIELD NO. 2912

Dawes' Roll No.	NAME	Relationship to Person Named	AGE	SEX	BLOOD	TRIBAL ENROLLMENT Year	County	No.
16048	1 Autrey, Columbus B 24	First Person Named	21	M	1/8	1896	Chick Dist	538
16049	2 Green, Lenora 26	Sister	23	F	1/8	1896	" "	539
16050	3 Green, Teddy 1	Son of N°2	22mo	M	1/16			
	4							
	5							
	6							
	7							
	8							
	9							
	10							
	11							
	12							
	13							
	14							
	15							
	16							
	17							

ENROLLMENT
OF NOS. ~~ 1-2 and 3 ~ HEREON
APPROVED BY THE SECRETARY
OF INTERIOR AUG 22 1906

Nos 1, 2 and 3 restored to roll by Departmental authority of January [illegible]
Enrollment of Nos. 1, 2 and 3 cancelled by Department March [illegible]

No2 is wife of Fin Green a non citizen. Evidence of marriage filed Jan. 6, 1903

GRANTED
JUN 13 1906

TRIBAL ENROLLMENT OF PARENTS

	Name of Father	Year	County	Name of Mother	Year	County
1	Enoch Autrey	1896	Non Citz	Adlade Autrey	Dead	Sans Bois
2	" "	1896	" "	" "	"	" "
3	Fin Green		non-citz	N°2		
4						
5	No1 on 1896 roll as Lem Autrey					
6	No2 " 1896 " " Rosa "					
7	N°3 Born Feby 14, 1901; application received Dec 22, 1902, proof of birth filed March 24 1903 For child of No.2 see NB (Apr 26, 1905[sic]) Card No. 38					
8	Sept 11-99: Said not to have been admitted to citizenship in					
9	Choctaw Nation: See testimony of Simon E Lewis					
10	and Freeman Spann.					
11	Dec 24, 1904 Record forwarded Department in compliance with its request of Dec 3 1904 for reconsideration in case of Hezekiah Enoch Autry Micoo 123					
12						
13						
14						
15					Date of Application for Enrollment.	
16					6/20/99	
17	PO Briartown IT 3/13/05					

Choctaw By Blood Enrollment Cards 1898-1914

RESIDENCE:	Sugar Loaf	COUNTY.	**Choctaw Nation**		**Choctaw Roll**	CARD NO.	
POST OFFICE:	Red Oak, I.T.				*(Not Including Freedmen)*	FIELD NO.	2913

Dawes' Roll No.		NAME		Relationship to Person First Named	AGE	SEX	BLOOD	TRIBAL ENROLLMENT		
								Year	County	No.
DEAD.	1	~~Louis, Reuben~~	DEAD.	~~First Named~~	~~50~~	~~M~~	~~Full~~	~~1896~~	~~Sugar Loaf~~	~~7779~~
15047	2	" Jefferson	15	Son	12	M	"	1896	" "	7782
15575	3	" Ada	12	Dau	9	F	"	1896	" "	7783
15576	4	" Katie	11	"	8	"	"	1896	" "	7784
	5									
	6									
	7	No. 1 HEREON DISMISSED UNDER ORDER OF THE COMMISSION TO THE FIVE CIVILIZED TRIBES OF MARCH 31, 1905.								
	8									
	9									
	10	ENROLLMENT OF NOS. ~2~ HEREON APPROVED BY THE SECRETARY OF INTERIOR FEB 16 1904								
	11									
	12									
	13									
	14									
	15	ENROLLMENT OF NOS. 3 and 4 HEREON APPROVED BY THE SECRETARY OF INTERIOR SEP 22 1904								
	16									
	17									

TRIBAL ENROLLMENT OF PARENTS

	Name of Father	Year	County	Name of Mother	Year	County	
1	~~Pis-tom-bey~~	~~Dead~~	~~Sugar Loaf~~		~~Dead~~	~~Sugar Loaf~~	
2	No1			Siney Louis	"	"	"
3	No1			" "	"	"	"
4	No1			" "	"	"	"
5							
6							
7	No1 on 1896 roll as Roben Louis						
8	No2 " 1896 " " Jefferson Lewis						
9	No3 " 1896 " " Ada "						
10	No4 " 1896 " " Kittie "						
	Nº1 Died Feby 18, 1902, proof of death filed Oct. 24, 1902						
11							
12							
13							
14							
15							
16				Date of Application for Enrollment.	6/20/99		
17							

RESIDENCE:	Sans Bois	COUNTY.				Choctaw Roll		CARD No.	
POST OFFICE:	Red Oak, I.T.	**Choctaw Nation**				(Not Including Freedmen)		FIELD No.	2914

Dawes' Roll No.	NAME	Relationship to Person First Named	AGE	SEX	BLOOD	TRIBAL ENROLLMENT		
						Year	County	No.
DEAD	₁ Jefferson, Levicey		18	F	1/2	1896	Sans Bois	6413
8576	₂ Wall, Emiline ¹³	Cousin	10	"	1/2	1896	Gaines	12970
8577	₃ Jefferson, Lena ⁸	"	5	"	1/2	1896	"	6604
	₄							
	₅							
	₆							
	₇	No. 1 HEREON DISMISSED UNDER						
	₈	ORDER OF THE COMMISSION TO THE FIVE						
	₉	CIVILIZED TRIBES OF MARCH 31, 1905.						
	₁₀							
	₁₁							
	₁₂							
	₁₃							
	₁₄							
	₁₅	ENROLLMENT OF NOS. 2 and 3 HEREON						
	₁₆	APPROVED BY THE SECRETARY OF INTERIOR JAN 17 1903						
	₁₇							

TRIBAL ENROLLMENT OF PARENTS

Name of Father	Year	County	Name of Mother	Year	County
₁ Nicholas Jefferson	1896	Chick Roll	Ahs Jefferson	Dead	Sans Bois
₂ Jesse Wall	Dead	" "	Nancy Wall	"	Gaines
₃ Sweeny Jefferson	"	" "	Nicey Jefferson	"	"
₄					
₅					
₆		No1 Said to be dead			
₇					
₈	No1 Died October 9, 1900. Proof of death filed March 24, 1905				
₉					
₁₀					
₁₁					
₁₂					
₁₃					
₁₄					
₁₅				Date of Application for Enrollment.	
₁₆				6/20/99	
₁₇					

Choctaw By Blood Enrollment Cards 1898-1914

| RESIDENCE: Gaines | COUNTY. | **Choctaw Nation** | Choctaw Roll | CARD NO. |
| POST OFFICE: Wilburton, I.T. | | | *(Not Including Freedmen)* | FIELD NO. 2915 |

Dawes' Roll No.	NAME		Relationship to Person First Named	AGE	SEX	BLOOD	TRIBAL ENROLLMENT		
							Year	County	No.
8678	1 Wesley, Charles	57	Named	54	M	Full	1896	Sugar Loaf	12926
8579	2 Collin, Lena	19	G.Dau	16	F	"	1893	Gaines	596
8580	3 " Sena	17	"	14	"	"	1893	"	597
	4								
	5								
	6								
	7								
	8								
	9								
	10								
	11								
	12								
	13								
	14								
	15	ENROLLMENT OF NOS. 1, 2, 3 HEREON APPROVED BY THE SECRETARY OF INTERIOR JAN 17 1903							
	16								
	17								

TRIBAL ENROLLMENT OF PARENTS

	Name of Father	Year	County	Name of Mother	Year	County
1	Mo-shon-to-tubbee	Dead	Nashoba		Dead	Nashoba
2	Stephen Collin	"	"	Angie Collin	"	Cedar
3	" "	"	"	" "	'	"
4						
5						
6						
7	No2 on 1893 Pay Roll Gaines Co Page 63, No 596 as Lena Wesley					
8	No3 " 1896[sic] " " " " " 63 " 597 " Lucinda "					
9	No3 Died Sept. 15, 1898; proof of death filed Dec 24 1902 (This notation is					
10	in error as it refers to No(2) – 3/19/20 WHA					
11	Note: Evidence on file tending to show that Lena and Sena Collin are duplicates, and further, that there were no such persons.					
12						
13						
14						
15					Date of Application for Enrollment	
16					6/20/99	
17						

Choctaw By Blood Enrollment Cards 1898-1914

RESIDENCE: Sugar Loaf COUNTY.
POST OFFICE: Red Oak, I.T.

Choctaw Nation

Choctaw Roll
(Not Including Freedmen)

CARD NO.
FIELD NO. 2916

Dawes' Roll No.	NAME		Relationship to Person First Named	AGE	SEX	BLOOD	TRIBAL ENROLLMENT		
							Year	County	No.
8581	1 Carney, Morris	45	First Named	42	M	Full	1896	Sugar Loaf	2227
8582	2 " Elsie	40	Wife	37	F	"	1896	" "	2228
8583	3 " Isabelle	19	Niece	16	"	"	1896	" "	2267
8584	4 " Nelson	13	Nephew	10	M	"	1896	" "	2268
8585	5 " Lee	11	"	8	"	"	1896	" "	2269
8586	6 Paxton, Dora	14	Ward	11	F	"	1896	" "	10157
	7								
	8								
	9								
	10								
	11								
	12								
	13								
	14								
	15	ENROLLMENT OF NOS. 1,2,3,4,5,6 HEREON APPROVED BY THE SECRETARY OF INTERIOR JAN 17 1903							
	16								
	17								

TRIBAL ENROLLMENT OF PARENTS

	Name of Father	Year	County	Name of Mother	Year	County
1	Nelson Carney	Dead	Red River	Sally Ann Carney	Dead	Red River
2	Chas Wesley	1896	Sugar Loaf	Rhoda Wesley	"	Sugar Loaf
3	John Carney	Dead	" "	Serena Carney	"	Jacks Fork
4	" "	"	" "	" "	"	" " "
5	" "	"	" "	" "	"	" " "
6	Watson Paxton	"	" "	Malinda Paxton	"	Sugar Loaf
7						
8						
9		N⁰1 is legal guardian of N⁰6, July 13, 1903				
10						
11						
12						
13						
14						
15				Date of Application for Enrollment.		
16				6/20/99		
17						

Choctaw By Blood Enrollment Cards 1898-1914

RESIDENCE: Gaines COUNTY. **Choctaw Nation** Choctaw Roll CARD NO.
POST OFFICE: Wilburton, I.T. *(Not Including Freedmen)* FIELD NO. 2917

Dawes' Roll No.	NAME	Relationship to Person First Named	AGE	SEX	BLOOD	TRIBAL ENROLLMENT		
						Year	County	No.
8587	1 Wall, Gibson 22	First Named	19	M	Full	1896	Gaines	12972
	2							
	3							
	4							
	5							
	6							
	7							
	8							
	9							
	10							
	11							
	12							
	13							
	14							
	15	ENROLLMENT OF NOS. 1 HEREON APPROVED BY THE SECRETARY OF INTERIOR JAN 17 1903						
	16							
	17							

TRIBAL ENROLLMENT OF PARENTS

Name of Father	Year	County	Name of Mother	Year	County
1 Jesse Wall	Dead	Gaines	Nancy Wall	Dead	Gaines
2					
3					
4					
5					
6		For child of No1 see NB (Mar 3-05) Card #120			
7					
8					
9					
10					
11					
12					
13					
14					
15				Date of Application for Enrollment.	
16				6/20/99	
17					

Choctaw By Blood Enrollment Cards 1898-1914

RESIDENCE: Tobucksy COUNTY. **Choctaw Nation** Choctaw Roll CARD NO.
POST OFFICE: McAlester, I.T. (Not Including Freedmen) FIELD NO. 2918

Dawes' Roll No.	NAME		Relationship to Person First Named	AGE	SEX	BLOOD	TRIBAL ENROLLMENT		
							Year	County	No.
I.W. 966	1 McClure, Carrie L	37	First Named	34	F	I.W.	1896	Tobucksy	14863
8588	2 " Mary E	13	Dau	10	"	1/16	1896	"	9180
8589	3 " Margaret S	10	"	7	"	1/16	1896	"	9181
8590	4 " Sudye J	7	"	4	"	1/16	1896	"	9182
	5								

Jan 6 1904 Decision of Commission
enrolling No 1 rendered
Feb 12, 1904 Record and decision forwarded Department
8   Decision of Commission of Jan 6
9   1904 enrolling No 1 approved by
10   Department July 22, 1904
11   (I.T.D. 2222.5138 - 1904

ENROLLMENT
OF NOS. ~ 1 ~ HEREON
APPROVED BY THE SECRETARY
OF INTERIOR SEP 22 1904

ENROLLMENT
OF NOS. 2, 3, 4 HEREON
APPROVED BY THE SECRETARY
OF INTERIOR JAN 17 1903

TRIBAL ENROLLMENT OF PARENTS

Name of Father	Year	County	Name of Mother	Year	County
1 H. R. Schermerhorn	1896	Non Citz	Mary A Schermerhorn	1896	Non Citz
2 Preemon J McClure	1896	Tobucksy	No 1		
3 " " "	1896	"	No 1		
4 " " "	1896	"	No 1		

7 Marriage certificate dated June 16, 1886, of
8 marriage between Preeman[sic] J McClure
and Carrie L Schermerhorn, signed W.
9 B.J. Lond, exhibited, but not in a condition
10 to be filed. Does not disclose the fact
11 that Loyd was a Minister
See her testimony.
12 Certified copey[sic] of certificate of marriage between No 1 and
13 Preeman J McClure filed July 15, 1903.

Date of Application for Enrollment.
6/20/99

17 P.O. Hartshorne I.T. 7/20/03

218

Choctaw By Blood Enrollment Cards 1898-1914

RESIDENCE: Sugar Loaf	COUNTY.						CARD NO.	
POST OFFICE: Summerfield, I.T.	**Choctaw Nation**				Choctaw Roll (Not Including Freedmen)		FIELD NO. 2919	

Dawes' Roll No.	NAME	Relationship to Person First Named	AGE	SEX	BLOOD	TRIBAL ENROLLMENT		
						Year	County	No.
DEAD.	1 Shwinogee, Permelia DEAD.		18	F	Full	1896	Sugar Loaf	5213
8591	2 " Lucinda 3	Dau	2mo	"	"			
	3							
	4							
	5 No. 1 HEREON DISMISSED UNDER							
	6 ORDER OF THE COMMISSION TO THE FIVE CIVILIZED TRIBES OF MARCH 31, 1905.							
	7							
	8							
	9							
	10							
	11							
	12							
	13							
	14							
	15 ENROLLMENT OF NOS. 2 HEREON							
	16 APPROVED BY THE SECRETARY OF INTERIOR JAN 17 1903							
	17							

TRIBAL ENROLLMENT OF PARENTS

Name of Father	Year	County	Name of Mother	Year	County
1 Sweeny Holson	1896	Sugar Loaf	Sukey Holson	Dead	Sugar Loaf
2 Sam Shawonoli		Choctaw	No1		
3					
4					
5					
6 On 1896 roll as Termelia Holson					
7 Husband on Card D257					
8 N°1 Died Dec. 31, 1901, See testimony of her husband Sam Shawanoli[sic] taken April 7, 1902					
9 Husband of No1 transferred from Choctaw Card #D257 to					
10 Chickasaw card #D362 Aug 20 1902					
11					
12					
13					
14					
15				Date of Application for Enrollment.	
16				6/20/99	
17			No2 enrolled Dec 14/99		

RESIDENCE:	Sans Bois	COUNTY.	**Choctaw Nation**		Choctaw Roll	CARD NO.	
POST OFFICE:	Sans Bois, I.T				*(Not Including Freedmen)*	FIELD NO.	2920

Dawes' Roll No.	NAME	Relationship to Person First Named	AGE	SEX	BLOOD	TRIBAL ENROLLMENT		
						Year	County	No.
8592	1 Belvin, Lucinda		16	F	Full	1896	Sans Bois	591
8593	2 Carney, Allie May	Dau	10mo	F	1/2			
	3							
	4							
	5							
	6							
	7							
	8							
	9							
	10							
	11							
	12							
	13							
	14							
	15	ENROLLMENT OF NOS. 1 and 2 HEREON						
	16	APPROVED BY THE SECRETARY OF INTERIOR JAN 17 1903						
	17							

TRIBAL ENROLLMENT OF PARENTS

Name of Father	Year	County	Name of Mother	Year	County
1 Hagan Belvin	1896	Sans Bois	Elsie Moore	1896	Sans Bois
2 Robert Carney		Choc Freedman	No 1		
3					
4					
5					
6					
7		No2 Enrolled Aug 23, 1901			
8		No.2 Died June 23, 1902: Proof of death filed Dec 30 1902			
9					
10		For child of No.1 see NB (Apr. 26-06) No. 789			
11					
12					
13					
14					
15					
16			Date of Application for Enrollment.	6/20/99	
17					

Choctaw By Blood Enrollment Cards 1898-1914

RESIDENCE: Sugar Loaf COUNTY. **Choctaw Nation** **Choctaw Roll** CARD No.
POST OFFICE: Le Flore, I.T *(Not Including Freedmen)* FIELD No. 2921

Dawes' Roll No.	NAME	Relationship to Person First Named	AGE	SEX	BLOOD	TRIBAL ENROLLMENT		
						Year	County	No.
8594	1 Roberson, James 55	First Named	53	M	Full	1896	Sugar Loaf	10715
8595	2 " Pollie 36	Wife	33	F	"	1896	" "	10716
8596	3 " Gibson 17	Son	14	M	"	1896	" "	10718
8597	4 " Caldwell 11	"	8	"	"	1896	" "	10719
8598	5 Loman, Kizzie 18	S.Dau	15	F	3/4	1896	" "	10717
	6							
	7							
	8							
	9							
	10							
	11							
	12							
	13							
	14							
	15	ENROLLMENT OF NOS. 1,2,3,4,5 HEREON APPROVED BY THE SECRETARY OF INTERIOR JAN 17 1903						
	16							
	17							

TRIBAL ENROLLMENT OF PARENTS

	Name of Father	Year	County	Name of Mother	Year	County
1	Co-le-cha	Dead	Sugar Loaf		Dead	Gaines
2	Tom Holloway	"	Skullyville		"	Skullyville
3	No 1			Sibbie Roberson	"	Sugar Loaf
4	No 1			No 2		
5	Ismon Loman	Dead	Gaines	No 2		
6						
7						
8						
9						
10	No5 on 1896 roll as Kizzie Roberson					
11	No.5 also on 1896 roll as Lizzie Loman: page 194: #7797					
12						
13						
14						
15						
16				Date of Application for Enrollment.	6/20/99	
17						

221

Choctaw By Blood Enrollment Cards 1898-1914

RESIDENCE:	Sugar Loaf	COUNTY.	**Choctaw Nation**	**Choctaw Roll**	CARD No.	
POST OFFICE:	Red Oak, I.T.			*(Not Including Freedmen)*	FIELD No.	2922

Dawes' Roll No.	NAME	Relationship to Person	AGE	SEX	BLOOD	TRIBAL ENROLLMENT		
						Year	County	No.
8599	1 Wright, Steward 22	First Named	19	M	Full	1896	Sugar Loaf	12910
	2							
	3							
	4							
	5							
	6							
	7							
	8							
	9							
	10							
	11							
	12							
	13							
	14							
	15	ENROLLMENT OF NOS. 1 HEREON						
	16	APPROVED BY THE SECRETARY OF INTERIOR JAN 17 1903						
	17							

TRIBAL ENROLLMENT OF PARENTS

Name of Father	Year	County	Name of Mother	Year	County
1 Simon Wright	Dead	Sugar Loaf	Sophie Wright	Dead	Sugar Loaf
2					
3					
4					
5					
6					
7					
8					
9					
10					
11					
12					
13					
14					
15					
16			Date of Application for Enrollment.	6/20/99	
17					

Choctaw By Blood Enrollment Cards 1898-1914

RESIDENCE: Sugar Loaf COUNTY. **Choctaw Nation** **Choctaw Roll** CARD NO.
POST OFFICE: Red Oak, I.T. *(Not Including Freedmen)* FIELD NO. 2923

Dawes' Roll No.	NAME		Relationship to Person	AGE	SEX	BLOOD	TRIBAL ENROLLMENT		
							Year	County	No.
8600	1 Harlen, Logan	30	First Named	27	M	1/2	1896	Gaines	5319
8601	2 " Amey	20	Sister	17	F	1/2	1896	"	5323
8602	3 " Bency	19	"	16	"	1/2	1896	"	5324
	4								
	5								
	6								
	7								
	8								
	9								
	10								
	11								
	12								
	13								
	14								
	15	ENROLLMENT OF NOS. 1, 2, 3 HEREON APPROVED BY THE SECRETARY OF INTERIOR JAN 17 1903							
	16								
	17								

TRIBAL ENROLLMENT OF PARENTS

	Name of Father		Year	County	Name of Mother		Year	County
1	Edmond Harlen		Dead	Chickasaw	Sis Harlen		Dead	Gaines
2	"	"	"	"	"	"	"	"
3	"	"	"	"	"	"	"	"
4								
5								
6								
7								
8								
9			No3 on 1896 roll as Densey Harlen					
10								
11			Wife of No1 on Chickasaw Card No 1469					
12			For child of No.1 see NB (Mar 3 '05) #407					
13								
14								Date of Application for Enrollment.
15								
16								6/20/99
17								

Roll No. 2583

No.1 is duplicate of Bency Harlen on Choctaw Card #976 Enrollment [illegible] cancelled by Department January 21, 1903 [illegible]

Choctaw By Blood Enrollment Cards 1898-1914

| RESIDENCE: Sugar Loaf COUNTY. | Choctaw Nation | Choctaw Roll | CARD NO. |
| POST OFFICE: Le Flore, I.T. | | (Not Including Freedmen) | FIELD NO. 2924 |

Dawes' Roll No.	NAME		Relationship to Person First Named	AGE	SEX	BLOOD	TRIBAL ENROLLMENT		
							Year	County	No.
8603	1 Jones, Willis	55	First Named	52	M	Full	1896	Sugar Loaf	6549
8604	2 " Mary	56	Wife	53	F	"	1896	" "	6550
8605	3 Nancy DIED PRIOR TO SEPTEMBER 25, 1902		Ward	20	"	"	1893	" "	543
	4								
	5								
	6								
	7								
	8								
	9								
	10								
	11								
	12								
	13								
	14								
	15	ENROLLMENT OF NOS. 1, 2, 3 HEREON APPROVED BY THE SECRETARY OF INTERIOR JAN 17 1903							
	16								
	17								

TRIBAL ENROLLMENT OF PARENTS

	Name of Father	Year	County	Name of Mother	Year	County
1	Jesse Jones	Dead	Sans Bois	E-la-ho-to-na	Dead	Sans Bois
2	E-la-po-tubbee	"	Jacks Fork	E-ka-nalle	"	Sugar Loaf
3	Johnson Jones	"	Gaines	Louisiana Jones	"	Gaines
4						
5						
6						
7						
8						
9						
10	No3 on 1893 Pay Roll, Gaines Co. Page 58 No 543					
11	No3 died Nov 14, 1902; proof of death filed Dec 20 1902					
12						
13						
14						
15						
16				Date of Application for Enrollment.	6/20/99	
17						

Choctaw By Blood Enrollment Cards 1898-1914

RESIDENCE: Sugar Loaf COUNTY. **Choctaw Nation** Choctaw Roll CARD No.
POST OFFICE: Fanshaw, I.T. (Not Including Freedmen) FIELD No. 2925

Dawes' Roll No.	NAME	Relationship to Person First Named	AGE	SEX	BLOOD	TRIBAL ENROLLMENT Year	County	No.
8606	1 McCurtain, Sliphy	DIED PRIOR TO SEPTEMBER 25, 1902	27	F	Full	1896	Sugar Loaf	9086
	2							
	3							
	4							
	5							
	6							
	7							
	8							
	9							
	10							
	11							
	12							
	13							
	14							
	15	ENROLLMENT OF NOS. 1 HEREON APPROVED BY THE SECRETARY OF INTERIOR JAN 17 1903						
	16							
	17							

TRIBAL ENROLLMENT OF PARENTS

	Name of Father	Year	County	Name of Mother	Year	County
1	Cornelius McCurtain	Dead	Sugar Loaf	Wacey McCurtain	Dead	Sugar Loaf
2						
3						
4						
5						
6						
7						
8	Nº1 Died March 14, 1902, proof of death filed Jany 5, 1903					
9	No1 died March 14, 1902; Enrollment cancelled by Department July 5, 1904					
10						
11						
12						
13						
14						
15					Date of Application for Enrollment.	
16					6/20/99	
17						

225

Choctaw By Blood Enrollment Cards 1898-1914

RESIDENCE: Sugar Loaf	COUNTY.		**Choctaw Nation**			**Choctaw Roll**	CARD No.	
POST OFFICE: Le Flore, I.T.						*(Not Including Freedmen)*	FIELD No.	2926

Dawes' Roll No.	NAME	Relationship to Person First Named	AGE	SEX	BLOOD	TRIBAL ENROLLMENT		
						Year	County	No.
8607	1 Jones, Jackson 33		30	M	Full	1896	Sugar Loaf	6547
8608	2 Annie DIED PRIOR TO SEPTEMBER 25, 1902	Dau	1½	F	"			
	3							
	4							
	5							
	6							
	7							
	8							
	9							
	10							
	11							
	12							
	13							
	14							
	15	ENROLLMENT OF NOS. 1 and 2 HEREON						
	16	APPROVED BY THE SECRETARY OF INTERIOR JAN 17 1903						
	17							

TRIBAL ENROLLMENT OF PARENTS

Name of Father	Year	County	Name of Mother	Year	County	
1 Lemon Jones	Dead	Sugar Loaf	Ish-te-chi	Dead	Sugar Loaf	
2 No1			Sophie Jones	"	"	"
3						
4						
5 No1 died in October 1901. Enrollment cancelled by Department Nov 22, 1906						
6 No2 died July 23, 1902. Enrollment cancelled by Department Dec 24 1904						
7						
8						
9 March 19, 1909 Department requests report as to No1 hereon						
10 March 31, 1909 Report to Department						
11						
12						
13						
14						
15			Date of Application for Enrollment			
16			6/20/99			
17						

226

Choctaw By Blood Enrollment Cards 1898-1914

RESIDENCE: Sugar Loaf	COUNTY.								
POST OFFICE: Fanshaw, I.T.	**Choctaw Nation**					Choctaw Roll *(Not Including Freedmen)*		CARD No. FIELD No. 2927	

Dawes' Roll No.	NAME		Relationship to Person First Named	AGE	SEX	BLOOD	TRIBAL ENROLLMENT		
							Year	County	No.
8609	1 Ripley, Dixon	25	First Named	22	M	Full	1896	Sugar Loaf	11234
	2								
	3								
	4								
	5								
	6								
	7								
	8								
	9								
	10								
	11								
	12								
	13								
	14								
	15	ENROLLMENT OF NOS. 1 HEREON APPROVED BY THE SECRETARY OF INTERIOR JAN 17 1903							
	16								
	17								

TRIBAL ENROLLMENT OF PARENTS

	Name of Father	Year	County	Name of Mother	Year	County
1	Simon Ripley	Dead	in Mississippi	Cisby Ripley	Dead	in Mississippi
2						
3						
4						
5						
6						
7			On 1896 roll as Dixon Sockey			
8			For child of No1 see NB (March 3, 1905) #1001			
9						
10						
11						
12						
13						
14						
15					Date of Application for Enrollment.	
16					6/20/99	
17						

Choctaw By Blood Enrollment Cards 1898-1914

RESIDENCE:	Sugar Loaf	COUNTY.	Choctaw Nation		Choctaw Roll	CARD NO.	
POST OFFICE:	Le Flore, I.T.				(Not Including Freedmen)	FIELD NO.	2928

Dawes' Roll No.	NAME		Relationship to Person First Named	AGE	SEX	BLOOD	TRIBAL ENROLLMENT		
							Year	County	No.
8610	₁ M°Curtain, Joseph	DIED PRIOR TO SEPTEMBER 25 1902	First Named	40	M	Full	1896	Sugar Loaf	9129
8611	₂ " Silly ⁵³		Wife	50	F	"	1896	" "	9130
8612	₃ " Thomas ¹⁷		Son	14	M	"	1896	" "	9131
8613	₄ " Martha ¹⁴		Dau	11	F	"	1896	" "	9132
8614	₅ " Mary ⁹		"	6	"	"	1896	" "	9133
	₆								
	₇								
	₈								
	₉								
	10								
	11								
	12								
	13								
	14								
	15								
	16								
	17								

ENROLLMENT
OF NOS. 1,2,3,4,5 HEREON
APPROVED BY THE SECRETARY
OF INTERIOR JAN 17 1903

TRIBAL ENROLLMENT OF PARENTS

	Name of Father	Year	County	Name of Mother	Year	County	
₁	Pooley M°Curtain	Dead	Sans Bois	Te-la-ma	Dead	Sugar Loaf	
₂	Al-yo-tubbee	"	Sugar Loaf	Pe-sa-ten-la	"	" "	
₃	No1			No2			
₄	No1			No2			
₅	No1			No2			
₆							
₇							
₈							
₉	No1 died March 12, 1902: proof of death filed Dec 20 1902						
10	No1 died March 12, 1902: Enrollment cancelled by Department July 8, 1904						
11	No.3 is now husband of No1 on Choctaw card #2407				12/17/02		
12	For child of No3 see NB (Mar 3-1905) Card No 144						
13							
14							
15							
16				Date of Application for Enrollment.	6/20/99		
17	PO Red Oak I.T.						

12/12/02

Choctaw By Blood Enrollment Cards 1898-1914

RESIDENCE:	Sugar Loaf	COUNTY.							
POST OFFICE:	Summerfield, I.T.	**Choctaw Nation**				**Choctaw Roll** (Not Including Freedmen)		CARD NO. FIELD NO.	2929

Dawes' Roll No.	NAME		Relationship to Person	AGE	SEX	BLOOD	TRIBAL ENROLLMENT		
							Year	County	No.
8615	1 Harris, Albert	26	First Named	23	M	Full	1896	Sugar Loaf	5241
	2								
	3								
	4								
	5								
	6								
	7								
	8								
	9								
	10								
	11								
	12								
	13								
	14								
	15	ENROLLMENT OF NOS. 1 HEREON APPROVED BY THE SECRETARY OF INTERIOR JAN 17 1903							
	16								
	17								

TRIBAL ENROLLMENT OF PARENTS

Name of Father	Year	County	Name of Mother	Year	County
1 Solomon Harris	Dead	Sugar Loaf	Mamis Freemon	1896	Sugar Loaf
2					
3					
4					
5					
6					
7					
8					
9					
10					
11					
12					
13					
14					
15					
16			Date of Application for Enrollment.	6/20/99	
17					

Choctaw By Blood Enrollment Cards 1898-1914

RESIDENCE: Sans Bois	COUNTY.				Choctaw Roll	CARD NO.	
POST OFFICE: Enterprise, I.T.	**Choctaw Nation**				(Not Including Freedmen)	FIELD NO. 2930	

Dawes' Roll No.	NAME	Relationship to Person First Named	AGE	SEX	BLOOD	TRIBAL ENROLLMENT		
						Year	County	No.
I.W. 916	1 Bickle, James A 44		41	M	I.W.	1896	Sans Bois	14278
8616	2 " Susan 37	Wife	34	F	1/2	1896	" "	622
8617	3 " Serina DIED PRIOR TO SEPTEMBER 25, 1902	Dau	16	"	1/4	1896	" "	623
8618	4 " Lula 13	"	10	"	1/4	1896	" "	624
8619	5 " Lona 11	"	8	"	1/4	1896	" "	625
8620	6 " Scott 9	Son	6	M	1/4	1896	" "	626
8621	7 " Jack 7	"	4	"	1/4	1896	" "	627
8622	8 " Roxy 4	Dau	1	dF	1/4			
8623	9 " Greenwood 3	Son	3mo	M	1/4			
8624	10 " Fannie 1	Dau	3wks	F	1/4			
	11 No.3 Died Feby 6,1901: Proof of death filed Dec 23, 1902							
	12 No.3 died Feb 6, 1901. Enrollment							
	13 cancelled by Department July 8, 1904							
	14					ENROLLMENT		
	15 ENROLLMENT OF NOS. 2,3,4,5,6,7,8,9,10 HEREON					OF NOS. 1 HEREON APPROVED BY THE SECRETARY		
	16 APPROVED BY THE SECRETARY					OF INTERIOR AUG 3 1904		
	17 OF INTERIOR JAN 17 1903							

TRIBAL ENROLLMENT OF PARENTS

	Name of Father	Year	County	Name of Mother	Year	County
1	George Bickle	Dead	Non Citz	Brasha Bickle	Dead	Non Citz
2	Kelly Frazier	"	Tobucksy	Lizzie Frazier	1896	white woman
3	No1			No2		
4	No1			No2		
5	No1			No2		
6	No1			No2		
7	No1			No2		
8	No1			No2		
9	No.1			No.2		
10	No.1			No.2		
11	No3 on 1896 roll as Bessie Bickle					
12	No4 " 1896 " " Lula "					
13	No6 " 1896 " " Scott B "					
13	No8 Affidavit of birth to be supplied: Recd Oct 6/99					
14	As to proof of marriage of parents				#1 to 8	
15	of No2, see Card of Lizzie Frazier				Date of Application for Enrollment.	
16	No.10 born Dec. 6, 1901: Enrolled Dec. 26, 1901.				6/20/99	
16	No.9 Enrolled May 24, 1900					
17	For child of Nos 1&2 see NB (March 3, 1905) #1041					

P.O. Quinton I.T. 4/3/05

Choctaw By Blood Enrollment Cards 1898-1914

RESIDENCE: Sans Bois   COUNTY. **Choctaw Nation**   **Choctaw Roll** CARD NO.

POST OFFICE: Sans Bois, I.T.   *(Not Including Freedmen)* FIELD NO. 2931

Dawes' Roll No.	NAME		Relationship to Person First Named	AGE	SEX	BLOOD	TRIBAL ENROLLMENT		
							Year	County	No.
15788	1 Fargo, Robert L	30		27	M	3/16			
	2								
	3								
	4								
	5								
	6								
	7								
	8								
	9								
	10								
	11								
	12								
	13								
	14								
	15	ENROLLMENT OF NOS. 1 HEREON APPROVED BY THE SECRETARY OF INTERIOR MAR 15 1905							
	16								
	17								

TRIBAL ENROLLMENT OF PARENTS

	Name of Father	Year	County	Name of Mother	Year	County
1	Charles A Fargo	1896	Cherokee	Narcissa Fargo	Dead	Choctaw
2						
3	No 1 on 1880 Cherokee roll Sequoyah Dist page 696, No. 501, as Robert Fargo					
4	No.1 " 1894 " " " page 956 No. 541					
5	No.1 " 1896 " " " page 1068 No. 555					
6						
7	Admitted by Dawes Commission Case No 489 No appeal					
8						
9	Is also enrolled and has always lived in					
10	the Cherokee Nation on 1880 Roll Elects to enroll in					
11	the Choctaw Nation.					
12	See that this is noted upon Cherokee Rolls. Properly noted on Cherokee Rolls Jany 16, 1901					
13						
14	No1 is now residing in California Feby 19, 1902				Date of Application for Enrollment. 6/20/99	
15						
16						
17	P.O. Muldrow I.T. 11/7/04					

Choctaw By Blood Enrollment Cards 1898-1914

RESIDENCE: Sugar Loaf COUNTY. **Choctaw Nation**
POST OFFICE: Le Flore, I.T.

Choctaw Roll CARD NO.
(Not Including Freedmen) FIELD NO. 2932

Dawes' Roll No.	NAME	Relationship to Person First Named	AGE	SEX	BLOOD	TRIBAL ENROLLMENT Year	TRIBAL ENROLLMENT County	TRIBAL ENROLLMENT No.
8625	1 Pearse, George	25 First Named	22	M	Full	1896	Sugar Loaf	10133
	2							
	3							
	4							
	5							
	6							
	7							
	8							
	9							
	10							
	11							
	12							
	13							
	14							
	15							
	16							
	17							

ENROLLMENT
OF NOS. 1 HEREON
APPROVED BY THE SECRETARY
OF INTERIOR JAN 17 1903

TRIBAL ENROLLMENT OF PARENTS

Name of Father	Year	County	Name of Mother	Year	County
1 Mih-yo-tubbee	Dead	Sugar Loaf	Susie Amos	Dead	Sugar Loaf
2					
3					
4					
5					
6					
7					
8					
9					
10					
11					
12					
13					
14					
15				Date of Application for Enrollment.	
16				6/20/99	
17					

Choctaw By Blood Enrollment Cards 1898-1914

RESIDENCE:	Sans Bois	COUNTY.	**Choctaw Nation**		**Choctaw Roll**	CARD NO.	
POST OFFICE:	Red Ok I.T.				(Not Including Freedmen)	FIELD NO.	2933

Dawes' Roll No.	NAME		Relationship to Person First Named	AGE	SEX	BLOOD	TRIBAL ENROLLMENT		
							Year	County	No.
8626	1 Pope Lucy	26	First Named	23	F	Full	1893	Tobucksey[sic]	722
8627	2 Silmon Jennie	5	Dau	2	F	"			
8628	3 Pope, Onie	DIED PRIOR TO SEPTEMBER 25, 1902	Dau	8mo	F	3/4			
8629	4 " Winnie	1	"	4mo	"	3/4			
	5								
	6								
	7								
	8								
	9								
	10								
	11								
	12								
	13								
	14								
	15	ENROLLMENT OF NOS. 1,2,3,4 HEREON							
	16	APPROVED BY THE SECRETARY							
	17	OF INTERIOR JAN 17 1903							

TRIBAL ENROLLMENT OF PARENTS

	Name of Father	Year	County	Name of Mother	Year	County
1	Wallace Sam	Dead	Tobucksey[sic]	Fannie Sam	1896	Tobucksey
2	Lee Silmon	1896	"	No 1		
3	Gilbert Pope		Chickasaw roll	No 1		
4	" "			No 1		
5						
6						
7	No1 On 1896 roll as Lou Sam					
8	Husband on Chick Card No. 1458 → transferred to Choctaw card #5578					
9	No3 died Sept 19 1902, enrollment cancelled by Department July 1, 1903					
10	No.1 On page 85 #722 – 93 P.R. Tobucksy Co as Rosa Sam					
	No.3 Enrolled April 15, 1901					
11	No4 Born June 18, 1902 – Proof of birth filed Oct. 25, 1902					
12	For child of No1 see NB (Apr 26-06) Card #728					
	" " " " " (Mar 3-05) " #221					
13						
14						
15						9/8/99
16					Date of Application for Enrollment.	6/20/99
17	PO Krebs IT 1/9/05					

Choctaw By Blood Enrollment Cards 1898-1914

RESIDENCE:	Sans Bois	COUNTY.	**Choctaw Nation**	Choctaw Roll	CARD NO.	
POST OFFICE:	Red Oak I.T.			(Not Including Freedmen)	FIELD NO.	2934

Dawes' Roll No.	NAME	Relationship to Person First Named	AGE	SEX	BLOOD	TRIBAL ENROLLMENT		
						Year	County	No.
8630	1 Pope Battiest 53	First Named	50	M	Full	1896	Skullyville	10101
	2							
	3							
	4							
	5							
	6							
	7							
	8							
	9							
	10							
	11							
	12							
	13							
	14							
	15	ENROLLMENT OF NOS. 1 HEREON APPROVED BY THE SECRETARY OF INTERIOR JAN 17 1903						
	16							
	17							

TRIBAL ENROLLMENT OF PARENTS

	Name of Father	Year	County	Name of Mother	Year	County
1	Alexander Pope	Dead	Skullyville	Shah-we	Dead	Skullyville
2						
3						
4						
5						
6						
7		On 1896 roll as Battice Pope				
8						
9						
10						
11						
12						
13						
14						
15					Date of Application for Enrollment.	
16					6/20/99	
17						

234

Choctaw By Blood Enrollment Cards 1898-1914

RESIDENCE: Sugar Loaf   COUNTY.   **Choctaw Nation**   Choctaw Roll *(Not Including Freedmen)*   CARD NO.
POST OFFICE: Le Flore I.T.   FIELD NO. 2935

Dawes' Roll No.	NAME	Relationship to Person First Named	AGE	SEX	BLOOD	TRIBAL ENROLLMENT		
						Year	County	No.
8631	1 Yota Dave ³³	First Named	30	M	Full	1896	Sugar Loaf	14199
8632	2 DIED PRIOR TO SEPTEMBER 25, 1902 Sissie	Wife	20	F	"	1896	" "	14200
8633	3 " Calvin ¹⁰	StepSon	7	M	"	P.R. 1893	" "	856
8634	4 DIED PRIOR TO SEPTEMBER 25, 1902 Manda	Dau	4	F	"	1896	" "	14201
	5							
	6							
	7							
	8							
	9							
	10							
	11							
	12							
	13							
	14							
	15	ENROLLMENT OF NOS. 1,2,3,4, HEREON						
	16	APPROVED BY THE SECRETARY OF INTERIOR JAN 17 1903						
	17							

TRIBAL ENROLLMENT OF PARENTS

	Name of Father	Year	County	Name of Mother	Year	County
1	Thomas Yota	Dead	Sugar Loaf	Melvina Yota	Dead	Sugar Loaf
2	Charleson Wesley	1896	" "	Annie Wesley	"	Gaines
3	George Burney	Dead	Gaines	No 2		
4	No 1			No 2		
5						
6	No3 On page 93 No 856 1893 Pay Roll Sugar Loaf Co					
7	as Calvin Yutah					
8	All on roll as Yoter					
9	No2 died January – 1900 proof of death filed Dec 20 1902					
10	No4 " November 1,1900; " " " " " " "					
11	No2 died Jan-1900; No4 died March 1, 1900; Enrollment cancelled by Department July 8, 1904					
11	N°3 also on 1896 Choctaw Census roll page 184 #7473 as Calvin Ketubbee					
12	N°1 now married to Celis Yotah					
13	N°3 is now known by both surnames Yotah and Ketubbee					
14						
15						
16					Date of Application for Enrollment.	6/20/99
17						

Choctaw By Blood Enrollment Cards 1898-1914

RESIDENCE: Sans Bois COUNTY.
POST OFFICE: Iron Bridge I.T.

Choctaw Nation
(Not Including Freedmen)

Choctaw Roll

CARD NO.
FIELD NO. 2936

Dawes' Roll No.	NAME	Relationship to Person First Named	AGE	SEX	BLOOD	TRIBAL ENROLLMENT Year	County	No.
8635	1 Bascom John 31	First Named	28	M	Full	1896	Sans Bois	685
	2							
	3							
	4							
	5							
	6							
	7							
	8							
	9							
	10							
	11							
	12							
	13							
	14							
	15							
	16							
	17							

ENROLLMENT
OF NOS. 1 HEREON
APPROVED BY THE SECRETARY
OF INTERIOR JAN 17 1903

TRIBAL ENROLLMENT OF PARENTS

Name of Father	Year	County	Name of Mother	Year	County
1 Cornelius Bascom	Dead	Skullyville	Wicey Bascom	Dead	Skullyville
2					
3					
4					
5					
6					
7					
8					
9					
10					
11					
12					
13					
14					
15					
16					
17					

Nº1 is husband of Alice Hickman and father of
Charlotte Bascom on Choctaw Card #2004
For child of No.1 see NB (Mar 3 '05) #523

DATE OF APPLICATION FOR ENROLLMENT. 6/20/99

236

Choctaw By Blood Enrollment Cards 1898-1914

RESIDENCE: **Sans Bois**   COUNTY.

POST OFFICE: **Red Oak I.T.**

Choctaw Nation
(Not Including Freedmen)

Choctaw Roll

CARD NO.

FIELD NO. **2937**

Dawes' Roll No.	NAME		Relationship to Person	AGE	SEX	BLOOD	TRIBAL ENROLLMENT		
							Year	County	No.
8636	1 James Joseph	48	First Named	45	M	Full	1896	Sans Bois	6416
8637	2 " Nellie	28	Wife	25	F	"	1896	" "	6417
8638	3 " Collin	25	Son	22	M	"	1896	" "	6418
8639	4 " William	9	"	6	M	"	1896	" "	6420
8640	5 " Levi	DIED PRIOR TO SEPTEMBER 25, 1902	"	4	M	"	1896	" "	6421
8641	6 " Dallas	5	"	17mo	M	"		" "	
8642	7 " Vina	3	Dau	2mo	F	"			
8643	8 " Elmer	1	Son	6mo	M	"			
	9								
	10								
	11								
	12								
	13								
	14								
	15	ENROLLMENT OF NOS 1,2,3,4,5,6,7,8 HEREON APPROVED BY THE SECRETARY OF INTERIOR JAN 17 1903							
	16								
	17								

TRIBAL ENROLLMENT OF PARENTS

	Name of Father	Year	County	Name of Mother	Year	County
1	Joshua James	Dead	Sans Bois	Biney James	Dead	Skullyville
2	Ay-a-kan-ta-be	"	Skullyville	Mary Jefferson	1896	"
3	No 1			Tennessee James	Dead	Sans Bois
4	No 1			No 2		
5	No 1			No 2		
6	No 1			No 2		
7	No 1			No 2		
8	No.1			No.2		
9	No1 On 1896 roll as Joe James					
10	No4 " 1896 " " Willis "					
11	No4 Brother John on Chickasaw Roll, Card No. 1461					
12	No.8 born May 15, 1901: Enrolled Nov. 22d, 1901					
13	Nº5 Died Nov 15, 1900; proof of death filed Dec 24 1902					
	No5 died Nov. 15, 1900: Enrollment cancelled by Department July 8, 1904					
14	For children of Nos 1&2 see NB (Mar 3, 1905) #617					
15					#1 to 6	
16					Date of Application for Enrollment.	6/20/99
17					No7 enrolled Nov 1/99	

Choctaw By Blood Enrollment Cards 1898-1914

RESIDENCE: Sans Bois	COUNTY.	Choctaw Nation		Choctaw Roll	CARD NO.
POST OFFICE: Red Oak I.T.				(Not Including Freedmen)	FIELD NO. 2938

Dawes' Roll No.	NAME	Relationship to Person	AGE	SEX	BLOOD	TRIBAL ENROLLMENT		
						Year	County	No.
8644	1 Hancock Israel 25	First Named	22	M	Full	1896	Gaines	5303
	2							
	3							
	4							
	5							
	6							
	7							
	8							
	9							
	10							
	11							
	12							
	13							
	14							
	15							
	16							
	17							

ENROLLMENT
OF NOS. 1 HEREON
APPROVED BY THE SECRETARY
OF INTERIOR JAN 17 1903

TRIBAL ENROLLMENT OF PARENTS

	Name of Father	Year	County	Name of Mother	Year	County
1	Benjamin Hancock	Dead	Gaines	Eliza Hancock	Dead	Gaines
2						
3						
4						
5						
6						
7						
8						
9						
10						
11						
12						
13						
14						
15						
16				Date of Application for Enrollment.	6/20/99	
17						

Choctaw By Blood Enrollment Cards 1898-1914

RESIDENCE: Sugar Loaf COUNTY. **Choctaw Nation** Choctaw Roll CARD No.
POST OFFICE: Le Flore I.T. *(Not Including Freedmen)* FIELD NO. 2939

Dawes' Roll No.	NAME	Relationship to Person First Named	AGE	SEX	BLOOD	TRIBAL ENROLLMENT Year	County	No.
8645	1 Sockey Vincy DIED PRIOR TO SEPTEMBER 25 1902		60	F	Full	1896	Sugar Loaf	11233
8646	2 Amos, Lena 17	Niece	14	F	"	1896	" "	12892
8647	3 Wishock, Dora DIED PRIOR TO SEPTEMBER 25 1902	"	12	F	"	1896	" "	12893
8648	4 " Cora 11	"	8	F	"	1896	" "	12894
8649	5 Amos Allen Wesley 2	G. N	3mo	M	"			
14894	6 Sockey Willie 1	Son of Nº2	10mo	M	"			
	7							
	8					ENROLLMENT OF NOS. 6 HEREON		
	9					APPROVED BY THE SECRETARY OF INTERIOR MAY 21 1903		
	10							
	11							
	12							
	13							
	14							
	15	ENROLLMENT OF NOS. 1,2,3,4,5 HEREON						
	16	APPROVED BY THE SECRETARY						
	17	OF INTERIOR JAN 17 1903						

TRIBAL ENROLLMENT OF PARENTS

	Name of Father	Year	County	Name of Mother	Year	County
1	Ta-hom-ba	Dead	Red River	Betsy	Dead	Miss.
2	Wesley W. Wishock	"	Sugar Loaf	Maria Wishock	"	Jack's Fork
3	" " "	"	" "	" "	"	" " "
4	" " "	"	" "	" "	"	" " "
5	Sexton Amos			No 2		
6	Dixon Sockey			Nº2		
7						
8	No2 On 1896 roll as Lena Williams					
9	No3 " 1896 ' " Dora Williams					
10	No4 " 1896 ' " Cora Williams					
11	No1 " 1896 ' " Vince Sockey					
	No5 Enrolled Oct 9th 1900					
12	No1 Died in August 1901. Proof of death filed Dec 24 1902					
13	No3 Died March 12, 1900: Proof of death filed Dec 24 1902					
	Father of No5 is Amos Sexton on Choctaw card #3051					
14	Nº6 Born Feby 3,1902. Application made Dec 18,1902 Proof of birth filed Feb 6,1903					
15	No1 died Aug-1901: No3 died March 12, 1900: Enrollment cancelled by Department 8, 1904					
16	For child of No.2 see NB (March 3, 1905) #1001				6/20/99
17	No2 PO Hughes IT 4/8/05					

#1 to 4 in Date of application for enrollment

Choctaw By Blood Enrollment Cards 1898-1914

RESIDENCE:	Skullyville	COUNTY.	Choctaw Nation		Choctaw Roll	CARD NO.	
POST OFFICE:	Lodi I.T.				(Not Including Freedmen)	FIELD NO.	2940

Dawes' Roll No.	NAME	Relationship to Person First Named	AGE	SEX	BLOOD	TRIBAL ENROLLMENT		
						Year	County	No.
8650	1 Adams Cornelius DIED PRIOR TO SEPTEMBER 25, 1902		39	M	Full	1896	Skullyville	35
	2							
	3							
	4							
	5							
	6							
	7							
	8							
	9							
	10							
	11							
	12							
	13							
	14							
	15							
	16							
	17							

ENROLLMENT
OF NOS. 1 HEREON
APPROVED BY THE SECRETARY
OF INTERIOR JAN 17 1903

TRIBAL ENROLLMENT OF PARENTS

	Name of Father	Year	County	Name of Mother	Year	County
1	John Williams	Dead	Skullyville	Chi-an-ho-ke	Dead	Skullyville
2						
3						
4						
5						
6						
7	Nº1 Died Aug 13, 1901, proof of death filed Dec 24 1902					
8	No1 died Aug 13, 1901; Enrollment cancel July 8, 1904					
9						
10						
11						
12						
13						
14						
15					Date of Application for Enrollment.	
16					6/20/99	
17						

Choctaw By Blood Enrollment Cards 1898-1914

RESIDENCE: Skullyville COUNTY.
POST OFFICE: Walls I.T.

Choctaw Nation

Choctaw Roll *(Not Including Freedmen)*

CARD No.
FIELD No. 2941

Dawes' Roll No.	NAME		Relationship to Person First Named	AGE	SEX	BLOOD	TRIBAL ENROLLMENT		
							Year	County	No.
8651	1 Takkubbee	Kelly	DIED PRIOR TO SEPTEMBER 25, 1902	28	M	Full	1896	Skullyville	11932
8652	2 "	Anna 41	Wife	38	F	"	1896	"	11933
8653	3 "	Susanna 12	Dau	9	F	"	1896	"	11934
8654	4 "	Artemissa 10	"	7	F	"	1896	"	11935
8655	5 "	Ida 7	"	4	F	"	1896	"	11936
8656	6 "	Joe A.	Son DIED PRIOR TO SEPTEMBER 25, 1902	2	M	"		"	
	7								
	8								
	9								
	10								
	11								
	12								
	13								
	14								
	15	ENROLLMENT OF NOS. 1,2,3,4,5,6 HEREON APPROVED BY THE SECRETARY OF INTERIOR JAN 17 1903							
	16								
	17								

TRIBAL ENROLLMENT OF PARENTS

	Name of Father	Year	County	Name of Mother	Year	County
1	Wallace Takkubbee	Dead	Sans Bois	Ho-li-a-ke	Dead	Sans Bois
2	Ben Lewis	"	Towson	Sakey Lewis	"	" "
3	No 1			No 2		
4	No 1			No 2		
5	No 1			No 2		
6	No 1			No 2		
7						
8	No3 On 1896 roll as Susann Takkubbee					
9	No4 " 1896 " " Timicy			"		
10						
11	For child of No2 see NB (Mar 3-1905) Card #146					
12	" " " " 3 " " (Apr 26-1906) " #159					
13						
14						
15						
16				Date of Application for Enrollment.	6/20/99	
17						

Choctaw By Blood Enrollment Cards 1898-1914

RESIDENCE:	Sugar Loaf	COUNTY.							
POST OFFICE:	Red Oak, I.T.								

Choctaw Nation

Choctaw Roll (Not Including Freedmen)

CARD NO.

FIELD NO. 2942

Dawes' Roll No.	NAME	Relationship to Person First Named	AGE	SEX	BLOOD	TRIBAL ENROLLMENT		
						Year	County	No.
8657	1 Thompson, Nelson 35	First Named	32	M	Full	1893	Sugar Loaf	752
8658	2 " Malinda 32	Wife	29	F	"	1893	" "	753
8659	3 " Rosa 9	Dau	6	"	"	1893	" "	754
8660	4 " Grace 6	"	3	"	"			
8661	5 DIED PRIOR TO SEPTEMBER 25, 1902 Serena 4	"	1	"	"			
	6							
	7							
	8							
	9							
	10							
	11							
	12							
	13							
	14							
	15	ENROLLMENT OF NOS. 1,2,3,4,5 HEREON APPROVED BY THE SECRETARY OF INTERIOR JAN 17 1903						
	16							
	17							

TRIBAL ENROLLMENT OF PARENTS

	Name of Father	Year	County	Name of Mother	Year	County
1	Isom Thompson	Dead	Sans Bois	Sally Thompson	Dead	Sans Bois
2	James Wright	"	Sugar Loaf	Agnes Wright		Gaines
3	No1			No2		
4	No1			No2		
5	No1			No2		
6						
7	No1 on 1893 Pay Roll, Page 82, No 752, Sugar Loaf Co					
8	No2 " 1893 " " " 82 " 753 " " " as Rose Thompson					
9	No3 " 1893 " " " 82 " 754 " " "					
10	No5 died Nov 27, 1901, proof of death filed Dec 20 1902					
11	No5 died Nov 27, 1901. Enrollment cancelled by Department July 8, 1904					
12						
13	For child of Nos 1&2 see NB (Mar 3-1905) Card #201					
14				Date of Application for Enrollment.	June 20/99	
15						
16			Date of application for enrollment			
17						

Choctaw By Blood Enrollment Cards 1898-1914

RESIDENCE: Sugar Loaf	COUNTY. **Choctaw Nation**				Choctaw Roll *(Not Including Freedmen)*	CARD NO.	
POST OFFICE: Red Oak I.T.						FIELD NO. 2943	

Dawes' Roll No.	NAME	Relationship to Person First Named	AGE	SEX	BLOOD	Year	County	No.
DEAD. 1	Colbert Nat ⁵¹	Named	48	M	1/2	1896	Sugar Loaf	2234
8662 2	DIED PRIOR TO SEPTEMBER 25 1902 Jane	Dau	18	F	3/4	1896	" "	2236
3								
4								
5	No. 1 HEREON DISMISSED UNDER							
6	ORDER OF THE COMMISSION TO THE FIVE CIVILIZED TRIBES OF MARCH 31, 1905.							
7								
8								
9								
10								
11								
12								
13								
14								
15	ENROLLMENT OF NOS. 2 HEREON							
16	APPROVED BY THE SECRETARY OF INTERIOR JAN 17 1903							
17								

TRIBAL ENROLLMENT OF PARENTS

	Name of Father	Year	County	Name of Mother	Year	County
1	Dave Colbert	Dead	Chick Nation	Amy Colbert	Dead	C
2	No 1			Elsie Wa-ka-ya	"	S
3						
4						
5						
6			Wife and children on Chick card No 1464			
7			No1 Died Decr 17" 1901: Proof of death filed Dec 23rd 1902			
8			No2 Died in January 1901: Proof of death filed Dec 23rd 1902			
9						
10						
11						
12						
13						
14						
15					Date of Application for Enrollment.	
16					6/20/99	
17						

243

Choctaw By Blood Enrollment Cards 1898-1914

Choctaw Nation

Choctaw Roll *(Not Including Freedmen)*

CARD No.
FIELD No. 2944

Dawes' Roll No.	NAME	Relationship to Person First Named	AGE	SEX	BLOOD	TRIBAL ENROLLMENT Year	County	No.
8663	1 Thomas Leonidas DIED PRIOR TO SEPTEMBER 25, 1902	First Named	45	M	Full	1896	Skullyville	11928
8664	2 " Lomida 27	Wife	24	F	"	1896	"	11929
8665	3 " Robert 17	Son	14	M	"	1896	"	11930
8666	4 " Wicey 8	Dau	5	F	"	1896	"	11931
8667	5 Serius DIED PRIOR TO SEPTEMBER 25, 1902	Son	15days	M	"			
	6							
	7							
	8							
	9							
	10							
	11							
	12							
	13							
	14							
	15							
	16							
	17							

ENROLLMENT
OF NOS. 1,2,3,4,5 HEREON
APPROVED BY THE SECRETARY
OF INTERIOR JAN 17 1903

TRIBAL ENROLLMENT OF PARENTS

	Name of Father	Year	County	Name of Mother	Year	County
1	Ta-nap-a-ya	Dead	Skullyville	Kan-chi-to-na	Dead	Skullyville
2	Jackson Webster	"	Sans Bois	An-oyo-te-ma	"	"
3	No 1			Is-be-lin	"	"
4	No 1			No 2		
5	No 1			No 2		
6						
7						
8	No 1 On 1896 roll as Leanders Thomas					
9	No 4 " 1896 " " Vicey "					
10						
11	No 1 died in 1900; proof of death filed Dec 19 1902 No 5 " Jany 1902; " " " " " "					
12						
13	For child of No.2 see NB (March 3, 1905) #1386					
14						
15						
16				Date of Application for Enrollment	6/20/99	
17	No 2 P.O. Le Flore IT 4/20/05					

244

Choctaw By Blood Enrollment Cards 1898-1914

RESIDENCE: Sans Bois COUNTY. **Choctaw Nation** **Choctaw Roll** CARD NO.
POST OFFICE: Iron Bridge I.T. *(Not Including Freedmen)* FIELD NO. 2945

Dawes' Roll No.	NAME	Relationship to Person First Named	AGE	SEX	BLOOD	TRIBAL ENROLLMENT Year	County	No.
8668	1 Bell Wilson 41	First Named	38	M	Full	1896	Sans Bois	633
	2							
	3							
	4							
	5							
	6							
	7							
	8							
	9							
	10							
	11							
	12							
	13							
	14							
	15							
	16							
	17							

ENROLLMENT
OF NOS. 1 HEREON
APPROVED BY THE SECRETARY
OF INTERIOR JAN 17 1903

TRIBAL ENROLLMENT OF PARENTS

	Name of Father	Year	County	Name of Mother	Year	County
1	Hampton Bell	Dead	Sugar Loaf	Ona-chi-he-ma	Dead	Skullyville
2						
3						
4						
5						
6						
7						
8						
9						
10						
11						
12						
13						
14						
15						Date of Application for Enrollment. 6/20/99
16						
17						

Choctaw By Blood Enrollment Cards 1898-1914

RESIDENCE: Sugar Loaf	COUNTY. **Choctaw Nation**	**Choctaw Roll** CARD No.
POST OFFICE: Red Oak I.T.		(Not Including Freedmen) FIELD No. 2946

Dawes' Roll No.	NAME	Relationship to Person First Named	AGE	SEX	BLOOD	TRIBAL ENROLLMENT		
						Year	County	No.
8669	1 Cargill Lucinda ⁵¹		48	F	1/4	1896	Gaines	2289
	2							
	3							
	4							
	5							
	6							
	7							
	8							
	9							
	10							
	11							
	12							
	13							
	14							
	15	ENROLLMENT						
	16	OF NOS. 1 HEREON APPROVED BY THE SECRETARY						
	17	OF INTERIOR JAN 17 1903						

TRIBAL ENROLLMENT OF PARENTS

	Name of Father	Year	County	Name of Mother	Year	County
1	James Loving	Dead	Non Citz	Mary Loving	Dead	Sugar Loaf
2						
3						
4						
5						
6						
7						
8						
9						
10						
11						
12						
13						
14					Date of Application for Enrollment.	
15						
16					6/20/99	
17						

Choctaw By Blood Enrollment Cards 1898-1914

RESIDENCE: Gaines COUNTY.	Choctaw Nation	Choctaw Roll (Not Including Freedmen)	CARD NO.
POST OFFICE: Wilburton I.T.			FIELD NO. 2947

Dawes' Roll No.	NAME	Relationship to Person First Named	AGE	SEX	BLOOD	TRIBAL ENROLLMENT		
						Year	County	No.
8670	1 Wall Jefferson 21	First Named	18	M	Full	1896	Gaines	12973
	2							
	3							
	4							
	5							
	6							
	7							
	8							
	9							
	10							
	11							
	12							
	13							
	14							
	15	ENROLLMENT OF NOS. 1 JAN 17 1903 HEREON APPROVED BY THE SECRETARY						
	16							
	17							

TRIBAL ENROLLMENT OF PARENTS

Name of Father	Year	County	Name of Mother	Year	County
1 Jessie Wall	Dead	Gaines	Nancy Wall	Dead	Gaines
2					
3					
4					
5					
6					
7					
8					
9					
10					
11					
12					
13					
14					
15					Date of Application for Enrollment.
16					6/20/99
17					

Choctaw By Blood Enrollment Cards 1898-1914

RESIDENCE: Sans Bois   COUNTY. **Choctaw Nation**   **Choctaw Roll**   CARD No.

POST OFFICE: Red Oak I.T.   (Not Including Freedmen)   FIELD No. **2948**

Dawes' Roll No.	NAME	Relationship to Person First Named	AGE	SEX	BLOOD	TRIBAL ENROLLMENT		
						Year	County	No.
8671	1 Wall Johnson 26	First Named	23	M	Full	1896	Sans Bois	12680
	2							
	3							
	4							
	5							
	6							
	7							
	8							
	9							
	10							
	11							
	12							
	13							
	14							
	15							
	16							
	17							

ENROLLMENT
OF NOS. 1 HEREON
APPROVED BY THE SECRETARY
OF INTERIOR JAN 17 1903

TRIBAL ENROLLMENT OF PARENTS

	Name of Father	Year	County	Name of Mother	Year	County
1	Jessie Wall	Dead	Gaines	Nancy Wall	Dead	Gaines
2						
3						
4						
5						
6						
7						
8						
9						
10						
11						
12						
13						
14					Date of Application for Enrollment.	
15						
16					6/20/99	
17						

Choctaw By Blood Enrollment Cards 1898-1914

RESIDENCE: Sans Bois   COUNTY.   **Choctaw Nation**   Choctaw Roll   CARD No.
POST OFFICE: Sans Bois I.T.   (Not Including Freedmen)   FIELD NO. 2949

Dawes' Roll No.	NAME	Relationship to Person First Named	AGE	SEX	BLOOD	TRIBAL ENROLLMENT		
						Year	County	No.
8672	1 Johnson Simon 58	First Named	55	M	Full	1896	Sans Bois	6392
8673	2 " Levina 46	Wife	43	F	"	1896	" "	6393
8674	3 Wright, Emeline 25	Dau	22	F	"	1896	" "	6394
8675	4 Wright, George Simon 1	G.Son	4mo	M	1/2			
	5							
	6							
	7							
	8							
	9							
	10							
	11							
	12							
	13							
	14							
	15							
	16							
	17							

ENROLLMENT
OF NOS. 1,2,3,4 HEREON
APPROVED BY THE SECRETARY
OF INTERIOR   JAN 17 1903

TRIBAL ENROLLMENT OF PARENTS

Name of Father	Year	County	Name of Mother	Year	County
1 Acha-kan-li	Dead	Skullyville	Elai Yi-ma	Dead	Sans Bois
2 Charles James	"	"	Sallie James	"	Sugar Loaf
3 No 1			No 2		
4 W.H. Wright		noncitizen	No 3		
5					
6					
7	No.3 is now wife of W. H. Wright a noncitizen. Evidence of marriage				
8	filed Sept 4, 1901				
9	No4 Enrolled Sept 4, 1901				
10					
11					
12					
13					
14					
15			#1 to 3		
16			Date of Application for Enrollment.		6/20/99
17					

Choctaw By Blood Enrollment Cards 1898-1914

RESIDENCE:	Sugar Loaf	COUNTY.							CARD No.	
POST OFFICE:	Red Oak I.T.		**Choctaw Nation**			Choctaw Roll (Not Including Freedmen)			FIELD No.	2950

Dawes' Roll No.	NAME	Relationship to Person First Named	AGE	SEX	BLOOD	TRIBAL ENROLLMENT		
						Year	County	No.
DEAD.	1 McCurtain Nicholas	Named	50	M	Full	1896	Sugar Loaf	9137
8676	2 " Bicey 63	Wife	60	F	"	1896	" "	9128
8677	3 Loman Johnson DIED PRIOR TO SEPTEMBER 25 1902	Ward	18	M	"	1896	" "	7813
	4							
	5							
	6	No2 – Died prior to September 25, 1902; not entitled to land or money						
	7	(See Indian Office letter September 16, 1910 – DC 41273-1910)						
	8							
	9							
	10							
	11	No. 1 HEREON DISMISSED UNDER						
	12	ORDER OF THE COMMISSION TO THE FIVE						
	13	CIVILIZED TRIBES OF MARCH 31, 1905.						
	14							
	15	ENROLLMENT OF NOS. 2 and 3 HEREON						
	16	APPROVED BY THE SECRETARY OF INTERIOR JAN 17 1903						
	17							

TRIBAL ENROLLMENT OF PARENTS

Name of Father	Year	County	Name of Mother	Year	County
1 Patrick McCurtain	Dead	Sugar Loaf	On-til-li-ma-ho-na	Dead	Sugar Loaf
2	"	Sans Bois		Dead	Sans Bois
3 Jack Loman	1896	Sugar Loaf	Rhoda Loman	"	Sugar Loaf
4					
5					
6					
7	No2 On 1896 roll as Bizie McCurtain				
8	No3 On 1896 " " Johnson Lomon				
9					
10	No letter returned Oct 5, 1902, marked "Dead."				
11	No1 Died Feby 10, 1901, proof of death filed Sept 16, 1904				
12					
13					
14					Date of Application for Enrollment.
15					
16					6/20/99
17					

Choctaw By Blood Enrollment Cards 1898-1914

RESIDENCE: Sugar Loaf   COUNTY. **Choctaw Nation**   **Choctaw Roll** (Not Including Freedmen)   CARD No.

POST OFFICE: Red Oak I.T.   FIELD NO. 2951

Dawes' Roll No.	NAME		Relationship to Person First Named	AGE	SEX	BLOOD	TRIBAL ENROLLMENT Year	County	No.
8678	1 Sockey Ben	43	First Named	40	M	Full	1896	Sugar Loaf	11218
8679	2 " Elizabeth	33	Wife	30	F	"	1896	" "	11219
8680	3 " Davis	12	Son	9	M	"	1896	" "	11221
8681	4 " Melvin	8	"	5	M	"	1896	" "	11222
8682	5 " Martha	11	Dau	8	F	"	1896	" "	11223
~~8683~~	~~6 " Britton~~ DIED PRIOR TO SEPTEMBER 25, 1902		~~Son~~	~~3~~	~~M~~	"	~~1896~~	~~" "~~	~~11224~~
8684	7 " John	1	"	10mo	M	"			
14776	8 Lewis Minnie	13	Niece	10	F	"	1896	" "	7812
~~DEAD~~	~~9 " William~~ DEAD.	11	~~Neph~~	~~8~~	~~M~~	"	~~1896~~	~~" "~~	~~7811~~
	10 NO. 9 HEREON DISMISSED UNDER								
	11 ORDER OF THE COMMISSION TO THE FIVE								
	12 CIVILIZED TRIBES OF MARCH 31, 1905.								
	13 No6 died Oct 16 1901: Enrollment								
	14 cancelled by Department July 8, 1904						ENROLLMENT		
	15 ENROLLMENT OF NOS. 1,2,3,4,5,6,7 HEREON						OF NOS. 8 HEREON APPROVED BY THE SECRETARY		
	16 APPROVED BY THE SECRETARY						OF INTERIOR MAY 20 1903		
	17 OF INTERIOR JAN 17 1903								

TRIBAL ENROLLMENT OF PARENTS

	Name of Father	Year	County	Name of Mother	Year	County
1	Mat Sockey	Dead	Sugar Loaf	Viney Sockey	1896	Sugar Loaf
2	Thomas Isaac	"	Miss	Polly Isaac	1896	Miss
3	No 1			No 2		
4	No 1			No 2		
5	No 1			No 2		
6	No 1			No 2		
7	No 1			No 2		
8				Sallie Lewis	Dead	Sugar Loaf
9				" "	"	" " "
10	No4 On 1896 roll as Malvin Sockey					
11	N°9 Died Sept 17, 1901, proof of death filed Nov. 11, 1902					
12	See affidavit of N°1 as to degree of Choctaw blood possessed by N°s 8 and 9, filed Nov. 11, 1902.					
13	No6 died October 16, 1901, proof of death filed Dec 19 1902					
14	For child of Nos 1 and 2 see NB (March 3, 1905) #1290					
15						
16						Date of Application for Enrollment 6/20/99
17						

Choctaw By Blood Enrollment Cards 1898-1914

RESIDENCE:	Sans Bois	COUNTY.	**Choctaw Nation**	**Choctaw Roll**	CARD NO.	
POST OFFICE:	Sans Bois I.T.			(Not Including Freedmen)	FIELD NO.	2952

Dawes' Roll No.	NAME		Relationship to Person First Named	AGE	SEX	BLOOD	TRIBAL ENROLLMENT		
							Year	County	No.
8685	1 Moore Elsie	43	First Named	40	F	Full	1896	Sans Bois	589
8686	2 Bond Lizzie	23	Dau	20	F	"	1896	" "	590
8687	3 Bond, Cynthia Renie	1	Grand dau	3mo	F	"			
	4								
	5								
	6								
	7								
	8								
	9								
	10								
	11								
	12								
	13								
	14								
	15	ENROLLMENT OF NOS. 1, 2, 3 HEREON							
	16	APPROVED BY THE SECRETARY OF INTERIOR JAN 17 1903							
	17								

TRIBAL ENROLLMENT OF PARENTS

Name of Father	Year	County	Name of Mother	Year	County
1 Wm Peter	Dead	Gaines	Wa-yo-he	Dead	Atoka
2 Hagan Belvin	1896	Sans Bois	No 1		
3 Swiney Bond	1896	Sans Bois	No. 2		
4					
5					
6					
7					
8		No1 On 1896 roll as Elsey Belvin			
9		No.2 is now the wife of Sweeny Bond on Choctaw card #2458			
10		Copy of marriage certificate filed Jany 29, 1901			Jany 17, 1901
		No.3 Enrolled Jany 17, 1901			
11					
12					
13					
14					
15				#1 & 2	
16			Date of Application for Enrollment.		6/20/99
17					

Choctaw By Blood Enrollment Cards 1898-1914

RESIDENCE: Sugar Loaf	COUNTY.	**Choctaw Nation**	**Choctaw Roll** _(Not Including Freedmen)_	CARD No.
POST OFFICE: Le Flore I.T.				FIELD No. 2953

Dawes' Roll No.	NAME		Relationship to Person First Named	AGE	SEX	BLOOD	TRIBAL ENROLLMENT		
							Year	County	No.
8688	1 Wilkins Jefferson	26	First Named	23	M	Full	1896	Skullyville	12735
	2								
	3								
	4								
	5								
	6								
	7								
	8								
	9								
	10								
	11								
	12								
	13								
	14								
	15	ENROLLMENT OF NOS. 1 HEREON APPROVED BY THE SECRETARY OF INTERIOR JAN 17 1903							
	16								
	17								

TRIBAL ENROLLMENT OF PARENTS

	Name of Father	Year	County	Name of Mother	Year	County
1	Allen Wilkins	Dead	Skullyville	Adaline Wilkins	Dead	Sugar Loaf
2						
3						
4						
5						
6						
7						
8	No 1 died Sept 11, 1901. enrollment cancelled by Department Sept 15, 1903					
9						
10						
11						
12						
13						
14						
15						Date of Application for Enrollment.
16						6/20/99
17						

Choctaw By Blood Enrollment Cards 1898-1914

Dawes' Roll No.	NAME	Relationship to Person First Named	AGE	SEX	BLOOD	TRIBAL ENROLLMENT		
						Year	County	No.
I.W.653 1	Bullard Andrew C ⁴⁸	First Named	44	M	I.W.	1896	Sans Bois	14277
8689 2	" Villey M ²³	Wife	20	F	1/2	1896	" "	584
8690 3	" Pocahontas ⁵	Dau	2	F	1/4			
8691 4	" Lu Orenia ²	Dau	1mo	F	1/4			
5								
6								
7								
8								
9								
10								
11	ENROLLMENT							
12	OF NOS. 1 HEREON							
13	APPROVED BY THE SECRETARY							
	OF INTERIOR MAR 26 1904							
14								
15	ENROLLMENT							
16	OF NOS. 2, 3, 4 HEREON							
	APPROVED BY THE SECRETARY							
17	OF INTERIOR JAN 17 1903							

TRIBAL ENROLLMENT OF PARENTS

	Name of Father	Year	County	Name of Mother	Year	County
1	Straid Bullard	Dead	Non Citz	Mary Bullard	Dead	Non Citz
2	John L Heron	1896	Non Citz	Susan Folsom	1896	Sans Bois
3	No 1			No 2		
4	No.1			No.2		
5						
6						
7			No1 On 1896 roll as A C Bullard			
8			No.4 Enrolled Aug. 22d, 1900			
9			For child of Nos 1&2 see NB (Mar 3-05) #579			
10						
11						
12						
13						
14						
15					#1 to 3	
16				Date of Application for Enrollment.	6/20/99	
17						

Choctaw By Blood Enrollment Cards 1898-1914

RESIDENCE: Gaines COUNTY.
POST OFFICE: Red Oak I.T.

Choctaw Nation

Choctaw Roll
(Not Including Freedmen)

CARD NO.
FIELD NO. 2955

Dawes' Roll No.	NAME	Relationship to Person First Named	AGE	SEX	BLOOD	TRIBAL ENROLLMENT		
						Year	County	No.
8692	1 Dunlap Rena G 10	First Named	7	F	1/4	1896	Gaines	3275
8693	2 " Kitty I 9	Sister	6	F	1/4	1896	"	3276
8694	3 " Susie E 7	"	4	F	1/4	1896	"	3277
I.W. 1115	4 " Christopher C 36	Father	36	M	I.W.	1896	"	14459
	5							
	6							
	7							
	8							
	9							
	10	ENROLLMENT OF NOS. ____4____ HEREON APPROVED BY THE SECRETARY OF INTERIOR NOV 16 1904						
	11							
	12							
	13							
	14							
	15	ENROLLMENT OF NOS. 1, 2, 3 HEREON APPROVED BY THE SECRETARY OF INTERIOR JAN 17 1903						
	16							
	17							

TRIBAL ENROLLMENT OF PARENTS

Name of Father	Year	County	Name of Mother	Year	County
1 Christopher C Dunlap	1896	Non Citz	Virginia Dunlap	Dead	Gaines
2 " " "	1896	" "	" "	"	"
3 " " "	1896	" "	" "	"	"
4 G. W. Dunlap	dead	" "	Aurena Dunlap	"	Non Citz
5					
6					
7					
8		Father on W.C.D. 258			
9					
10	No.4 transferred from Choctaw card #D-258 Oct. 31, 1904: See decision of Oct. 15, 1904				
11	No.4 Admitted by Dawes Com as an intermarried citizen as C.C. Dunlap Case #314				
	No.4 on 1896 roll as C C. Dunlap				
12					
13					
14					
15				#1 to 3	
16				Date of Application for Enrollment.	6/20/99
17					

255

Choctaw By Blood Enrollment Cards 1898-1914

Dawes' Roll No.	NAME	Relationship to Person First Named	AGE	SEX	BLOOD	TRIBAL ENROLLMENT		
						Year	County	No.
8695	1 McCann Cornelius 34	First Named	31	M	1/2	1896	Skullyville	9074
I.W. 654	2 " Leonia 25	Wife	21	F	IW		"	
8696	DIED PRIOR TO SEPTEMBER 25, 1902 Jesse 4	Son	7mo	M	1/4		"	
8697	4 " Isophine 11	Dau	8	F	1/2	1896	"	9076
8698	5 " Julia 7	"	4	F	1/2	1896	"	9077
8699	DIED PRIOR TO SEPTEMBER 25, 1902 William B 6	Son	3	M	1/2	1896	"	9078
14777	7 " Edna Algia 4	Dau	1½	F	1/4			
14778	8 " Thelmer 1	"	4mo	F	1/4			
	9							
	10							
	11	ENROLLMENT						
	12	OF NOS. 2 HEREON APPROVED BY THE SECRETARY						
	13	OF INTERIOR MAR 26 1904						
	14							
	15	ENROLLMENT OF NOS. 1,3,4,5,6 HEREON				ENROLLMENT OF NOS. 7 and 8 HEREON		
	16	APPROVED BY THE SECRETARY				APPROVED BY THE SECRETARY		
	17	OF INTERIOR JAN 17 1903				OF INTERIOR MAY 29 1903		

RESIDENCE: Skullyville **COUNTY:** **POST OFFICE:** Walls I.T.

Choctaw Nation

Choctaw Roll (Not Including Freedmen) **CARD NO.**

FIELD NO. 2956

TRIBAL ENROLLMENT OF PARENTS

	Name of Father	Year	County	Name of Mother	Year	County
1	Simpson McCann	Dead	Skullyville	Sarah McCann	Dead	Non Citz
2	G. W. Ollar	18 6[sic]	Non Citz	Emily Ollar	1786	Non Citz
3	No 1			No 2		
4	No 1			Leatha A McCann	Dead	Skullyville
5	No 1			" " "	"	"
6	No 1			" " "	"	"
7						
8	No1 As to marriage of father and mother see testimony					
9	of Jesse H Hardaway					
10	No4 On 1896 roll as Josephine McCann No6 " 1896 " " Wm B. McCann					
11	For child of Nos 1&2 see NB (Apr 26-06) Card No 722					
12	No7 Father of No7 is No1, Mother of No7 is No2; Born April 18 1901: Enrolled Decr 23, 1902 No8 " " " 8 " " " " 8 " Born Aug 5 1902: Enrolled Decr 23 1902					
13	No6 Died July 15, 1899. Proof of death received and filed Dec 30 1902					
14	No.3 Died July 20, 1899. Proof of death received and filed Dec 30 1902					
15	No3 died July 20, 1899; No6 died July 15, 1899; Enrollment cancelled by Department July 8, 1903					
16	For child of Nos 1&2 see NB (March 3 1905) #1062			Date of Application for Enrollment. 6/20/99 1 to 6 inc		
17						

Choctaw By Blood Enrollment Cards 1898-1914

RESIDENCE:	Sugar Loaf	COUNTY.							
POST OFFICE:	Le Flore I.T.								

Choctaw Nation

Choctaw Roll *(Not Including Freedmen)*

CARD No. FIELD No. 2957

Dawes' Roll No.	NAME	Relationship to Person First Named	AGE	SEX	BLOOD	TRIBAL ENROLLMENT		
						Year	County	No.
8700	1 Lewis Alexander J 33	First Named	30	M	Full	1896	Sugar Loaf	7821
	2							
	3							
	4							
	5							
	6							
	7							
	8							
	9							
	10							
	11							
	12							
	13							
	14							
	15	ENROLLMENT OF NOS. 1 HEREON APPROVED BY THE SECRETARY OF INTERIOR JAN 17 1903						
	16							
	17							

TRIBAL ENROLLMENT OF PARENTS						
Name of Father	Year	County	Name of Mother	Year	County	
1 Amaziah Lewis	Dead	Sugar Loaf	Lucy Lewis	Dead	Sugar Loaf	
2						
3						
4						
5						
6						
7	Nº1 is now the husband of Adeline Hudson on Choctaw card #3050 Sept 15, 1902					
8						
9						
10	Half sister Nied on card 3065					
11						
12						
13						
14						
15					Date of Application for Enrollment.	
16					6/20/99	
17						

Choctaw By Blood Enrollment Cards 1898-1914

RESIDENCE: Sugar Loaf	COUNTY.	Choctaw Nation	Choctaw Roll	CARD NO.
POST OFFICE: Red Oak I.T.			(Not Including Freedmen)	FIELD NO. 2958

Dawes' Roll No.	NAME	Relationship to Person First Named	AGE	SEX	BLOOD	TRIBAL ENROLLMENT Year	County	No.
8701	1 Carshall James DIED PRIOR TO SEPTEMBER 25 1902		20	M	Full	1896	Sugar Loaf	2264
8702	2 " Susan 23	Wife	20	F	"	1896	" "	80
8703	3 " Simon 5	Son	1	M	"			
DEAD.	4 DEAD. Eugene	Dau	3mo	F	"			
	5							
	6							
	7 No. 4 HEREON DISMISSED UNDER							
	8 ORDER OF THE COMMISSION TO THE FIVE							
	9 CIVILIZED TRIBES OF MARCH 31, 1905.							
	10							
	11							
	12							
	13							
	14							
	15 ENROLLMENT OF NOS. 1, 2, 3 HEREON							
	16 APPROVED BY THE SECRETARY							
	17 OF INTERIOR JAN 17 1903							

TRIBAL ENROLLMENT OF PARENTS

	Name of Father	Year	County	Name of Mother	Year	County
1	Simon Carshall	1896	Sugar Loaf	Louisiana Anderson	1896	Sugar Loaf
2	Simeon Atokko	Dead	" "	Marcey Atokko	Dead	" "
3	No1			No2		
4	No.1			No.2		
5						
6			On 1896 roll as Susan Atokko			
7						
8						
9						
10			Proper name of No 4 is Agnes			
11						
12			No1 died October 9, 1901; proof of death filed Dec 19, 1902			
13			No4 " April 10, 1902; " " " " " " "			
14			No1 died Oct 9, 1900: Enrollment cancelled by Department July 8, 1904			
15			No.4 Enrolled June 25, 1900.			
16				Date of Application for Enrollment.		6/20/99
17	PO Le Flore I.T.					

12/16/02

Choctaw By Blood Enrollment Cards 1898-1914

RESIDENCE:	Sugar Loaf	COUNTY.				
POST OFFICE:	Le Flore I.T.					

Choctaw Nation

Choctaw Roll (Not Including Freedmen)

CARD NO.

FIELD NO. 2959

Dawes' Roll No.	NAME		Relationship to Person First Named	AGE	SEX	BLOOD	TRIBAL ENROLLMENT		
							Year	County	No.
8704	1 Winlock Wattie	41	First Named	38	M	Full	1896	Sugar Loaf	12899
8705	2 ~~Eliza~~ DIED PRIOR TO SEPTEMBER 25 1902		Wife	34	F	1/2	1896	" "	12900
8706	3 Adams Abel	17	Son	14	M	3/4	1896	" "	71
8707	4 Winlock Johnny	11	"	8	M	3/4	1896	" "	12902
8708	5 " Ellis	6	"	2	M	"		" "	
	6								
	7								
	8								
	9								
	10								
	11								
	12								
	13								
	14								
	15	ENROLLMENT OF NOS. 1,2,3,4,5 HEREON APPROVED BY THE SECRETARY OF INTERIOR JAN 17 1903							
	16								
	17								

TRIBAL ENROLLMENT OF PARENTS

	Name of Father	Year	County	Name of Mother	Year	County
1	Tom Winlock	Dead	Red River	Betsy Winlock	Dead	Red River
2	~~Jacob Boland~~	"	~~Gaines~~	~~Hetty Jones~~	"	~~Gaines~~
3	Simon Adams	1896	Sugar Loaf	No 2		
4	No 1			No 2		
5	No 1			No 2		
6						
7						
8						
9			No3 On 1896 roll as Abe Adam			
10						
11			No.3 Died May 18, 1901. Proof of death received filed Dec 24 1902			
12			No.2 died May 18, 1901. Enrollment cancelled by Department July 8, 1904			
13						
14						
15						
16						6/20/99
17						

259

Choctaw By Blood Enrollment Cards 1898-1914

RESIDENCE: Sugar Loaf COUNTY. **Choctaw Nation** Choctaw Roll CARD NO.
POST OFFICE: Red Oak I.T. (Not Including Freedmen) FIELD NO. 2960

Dawes' Roll No.	NAME	Relationship to Person Named	AGE	SEX	BLOOD	TRIBAL ENROLLMENT		
						Year	County	No.
8709	1 Wade Dennis 39	First Named	36	M	Full	1896	Sugar Loaf	12911
8710	2 " Elizabeth 36	Wife	33	F	"	1896	" "	12912
8711	3 DIED PRIOR TO SEPTEMBER 25, 1902 Grover C	Son	4	M	"	1896	" "	12913
8712	4 DIED PRIOR TO SEPTEMBER 25, 1902 Mary J	Dau	2	F	"			
8713	5 DIED PRIOR TO SEPTEMBER 25, 1902 Gibson	Son	7mo	M	"			
8714	6 " Bessie 1	Dau	6wks	F				
	7							
	8							
	9							
	10							
	11							
	12							
	13							
	14							
	15	ENROLLMENT OF NOS. 1,2,3,4,5,6 HEREON APPROVED BY THE SECRETARY OF INTERIOR JAN 17 1903						
	16							
	17							

TRIBAL ENROLLMENT OF PARENTS

Name of Father	Year	County	Name of Mother	Year	County
1 Loma Wade	Dead	Sugar Loaf	Ta-m-ho-na	Dead	Sugar Loaf
2 Jack Loman	1896	" "		"	" "
3 No 1			No 2		
4 No 1			No 2		
5 No 1			No 2		
6 N⁰1			N⁰2		
7					
8					
9					
10	N⁰6 Born July 8, 1902 – enrolled Aug 21, 1902				
11	No3 died August 25, 1900; proof of death filed Dec 19 1902				
12	No4 " July 15, 1900; " " " " " " "				
	No5 " January 6, 1901; " " " " " " "				
13	No 3 died Aug 25, 1900; No 4 died July 15, 1900; No 5 died Jan 6, 1901; Enrollment				
14	cancelled by Department July 6, 1904				#1 to 5
15					Date of Application for Enrollment.
16					6/20/99
17					

Choctaw By Blood Enrollment Cards 1898-1914

RESIDENCE: Sugar Loaf	COUNTY. **Choctaw Nation**	**Choctaw Roll** (Not Including Freedmen)	CARD NO.
POST OFFICE: Le Flore I.T.			FIELD NO. 2961

Dawes' Roll No.	NAME		Relationship to Person First Named	AGE	SEX	BLOOD	TRIBAL ENROLLMENT		
							Year	County	No.
8715	1 Choate Jincy	20	First Named	17	F	1/2	P R 1893	Sugar Loaf	146
	2								
	3								
	4								
	5								
	6								
	7								
	8								
	9								
	10								
	11								
	12								
	13								
	14								
	15	ENROLLMENT OF NOS. 1 HEREON APPROVED BY THE SECRETARY OF INTERIOR Jan 17 1903							
	16								
	17								

TRIBAL ENROLLMENT OF PARENTS							
Name of Father	Year	County	Name of Mother		Year	County	
1 James Choate	Dead	Sugar Loaf	Louie Choate		Dead	Sugar Loaf	
2							
3							
4							
5							
6							
7 On page 14 No 146 Sugar Loaf Co 1893 P.R. as Sinsey Choat							
8 For child of No.1 see NB (March 3 1905) #1201							
9							
10							
11							
12							
13							
14							
15						Date of Application for Enrollment.	
16						6/20/99	
17							

261

RESIDENCE:	Sugar Loaf	COUNTY.	**Choctaw Nation**	**Choctaw Roll**	CARD NO.	
POST OFFICE:	Red Oak I.T.			*(Not Including Freedmen)*	FIELD NO.	2962

Dawes' Roll No.	NAME	Relationship to Person First Named	AGE	SEX	BLOOD	TRIBAL ENROLLMENT Year	TRIBAL ENROLLMENT County	TRIBAL ENROLLMENT No.
8716	1 Sam Stanford 31	First Named	28	M	Full	P R 1893	Gaines	505
8717	2 " Susan 25	Wife	22	F	"	P R 1893	Towson	6
8718	3 " Sallie 3	Dau	1 wk	F	"			
8719	4 " Silas 1	Son	5 mo	M	"			
	5							
	6							
	7							
	8							
	9							
	10							
	11							
	12							
	13							
	14							
	15	ENROLLMENT OF NOS. 1,2,3,4 HEREON						
	16	APPROVED BY THE SECRETARY						
	17	OF INTERIOR JAN 17 1903						

TRIBAL ENROLLMENT OF PARENTS

	Name of Father	Year	County	Name of Mother	Year	County
1	James Sam	Dead	Skullyville	Sally Sam	Dead	Gaines
2	Sampson Atokobee	"		Rhoda Atokobee	"	
3	No 1			No 2		
4	Nº1			Nº2		
5						
6						
7						
8	No 1 On P. 53 No 505, 1893 Gaines Co Pay Roll					
9	No 2 " P 53 " 6 , 1893 Towson Co " " as Susan Howard					
10	No 3 Affidavit of birth to be supplied. Recd June 20/99					
11	Nº 4 Born March 11, 1902; enrolled Aug. 16, 1902					
12	For child of Nos 1&2, see NB (Apr. 26, 1906) Card No 127.					
13	" " " " " " (March 3 1905) " " 824					
14					6/20/99	
15					Date of Application for Enrollment	
16					6/2?	
17						

RESIDENCE: Sans Bois	COUNTY:	Choctaw Nation	Choctaw Roll	CARD NO.
POST OFFICE: Enterprise I.T.			(Not Including Freedmen)	FIELD NO. 2963

Dawes' Roll No.	NAME		Relationship to Person First Named	AGE	SEX	BLOOD	TRIBAL ENROLLMENT		
							Year	County	No.
8720	1 Dixon Jesse	22	First Named	19	M	1/2	1896	Sans Bois	3176
I.W. 736	2 " Melvina	23	Wife	19	F	I.W.		" "	
8721	3 " Bertha M	4	Dau	7mo	F	1/4		" "	
8722	4 " Clyde	1	Son	2mo	M	1/4			
	5								
	6								
	7								
	8	DECISION PREPARED							
	9								
	10	ENROLLMENT							
	11	OF NOS. ~~~~ 2 ~~~~ HEREON APPROVED BY THE SECRETARY							
	12	OF INTERIOR MAY -7 1904							
	13								
	14								
	15	ENROLLMENT OF NOS. 1, 3, 4, HEREON							
	16	APPROVED BY THE SECRETARY							
	17	OF INTERIOR JAN 17 1904							

TRIBAL ENROLLMENT OF PARENTS

	Name of Father	Year	County	Name of Mother	Year	County
1	Silas Dixon	Dead	Sans Bois	Elizabeth Dixon	1896	Non Citz
2	Budd Harris	1896	Non Citz	Ellen Harris	1896	" "
3	No 1			No 2		
4	№ 1			№ 2		
5						
6						
7						
8			No2 See Decision of [Illegible] 2 '04			
9			No1 On 1896 roll as Jessee Dixon			
10			No1 As to marriage of father and mother see testimony of Sam Bench			
11			No3 Affidavit of birth to be supplied. Recd July 27/99			
12			№4 Born March 8, 1902; enrolled May 1, 1902			
13						
14						#1 to 3
15						Date of Application for Enrollment.
16						6/20/99.
17						

Choctaw By Blood Enrollment Cards 1898-1914

| | RESIDENCE: Sugar Loaf | COUNTY. Choctaw Nation | | | | Choctaw Roll (Not Including Freedmen) | CARD NO. | |
| | POST OFFICE: Red Oak I.T. | | | | | | FIELD NO. 2964 | |

Dawes' Roll No.	NAME	Relationship to Person	AGE	SEX	BLOOD	TRIBAL ENROLLMENT Year	County	No.
8723	1 Folsom Alexander 31	First Named	28	M	Full	1896	Sugar Loaf	3953
	2							
	3							
	4							
	5							
	6							
	7							
	8							
	9							
	10							
	11							
	12							
	13							
	14							
	15	ENROLLMENT OF NOS. 1 HEREON APPROVED BY THE SECRETARY OF INTERIOR JAN 17 1903						
	16							
	17							

TRIBAL ENROLLMENT OF PARENTS

	Name of Father	Year	County	Name of Mother	Year	County
1	Alex Folsom	Dead	Sans Bois	Artemissia Folsom	Dead	Sans Bois
2						
3						
4						
5						
6						
7						
8						
9						
10						
11						
12						
13						
14						
15						Date of Application for Enrollment.
16						6/20/99
17	PO Poteau I.T. 2/4/03					

264

Choctaw By Blood Enrollment Cards 1898-1914

RESIDENCE: Gaines COUNTY. **Choctaw Nation** Choctaw Roll CARD NO.
POST OFFICE: Wilburton I.T. *(Not Including Freedmen)* FIELD NO. 2965

Dawes' Roll No.	NAME	Relationship to Person First Named	AGE	SEX	BLOOD	TRIBAL ENROLLMENT		
						Year	County	No.
✓ * 1	Broome James E	Named	47	M	1/4		Gaines	
✓ 2	" Abbie J	Wife	41	F	I.W.		"	
3								
4								
5								
6	No.2 DISMISSED MAY 7 1904							
7								
8								
9								
10								
11								
12								
13								
14								
15								
16								
17								

TRIBAL ENROLLMENT OF PARENTS

Name of Father	Year	County	Name of Mother	Year	County
1 J. C. Broome	Dead	Non Citz	M.E. Broome	Dead	Ark.
2 Walter Beardsley	"	" "	Jane Beardsley	"	Non Citz
3					

DENIED CITIZENSHIP BY THE CHOCTAW AND
CHICKASAW CITIZENSHIP COURT

No1 Denied on 96 Case #1268
No1 Admitted by U.S. Court, So. McAlester,, Sept. 1- 1897,
Case No 241, as to residence see his testimony
No2 married to James E. Broome, Oct 29, 1897
Judgement[sic] of US Court [remainder illegible]
No1 [remainder illegible]

No1 denied by C.C.C.C. Case #55 March 14 04

Date of Application for Enrollment.

6/20/99

265

RESIDENCE: Gaines	COUNTY.	Choctaw Nation	Choctaw Roll	CARD No.	
POST OFFICE: Wilburton I.T.			(Not Including Freedmen)	FIELD No. 2966	

Dawes' Roll No.	NAME	Relationship to Person First Named	AGE	SEX	BLOOD	TRIBAL ENROLLMENT		
						Year	County	No.
✓ ✗ 1	Langford Rachael	Named	59	F	1/4			
2								
3								
4								
5								
6								
7								
8								
9								
10								
11								
12								
13								
14								
15								
16								
17								

TRIBAL ENROLLMENT OF PARENTS

	Name of Father	Year	County	Name of Mother	Year	County
1	James Biddy	Dead	Skullyville	Mary Jane Biddy	Dead	Non Citz
2						
3						
4						
5						
6	No 1 Denied by Dawes Com in '96 Choctaw Cit Case #598					
7	Admitted by U.S. Court, at So. McAlester Aug 24, 1897					
8	Case No 94. As to residence see her testimony					
9						
10						
11						
12						
13						
14					Date of Application for Enrollment.	
15						
16					6/20/99	
17						

Choctaw By Blood Enrollment Cards 1898-1914

RESIDENCE: Sans Bois COUNTY. **Choctaw Nation** **Choctaw Roll** CARD NO.
POST OFFICE: Lodi I.T. (Not Including Freedmen) FIELD NO. 2967

Dawes' Roll No.	NAME		Relationship to Person First Named	AGE	SEX	BLOOD	TRIBAL ENROLLMENT		
							Year	County	No.
8724	1 Hulsey Mary A	39	First Named	36	F	1/32	1896	Sans Bois	5152
8725	2 " Lora B	16	Dau	13	F	1/64	1896	" "	5153
8726	3 " Willard E	13	Son	10	M	1/64	1896	" "	5154
8727	4 " Alonzo L	11	"	8	M	1/64	1896	" "	5155
8728	5 " Lemuel V	10	"	7	M	1/64	1896	" "	5156
8729	6 " Claude M	7	"	4	M	1/64	1896	" "	5157
8730	7 DIED PRIOR TO SEPTEMBER 25, 1902 Ollie I		Dau	20mo	F	1/64			
8731	8 " Oral Clarence	1	Son	2mo	M	1/64			
	9								
	10								
	11								
	12								
	13								
	14								
	15	ENROLLMENT OF NOS. 1,2,3,4,5,6,7,8 HEREON							
	16	APPROVED BY THE SECRETARY OF INTERIOR JAN 17 1903							
	17								

TRIBAL ENROLLMENT OF PARENTS

Name of Father	Year	County	Name of Mother	Year	County
1 Henry Boron	Dead	Non Citz	Luercey Boron	Dead	Kiamitia
2 M. T. Hulsey	1896	Non Citz	No 1		
3 " " "	1896	" "	No 1		
4 " " "	1896	" "	No 1		
5 " " "	1896	" "	No 1		
6 " " "	1896	" "	No 1		
7 " " "	1896	" "	No 1		
8 " " "	1896	" "	No 1		

9 No3 On 1896 roll as Wm D. Hulsey
10 No4 " 1896 " " Alonzo "
11 No7 Affidavit of birth to be supplied
    Rec'd & filed June 20, 1899
12 No 8 Born Sept. 23, 1901; Enrolled Nov. 11, 1901
13 No.7 Died July 15, 1899: Proof of death filed Dec 23 1902.
14 No.7 died July 15, 1899: Enrollment cancelled by Department July 8, 1904
15 For child of No1 see NB (Mar 3-05) Card #203   #1 to 7
16 " " " No2 " " " " " " " #1022   DATE OF APPLICATION FOR ENROLLMENT. 6/20/99
17 No2 PO Pauls Valley IT 4/4/05

Wilburton IT 11/1/04

Choctaw By Blood Enrollment Cards 1898-1914

RESIDENCE: Sans Bois	COUNTY.	**Choctaw Nation**	Choctaw Roll	CARD NO.	
POST OFFICE: Sans Bois I.T.			(Not Including Freedmen)	FIELD NO.	2968

Dawes' Roll No.	NAME	Relationship to Person First Named	AGE	SEX	BLOOD	TRIBAL ENROLLMENT Year	County	No.
8732	1 Johnson Alexander 33	First Named	30	M	Full	1896	Sans Bois	6395
DEAD.	2 " Ada E. B. DEAD	Wife	19	F	I.W.	1896	" "	14682
	3							
	4							
	5							
	6							
	7							
	8							
	9							
	10							
	11	No. 2 HEREON DISMISSED UNDER ORDER OF THE COMMISSION TO THE FIVE CIVILIZED TRIBES OF MARCH 31, 1905.						
	12							
	13							
	14							
	15	ENROLLMENT OF NOS. 1 HEREON APPROVED BY THE SECRETARY OF INTERIOR JAN 17 1903						
	16							
	17							

TRIBAL ENROLLMENT OF PARENTS

Name of Father	Year	County	Name of Mother	Year	County
1 Simon Johnson	1896	Sans Bois	Amy Johnson	Dead	Skullyville
2 William Ramsey	Dead	Non Citz	Catherine Ramsey	Dead	Non Citz
3					
4					
5					
6					
7	No 1 On 1896 roll as Alick Johnson				
8	No 2 " 1896 " " Ada "				
9	No.1 is now the husband of Elizabeth Wenlock on Choctaw card #4489			Jany 11, 1902	
10	N°2 Died Jany 9, 1900; proof of death filed April 17 1902				
11	For child of No.1 see N.B. (Apr. 26, 1906) Card No 174				
12	" " " " " " (Mar 3, 1905) " " 616				
13					
14					
15				Date of Application for Enrollment.	
16				6/20/99	
17					

Choctaw By Blood Enrollment Cards 1898-1914

RESIDENCE: Sans Bois   COUNTY. **Choctaw Nation**   **Choctaw Roll**   CARD NO.
POST OFFICE: Sans Bois I.T.   *(Not Including Freedmen)*   FIELD NO. 2969

Dawes' Roll No.	NAME	Relationship to Person First Named	AGE	SEX	BLOOD	TRIBAL ENROLLMENT		
						Year	County	No.
8733	1 Austin James *DIED PRIOR TO SEPTEMBER 25 1902*		19	M	Full	1896	Sans Bois	d24
	2							
	3							
	4							
	5							
	6							
	7							
	8							
	9							
	10							
	11							
	12							
	13							
	14							
	15							
	16							
	17							

ENROLLMENT
OF NOS. 1 HEREON
APPROVED BY THE SECRETARY
OF INTERIOR JAN 17 1903

TRIBAL ENROLLMENT OF PARENTS

	Name of Father	Year	County	Name of Mother	Year	County
1	Lewis Austin	Dead	Sugar Loaf	Sophy Austin	1896	Sans Bois
2						
3						
4						
5						
6						
7	No 1 died January 21, 1901; proof of death filed Dec 19 1902					
8	No. 1 died Jan 21, 1901; Enrollment cancelled by Department July 8, 1904					
9						
10						
11						
12						
13						
14						
15						Date of Application for Enrollment.
16						6/20/99
17						

Choctaw By Blood Enrollment Cards 1898-1914

RESIDENCE:	Sugar Loaf	COUNTY.					CARD NO.	
POST OFFICE:	Le Flore I.T.	**Choctaw Nation**			**Choctaw Roll** (Not Including Freedmen)		FIELD NO.	2970

Dawes' Roll No.	NAME	Relationship to Person	AGE	SEX	BLOOD	TRIBAL ENROLLMENT		
						Year	County	No.
8734 1	LeFlore Jacob ~~DIED PRIOR TO SEPTEMBER 25 1902~~	First Named	48	M	Full	1896	Sugar Loaf	7798
8735 2	" Rhoda ~~DIED PRIOR TO SEPTEMBER 25 1902~~	Dau	10	F	"	1896	" "	7801
8736 3	" Wilmond 7	Son	4	M	"	1896	" "	7800
4								
5								
6								
7								
8								
9								
10								
11								
12								
13								
14								
15	ENROLLMENT OF NOS. 1, 2, 3, HEREON							
16	APPROVED BY THE SECRETARY OF INTERIOR JAN 17 1903							
17								

TRIBAL ENROLLMENT OF PARENTS

	Name of Father	Year	County	Name of Mother	Year	County
1	Wallace LeFlore	Dead	Kiamatia[sic]	Josie Wright	Dead	Skullyville
2	No 1			Liney LeFlore	"	Sugar Loaf
3	No 1			Eliza LeFlore	"	" "
4						
5						
6						
7						
8	No3 On 1896 roll as William LeFlore					
9						
10	No1 died January – 1900; proof of death filed Dec 19 1902					
11	No2 " in 1900 " " " " " " " "					
12	No1 died Jany – 1900; No2 [remainder illegible]					
13						
14						
15					Date of Application for Enrollment	
16					6/20/99	
17						

270

Choctaw By Blood Enrollment Cards 1898-1914

RESIDENCE: Gaines COUNTY.
POST OFFICE: Hartshorne I.T.

Choctaw Nation

Choctaw Roll *(Not Including Freedmen)*

CARD NO.
FIELD NO. 2971

Dawes' Roll No.	NAME	Relationship to Person First Named	AGE	SEX	BLOOD	TRIBAL ENROLLMENT Year	County	No.
✓ ✗ 1	Dehart Susan	Named	41	F	1/8			
2								
3								
4								
5								
6								
7								
8								
9								
10								
11								
12								
13								
14								
15								
16								
17								

TRIBAL ENROLLMENT OF PARENTS

	Name of Father	Year	County	Name of Mother	Year	County
1	Henry Langford	Dead Non Citz		Rachel Langford	1896	Gaines
2						
3						
4						
5						
6	No1 Denied by Dawes Com in '96 Choc Cit Case #598					
7	No1 Admitted by U.S. Court at So. McAlester Aug 24, 1896					
8	Case No 94. As to residence see her testimony.					
9	No1 denied by [remainder illegible]					
10						
11						
12						
13						
14					Date of Application for Enrollment.	
15						
16					6/20/99	
17						

Choctaw By Blood Enrollment Cards 1898-1914

RESIDENCE: Gaines   COUNTY. **Choctaw Nation**   Choctaw Roll   CARD NO.

POST OFFICE: Wilburton I.T.   (Not Including Freedmen)   FIELD NO. 2972

Dawes' Roll No.	NAME	Relationship to Person First Named	AGE	SEX	BLOOD	TRIBAL ENROLLMENT		
						Year	County	No.
1	Murphy Mary		19	F	1/16			
2								
3								
4								
5								
6								
7								
8								
9								
10								
11								
12								
13								
14								
15								
16								
17								

TRIBAL ENROLLMENT OF PARENTS

	Name of Father	Year	County	Name of Mother	Year	County
1	Jasper Williams	1896	Not Citz.	Susan Dehart	1896	Gaines
2						
3						
4						
5						
6						
7	No1 Denied by Dawes Com in '96 Choctaw Ct Case # 598					
8	Admitted by U.S. Court at So McAlester Aug 24, 1896 Case No 94 as Mary Williams As to residence see her testimony					
9	[Reminder illegible]					
10						
11						
12						
13						
14						
15					Date of Application for Enrollment.	
16					6/20/99	
17						

DENIED CITIZENSHIP BY THE CHOCTAW AND CHICKASAW CITIZENSHIP COURT

272

Choctaw By Blood Enrollment Cards 1898-1914

RESIDENCE: Gaines COUNTY. **Choctaw Nation** Choctaw Roll CARD NO.
POST OFFICE: Wilburton I.T. *(Not Including Freedmen)* FIELD NO. 2973

Dawes' Roll No.	NAME	Relationship to Person First Named	AGE	SEX	BLOOD	TRIBAL ENROLLMENT		
						Year	County	No.
✓	1 Langford Edward		26	M	1/8			
✓ ✗	2 " Dora	Wife	28	F	IW			
✓ ✗	3 " Albert	Son	3	M	1/16			
	4							
	5							
	6							
	7							
	8							
	9							
	10							
	11							
	12							
	13							
	14							
	15							
	16							
	17							

TRIBAL ENROLLMENT OF PARENTS

	Name of Father	Year	County	Name of Mother	Year	County
1	Henry Langford	Dead	Non Citz	Rachel Langford	1896	Gaines
2	Abe Deaton	1897		Susan Deaton	Dead	Non Citz
3	No 1			No2		
4						
5						
6	No1,2 and 3 Denied by Dawes Com in '96 Choctaw Cit Case #598					
7	Nos 1,2 and 3 Admitted by U.S. Court at So McAlester Aug					
8	24, 1896 Case No 94. Dora as an intermarried citizen					
9	As to residence see his testimony [Remainder illegible]					
10						
11						
12						
13						
14					Date of Application for Enrollment.	
15						
16					6/20/99	
17						

Choctaw By Blood Enrollment Cards 1898-1914

RESIDENCE: Sans Bois			COUNTY.					
POST OFFICE: Hoyt I.T.						Choctaw Roll (Not Including Freedmen)	CARD NO. FIELD NO.	2974

COUNTY. **Choctaw Nation**

Dawes' Roll No.	NAME		Relationship to Person	AGE	SEX	BLOOD	TRIBAL ENROLLMENT		
							Year	County	No.
8737	1 Piears[sic] Joseph	20	First Named	17	M	1/4	1896	Sans Bois	10037
	2								
	3								
	4								
	5								
	6								
	7								
	8								
	9								
	10								
	11								
	12								
	13								
	14								
	15								
	16								
	17								

ENROLLMENT OF NOS. 1 APPROVED BY THE SECRETARY OF INTERIOR HEREON JAN 17 1903

TRIBAL ENROLLMENT OF PARENTS

Name of Father	Year	County	Name of Mother	Year	County
1 Franklin Piears	Dead	Non Citz	Dona Piears	Dead	Sans Bois
2					
3					
4					
5					
6					
7	On 1896 roll as Joseph Piers				
8					
9					
10					
11					
12					
13					
14					
15				Date of Application for Enrollment.		
16				6/20/99		
17						

Choctaw By Blood Enrollment Cards 1898-1914

RESIDENCE:	Sugar Loaf	COUNTY.	**Choctaw Nation**	**Choctaw Roll** *(Not Including Freedmen)*	CARD No.
POST OFFICE:	Summerfield, I.T.				FIELD No. 2975

Dawes' Roll No.	NAME	Relationship to Person First Named	AGE	SEX	BLOOD	TRIBAL ENROLLMENT		
						Year	County	No.
8738	1 Holloway, John ²³	First Named	20	M	Full	1896	Sugar Loaf	5246
	2							
	3							
	4							
	5							
	6							
	7							
	8							
	9							
	10							
	11							
	12							
	13							
	14							
	15	ENROLLMENT OF NOS. 1 HEREON APPROVED BY THE SECRETARY OF INTERIOR JAN 17 1903						
	16							
	17							

TRIBAL ENROLLMENT OF PARENTS

	Name of Father	Year	County	Name of Mother	Year	County
1	Lincoln Holloway	Dead	Skullyville	Elizabeth Sain	Dead	Skullyville
2						
3						
4						
5						
6						
7			For child of No1 see NB (March 3 1905) #1433			
8						
9						
10						
11						
12						
13						
14					Date of Application for Enrollment.	
15						
16					6/20/99	
17						

Choctaw By Blood Enrollment Cards 1898-1914

RESIDENCE:	Sans Bois	COUNTY.									

RESIDENCE: Sans Bois   **COUNTY.** Choctaw Nation   **Choctaw Roll** (Not Including Freedmen)   **CARD NO.**
POST OFFICE: Sans Bois, I.T.   **FIELD NO.** 2976

Dawes' Roll No.	NAME	Relationship to Person First Named	AGE	SEX	BLOOD	TRIBAL ENROLLMENT		
						Year	County	No.
8739	1 Thompson, Billy 39	First Named	36	M	Full	1896	Sans Bois	11820
8740	2 " Elizabeth 43	Wife	40	F	"	1896	" "	11821
8741	3 " Isom 12	Son	9	M	"	1896	" "	11822
	4							
	5							
	6							
	7							
	8							
	9							
	10							
	11							
	12							
	13							
	14							
	15	ENROLLMENT OF NOS. 1, 2, 3 HEREON APPROVED BY THE SECRETARY OF INTERIOR JAN 17 1903						
	16							
	17							

TRIBAL ENROLLMENT OF PARENTS

	Name of Father	Year	County	Name of Mother	Year	County
1	Jimson Thompson	1896	Sans Bois	Losie Thompson	Dead	Sans Bois
2	Kanabbi	Dead	Tobucksy	[Illegible]	"	Tobucksy
3	No1			No2		
4						
5						
6						
7						
8						
9						
10						
11						
12						
13						
14						
15						
16				Date of Application for Enrollment.	6/20/99	
17						

276

Choctaw By Blood Enrollment Cards 1898-1914

RESIDENCE: Sans Bois   COUNTY.   **Choctaw Nation**   Choctaw Roll *(Not Including Freedmen)*   CARD NO.

POST OFFICE: Sans Bois, I.T.   FIELD NO. 2977

Dawes' Roll No.	NAME		Relationship to Person First Named	AGE	SEX	BLOOD	TRIBAL ENROLLMENT		
							Year	County	No.
8742	1 Belvin, Hagin	47	First Named	44	M	Full	1896	Gaines	847
8743	2 " Annie	46	Wife	43	F	"	1896	"	848
	3								
	4								
	5								
	6								
	7								
	8								
	9								
	10								
	11								
	12								
	13								
	14								
	15	ENROLLMENT OF NOS. 1 and 2 HEREON APPROVED BY THE SECRETARY OF INTERIOR JAN 17 1903							
	16								
	17								

TRIBAL ENROLLMENT OF PARENTS

	Name of Father	Year	County	Name of Mother	Year	County
1	Wilson Belvin	Dead	Red River		Dead	Red River
2		"	Cedar		"	Cedar
3						
4						
5						
6	No1 died prior to September 25, 1902; Enrollment cancelled by Department February					
7	13, 1907 (I.T.D. 296-8= 1907) DC 4332-1907)					
8	June 16, 1909 Department holds case is not analogous to Goldsby case and declines to take action looking to restoration of No.1 to the roll					
9						
10						
11						
12						
13						
14						
15					Date of Application for Enrollment.	
16					6/20/99	
17						

Choctaw By Blood Enrollment Cards 1898-1914

RESIDENCE: Sugar Loaf	COUNTY. **Choctaw Nation**				**Choctaw Roll** (Not Including Freedmen)	CARD NO.		
POST OFFICE: Le Flore, I.T.						FIELD NO. 2978		

Dawes' Roll No.	NAME		Relationship to Person First Named	AGE	SEX	BLOOD	TRIBAL ENROLLMENT		
							Year	County	No.
8744	1 Lewis, Israel	31		28	M	Full	1896	Sugar Loaf	7795
8745	2 " Eliza	33	Wife	30	F	"`	1896	" "	7796
	3								
	4								
	5								
	6								
	7								
	8								
	9								
	10								
	11								
	12								
	13								
	14								
	15								
	16								
	17								

ENROLLMENT OF NOS. 1 and 2 APPROVED BY THE SECRETARY HEREON OF INTERIOR JAN 17 1903

TRIBAL ENROLLMENT OF PARENTS

Name of Father	Year	County	Name of Mother	Year	County
1 Amaziah Lewis	Dead	Sugar Loaf	Lucy Lewis	Dead	Sugar Loaf
2 E-ma-tha-tubbee	"	Gaines		"	Gaines
3					
4					
5					
6	No.1 died in June 1902				
7	allotment Jacket 8744				
8	* Died prior to Sept 25, 1902 not entitled to land or money				
9	(See Indian Office letter of Aug 22, 1911 No. 1871-1911)				
10					
11					
12					
13				Date of Application for Enrollment.	
14					
15					
16				6/20/99	
17					

Choctaw By Blood Enrollment Cards 1898-1914

RESIDENCE: Sans Bois   COUNTY. **Choctaw Nation**   **Choctaw Roll** CARD NO.
POST OFFICE: Sans Bois, I.T.   *(Not Including Freedmen)* FIELD NO. 2979

Dawes' Roll No.	NAME	Relationship to Person First Named	AGE	SEX	BLOOD	TRIBAL ENROLLMENT Year	County	No.
8746	1 Drake, Rosa ²⁸	First Named	25	F	Full	1896	Sans Bois	3175
14779	2 Cooper, Mary Belle ³	Dau	3	F	1/2			
	3							
	4							
	5							
	6							
	7							
	8							
	9							
	10							
	11							
	12				ENROLLMENT OF NOS. 2 HEREON			
	13				APPROVED BY THE SECRETARY OF INTERIOR MAY 20 1903			
	14							
	15	ENROLLMENT OF NOS. 1 HEREON						
	16	APPROVED BY THE SECRETARY OF INTERIOR JAN 17 1903						
	17							

TRIBAL ENROLLMENT OF PARENTS

	Name of Father	Year	County	Name of Mother	Year	County
1	Joe Coley	Dead	Sans Bois	Sophie Coley	1896	Sans Bois
2	Jeff Cooper		Sans Bois	No 1		
3						
4						
5						
6						
7	No2 born October 13 1899; enrolled September 15, 1902					
8	For child of No1 see NB (March 8, 1905) #792					
9						
10						
11						
12						
13						
14					Date of Application for Enrollment.	
15						
16					6/20/99	
17	P.O. Quinton, 12/15/02					

Choctaw By Blood Enrollment Cards 1898-1914

RESIDENCE:	Sans Bois	COUNTY.	**Choctaw Nation**	**Choctaw Roll**	CARD No.	
POST OFFICE:	Panther, I.T.			(Not Including Freedmen)	FIELD No.	2980

Dawes' Roll No.	NAME	Relationship to Person	AGE	SEX	BLOOD	TRIBAL ENROLLMENT		
						Year	County	No.
8747	1 Franklin, Billy	First Named	28	M	Full	1896	Sans Bois	3895
	2							
	3							
	4							
	5							
	6							
	7							
	8							
	9							
	10							
	11							
	12							
	13							
	14							
	15	ENROLLMENT OF NOS. 1 HEREON APPROVED BY THE SECRETARY OF INTERIOR JAN 17 1903						
	16							
	17							

DIED DECEMBER 29 1902

TRIBAL ENROLLMENT OF PARENTS

	Name of Father	Year	County	Name of Mother	Year	County
1	Ben Franklin	Dead	Skullyville	Tolean Franklin	1896	Sans Bois
2						
3						
4						
5						
6	On 1896 roll as William Franklin					
7	No1 Died Jany 29, 1902, proof of death filed Jany 21, 1903					
8	No. 1 died Jany 29, 1902; Enrollment cancelled by Department July 8, 1904					
9						
10						
11						
12						
13						
14					Date of Application for Enrollment.	
15						
16					6/20/99	
17						

RESIDENCE: Gaines COUNTY. **Choctaw Nation** **Choctaw Roll** (Not Including Freedmen) CARD NO.
POST OFFICE: Wilburton, I.T. FIELD NO. 2981

Dawes' Roll No.		NAME	Relationship to Person First Named	AGE	SEX	BLOOD	TRIBAL ENROLLMENT Year	County	No.
✓ *	1	~~Langford, James~~	~~First Named~~	~~43~~	~~M~~	~~1/8~~			
✓ *	2	~~" Alice~~	~~Dau~~	~~19~~	~~F~~	~~1/16~~			
✓ *	3	~~" Rebecca~~	~~"~~	~~14~~	~~"~~	~~1/16~~			
✓ *	4	~~" Martin~~	~~Son~~	~~8~~	~~M~~	~~1/16~~			
✓ *	5	~~" Nellie~~	~~Dau~~	~~5~~	~~F~~	~~1/16~~			
	6								
	7								
	8								
	9								
	10								
	11								
	12								
	13								
	14								
	15								
	16								
	17								

DENIED CITIZENSHIP BY THE CHOCTAW AND CHICKASAW CITIZENSHIP COURT

TRIBAL ENROLLMENT OF PARENTS

	Name of Father	Year	County	Name of Mother	Year	County
1	~~Henry Langford~~	~~Dead~~	~~Non Citz~~	~~Rachel Langford~~	~~1896~~	~~Choctaw~~
2	~~No1~~			~~Nancy Langford~~	~~Dead~~	~~Non Citz~~
3	~~No1~~			~~" "~~	~~"~~	~~" "~~
4	~~No1~~			~~" "~~	~~"~~	~~" "~~
5	~~No1~~			~~" "~~	~~"~~	~~" "~~
6						
7						
8	No1 to 5 inclusive Denied by Dawes Com in '96 Choctaw Cit Case # 598					
9	Admitted by the U.S. Court Central					
10	District Aug 24/97, Case No 94.					
11	~~As to residence. see testimony~~ of No1					
12	[Remainder illegible]					
13						
14						
15					Date of Application for Enrollment.	
16					6/20/99	
17						

Choctaw By Blood Enrollment Cards 1898-1914

RESIDENCE: Gaines COUNTY.	Choctaw Nation	Choctaw Roll (Not Including Freedmen)	CARD NO.
POST OFFICE: Wilburton, I.T.			FIELD NO. 2982

Dawes' Roll No.	NAME	Relationship to Person First Named	AGE	SEX	BLOOD	TRIBAL ENROLLMENT		
						Year	County	No.
* 1	Steward, Savanna	Named	21	F	1/8			
* 2	" Elmer	Son	3	M	1/16			
3	" Cosma	Son	5mo	M	1/16			
4	" Willie	Son	1mo	M	1/16			
5								
6								
7								
8								
9	NOS DISMISSED							
10	MAY 24 1904							
11								
12								
13								
14								
15								
16								
17								

TRIBAL ENROLLMENT OF PARENTS

	Name of Father	Year	County	Name of Mother	Year	County
1	Mack Henry	Dead	Non Citz	Rachel Langford	1896	Choctaw
2	John Steward	1896	" "	No1		
3	" "	"	" "	No1		
4	" "	"	" "	No1		
5						
6	DENIED CITIZENSHIP BY THE CHOCTAW AND					
7	CHICKASAW CITIZENSHIP COURT					
8						
9	Nos 1&2 Denied by Dawes Com in '96 Choctaw Cit Case #598					
10	Admitted by U.S. Court Central District					
11	August 24/97, Case No 94					
11	As to residence, see testimony of No1					
12	No.3 Enrolled February 25th 1901					
13	No.4 Born Sept. 18, 1902. Enrolled Oct. 24, 1902					
14	Judgment of U.S. Court C.D. admitting No 1&2 vacated and set aside by Decree of Choctaw Chickasaw Cit Court Dec 17/02					
15	No 1&2 Denied by Choctaw Chickasaw Citizenship Court Dec 17, 1902 Dec #79			Date of Application for Enrollment.		
16				6/20/99		
17						

Choctaw By Blood Enrollment Cards 1898-1914

RESIDENCE:	Wade	COUNTY.								

RESIDENCE: Wade   **COUNTY.**   **Choctaw Nation**   **Choctaw Roll** *(Not Including Freedmen)*   **CARD NO.**
POST OFFICE: Lyceum I.T.   **FIELD NO.** 2983

Dawes' Roll No.	NAME		Relationship to Person First Named	AGE	SEX	BLOOD	TRIBAL ENROLLMENT		
							Year	County	No.
8748	1 Pope Tecumseh	27	First Named	24	M	Full	1896	Skullyville	10100
	2								
	3								
	4								
	5								
	6								
	7								
	8								
	9								
	10								
	11								
	12								
	13								
	14								
	15								
	16								
	17								

ENROLLMENT
OF NOS 1 HEREON
APPROVED BY THE SECRETARY
OF INTERIOR JAN 17 1903

TRIBAL ENROLLMENT OF PARENTS

Name of Father	Year	County	Name of Mother	Year	County
1 Tobias Pope	Dead	Sans Bois	Kaizie Pope	Dead	Skullyville
2					
3					
4					
5					
6					
7					
8					
9					
10					
11					
12					
13					
14					
15				Date of Application for Enrollment.		
16				6/20/99		
17						

Choctaw By Blood Enrollment Cards 1898-1914

RESIDENCE: Sans Bois COUNTY. **Choctaw Nation** **Choctaw Roll** CARD NO.
POST OFFICE: Featherstone I.T. (Not Including Freedmen) FIELD NO. 2984

Dawes' Roll No.	NAME	Relationship to Person First Named	AGE	SEX	BLOOD	TRIBAL ENROLLMENT		
						Year	County	No.
8749	1 Carney Silway 26		23	F	Full	P.R. 1893	Sugar Loaf	7
	2							
	3							
	4							
	5							
	6							
	7							
	8							
	9							
	10							
	11							
	12							
	13							
	14							
	15							
	16							
	17							

ENROLLMENT
OF NOS. 1 HEREON
APPROVED BY THE SECRETARY
OF INTERIOR JAN 17 1903

TRIBAL ENROLLMENT OF PARENTS

Name of Father	Year	County	Name of Mother	Year	County
1 Solomon Nelson	Dead	Sugar Loaf	Caroline Nelson	Dead	Sugar Loaf
2					
3					
4					
5					
6 As Selney Alexander on page 1 No7, 1893 P.R. Sugar Loaf Co					
7 For child of No.1 see NB (March 3 1905) #1289					
8					
9					
10					
11					
12					
13					
14					
15				Date of Application for Enrollment.		
16				6/20/99		
17 PO Quinton IT 4/26/05					

Choctaw By Blood Enrollment Cards 1898-1914

RESIDENCE: Sugar Loaf COUNTY. **Choctaw Nation** Choctaw Roll CARD No.
POST OFFICE: Summerfield I.T. *(Not Including Freedmen)* FIELD No. 2985

Dawes' Roll No.	NAME	Relationship to Person First Named	AGE	SEX	BLOOD	TRIBAL ENROLLMENT		
						Year	County	No.
8750	1 Colbert Dave 24	First Named	21	M	Full	1896	Sugar Loaf	2270
	2							
	3							
	4							
	5							
	6							
	7							
	8							
	9							
	10							
	11							
	12							
	13							
	14							
	15	ENROLLMENT OF NOS. 1 HEREON APPROVED BY THE SECRETARY OF INTERIOR JAN 17 1903						
	16							
	17							

TRIBAL ENROLLMENT OF PARENTS

	Name of Father	Year	County	Name of Mother	Year	County
1	Nat Colbert	1896	Sugar Loaf	Elsie Colbert	Dead	Skullyville
2						
3						
4						
5						
6	Nº1 is now the husband of Lena Edward on Choctaw card #1031 Nov 1, 1902					
7						
8						
9						
10						
11						
12						
13						
14						
15						
16				Date of Application for Enrollment.	6/20/99	
17						

RESIDENCE:	Sugar Loaf	COUNTY.						CARD NO.	
POST OFFICE:	Red Oak I.T.		**Choctaw Nation**			**Choctaw Roll** (Not Including Freedmen)		FIELD NO.	2986

Dawes' Roll No.	NAME	Relationship to Person First Named	AGE	SEX	BLOOD	TRIBAL ENROLLMENT		
						Year	County	No.
DEAD.	1 Collin Artemissa		60	F	Full	1893	Sugar Loaf	135
	2							
	3							
	4							
	5							
	6 No. 1 HEREON DISMISSED UNDER							
	7 ORDER OF THE COMMISSION TO THE FIVE CIVILIZED TRIBES OF MARCH 31, 1905							
	8							
	9							
	10							
	11							
	12							
	13							
	14							
	15							
	16							
	17							

TRIBAL ENROLLMENT OF PARENTS

	Name of Father	Year	County	Name of Mother	Year	County
1	Bo-nach-it-a-bo	Dead	Miss	A-no-li-ho-na	Dead	Sugar Loaf
2						
3						
4						
5						
6	On page 14 No 135, 1893 P.R. Sugar Loaf Co as Artemary Collen					
7						
8	Nº 1 Died May 21, 1901, proof of death filed March 12, 1903					
9						
10						
11						
12						
13						
14						
15						
16					Date of Application for Enrollment.	6/20/99
17						

Choctaw By Blood Enrollment Cards 1898-1914

RESIDENCE: Sugar Loaf COUNTY. **Choctaw Nation** **Choctaw Roll** *(Not Including Freedmen)* CARD No.
POST OFFICE: Red Oak I.T. FIELD No. 2987

Dawes' Roll No.	NAME	Relationship to Person	AGE	SEX	BLOOD	TRIBAL ENROLLMENT		
						Year	County	No.
8751	1 Harkins Sillen 43	First Named	40	F	Full	1896	Sans Bois	2126
	2							
	3							
	4							
	5							
	6							
	7							
	8							
	9							
	10							
	11							
	12							
	13							
	14							
	15	ENROLLMENT OF NOS. 1 HEREON APPROVED BY THE SECRETARY OF INTERIOR JAN 17 1903						
	16							
	17							

TRIBAL ENROLLMENT OF PARENTS

	Name of Father	Year	County	Name of Mother	Year	County
1	Ish-tam-be	Dead	Sugar Loaf	He-mo-na-ho-na	Dead	Sugar Loaf
2						
3						
4						
5						
6						
7		On 1896 roll as Salina Christy				
8						
9						
10						
11						
12						
13						
14						
15						
16				Date of Application for Enrollment.	6/20/99	
17						

Choctaw By Blood Enrollment Cards 1898-1914

RESIDENCE: Skullyville	COUNTY. Choctaw Nation		Choctaw Roll	CARD No.	
POST OFFICE: Lodi I.T.			(Not Including Freedmen)	FIELD No. 2988	

Dawes' Roll No.	NAME	Relationship to Person First Named	AGE	SEX	BLOOD	TRIBAL ENROLLMENT Year	County	No.
8752	1 Harrison Charlie 48		45	M	Full	1896	Skullyville	5183
14780	2 " Awachima 63	Wife	60	F	"	P R 1893	Sans Bois	129
	3							
	4							
	5							
	6							
	7							
	8							
	9							
	10							
	11							
	12							
	13							
	14							
	15							
	16							
	17							

ENROLLMENT
OF NOS. 1 HEREON
APPROVED BY THE SECRETARY
OF INTERIOR JAN 17 1903

ENROLLMENT
OF NOS. 2 HEREON
APPROVED BY THE SECRETARY
OF INTERIOR MAY 20 1903

TRIBAL ENROLLMENT OF PARENTS

	Name of Father	Year	County	Name of Mother	Year	County
1	Wm Harrison	Dead	Sans Bois		Dead	Sans Bois
2		"	Miss		"	Miss
3						
4						
5						
6	No2 On page 92 No 929, 1893 P.R. Sans Bois Co, as Eliza Dixon					
7						
8						
9						
10						
11						
12						
13						
14						
15					Date of Application for Enrollment	
16					6/20/99	
17						

Choctaw By Blood Enrollment Cards 1898-1914

RESIDENCE: Sugar Loaf POST OFFICE: Red Oak I.T.	COUNTY. **Choctaw Nation**	Choctaw Roll (Not Including Freedmen)	CARD NO. FIELD NO. 2989

Dawes' Roll No.	NAME		Relationship to Person First Named	AGE	SEX	BLOOD	TRIBAL ENROLLMENT		
							Year	County	No.
8753	1 Stallaby James	38	First Named	36	M	Full	1896	Sugar Loaf	11176
8754	2 " Sallie	37	Wife	34	F	"	1896	" "	11177
8755	3 " Robert	21	Son	18	M	"	1896	" "	11178
8756	4 " Selaney	19	Dau	16	F	"	1896	" "	11179
8757	5 " Nattie	16	"	13	F	"	1896	" "	11180
8758	6 " Tenni	13	Son	10	M	"	1896	" "	11181
8759	7 " Dukes	11	"	8	M	"	1896	" "	11182
8760	8 " James N	9	"	6	M	"	1896	" "	11183
8761	9 " Forbis	6	"	3	M	"	1896	" "	11184
8762	10 " Nannie	2	Dau	3mos	F	"			
8763	11 " Lizzie	1	Dau	4mo	F	"			
	12 No9 on 1896 roll as Ferbis Stilibay								
	13								
	14 Father of No.11 is No.1								
	15 Mother of No.11 is No.2								
	16								
	17								

ENROLLMENT OF NOS. 1 2 3 4 5 6 7 8 9 10 11 HEREON APPROVED BY THE SECRETARY OF INTERIOR JAN 17 1903

TRIBAL ENROLLMENT OF PARENTS

	Name of Father	Year	County	Name of Mother	Year	County
1	John Stallaby	Dead	Miss	Mary Stallaby	Dead	Miss
2	Charley White	"	Nashoba	Amy White	1896	Sugar Loaf
3	No 1			No 2		
4	No 1			No 2		
5	No 1			No 2		
6	No 1			No 2		
7	No 1			No 2		
8	No 1			No 2		
9	No 1			No 2		
10	No 1			No 2		
11	No 1			No 2		
12	No1 On 1896 roll as James Stiliby					
13	No2 " 1896 " " Silie "			No.11 Born Dec 10, 1901. Enrolled April 8,		
14	No3 " 1896 " " Bob "					
	No4 " 1896 " " Silinia "			#1 to 11		
15	No5 " 1896 " " Hige "			Date of Application for Enrollment		
16	No6 " 1896 " " Danes "			6/20/99		
	No7 " 1896 " " Dank "					
17	No8 " 1896 " " Nation "					

Wynnewood I.T. 1/5/03   For child of No4 see NB (Mar 3-1905) Card #202

RESIDENCE:	Sans Bois	COUNTY.	Choctaw Nation	Choctaw Roll	CARD NO.	
POST OFFICE:	Hoyt, I.T.			(Not Including Freedmen)	FIELD NO.	2990

Dawes' Roll No.	NAME		Relationship to Person First Named	AGE	SEX	BLOOD	TRIBAL ENROLLMENT		
							Year	County	No.
15434	1 Hoyt, Milo A	34	First Named	31	M	1/8	1896	Sans Bois	5136
I.W. 917	2 " Lizzie	27	Wife	23	F	I.W.	1896	" "	14594
15435	3 " Flossie L	6	Dau	3	"	1/16	1896	" "	5137
DEAD.	4 " Milo A Jr	4	Son	3mo	M	1/16			
15436	5 " Homer	2	Son	6wks	M	1/16			
	6								
	7								
	8								
	9								
	10								
	11								
	12								
	13								
	14								
	15								
	16								
	17								

ENROLLMENT
OF NOS. 1 – 3 – 5 – HEREON
APPROVED BY THE SECRETARY
OF INTERIOR MAY 9 1904

ENROLLMENT
OF NOS. 2 HEREON
APPROVED BY THE SECRETARY
OF INTERIOR AUG 3 1904

No. 4 HEREON DISMISSED UNDER
ORDER OF THE COMMISSION TO THE FIVE
CIVILIZED TRIBES OF MARCH 31, 1905

TRIBAL ENROLLMENT OF PARENTS

	Name of Father	Year	County	Name of Mother	Year	County
1	Milo Hoyt	Dead	Cherokee	Harriet Hoyt	1896	Tobucksy
2	Robert Smith	1896	Non-Citz	Nannie Smith	Dead	Non Citz
3	No 1			No 2		
4	No 1			No 2		
5	No. 1			No. 2		
6						
7						
8						
9	No 1 Elects [remainder illegible]					
10	No 1 Elects for himself and family to be enrolled as Choctaws Oct 4 '03					
11	No 3 on 1896 roll as Frances Hoyt					
12	No 4 Affidavit of birth to be supplied: Recd July 1/99					
13	No. 5 Enrolled April 9, 1901					
14	Nº 4 Died June 27, 1900; proof of death filed Nov 11 1902 Additional proof filed Dec 23, 1902 On Cherokee roll. See enrollment of					
15	Serena Parnell, D. Card 465					
16	For child of Nos 1&2 see NB (Apr 26-06) Card #399		Date of Application for Enrollment:	6/20/99		
17	" " " " " " " (Mar 3'05) " #1282					

Choctaw By Blood Enrollment Cards 1898-1914

RESIDENCE: Sugar Loaf	COUNTY.					
POST OFFICE: Red River, I.T.						

Choctaw Nation

Choctaw Roll (Not Including Freedmen)

CARD NO. FIELD NO. 2991

Dawes' Roll No.	NAME		Relationship to Person First Named	AGE	SEX	BLOOD	TRIBAL ENROLLMENT		
							Year	County	No.
8764	1 Baker, Sillin	25	First Named	22	F	Full	1896	Sugar Loaf	76
8765	2 Baker, Elliott	2	Son	1yr	M	"			
8766	3 " Francis	1	Dau	3mo	F	"			
	4								
	5								
	6								
	7								
	8								
	9								
	10								
	11								
	12								
	13								
	14								
	15	ENROLLMENT OF NOS. 1, 2, 3 HEREON APPROVED BY THE SECRETARY OF INTERIOR JAN 17 1903							
	16								
	17								

TRIBAL ENROLLMENT OF PARENTS

	Name of Father	Year	County	Name of Mother	Year	County
1	John Slaughter	Dead	Sugar Loaf	Bicey Slaughter	Dead	Sugar Loaf
2	Elum Baker	1896	Skullyville	No1		
3	" "	1896	"	Nº1		
4						
5						
6						
7	On 1896 roll as Sillin Anderson					
8	No.1 is now the wife of Elum Baker on Choctaw Card No 2888 and					
9	Evidence of marriage is filed herein this day May 8, 1901					
10	No2 Enrolled May 8, 1901					
	Nº3 Born May 30, 1902; enrolled Aug. 25, 1902					
11						
12	For child of No1 see NB (Apr 26-06) Card #458					
13						
14					#1	
15					Date of Application for Enrollment.	
16					6/20/99	
17						

Choctaw By Blood Enrollment Cards 1898-1914

RESIDENCE: Sugar Loaf COUNTY.	**Choctaw Nation**	Choctaw Roll	CARD NO.
POST OFFICE: Red Oak, I.T.		(Not Including Freedmen)	FIELD NO. 2992

Dawes' Roll No.	NAME		Relationship to Person	AGE	SEX	BLOOD	TRIBAL ENROLLMENT		
							Year	County	No.
8767	1 Sam, Morris	27	First Named	24	M	Full	1893	Blue	8
8768	2 " Sophia	25	Wife	22	F	"	1896	Sans Bois	5144
14781	3 " Clifford	3	Son	2	M	"			
14782	4 " Nancy	1	Dau	4mo	F	"			
14783	5 " James	1	Son	4mo	M	"			
	6								
	7								
	8								
	9								
	10								
	11								
	12								
	13								
	14								
	15	ENROLLMENT OF NOS. 1 and 2 HEREON APPROVED BY THE SECRETARY OF INTERIOR JAN 17 1903		ENROLLMENT OF NOS 3, 4 and 5 HEREON APPROVED BY THE SECRETARY OF INTERIOR MAY 20 1903					
	16								
	17								

TRIBAL ENROLLMENT OF PARENTS

	Name of Father	Year	County	Name of Mother	Year	County
1	James Sam	Dead	Skullyville	Sallie Sam	Dead	Gaines
2	Cornelius Hancock	"	Sans Bois	Betsy Hancock	1896	Sans Bois
3	No 1			No 2		
4	No 1			No 2		
5	No 1			No 2		
6						
7	No1 on 1893 Pay Roll, Blue County, Page 117, No8, as Morris Sams					
8	No2 " 1896 roll as Sophia Hancock					
9	No3 born March 24, 1900: enrolled Dec 11, 1902					
	Nos 4 and 5 born August 19, 1902: enrolled Dec. 11, 1902					
10	For child of Nos 1&2 see NB (Apr 26-06) Card #321					
11						
12						
13						
14					Date of Application for Enrollment.	
15						
16					6/20/99	
17	Leflore IT 11/1/04					

292

Choctaw By Blood Enrollment Cards 1898-1914

RESIDENCE: Sans Bois COUNTY. **Choctaw Nation** **Choctaw Roll** CARD No.
POST OFFICE: Enterprise, I.T. (Not Including Freedmen) FIELD NO. 2993F

Dawes' Roll No.	NAME	Relationship to Person First Named	AGE	SEX	BLOOD	TRIBAL ENROLLMENT		
						Year	County	No.
8769	1 Quinton, Elizabeth 62	First Named	59	F	1/8	1896	Sans Bois	10643
8770	2 " Samuel 25	Son	22	M	1/16	1896	" "	10644
8771	3 " Charles 22	"	19	"	1/16	1896	" "	10645
8772	4 Breedlove, Margaret E 13	G.Dau	10	F	1/32	1896	" "	594
8773	5 " James 11	G.Son	8	M	1/32	1896	" "	593
	6							
	7							
	8							
	9							
	10							
	11							
	12							
	13							
	14							
	15	ENROLLMENT OF NOS. 1,2,3,4,5 HEREON APPROVED BY THE SECRETARY OF INTERIOR JAN 17 1903						
	16							
	17							

TRIBAL ENROLLMENT OF PARENTS

	Name of Father	Year	County	Name of Mother	Year	County
1	S. L. Jacobs	Dead	Skullyville		Dead	
2	Sam Quinton	"	Non Citz	No1		
3	" "	"	" "	No1		
4	Wm Breedlove	"	" "	Roxie E Breedlove	Dead	Sans Bois
5	" "	"	" "	" " "	"	" " "
6						
7						
8	For child of No3 see NB (Apr 26-06) Card #684					
9	No4 on 1896 roll as Breedlove					
10						
11	Information as to mother of No1					
12	waived by Commissioner McKinnon					
13						
14						
15						
16			Date of Application for Enrollment.	6/20/99		
17						

Choctaw By Blood Enrollment Cards 1898-1914

RESIDENCE: Sans Bois	COUNTY.					Choctaw Roll	CARD NO.
POST OFFICE: Red Oak, I.T.		Choctaw Nation				(Not Including Freedmen)	FIELD NO. 2994

Dawes' Roll No.	NAME	Relationship to Person First Named	AGE	SEX	BLOOD	TRIBAL ENROLLMENT		
						Year	County	No.
8774 1	Jefferson, Smallwood 27	Named	24	M	Full	1896	Sans Bois	6412
8775 2	" Mary 23	Wife	20	F	"	1896	" "	3174
8776 3	" Eliza 1	Dau	3mo	F	"			
4								
5								
6								
7								
8								
9								
10								
11								
12								
13								
14								
15	ENROLLMENT OF NOS. 1,2,3 HEREON							
16	APPROVED BY THE SECRETARY OF INTERIOR JAN 17 1903							
17								

TRIBAL ENROLLMENT OF PARENTS

	Name of Father	Year	County	Name of Mother	Year	County
1	Nicholas Jefferson	1896	Sans Bois	Alis Jefferson	Dead	Sans Bois
2	Johnson Dwight	Dead	Skullyville	Sallie Dwight	"	" " "
3	No 1			No 2		
4						
5						
6						
7						
8	No1 on 1896 roll as Small Jefferson					
9	No2 " 1896 " " Mary Daggs					
10	No3 Born August 11-1901: Enrolled November 1, 1901					
11						
12						
13						
14					#1&2	
15					Date of Application for Enrollment.	
16					6/20/99	
17						

294

Choctaw By Blood Enrollment Cards 1898-1914

Dawes' Roll No.	NAME		Relationship to Person First Named	AGE	SEX	BLOOD	TRIBAL ENROLLMENT		
							Year	County	No.
8777	1 Jones, Marteson	29	First Named	26	M	Full	1896	Sans Bois	6425
8778	2 " Lucy DIED PRIOR TO SEPTEMBER 25 1902	30	Wife	36	F	"	1893	Sugar Loaf	2
8779	3 " Wilson	6	Son	3	M	"	1896	"	6566
8780	4 " Mary	4	Dau	4mo	F	"			
8781	5 Baker, Annie	11	S.Dau	8	"	"	1896	Sugar Loaf	770
8782	6 " Sallie	12	"	9	"	"	1896	" "	771
	7								
	8								
	9								
	10								
	11								
	12								
	13								
	14								
	15	ENROLLMENT OF NOS. 1,2,3,4,5,6 HEREON							
	16	APPROVED BY THE SECRETARY OF INTERIOR JAN 17 1903							
	17								

TRIBAL ENROLLMENT OF PARENTS

	Name of Father	Year	County	Name of Mother	Year	County
1	James Jones	1896	Sugar Loaf	Selina Jones	Dead	Sugar Loaf
2	Columbus Jack	Dead	" "	Winnie Jack	"	in Mississippi
3	No1			No2		
4	No1			No2		
5	Billy Baker	Dead	Sugar Loaf	No2		
6	" "	"	" "	No2		
7		No2 on 1893 Pay Roll, Page 1, No2, Sugar Loaf Co as Lucy Amos				
8		No2 also on 1896 Roll " 161 " 6565 " " " " Locin Jones				
9		For child of No.5 see NB (April 26,1906) No 529				
10		No.3 on 1896 census roll, Choctaw Nation as Johnnie Jones: page 161: #6566 3/29, 1900				
11		No.2 died January – 1901; proof of death filed Dec 19, 1902				
12		No.2 died Jan – 1901: Enrollment cancelled by Department July 8, 1904				
13						
14						
15	P.O. Red Oak 9/29/10					
16				Date of Application for Enrollment	6/20/99	
17						

Choctaw By Blood Enrollment Cards 1898-1914

RESIDENCE: Sans Bois   COUNTY. **Choctaw Nation**   Choctaw Roll   CARD NO.
POST OFFICE: Featherstone, I.T.   *(Not Including Freedmen)*   FIELD NO. 2996

Dawes' Roll No.	NAME		Relationship to Person	AGE	SEX	BLOOD	TRIBAL ENROLLMENT		
							Year	County	No.
8783	1 Quinton, Joel	30	First Named	27	M	1/32	1896	Sans Bois	10646
I.W 1317	2 " Katie	29	Wife	25	F	I.W			
8784	3 " Elizabeth	8	Dau	5	"	1/64	1896	Sans Bois	10647
8785	4 " Edward	5	Son	3	M	1/64			
8786	5 ~~DIED PRIOR TO SEPTEMBER 25 1902~~ Lee		"	4mo	"	1/64			
8787	6 " Lillie	4	Dau	4mo	F	1/64			
14895	7 " Myrtle	6	"	16"	"	1/64			
	8								
	9								
	10								
	11								
	12								
	13								
	14								
	15								
	16								
	17								

ENROLLMENT
OF NOS. 7 HEREON
APPROVED BY THE SECRETARY
OF INTERIOR MAY 21 1903

ENROLLMENT
OF NOS. 2 HEREON
APPROVED BY THE SECRETARY
OF INTERIOR MAR 14 1905

ENROLLMENT
OF NOS. 1,3,4,5,6 HEREON
APPROVED BY THE SECRETARY
OF INTERIOR JAN 17 1903

TRIBAL ENROLLMENT OF PARENTS

	Name of Father	Year	County	Name of Mother	Year	County
1	Sam'l Quinton	Dead	Non Citz	Eliz. Quinton	1896	Sans Bois
2	Edw. Salon	"	" "	Ella Sanders	1896	Non Citz
3	No 1			No 2		
4	No 1			No 2		
5	~~No 1~~			~~No 2~~		
6	No 1			No 2		
7	No.1			No.2		
8						
9	For child of Nos 1&2 see NB (Apr 26-06) Card #853					
10	As to marriage, see testimony of No1 and ~~Matilda Bench~~					
11						
12	Nos 4-5-6 Affidavits of birth to be supplied: Recd 7/1/99					
13	No.7 Born Sept 9, 1901: application made Dec 23, 1902 Proof of birth filed 2/11/1903 ~~No.5 Died Oct, 1899. Proof of death filed Dec 23 1902~~					
14						
15	For child of Nos 1&2 see NB (March 3,1905) Card #1402			Date of Application for Enrollment. #1 to 6 inc		
16				6/21/99		
17	No2 PO Quinton IT 7/16/04					

Choctaw By Blood Enrollment Cards 1898-1914

RESIDENCE: Skullyville COUNTY.	**Choctaw Nation**	Choctaw Roll (Not Including Freedmen)	CARD NO.
POST OFFICE: Shady Point, I.T.			FIELD NO. 297

Dawes' Roll No.	NAME	Relationship to Person First Named	AGE	SEX	BLOOD	TRIBAL ENROLLMENT		
						Year	County	No.
8788	1 Jacob, David DIED PRIOR TO SEPTEMBER 25 1902	First Named	19	M	Full	1896	Skullyville	6435
8789	2 " Lizzie 19	Wife	16	F	"	1893	Sugar Loaf	245
15577	3 Jackson Minnie 1	Dau of Nº2	2	F	"			
	4							
	5							
	6							
	7							
	8							
	9							
	10							
	11							
	12							
	13							
	14							
	15							
	16							
	17							

ENROLLMENT
OF NOS. ~ 3 ~~~ HEREON
APPROVED BY THE SECRETARY
OF INTERIOR   SEP 22 1904

ENROLLMENT
OF NOS. 1 and 2 HEREON
APPROVED BY THE SECRETARY
OF INTERIOR   JAN 17 1903

TRIBAL ENROLLMENT OF PARENTS

Name of Father	Year	County	Name of Mother	Year	County
1 Thos. Jacob	Dead	Skullyville	Rhoda Thomas	Dead	Skullyville
2 Shot-ho-ma	"	Gaines	Phoebe	"	Gaines
3 Joseph Jackson	1896	"	Nº2		
4					
5					
6					
7					

No1 Died in 1899: Proof of death filed Decᴸ 23ʳᵈ 1902

No2 on 1893 Pay roll, Sugar Loaf Co, Page 24, No 245 as Lizzie Homma

No1 died - - 1899. Enrollment cancelled [remainder illegible]

For child of No.2 see NB (March 3, 1905) #970

Nº3 Born Feby 15, 1902, application said to have been made at Wister I.T. in December 1902. See affidavits of witnesses, also copy of letter of Joe Jackson.

Nº3 enrolled May 2, 1904.

		Date of Application for Enrollment.	6/21/99

RESIDENCE:	Sans Bois	COUNTY.							
POST OFFICE:	Sans Bois, I.T.							CARD NO. FIELD NO.	2998

Choctaw Nation

Choctaw Roll (Not Including Freedmen)

Dawes' Roll No.	NAME	Relationship to Person First Named	AGE	SEX	BLOOD	TRIBAL ENROLLMENT		
						Year	County	No.
8790	1 Tom, Simon	38	35	M	Full	1893	Sans Bois	803
	2							
	3							
	4							
	5							
	6							
	7							
	8							
	9							
	10							
	11							
	12							
	13							
	14							
	15							
	16							
	17							

ENROLLMENT
OF NOS. 1 HEREON
APPROVED BY THE SECRETARY
OF INTERIOR Jan 17 1903

TRIBAL ENROLLMENT OF PARENTS

	Name of Father	Year	County	Name of Mother	Year	County
1	En-sha-lih-tubbee	Dead	Sans Bois	Ish-ta-lin-na	1896	Sans Bois
2						
3						
4						
5						
6			On 1893 Pay Roll, Sans Bois Co, Page 77, No 803			
7						
8			N° 1 is duplicate of Simon Tom on Choctaw card N° 2667 approved roll			
9			of Choctaws by blood N° [illegible] Enrollment of N°1 cancelled by [illegible]			
10			September 2, 1904. See Departmental letter of that date [illegible]			
11						
12						
13						
14						Date of Application for Enrollment.
15						
16						6/21/99
17						

Choctaw By Blood Enrollment Cards 1898-1914

RESIDENCE: Sugar Loaf **COUNTY.** **Choctaw Nation** **Choctaw Roll** (Not Including Freedmen) **CARD No.**
POST OFFICE: Red Oak, I.T. **FIELD No.** 2999

Dawes' Roll No.	NAME		Relationship to Person First Named	AGE	SEX	BLOOD	TRIBAL ENROLLMENT		
							Year	County	No.
I.W 655	1 Williams, Jasper	35	First Named	30	M	I.W	1896	Sans Bois	15141
8791	2 " Eli	12	Son	9	"	1/8	1896	" "	12642
8792	3 " Eddie	10	"	7	"	1/8	1896	" "	12643
	4								
	5								
	6								
	7								
	8								
	9								
	10								
	11	ENROLLMENT							
	12	OF NOS. 1 HEREON							
	13	APPROVED BY THE SECRETARY OF INTERIOR MAR 26 1904							
	14								
	15	ENROLLMENT							
	16	OF NOS. 2 and 3 HEREON APPROVED BY THE SECRETARY							
	17	OF INTERIOR JAN 17 1903							

TRIBAL ENROLLMENT OF PARENTS

	Name of Father	Year	County	Name of Mother	Year	County
1	Jas. Williams	Dead	Non Citz	Mary Williams	Dead	Non Citz
2	No1			Cassie Williams	"	Sans Bois
3	No1			" "	"	" " "
4						
5						
6						
7						
8			No1 As to marriage, see testimony			
9			of himself and G. W. Dukes			
10						
11						
12						
13						
14						
15						
16				Date of Application for Enrollment.	6/21/99	
17						

Choctaw By Blood Enrollment Cards 1898-1914

RESIDENCE:	Sugar Loaf							

RESIDENCE: Sugar Loaf **COUNTY.** **Choctaw Nation** **Choctaw Roll** CASE No.
POST OFFICE: Le Flore, I.T. (Not Including Freedmen) **FIELD NO.** 3000

Dawes' Roll No.	NAME	Relationship to Person First Named	AGE	SEX	BLOOD	TRIBAL ENROLLMENT		
						Year	County	No.
8793	1 Burns, William 23	First Named	20	M	1/2	1896	Sugar Loaf	812
8794	2 " Jane 24	Wife	21	F	3/4	1896	" "	8489
8795	3 " Alphy 3	Dau	2mo	"	3/8			
	4							
	5							
	6							
	7							
	8							
	9							
	10							
	11							
	12							
	13							
	14							
	15	ENROLLMENT OF NOS. 1, 2, 3 HEREON APPROVED BY THE SECRETARY OF INTERIOR JAN 17 1903						
	16							
	17							

TRIBAL ENROLLMENT OF PARENTS

	Name of Father	Year	County	Name of Mother	Year	County
1	Buckner Burns	1896	Non Citz	Isabelle Burns	Dead	Sugar Loaf
2	Thos Moore	Dead	Sugar Loaf	Phoebe Moore	"	" " "
3	No1			No2		
4						
5						
6						
7	No1 on 1896 roll as Wᵐ Burns					
8	No2 " 1896 " " Jane Moore					
9						
10	Nos 1 and 2 are divorced					
11	For child of No.2 see NB (Mar 3, 1905) #484					
12						
13						
14						
15					Date of Application for Enrollment.	
16					6/21/99	
17					No3 enrolled Dec. 14/99	

ACHA-KAN-LI................................249
A-CHUK-MAT-HE-KET-A-BE.....164
ADAM, Abe...................................259
ADAMS
    Abel..259
    Cornelius..................................240
    Davis...193
    Eliza..192
    Elizabeth...................................177
    James..192
    John..177
    Jonas...192
    Lawrence...................................192
    Lony..192
    Louina.......................................192
    Reuben......................................192
    Rhoda..192
    Seal...177
    Sebonn......................................192
    Selin..192
    Simon..259
A-HA-YO-TUBBEE.........................33
A-HE-LAT-AM-BE.........................164
AH-HUBBEE..................................183
AH-LE-HE-MA................................140
AH-NO-LA-TUBBEE.......................196
AH-PE-LA......................................174
AINSWORTH
    Alice..79
    Ally..79
    Chester...79
    Clifford..79
    D S..79
    J G..79
    Jas G..80
    Jesse B...79
    Jessie B..79
    Margaret.......................................79
    Martha.....................................79,80
    Nancy...79
AK-KOS-TO-NECHI.......................174
ALEXANDER, Selney.....................284
ALLEN
    Alex...75
    Callie...75
    David...75
    Mary..75

    Maud..75
    May..75
    Richard M.....................................75
    Spazzee..75
    W W...200
    Walter..75
    William...75
AL-YO-TUBBEE.............................228
AMOS
    Allen Wesley...............................239
    Lena...239
    Lucy...295
    Sexton..239
    Susie..232
ANDERSON
    Andee...197
    David..15
    Davis..197
    Isabelle...15
    Jincey...197
    Joseph..156
    Juliana..156
    Levisey...15
    Louisiana....................................258
    Lucy Ann....................................197
    Luvy S..197
    Martha..157
    Newman..15
    Richard.......................................197
    Sam..15
    Sillin..291
    Wm...157
A-NE-LI-HO-NA.............................286
AN-OYO-TE-MA.............................244
A-SHA-LIN-TUBBEE.........................93
A-TOB-BI......................................147
ATOKKO
    Marcey.......................................258
    Simeon.......................................258
    Susan...258
ATOKOBEE
    Rhoda..262
    Sampson.....................................262
A-TOM-BE.....................................145
    Nancy...145
AU-I-CHI......................................190
AUSTIN

James 269
Lewis 269
Sophy.................................269
AUTREY
   Adlade 212
   Columbus B......................212
   Enoch................................212
   Lem....................................212
   Rosa..................................212
AUTRY, Hezekiah Enoch 212
AY-A-KAN-TA-BE 237
BACON
   Amanda 156
   Mollie 156
   Reuben..............................156
   Reuben J...........................156
   Reuben, Jr.........................156
BAILEY
   Jack...................................107
   Rebecca 107
BAKER 161
   Annie 295
   Billy..................................295
   Elizabeth....................162,188
   Elliott................................291
   Elum 188,291
   Emeline.............................188
   Francis...............................291
   Houston 188
   Lewis 188
   Louis.................................188
   Milan 188
   Millin................................188
   Robert................................188
   Sallie.................................295
   Sillin 291
BARBER, David P 72
BARBOUR
   David Preston 72
   Hester A..............................72
   James William 72
BARNARD, Polly 78
BASCOM
   Charlotte............................236
   Cornelius 236
   Joe 129
   John 236

Oscar.................................129
Wicey 236
BATTIEST
   Andrew 158
   Eliza..................................158
   Gibson 158
   Harris 158
   Liza...................................158
BATTISE, Gibson 156
BATTLES
   Mattie D............................122
   Mattie E 122,149
   Wm...................................122
BEARDSLEY
   Jane...................................265
   Walter 265
BELL
   Agnes................................129
   Alice 129
   Amon.................................129
   Daniel 129
   Hampton 245
   Sweeny 129
   Wilson 245
BELLE
   Alice 129
   Baby 129
   Sweeny 129
BELVIN
   Annie 277
   Elsey 252
   Hagan 220,252
   Hagin 277
   Lucinda..............................220
   Wilson 277
BE-NACH-IT-A-BE......................286
BENCH
   Matilda 296
   Sam....................................263
BESSIE.....................................196
BETSY 239
BICE
   Beckie................................103
   Thomas 103
BICKLE
   Bessie 230
   Brasha................................230

Fannie 230
George 230
Greenwood 230
Jack 230
James A 230
Lona 230
Lula 230
Roxy 230
Scott 230
Scott B 230
Serina 230
Susan 230
BIDDIE
Elizabeth 173
James 173
BIDDY
James 266
Mary Jane 266
BILLY
Bicy 206
Cephus 206
Dixon 206
Eliza 206
Jennie 206
John 206
Lida 206
Lita 206
Milton 206
Nicey 206
Sodie 206
BISHOP
David 106
Myrah 106
BIXBY, Tams 9
BLAIR, John W 179
BLAKE, Fletcher 59
BOATRIGHT
Elias 63
Eva J 63
Joseph 63
Lou E 63
Martha Louzena 63
Robert E W 63
Ruth A 63
Ruth I 63
Viola M 63
BOATWRIGHT

Eva 63
Ruth 63
Viola 63
BOBO
Arrena 173
Estilla 173
Ethel B 173
Ethel P 173
James P 173
Josephine 173
Mary E 173
Ola Odessa 173
William 173
BOHANAN
Annie 54
Celia 54
Elmer Wear 54
James 54
James W 54
Joseph 138
Lyman 54
Rachel 138
Sy 138
BOLAND, Jacob 259
BOND
Cynthia Renie 252
Lizzie 252
Mary 132
Sweeny 252
Swiney 252
BORON
Henry 267
Luercey 267
BOWMAN
Jas H 82
Sarah 82
BRAKE
Amanda I 59
James Duval 59
Kully 59
Mary 59
BRANDY
Betsy 178
Jacob 178
James 178
BRASHEARS
Kate 200

Katie 11,70
Turner 11,70,200
BREEDLOVE
  James 293
  Margaret E 293
  Roxie E 293
  Wm 293
BROGDON
  Allaminta 69
  James M 69
  Jodie J 69
  Riley 69
  Sarah D 69
  Wesley H 69
BROOME
  Abbie J 265
  J C 265
  Jaes E 265
  James E 265
  M E 265
BROWN
  Laut 90
  Robert 47,90
  Shorty 47
  Tecumseh 47
BULLARD
  Andrew C 254
  A C 254
  Lu Orenia 254
  Mary 254
  Pocahontas 254
  Straid 254
  Villey M 254
BURGEVIN
  Edmond 98
  Edmond A 98
  Edward 98
  Ella 98
  Frances 98
  Francis 98
  Francis H 98
  Henry A 98
  John T 98
  Julia G 98
BURNEY, George 235
BURNS
  Alex 145

Alphy 300
Buckner 300
Isabelle 300
Jane 300
Martha 145
William 300
Wm 300
BURRIS
  Cassie 203
  Isaac 203
BURS
  Isaac 203
  Sidney 203
BURTIES 68
  James 68
  Leonard 68
  Rhoda 68
BUSH
  J D 20
  Rachel 20
BYINGTON
  Henry 37
  Joseph 126,176
  Lizzie 37
  Malinda 176
  Philip 37,126,176
  Phillip 52
  Sealy 176
  Silas 37
  Vicy 37
  Wycie 37
CANNON
  Elizabeth 62
  Isaac 62
CARGILL, Lucinda 246
CARNEY
  Allie May 220
  Caroline 284
  Elsie 216
  Frank W 100
  Isabelle 216
  John 216
  John S P 100
  Lee 216
  Maud E 100
  Morris 216
  Nelson 216

Robert...................................220
Sally Ann.............................216
Serena.................................216
Silway.................................284
William Mck........................100
CARSHALL
Agnes..................................258
Eugene................................258
James..................................258
Simon.................................258
Susan..................................258
CARTER
Beckey..................................48
John W..................................48
CARTWRIGHT, Hannah.............43,44
CASS.......................................27
Adam..................................131
Emma...................................29
Lewis..................................131
CHA-FA-HO-KE.................139,141
CHAPMAN
Providence.............................87
Sarah....................................87
CHI-LI-TA.............................198
CHI-MA-HE-KE......................193
CHI-MA-HO-KE.................192,240
CHOAT, Somseu......................261
CHOATE
Emily....................................21
James..................................261
Jincy...................................261
John......................................21
Louie..................................261
CHRISTY, Salina.....................287
CLOSSON
Christina................................56
John......................................56
V P....................................56,67
COGBILL
Frank.....................................69
Isabell...................................69
COLBERT
Amy....................................243
Cornelia...............................141
Dave...............................243,285
Edward................................140
Elsie....................................285

Jane....................................243
Jaspe.....................................15
Joe..15
Joseph...................................15
Nancy....................................15
Nat..................................243,285
Siney...............................135,140
Sophie...................................15
Thomas................................141
Thos.................................139,141
Willie..................................140
Winchester.............................15
CO-LE-CHA...........................221
COLEY
Anderson..............................125
Biney...................................125
Caldwell..............................125
Edmond...............................125
Edward................................125
Ella.....................................125
Jacob...................................125
Joe......................................279
Johnson................................125
Sema...................................125
Sophie.................................279
Wilburn...............................125
COLLEN, Artemary..................286
COLLIN
Angie..................................215
Artemissa.............................286
Claudie L...............................32
Gracie.................................104
Lena...................................215
Sena...................................215
Stephen...............................215
COLLINS
Andrew..................................32
Andrew J................................32
Andrew L...............................32
Artimissie............................184
Clara May............................106
Clarence Cole.......................106
Claudie C...............................32
Claudie L...............................32
Daisy..................................106
Elijah A...............................106
Foly D.................................106

Gracie 104
John 106
John F 106
Mamie A..................................104
Mary 32,104,106
Mary A 104
Mike 32
Miles...104
Miles Ricker 104
Miles S........................104,106
Mills 104
Nellie 32
Nettie 32
Stella...104
Tallia...106
Thomas Hugh 32
CONAWAY, Maud......................100
CONSTREET, Margaret 64
CONWAY
Ben 100
Wesley A 100
COOPER
Abel..116
Andrew J 149
Annie.................................123,149
Austin Albro 149
Charles.....................................123
Charley 123
Clara 116
Dora...201
Douglas.................................116,123
Eliza A 149
Estella...51
Frank...66
Henry.......................................110
Irena..66
Irene..66
A J 149
Jeff...279
John 151
Joseph C 123
Joseph S...................................123
Katie 201
Kirby...201
Liza..123
Maggie Jane.............................123
Margaret J................................123

Margaret Jane 123
Mary 110,138
Mary Belle................................279
Mattee......................................149
Mattie 149
Maud S 110
Sam...................................51,66
Samuel..........................66,110
Sarah...................122,123,149
Stephen................122,123,149
Sue E 66
Susan 110
Thompson.................................201
Willie Vera 110
COWART
Rhoda 8
Samuel J 8
COX
Caleb...92
Charles......................................20
Charley 19,20,124
Emma 19
John 20
Joseph.................................19,20
Joseph R 20
Letha...19
Mary Melzona 20
Prude...88
Rebecca A.................................20
CRICKLIN
Jesse...108
Jessie..108
John 108
CROP, Ben 131
DAGGS
Amanda 76,77
James M....................................76
James W 76
Jas M 76,77
John C.......................................76
Leonidas 76
Mary 294
Mollie.......................................76
Sarah E 76
W W 76
William W 76
DALTON, C L................................200

DANIELS
  Alfred 19
  Green 67
  Mary 19
  Minnie 67
  Susan 67
  Thelma 67
  Turner 67
DARNEAL
  Caroline 78
  Elias 78
  Fred S 78
  Henry 78
  James 78
  Jim 78
  Mary 78
  Stephen 78
  William 78
  Willy 78
DAVIS
  Bertie Lorena 124
  Dave E 124
  Eva 124
  Laithey 124
  Lennie 124
  Letha 124
  Maggie 124
  Mary 156
  Mollie J 57
  Oscar 156
DEATON
  Abe 273
  Susan 273
DEGGS
  James 76
  John 76
DEHART, Susan 271,272
DELOACH
  Annie 43
  Hannah 43
  Joseph 43,44
  Josie 43
  Jossie 43
  Mollie 44
  William 43
  Wm 43
DENTON

  Ada 122
  Emma 122
  James L 122
  Jas L 122
  John 122
  Johnnie 122
  Johnny 122
  Nancy I 122
DERRYBERRY
  Brandon 58
  Brandon B 58
  Clementine 58
  Emma R 58
  Garrison W 58
  John W 58
DESEVERIDGE, Harry 102
DIXON
  Bertha M 263
  Betsy 27
  Billy 27
  Clyde 263
  Eliza 288
  Elizabeth 263
  Hopson 27
  Jesse 263
  Jessee 263
  John 152
  Joseph 27
  Julia 152
  Lilly 27
  Lily 27
  Mamie 27
  Melvina 263
  Silas 263
  Susan 27
DODSON
  Charlie 17
  Elisha Thomas 17
  Eliza 17
  Emma 17
  Jno W 17
  John W 17
  Ludie 17
  Rolly 17
  Sudie 17
  Willie E 17
  Willy E 17

DOUGLASS, Kyle 8
DRAKE
    Cansada 142
    Canzada 142
    John 142
    John E 142
    Palmer................................142
    Rosa....................................279
DUKES, G W 31,299
DUNCAN, Nannie 32
DUNLAP
    Aurena................................255
    C C 142,255
    Christopher C 255
    G W 255
    Kitty I 255
    Rena G................................255
    Susie E................................255
    Virginia..............................255
DURANT
    Alfohns 156
    Sallie..................................156
DWIGHT
    Albert................................. 4
    Eden.................................... 4
    Johnson..............................294
    Lizzie.................................. 4
    Sallie..................................294
    Simon 4
E-CHE-KA-HUNA 178
EDWARD, Lena...........................285
EDWARDS
    Charles............................... 9
    David L............................... 9
    Joseph M 9
    Lula J................................. 9
    Luther W............................. 9
    Martha J............................. 9
    Ophelia S............................ 9
EGBERT, Elizabeth........................161
E-KA-NALLE 224
E-LA-CHE-HO-NA.,........................121
E-LA-CHI-HO-NA...........................151
E-LA-HO-NA..................................198
E-LA-HO-TEMA 33
E-LA-HO-TO-NA 224
ELAI YI-MA..................................249

E-LA-PO-TUBBEE..........................224
E-LA-TO-BA 158
ELIZA 164
E-MA-SPA-SUBBEE.......................28
E-MA-THA-TUBBEE...................278
EN-SHA-LIH-TUBBEE.................298
EVANS
    Edmond 24
    Edmund 24
    Edna.....................................24
    Harriet..................................24
    Harve...................................24
    Jesse.....................................24
    Jessee...................................24
    Lee.......................................24
    Lizzie...................................24
    Rufus....................................24
    Simpson 24
    Tandy....................................24
FANNIN
    Adaline 80
    Allice 80
    Elijah W................................80
    Florence................................80
    Florence Lorell 80
    Florence Loren......................80
    Freddie..................................80
    Fredrica.................................80
    Georgia 80
    Georgina 80
    Henry 80
    Joanna...................................80
    Johnanna...............................80
    Johnanna F............................80
    Kyle 80
    Madaline................................80
    Madaline F.............................80
    Mella Belle 80
    Myrtle I..................................80
    Pauline...................................80
    Wm H 80
FARGO
    Charles A 231
    Narcissa 231
    Robert....................................231
    Robert L.................................231
FARRELL

Eunice...........................133
Gertrude........................133
John Raymond...................133
Theodosia 133,134
Walter.........................133

FARRILL
Anna...........................160
Emry...........................160
Harriet........................160
Theodosia 160
Zelma Lee......................160

FE-LE-MA 37

FENNEL
Ann............................201
Jack...........................201
Louisa.........................201
Samuel.........................201

FENTON
Laura...........................65
William.........................65

FERRILL, Harriett 160
FERRIOLL, Theodosia A...........133

FISHER
Charles.........................41
Nicey 41

FOLSOM
Albert.......................70,84
Alex...........................264
Alexander 264
Alice...........................88
Allie M 70
Ann.............................85
Annie...........................61
Ar B...........................159
Ara D..........................159
Arnold.........................133
Artemissia.....................264
Artimissie 129
Bettie 143
Billy...........................36
Charlotte.......................36
Claude C 70
David........................20,86
David W 70
Edmond..........................85
Edwar...........................61
George......................47,88,90

George D 88
Ida.............................36
Isaac...........................86
Israel..........................36
James..........................159
James W........................159
Jane............................62
Jas W 159
Jerry...........................84
John............................85
Joseph S........................70
Laura..........................159
Levicey......................47,88
Lucinda.........................70
Lucy............................62
Millie..........................86
Nathaniel 62
Ollie E 70
Robbie 88
Robert..........................88
Robt, Jr........................88
Susan 254
Susie Irene 70
Susie K 70
Tandy..........................129
Walker 62
Ward...........................143
Willis F 162

FOLSUM...........................36
Albert..........................84
Walker 62

FORD
Victoria.......................112
William........................112
William W 112
Zack...........................112

FOREMAN
Ben 162
Ben G..........................162
Fannie.........................162
Josephine 162
Mattie 162

FORK, Zack 112
FOUCAR, Ida L 83

FRANKLIN
Ben 35,280
Billy..........................280

Jno W..35
John W..35
Louvinia 168
Sarah..35
Ta-mis-se...35
Tolean..280
Tolena..168
William...280
FRAZIER
  Elizabeth......................................162
  Kelly............................161,162,230
  Lizzie.....................................161,230
FREEMAN
  George...109
  John...109
FREEMON, Mamis.........................229
FREENEY
  Andrew..186
  Mary..186
FRY, Elijah.....................................113
FRYER
  Elijah...113
  Ella..113
FULSOM, John................................85
GAMMEL
  Sarah J...123
  Wm F...123
GARLAND
  James..154
  Jol..154
  Peggy...154
GERMAN, Rena..................................2
GGE
  Betsy..185
  Willie...185
GILL
  Henrietta..73
  John..73
GOLDSBY......................................277
GOUGER
  Estelle..51
  Frank..51
  J J...51
  Julia..51
GRADY
  Fannie E..74
  John M...74

Mrs Fannie.....................................91
GRAHAM
  John..179
  Orminda..179
GREEN
  Daniel...189
  Edmona..189
  Fin..212
  Ida...189
  Lenora...212
  Lewis...189
  Morris..189
  Nellie...189
  Robert..189
  Sophie..189
  Teddy...212
GREYTON
  Jno..95
  Lillith..95
GRIFFITH, Louisa 74
HAHA, Lily....................................184
HALL
  Ada B..175
  Ada V..175
  Ann..175
  Daisy C...134
  George B 175
  John...175
  Leo Bennett 134
  R H..175
  Robert H 175
  Robt H 175
  Susan 175
  William S.......................................134
HAMPTON 46
HANCOCK
  Benjamin 238
  Betsy..........................198,205,292
  Clayton..198
  Cornelius...........................205,292
  Eliza..238
  Israel...238
  Sophia...292
  Willis...............................198,205
HARDAWAY
  Edgar...166
  Jesse..........................115,146,166

Jesse H 166,256
Jno R 166
John 166
John R 166
Julia 166
Julius 166
Margaret 115,146,166
Sarah Ann 166
HARKINS 88
Adam 46
Edward 46
Elizabeth 30
Jim 89
Louvisa 90
Mary 39
Sillen 287
HARLEN
Amey 223
Bency 223
Densey 223
Edmond 223
Logan 223
Sis 223
HARLOW, Mary 61
HARPER
Edgar B 12
Leathy A 12
W W 12
HARRIS 5
Addell 65
Albert 229
Battice 163
Battiest 163
Benjamin 163
Budd 263
Daniel 163
Demon 68
Ellen 263
Emily 163
Lizzie 5
Moses 68
Rhoda 68
Rosa B 163
Rose B 163
Sarah A 40
Solomon 229
Walker 40

HARRISON
Addell 65
Albert 135
Awachima 288
Ben 31
Benjamin 31
Charlie 288
Chas 135
Daisy 134
Emma L 31
Golden 65
Henry 65
Jane 135
Milo H 134
Mitchell 31,134
Mrs D C 134
Wm 288
HARTSHORNE
David 71
David C 71
Edward D 71
Geo E 71
Geo S 71
George E 71
Jane E 71
Margaret 71
Robt D 71
HEARD
Martha 25
Thos 25
HECHA, Houston 184
HE-KE-AN-TA-BE 147
Amy 147
HE-KE-MA 150
HE-KIN-TUBBEE 206
HE-MO-NA-HO-NA 287
HENDRICKS
Ann 133,134
Anna 160
Harriet 160
Jesse 120
John 117,120,133,134,160
Martha M 120
Nancy 120
Theodosia 133
HENDRICKSON, Fannie 74
HENRY

Alexander 145
Amos 145
Arian.............................145
Lucy......................129,145
Mack.............................282
Roosevelt......................145
Susan 145
Wilburn.........................145
HERON, John L 254
HICKER
    Eddie.............................211
    Edward 211
    John Little.....................211
    Jonas............................211
    Lucinda.........................211
    Minnie 211
    Simon 211
HICKES, Ulric C.............10
HICKMAN
    Alice.............................236
    J H 166
    James 146
    James H 146
    Jesse J 146
    Jessie J 146
    Minnie 146,166
    Sarah............................146
    W A 146
HICKS
    Mollie.............................10
    Stephen P 10
    Ulrie Z 10
HISCHA
    Davis.............................184
    Houston 184
    Lillie.............................184
HO-BA-CHEE..................178
HO-KE-MA.................130,163
HO-LI-A-KE 241
HOLLOWAY
    John 275
    Lincoln 275
    Tom 221
HOLMES
    Betsy.............................150
    Charles..........................150
    Morris...........................150

Robinson........................150
HOLSON
    Ada...............................132
    Amanda 156
    Beckie...........................132
    Boyd 132
    Clara A 132
    Joseph...........................156
    Lizzie............................132
    Minnie 156
    N J 156
    Noel J............................132
    Rebecca 156
    Shony............................156
    Stephen.....................132,156
    Sukey.......................156,219
    Sweeney F 132,156
    Sweeny 156,219
    Termelia 219
HOMER, Ellen 119
HOMMA, Lizzie 297
HOM-MZ.......................188
HOWARD, Susan.............262
HOWELL
    Manda............................. 3
    Polk 3
HO-YA-HO-KE 128
HOYT
    Flossie L 290
    Frances 290
    Harriet...........................290
    Homer...........................290
    Lizzie............................290
    Milo..............................290
    Milo A...........................290
    Milo A, Jr 290
HOY-TEA-BE, Adaline 109
HUDSON, Adeline...........257
HULSEY
    Alonzo 267
    Alonzo L........................267
    Claude M........................267
    Henry.............................89
    J C.................................89
    Lavica............................89
    Lemuel V 267
    Lora B...........................267

Louvisa 89
M T 267
Mary A 267
May 89
Ollie I 267
Oral Clarence 267
Walter 89
Willard E 267
Wm D 267
ISAAC
    Polly 251
    Thomas 251
IS-BE-LIN 244
ISH-TA-LIN-NA 298
ISH-TAM-BE 287
ISH-TE-CHI 226
ISH-TE-MA-HOKE 28,36
ITH-KO-CHEE 125
IYAKTUBBE 170
I-YO-NA 93
I-YO-NO 16
JACK
    Columbus 295
    Winnie 295
JACKSON
    Ben 28
    Jas 297
    Joseph 297
    Minnie 297
    Mollie 97,131
    Robin 97
    Sicany 28
    William 135
    Willis 97
JACOB
    David 297
    Lizzie 297
    Thos. 297
JACOBS, S L 293
JAMES
    Adam 39
    Allen 39
    Amanda 109
    Ben 30
    Bennie 109
    Biney 237
    Charles 26,30,39,249

Clarissa 164
Collin 237
Cornelia 164
Dallas 237
Davis 57
Dennis 57
Eli 136
Eliza 39
Ella 36
Ellis 109
Elmer 237
Emiline 36
Emily 39
Etha M 57
Ettier 57
Frank 39
George 28,36
Harris 164
Isaac 39,136
Jackson 36
Jane 30
Jesse 39
Jessie 39
Joe 237
Joseph 237
Joshua 237
L W 148
Lena 136
Levi 109,237
Louisa 30,164
Malina 109
Malissa 26
Malissie 26
Mary 57,109
Mollie J 57
Nellie 237
Noel 26,96,109
Rhoda 30
Sallie 26,30,249
Sealy 109
Selina 36,109
Sely 109
Siley 39
Solomon 96
Susan 30
Sykney 28
Tennessee 237

Ticey 39
Vina 237
Walton 57
Walton D 57
Warlin 36
Warren 36
William 237
Willis 237
Winnie 136
JEFFERSON
Ada 191
Ahs 214
Alfred 184
Alis 294
Allen 191
Arian 191
Benjamin 184,191
Bessie 204
Betsy 199
Bicey 191
Calvin 191
Dixon 191
Eastman 207
Elas 170,171
Eli 204
Elis 184
Eliza 294
Jas 135,207
Jennie 135
Joseph 204
Layson 135
Lena 191,214
Levicey 214
Lina 191
Mary . 135,170,171,181,199,237,294
Mollie 181
Nicey 198,207,214
Nicholas 170,184,191,214,294
Sackey 204
Sampson 204
Sarah 204
Siley 204
Siney 184
Small 294
Smallwood 294
Stephen 135
Sweeny 214

Thoma 199
Thomas 191
Wallace 204
Watson 181
JOE
Adam 114
Elizabeth 114
Sophia 114
Sophie 114
JOHNSON
Ada 268
Ada E B 268
Albin 185
Alexander 268
Alick 268
Amy 268
Arbin 185
E J 32
J P 44
Jep 44
Leolena 185
Levina 249
Lizer 185
Lizzie 185
Lula 185
Lulu 185
Maud 44
Ola 44
Sarah 44
Simon 249,268
Susan 185,188
Wm 185
JONES
Ann 104
Annie 36,226
Edward 116
Eliza 116
Emma 131
Forbis 116
Hetty 259
J R 104
Jackson 226
James 295
Jesse 150,224
John 116
Johnson 224
Julia 29

Julius..................................29
Lemon................................226
Locin.................................295
Louisiana 224
Lucy..................................295
Marteson.............................295
Mary 224,295
Mike 29
Nancy 224
Selina................................295
Sophie................................226
Willie.................................36
Willis 224
Wilson 295
JONESON, Mike..................131
JORDAN
    Henry.............................. 8
    Lora 8
    Rhoda 8
KANABBI.............................276
KAN-CHI-TO-NA 244
KA-NEH-TA 182
KANEHTA
    Annette...........................182
    Arnetta...........................182
    Dave 182
    David 182
    Joseph 182
    Lola..............................182
    Morris............................182
    Rhoda 182
KA-NE-O-TUBBEE.......................121
KAYSER
    Elizabeth.........................25
    Elizabeth H.......................25
    H J 25
KEMP, B F............................32
KERSH
    Alice 32
    Samuel 32
KETUBBEE, Calvin.....................235
KINCADE
    Levina............................30
    Robert............................30
KING
    Abel 195
    Ellen 119

Harris...............................195
Mickie...............................119
Sammie...............................195
Susan 119
KINGCADE, Lavina 30
KINSEY
    Amison J..........................155
    Andrew J 155,186
    Callie 155
    Charles...........................155
    Charlotta 155
    Emily 186
    Francis 186
    Gertrude..........................186
    James H 155
    Samuel............................155
    Sarah A 186
    Sarah Ann 155
KINSIE, Callie 155
KNIGHT
    Fulton 128
    Liza..............................128
KREBBE, Oscar........................99
KREBBS
    Easter............................99
    Reuben............................99
KREBS, Oscar.........................99
LANGFORD
    Albert............................273
    Alice 281
    Benjamin 153
    Calvin 153
    Dora..............................273
    Edward 273
    Henry 153,165,271,273,281
    James 281
    Leberry 153
    Martin............................281
    Mary Ann 153
    Nancy 281
    Nellie 281
    Nettie 153
    Rachael 266
    Rachel 153,165,271,273,281,282
    Rebecca 281
    William...........................153
LANIER

Rebecca 71
Susan P 66
Thos......................................66
LEE, Kizzie 181
LEFLORE
  Ann....................................112
  Arizona 112
  Campbell 83
  Eliza...................................270
  F Greenwood 42
  Florence L.............................42
  Frank....................................83
  Frank T 83
  Gertrude................................83
  Greenwood 42
  Harriet...................................42
  Ida L 83
  Jacob..................................270
  Jos......................................208
  Joseph.................................208
  Joseph, Jr 208
  Jude....................................132
  Leona A 42
  Liney...................................270
  Louie....................................83
  Louis T 42
  Maniva................................208
  Martha 16
  McAlester 208
  Minerva 208
  Mitchell 16
  Polina..................................208
  Rhoda 270
  Selina..................................208
  Wallace........................132,270
  Walter..................................112
  William.................................270
  Wilmond...............................270
LE-MAN-LO-NA.........................125
LEWIS
  Ada 213
  Alexander J..........................257
  Alice 34
  Amaziah 257,278
  Annie 34
  Belle 34
  Ben 241

Benjamin 167
Bettie 34
Bettie A 34
Curtis 34
Eliza.....................................278
Frank.....................................34
Israel 278
Jefferson 213
Kittie....................................213
Lena....................................140
Lucy...............................257,278
Luisa....................................167
M 9
Mary 34,167
May..34
Minnie 211,251
Mrs Mary..............................180
Reuben.................................211
S E 200,202
Sakey...................................241
Sallie....................................251
Simon E 212
Siney....................................211
Wallis G..................................34
William..................................251
William A 34
Winnie 34
Zora P 9
LOMAN
  Ismon...................................221
  Jack................................250,260
  Johnson................................250
  Kizzie 221
  Lizzie 221
  Rhoda 250
LOMBY
  Hannah 132
  John 132
  Lucy....................................132
LOMON, Johnson 250
LOND, W B J 218
LONG
  Charley 92
  Jesse.....................................92
  Jessie.....................................92
  Julia 92
  Louisa....................................78

Milt 78
Parma 92
LORIN, Sampson 147
LOUIS
    Ada 213
    Jefferson 213
    Katie 213
    Reuben 213
    Roben 213
    Siney 213
LOVING
    Jackson 169
    James 246
    Lucinda 169
    Mary 246
    Milton 169
    Sampson 169
    Silsy 169
LUCAS
    Frank 6
    Jennie 6
    Joshua 6
    Lewis 6
    Mary 6
    Sally 7
LUKE, Emma 190
LUMBER, Lucy 132
LYLES
    John W 61
    Mary 61
MACKEY, Jerry 109
MADDIX, W T 200
MA-KA-HO-TE-MA 188
MARTIN, Louina 28
MASSEY
    Henry 74
    James 155
    Mattie 155
MAY
    Mary J 83
    Wm F 83
MCCANN
    Alex 128
    Alexander 128
    Betsy 128,131
    Charley 94
    Cornelius 26,256

Edna Algia 256
Isophine 256
Jesse A 256
Joseph 128
Josephine 256
Leatha A 256
Leonia 256
Melissa 96
Philip 94
Sarah 256
Silway 94
Simpson 256
Thelmer 256
William B 256
Wm B 256
MCCLURE
    Carrie L 218
    Margaret S 218
    Mary E 218
    Preeman J 218
    Preemon J 218
    Sudye J 218
MCCOY
    Milton 7
    Shemohoyo 7
MCCURTAIN
    Amy 201
    Bertha 201
    Bicey 250
    Bizie 250
    Cor 201
    Cornelius 152,201,225
    David 71
    Edmond 6
    George 152
    Green 137,166,201
    Jane 187
    Joseph 228
    Joshua 187
    Katie 201
    Kittie 137
    Lena 201
    Lester 201
    Martha 228
    Mary 228
    Miney 187
    Minnie 187

Mitchell 152
Nicholas......................250
Osborn......................152
Osborne 152
Pataley......................197
Patrick......................250
Pooley......................228
Sampson 152
Sillen......................152
Silly......................228
Silphy 225
Surie 6
Thomas......................187,228
Wacey......................225
Winnie......................152

MCDANIEL
   Ethie 31
   Jenett......................31
   Kate 86
   Thomas......................86
   Velma A 86

MCFERRAN
   Isabelle 102
   John 102
   Ruthie 102
   Walter......................102

MCGILBERRY
   Amsa......................84
   Charley 84

MCGILBERY, Allen......................116

MCGINTY
   Burney W 22
   Ida L 22
   Joseph......................22
   Joseph W 22
   Lois Lucile......................22
   Lucretia......................22
   Mary 22

MCKINNEY
   Adam 18
   Bertha W......................18
   Elizabeth......................57
   James 57
   John 18
   Martha 18
   Philip 31
   Pollie......................31

   Richard 31
   Sampson 31

MCKINNON, Commissioner..........293
MCMAHAN, Cornelia......................91
MCMAHON, Cornelia......................91
ME-HE-LE......................158
MEH-YO-LO-NA 15
MELISSA......................126

MERONEY
   Kate 80
   W D 80

MERRYMAN
   Abraham......................179
   Agnes......................194
   Allie......................82
   Anna......................107
   Annie 179
   Beloa......................107
   Belva......................107
   Cadelia......................194
   Caroline 42,82,87
   Cordelia 179,180
   Cordelia B......................179
   Daniel W......................87
   David C 179,180,194
   Earl Q 3
   Edgar B......................107
   Ellen 107
   Erie V 107
   Ezra Ruben 82
   Florence A 82
   Frances 129
   Frank......................82
   Frank S 82
   Gabe 180
   Gipson V 194
   Ivy V......................107
   Izora Lula 180
   James F 3
   Jas F...................... 3
   Jno D 180
   Jno Q 107
   Joanna......................3,107
   John 3,107,129
   John D 180
   John Q 107
   John S 107

Lee Roy 87
Leo E 179
Leonidas 87
Lillian Joanna 3
Lula...............................180
Mary 179,180
Mary J F 179
Minnie I 107
Nancy J.............................82
Ophelia............................107
Ora................................179
Pairlee............................194
Rosco..............................107
Roscoe C 107
Ruth............................... 3
Sally...............................87
Sarah...............................87
Sumner 42
Theodore............................87
Theodore Scott.....................107
W P.......................82,107,179
Walter G 180
William B 82
William H.......................82,179
Wm..................................82
Wm H...............................179
Wm P..............................42,87
Wm, Jr..............................82
Zado C.............................180
ME-SHA-FIH-NA-BE....................158
MESHEMAHTUBBEE
  Semelian.........................174
  Semmie...........................174
MIH-YO-TUBBEE 232
MINTON
  Barney............................90
  Robert............................90
  Winnie............................90
MOLLIE.............................183
MONTAGUE
  Joe 66
  Lottie Marie......................66
MOON
  Ann..............................200
  Joe J............................200
  Joseph J 200
  Levi.............................200

Levi L 200
Mattie 200
Susie O 200
MOORE
  Ada...............................60
  Andrew J 60
  Beuna.............................60
  Cecil 50
  Clara 50
  David A 50
  Dora M 50
  Elsie........................220,252
  Gertrude..........................60
  J J..............................200
  Jackson 60
  Jane.............................300
  Jeptha N.......................50,60
  Joe J............................200
  Laura.............................60
  Milberry..........................60
  Milberry J 50
  Ola May...........................50
  Phoebe.......................208,300
  Stacy.............................50
  Thomas............................50
  Thos.........................208,300
MORGAN
  Armstead 101
  Sibbie............................101
  Susan 101
  W B 101
  Wiley B 101
MOSBEY
  John M............................63
  Martha 63
MO-SHON-TO-TUBBEE 215
MURPHY, Mary 272
NAIL
  Cillen 144
  Elizabeth.........................144
  Emma 131
  Empsy.............................144
  Greenwood 144
  Jeff..............................128
  Louisa............................204
  Maggie............................144
  Manda.............................144

Morris 128,131,204
Nelson..144
Richard 144
Saline..144
William..144
NAK-IN-TO-LA.............................158
NELSON
Dannil..197
Jon 197
Smallwood......................................197
Solomon 284
NESSMITH
David..95
Frank..95
Mary V 95
Robert P..95
Susan K 95
NICHOLSON, Omer R 179
NOHIC, Jame 196
NORMAN
Ara B 23
Cilpha 23
Isaac M 23
Laura B 23
Maggie..86
Richard 23
Robert..86
NORRIS
E J...194
Neoma 194
O-KE-MA..125
OK-SAK-NIP-KU 140
OLLAR
Emily 256
G W 256
ONA-CHI-HE-MA..........................245
ON-TIL-LI-MA-HO-NA.................250
OVERSTREET
Lutitia 60
Thos...64
Wm..60
PAGE
Ann...95
Mary 95
Robt..95
PAIOR.. 8
PARNELL, Serena 290

PARRISH
Bethena..24
John 24
PATTERSON
Ethel 157
Green...157
J M...157
Kittie J 157
Maggie...157
Martha 157
Martha J 157
Martha Jane 157
Pearl A 157
Pearl O 157
Sarah..157
Walton 157
PAXTON
Dora...216
Malinda..216
Watson...216
PAYTON
Daniel 113
Mary 113
Philip 113
Sophie..113
PEARSE, George 232
PEARSON
Albert... 4
Jonas..183
Joseph 183
Limon 4
PERRY
Albert..52
Boland 5,30,36
Campbell 5
Caroline 5,114
Catherine 5
Daniel 114
Eastman 5
Edna...52
Emily 30
Eve... 5
Fanny...52
Gilbert..52
Jefferson 127
Jennie...114
Jonas..52

Joseph 5
Leo 5
Lyman 114
Martha 114
Milton 52
Nancy 5,114
Newton 5
Rachel 127
Rhodie 30
Siney 127
Stephen 127
Vicey 52
Wicy 52
PE-SA-LE-MA 116
PE-SA-TEN-LA 228
PE-SA-TO-NA 125
PE-SUN-TUBBEE 126
PETER
    Simon 39
    Wm 252
PHOEBE 297
PIEARS
    Dona 274
    Franklin 274
    Joseph 274
PIERS, Joseph 274
PIRTLE, Sarah 92
PISA-HO-TEMA 27
PIS-TOM-BEY 213
PITCHLYN
    Becky 201
    Joseph 201
PITTS
    Gore 166
    Martha 166
POLK
    Betsy 68
    James 68
    Rhoda 68
POPE
    Alexander 234
    Battice 234
    Battiest 234
    Gilbert 233
    Kaizie 283
    Lucy 233
    Onie 233

    Tecumseh 283
    Tobias 283
    Winnie 233
POTEET
    Joe 180
    Tishie 180
PRYOR
    Earl 8
    George 8
    James 8
    Mary E 8
    Oliver 8
    Olivia 8
    Sallie 8
    Saml V 8
    Samuel V 8
    Vernon 8
QUINTON
    Charles 293
    Edward 296
    Eliz. 296
    Elizabeth 293,296
    Joel 296
    Katie 296
    Lee 296
    Lillie 296
    Myrtle 296
    Sam 293
    Sam'l 296
    Samuel 293
RABERN
    Mary J 50
    Thomas 50
RABON
    Cora E 148
    Curtis 118
    Ethel M 118
    Eunice 148
    Floyd 118
    Frod 118
    Hazel 118
    Lee Ora 148
    Loucila 60
    Mary 118
    Mary Jane 148
    Ora 60
    R L 148

Richard A 60
Robert L................................148
Rufus 118
Thomas 148
Thos.......................................118
Wallace..................................148
William T 60
RAMSEY
Catherine 268
William..................................268
RAY
Jas W 110
Margaret 110
REAGAN, R L 200
REVARD, Mary 179
RIDDLE
George...................................175
Isabelle 175
Jack........................123,130,163
RIPLEY
Cisby......................................227
Dixon.....................................227
Simon 227
ROBERSON
Caldwell 221
Gibson 221
James 221
Kizzie 221
Pollie.....................................221
Sibbie....................................221
ROBERTSON
David 66
George......................................66
Irene...66
Susan 66
ROCKMAN
Joseph......................................47
Leona May...............................47
Lizzie.......................................47
William H.................................47
ROSE, Jensy..............................147
ROSS
Cora.......................................148
Cora E....................................148
Ethen......................................118
Lizzie.............................118,148
W T...148

William T 118,148
RUSSELL
Almira................................58,81
Campbell 64
Dora..40
Elmira.....................................40
Eva..40
Jacob............................40,58,81
Mamie.....................................64
Margaret 64
Mary 64
Mary A 64
Robert.....................................40
Thos D 64
SAGE
Malinda.................................176
Noel......................................176
Wincy 176
SAIN, Elizabeth.........................275
SAKKI.......................................111
William..................................156
SALLIE 68
SALON, Edw. 296
SAM
Clifford..................................292
Fannie....................................233
James 262,292
Morris....................................292
Nancy....................................292
Rosa.......................................233
Sallie..............................262,292
Sally......................................262
Silas 262
Sophia....................................292
Stanford 262
Susan 262
Wallace..................................233
SAMS, Morris 292
SANDERS
Ella 296
Jno A 202
John 202
Leona....................................202
Lizzie....................................202
Net 202
Newton 202
Nona 202

Norma..202
Robt..202
SCHERMERHORN
Carrie L 218
H R 218
Mary A 218
SCOTT
Alice 137
Clifford B 137
Daniel 16
Emma 137
George 137
Henry.......................................16,93
Phoebe 16,45,46
SEABOLT
Annie 210
W C 210
SEXTON
Amos 239
Claracy 130
Cora...130
Dave 130
David 130
Elisabeth 130
Gilbert..130
James 130
Mary 130
SHAH-WE.......................................234
SHAN-TAY-O 108
SHAWANOLI, Sam........................219
SHAWONOLI, Sam........................219
SHEPPARD, Scott 136
SHI-KONNEY 196
SHOT-HO-MA.................................297
SHROPSHIRE
Adolph...66
J J..66
Jackson 66
Joseph J 66
Levina...66
Susan 51,66
SHWINOGEE
Lucinda...219
Permelia..219
SILMON
Jennie..233
Lee...233

SIMCOE
Fannie...75
Gaines...75
SIMPSON
Baily 76
Betty 76
Edward R..81
Marion 81
Nettie R 81
Russel E...81
Sarah...16
W M...81
William N 81
Willis 16
Wm N 81
SIMSON, Walter 16
SLAUGHTER
Bicey...291
John...291
Sillin 188
SMITH
Bettie 142
Cora...105
Layman..206
Leathy...11
Letha...............................19,20,124
Mary F 105
Milton..206
Nannie 290
Onie 105
Robert..290
Robert F...105
Tom 142
Zach T 105
SOCKEY
Ben 251
Britton..251
Davis..251
Dixon.....................................227,239
Eliza...111
Elizabeth.................................111,251
Emmit..156
John...251
Josephine 156
Lula..111
Malvin 251
Martha 251

Mat...............................251
Melvin...........................251
Salina...........................111
Vince............................239
Viney.......................239,251
Wallace.........................111
William.........................111
Willie..........................239
SORRELS
 John............................165
 Martha..........................165
 Maud............................165
 Mollie..........................165
 Newton..........................165
 Sarah...........................165
SPANN
 Carrel M........................210
 Claud E.........................210
 Freeman.....................209,212
 Freeman R.......................209
 J H.............................210
 John H......................209,210
 Katie A.........................210
 Leona.......................209,210
SPRING
 John............................201
 Sally...........................201
STACY
 Andrew..........................14
 Andrew J........................14
 Henry J.........................14
 Julius V........................14
 Lucretia........................14
 Susie E.........................14
 William F.......................14
STALLABY
 Annie...........................289
 Dukes...........................289
 Forbis..........................289
 James...........................289
 James N.........................289
 John............................289
 Lizzie..........................289
 Mary............................289
 Nattie..........................289
 Robert..........................289
 Sallie..........................289

Selaney.........................289
Tenni...........................289
STARK
 Flissie.........................17
 Thos............................17
STEWARD
 Cosma...........................282
 Elmer...........................282
 John............................282
 Savanna.........................282
 Willie..........................282
STILIBAY, Ferbis....................289
STILIBY
 Bob.............................289
 Danes...........................289
 Dank............................289
 Hige............................289
 James...........................289
 Nation..........................289
 Silie...........................289
 Silinia.........................289
STRAWN
 Balaan..........................120
 Mary L..........................120
SURRATT
 Fena............................31
 Fona............................31
 Henry...........................31
 J D.............................31
 Jefferson D.....................31
 Lucy............................31
TACH-BON-TA, Johnson................41
TACH-KAH-KA.........................121
TA-HOM-BA...........................239
TAKKUBBEE
 Anna............................241
 Artemissa.......................241
 Ida.............................241
 Joe A...........................241
 Kelly...........................241
 Susann..........................241
 Susanna.........................241
 Timicy..........................241
 Wallace.........................241
TALIPOOSE
 Sampson.........................1
 Simeon..........................1

Tema....................................... 1
TALLAPOCH
   John 192
   Mary 192
TALLIPOOSE, Celey...................196
TA-LO-AT-E-MA...........................164
TA-M-HO-NA..................................260
TA-NAP-A-YA 35,244
TARBY, William 33
TASH-KAH-KE..............................151
TAYLOR
   Emiline 195
   General 117
   Green 162
   Hester 72
   James 72
   John 22,117
   Joseph..................................22
   Leathy.................................162
   Leitha.................................162
   Lina......................................91
   Lucretia.................................22
   M F 91
   Maimie 162
   Mamie.................................162
   Martha J..............................72
   Mary 117
   Newton 162
   Pamelia..............................162
   Sallie..................................162
   Tishy...................................162
TE-LA-MA.....................................228
TE-LE-MAH 197
TERREL...33
   Silen...................................33
TERRELL
   Daniel 33
   Emiline 33
   George 33
   Houston 49
   Mutsey...............................33
   Rhoda 49
   Sillen..................................33
   Solomon 33,49
THOMAS
   Alice 196
   Elias...................................196

Leanders 244
Leonidus.................................244
Loman.....................................38
Lomida....................................244
Minnie....................................196
Rhoda.....................................297
Robert.....................................244
Sacia.......................................38
Semus 244
Sophia.....................................38
Stephen...................................196
Vicey 244
Wicey 244
Wilson 196
THOMPSON
   Bicey.....................................126
   Billy.................................126,276
   Elizabeth.........................139,276
   Grace 242
   Henry....................................139
   Ishatanona.............................121
   Ishtohena 121
   Isom................................242,276
   James 121
   Jimpson.................................151
   Jimson..................................276
   Joanna...................................170
   Johana...................................170
   Jonas................................139,184
   Julia......................................170
   Losie.....................................276
   Lucy......................................151
   Malinda.................................242
   Nelson...................................242
   Rosa......................................242
   Rose......................................242
   Sally......................................242
   Serena...................................242
   Tona......................................139
THOMSON, Isham.........................170
THORNTON
   Beulah...................................61
   Eureka...................................61
   Frederick................................61
   Jesse W 61
   Jno V 61
   John V 61

Johnnie A.....................................61
Mabell...61
Maud...61
Paralee..61
Parlea..61
T V 61
TICKNESS
Frances 93
Frank...93
John 93
Lizzie...93
Sillian 93
Tillian 93
TOBLEY 114
Ellen 172
Sam...172
Willis...172
TOBLY, Sam..................................172
TO-KA-HALLE 178
TO-KAH-LI....................................190
TOK-FO-A-TA, Incy.......................38
TOLBERT
Elizabeth...................................177
John 177
Nellie 177
Washington................................177
TOM
Aaron...46
Abilena 46
Albert...46
Benjamin 46
Benny 46
Bicy 45
Ebeneezer 45
Ebenezer 45
Elias...46
Eliza......................................45,46
Elsie...45
Esias 46
Gency 46
Isabelle 46
John 45,52
Levi..46
Mandy..46
Phoebe...................................52,53
Sarah..45
Simeon.......................................46

Simon 46,298
Thomas......................................53
Tommy 53
Wilson 45,46,53
TRAHERN
Annie 102
Cornelia..................................... 2
Czarma 2
Docia 56
Don..19
James.....................................55,67
James N 56,67
Jas...102
Lysander....................................102
Minnie 67
Rebecca 43
Robert....................................... 2
Sallie...102
Sarah..55
Virginia......................................67
Virginia P 55,56
Walter..102
William.......................................43
TRAMMEL, Jack 54
VANDERGRIF
Hazey Ann.................................59
Wm..59
VANDERGRIFF, Amanda I 59
VICTOR
Alfred 103
Alfred W....................................103
Ether 103
Ether M......................................103
Ida E 103
Jane..103
Mary 103
Penson 103
Trudy May.................................103
WADE
Bessie 260
Connickey...................................183
Dennis..260
Elizabeth....................................260
Gibson 260
Grover C.....................................260
Loma.....................................125,260
Mary J..260

Phoebe 183
Sampson 183
Sarah 183
WA-KA-HA, Elsie 243
WA-KA-TA-BI 37
WALKER
    Agnes 73
    Cassie 203
    D Clifton 203
    Jesse A 203
    Jesse Allen 203
    John W 203
    K Tandy 73
    Kizzie 203
    Lucinda 203
    Mattie 73
    Oscar W 203
    R L 203
    Robert L 203
    Sillin 73
    Tandy 73
WALL
    Abbie E 142
    Abigail 115
    Abigail E 143
    Ben F 142
    Benj 115
    Benjamin 142
    Benjamin F 143
    Benjamin H 142
    Cervera M 142
    Cz rena B 115
    Ellis W 142
    Emiline 214
    Gibson 217
    Jefferson 247
    Jesse 214,217
    Jesse E 142
    Jessie 247,248
    Johnson 248
    Katie 143
    Lillie D 115
    Nancy 214,217,247,248
    Octavia 142
    Roena Estell 115
    Tom 143
    Walter T 142

    William W 115
WALLACE
    Isom 114
    Nellie 114
WALLEN
    Sam 38
    Sim 38
    Sophia 38
    Thompson 38
WALLS
    Abigail E 143
    Ben F 142,143
    Ben H 142
    Ellis W 142
    Jessie E 142
    Lillie 115
    Octave 142
    Walter F 142
    Willie W 115
WARD
    Addie L 105
    Cyrus B 24
    Maggie 84
    Robert J 103,105
WA-YO-HE 252
WEBSTER
    Albert 114
    Jackson 244
    Jincy 114
    Minnie 114
    Thomas 114
WENLOCK, Elizabeth 268
WESLEY
    Annie 235
    Charles 215
    Charleson 191,235
    Chas 216
    Harris 158
    Lena 215
    Lucinda 215
    Noel 158
    Rhoda 191,216
WHEELER
    Louisa 167
    Rhoda 167
    Wm P 167
WHISTLER

Etna 41
Martin 41
Nancy 41
WHITE
   Amy 289
   Charley 289
WHITEHEAD
   Ann M 18
   Geo E 18
WILKIN
   Cely 126
   Sealy 126
WILKINS
   Adaline 253
   Adam 13
   Adams 13
   Allen 253
   Henry 13
   Jefferson 253
   Wicey 13
WILLIAMS
   Albert J 48
   Amanda 48
   Betsy 33
   Cassie 299
   Coleman 198
   Cora 239
   Dora 239
   E,,A 48
   Easter 33
   Eddie 299
   Eli 299
   Emeline 199
   Fanne 33
   Forbis 181
   Forrest 170
   Freeman 170
   George 198
   Hickman 199
   Ida 33
   Jas 299
   Jasper 272,299
   Jensie 170
   Jincy 170
   Joel 199
   John 187,192,193,240
   Lena 239

Leona 170
Mary 33,272,299
Mattie 199
Mattie B 199
Meleanna 181
Melvina 33
Mollie 199
Phoebe 199
Reuben 98
S W 48
Sarah E 48
Senora W 48
Sophy 198
Stephen 33
Susanna 98
WILLIS
   John 180
   Ruth 180
WILMON
   Jincy 147
   John 147
   Lewis 147
   Martha 147
   Rose 147
   Sampson 147
WILSON
   Allington 183
   Caleb 149
   Cillen 183
   Cornelius 183
   Daniel 197
   Jonas 197
   Martha 197
   Sarah 149
   Sarah E 123
WINLOCK
   Betsy 259
   Eliza 259
   Ellis 259
   Johnny 259
   Lavinia 84
   Peter 84
   Polly 84
   Rufus 84
   Tom 259
   Wattie 259
WINTERS

Amanda 77
Daisy L 77
Frank..77
Hazel V 77
Lizzie..77
Walter B 77
WISHOCK
Cora..239
Dora..239
Maria 239
Wesley W 239
WOODS
George 84
James 84
Louis..84
Lyons...84
Martha J...84
Susan 84
WOODWARD, B B 148
WRIGHT
Agnes..242
Emeline...249
George Simon..............................249
James 242
Josie..270
Simon 222
Siney..41
Sophie...222
Steward...222
W H..249
WYERS
Bailey 11
Belle 11
Corena 11
Edna...11
Effie...11
Ellen 11
Irene...11
John N 11
John W.....................................11,70
Norman...11
Pearl...11
Sampson 11
William...11
YA-KAN-TA-BE 199
YA-MO-TAN-TUBBEE 141
YOTA

Calvin 235
Dave 235
Manda...235
Melvina...235
Sissie...235
Thomas 235
YOTAH, Celis................................235
YOTER...235
YUM-MI-HO-MA...........................39
YUTAH, Calvin 235

9 781649 680136

Other Books and Series by Jeff Bowen

1901-1907 Native American Census Seneca, Eastern Shawnee, Miami, Modoc, Ottawa, Peoria, Quapaw, and Wyandotte Indians (Under Seneca School, Indian Territory)

1932 Census of The Standing Rock Sioux Reservation with Births And Deaths 1924-1932

Census of The Blackfeet, Montana, 1897- 1901 Expanded Edition

Eastern Cherokee by Blood, 1906-1910, Volumes I thru XIII

Choctaw of Mississippi Indian Census 1929-1932 with Births and Deaths 1924-1931   Volume I

Choctaw of Mississippi Indian Census 1933, 1934 & 1937, Supplemental Rolls to 1934 & 1935 with Births and Deaths 1932-1938, and Marriages 1936-1938   Volume II

Eastern Cherokee Census Cherokee, North Carolina 1930-1939 Census 1930-1931 with Births And Deaths 1924-1931 Taken By Agent L. W. Page   Volume I

Eastern Cherokee Census Cherokee, North Carolina 1930-1939 Census 1932-1933 with Births And Deaths 1930-1932 Taken By Agent R. L. Spalsbury   Volume II

Eastern Cherokee Census Cherokee, North Carolina 1930-1939 Census 1934-1937 with Births and Deaths 1925-1938 and Marriages 1936 & 1938 Taken by Agents R. L. Spalsbury And Harold W. Foght Volume III

Seminole of Florida Indian Census, 1930-1940 with Birth and Death Records, 1930-1938

Texas Cherokees 1820-1839 A Document For Litigation 1921

Visit our website at **www.nativestudy.com** to learn more about these
and other books and series by Jeff Bowen

CHOCTAW BY BLOOD

ENROLLMENT CARDS

1898-1914

VOLUME X

TRANSCRIBED BY

JEFF BOWEN

NATIVE STUDY
Gallipolis, Ohio
USA